Ethnic Elements, Fashion Creative and Cultural Identity
民族元素、时尚创意与文化认同

———·中英对照·———

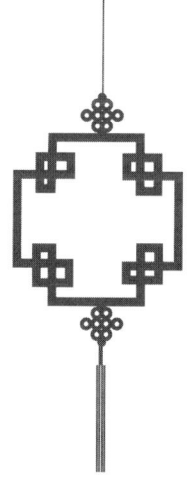

张贤根 著　Written by Xiange
陈奇敏 译　Translated by Qimin Chen

中国纺织出版社有限公司

内 容 提 要

《民族元素、时尚创意与文化认同》旨在揭示时尚创意中民族元素的运用、意义生成的机制，以及与之相关的审美与文化认同的问题。本书从时尚、创意与民族元素的生成性关联出发，探究与阐发民族元素及其时尚创意的建构。作者深入探讨了民族时尚创意的生成与视觉表现问题，以及民族生活方式与民族时尚创意的密切关联，并对全球化语境里的民族时尚与文化认同加以研究，以期将对民族时尚设计与创意文化产业的发展有所助益与启示。

Abstract

Ethnic Elements, Fashion Creative and Cultural Identity discusses the ways of applying ethnic elements to fashion creative, the mechanism of meaning generation, and relevant issues on the aesthetic and cultural identity. Based on the generative relationship between fashion, creative and ethnic elements, this book explored the mechanism of constructing fashion creative with ethnic elements. To that end, the generation and visualization of ethnic fashion creative are discussed, the close relationship between ethnic lifestyle and fashion creative is expounded, and the cultural identity with ethnic fashion in the context of globalization are studied. It is hoped that the book will be enlightening to ethnic fashion design and the development of creative cultural industries.

图书在版编目（CIP）数据

民族元素、时尚创意与文化认同：中英对照 / 张贤根著；陈奇敏译. -- 北京：中国纺织出版社有限公司，2024.3

ISBN 978-7-5229-1315-5

Ⅰ.①民… Ⅱ.①张… ②陈… Ⅲ.①民族文化－应用－服装设计－研究－中国－汉、英 Ⅳ.①K28 ①TS941.2

中国国家版本馆CIP数据核字（2024）第016756号

责任编辑：宗 静 刘 茸　　责任校对：高 涵
责任印制：王艳丽

中国纺织出版社有限公司出版发行
地址：北京市朝阳区百子湾东里 A407 号楼　邮政编码：100124
销售电话：010—67004422　传真：010—87155801
http://www.c-textilep.com
中国纺织出版社天猫旗舰店
官方微博 http://weibo.com/2119887771
三河市宏盛印务有限公司印刷　各地新华书店经销
2024 年 3 月第 1 版第 1 次印刷
开本：787×1092　1/16　印张：18.75
字数：390 千字　定价：98.00 元

凡购本书，如有缺页、倒页、脱页，由本社图书营销中心调换

导论

在当代人们的日常生活世界里，时尚不仅是衣生活的流行样式，而且具有越来越重要的社会与文化的意义和价值。因为，无论人们是否在乎自己着装的时尚性，他（她）们都不可避免地生活在一个日趋时尚化的世界。实际上，各种时尚艺术及其表现风格正在驱使人们了解时尚甚至建构自己的时尚感，以及对时尚的生活方式加以认识与理解。另外，当代时尚的设计与审美表现关涉民族元素的发掘、重构与阐释等问题。其实，一切时装设计乃至整个时尚业的创意，虽然都极其关注当代感的塑造与生成，但它们都不可能与民族元素、传统文化分割开来。

在这里，创意无疑是时尚艺术的根本性诉求，而审美表现又是创意实现的核心与关键。创意首先涉及的是新的观念如何发生的问题，这同时也关联到这些新观念的视觉化表现与实现，以及这种新观念与想法能否通过视觉化生成时尚感。因此，除了艺术设计与表现之外，时尚创意还涉及人们的审美接受与认同问题，这又是与特定的民族文化密切相关的。正因如此，时尚应当回归人类学与日常生活，对民族元素及其创意可能性加以审美重构，这样才能将当代时尚创意建基于历史与传统文化的语境之上。

时尚艺术与审美不仅涉及个人的品位与情趣，而且与民族或族群具有密切的关联，这显然也是一种艺术、审美与文化人类学的课题。比如，什么样的时尚艺术是美的？时尚美的本性究竟是什么？我们能否接受某种时尚样式与格调？这些既是艺术表现与审美的重要问题，无疑也与民族和人类文化相关。在当代，围绕民族时尚创意及其文化认同的问题凸显出来，引起了人们的广泛关注，并成为艺术与时尚界的热点问题，这就涉及对民族元素与传统文化的挖掘、整理与当代重构。

特别是在当今国际时尚界，各民族的时尚与风格正在受到广泛的借鉴与重构，这些源于民族的时尚趋势正在建构世界性时尚及其多元性特质。在这里，时装不仅是一种身体美化的独特艺术，而且是一种自我建构与认同的技术。显然，在时装的创意表现与设计过程中，艺术与技术不仅是密切相关的，而且是彼此渗透与难以分离的。与此同时，时尚创意与设计所凭借的艺术和技术手段，还与人们的生存方式、身体意识和日常生活相关联。

根据当代时尚创意及其视觉表现的现状与处境，分析与揭示创意进一步发展所面临的问题与受到的制约，无疑是民族时尚创意与文化认同研究的重要课题。同时，如何根据民族文化及其多样性特质，考虑各民族时尚艺术与文化的密切关联性，显然也是一个有待关注与探究的艺术与文化课题。实际上，还应将民族元素与时尚创意置于全球化语境，进而与不同民族或国家的时尚文化展开沟通和对话，以促成当代时尚创意在多元的文化传统中获得自身的自觉与文化认同。

基于时尚创意及其视觉化表现，把民族元素的视觉表现与文化内涵的研究，以及民族文化认同及其当代建构作为根本性诉求，将有助于民族时尚创意设计水平的提升及其在当代的发展，也会对人们日常生活审美化的实现有所裨益。因此，民族元素及其文化内涵的揭示与阐发，就成为民族时尚创意设计与表现不可或缺的基础。为此，还应对民族创意与服饰文化的视觉化表现的可能性与独特方式加以探究。虽然人类学家大都主张文化的多元化，但他（她）们往往只是从某一特定视角去揭示与阐释文化的本性。人们应当看到，在时尚创意及其与民族文化的关联性研究上，不同观点与思想之间的沟通、对话和讨论是非常必要的。

当然，当代艺术与日常生活的各种相关元素，以及这些元素的构成与社会、历史、文化语境的关联，显然也是值得关注与探究的设计问题。在时尚艺术与文化方面，不少设计师之所以创新性匮乏，虽然原因是多种多样的，但缺乏文化底蕴，无疑是不可忽视的重要原因。本书通过民族元素及其文化意义的深入研究，旨在为时尚创意与民族文化的当代发展，以及民族时尚向日常生活的介入与渗透，提供可供借鉴的观念引领、文化语境与理论建构。与此同时，力图经由对时尚创意及其存在问题的分析与研究，揭示时尚创意中民族元素的发掘与意义生成机制。特别是，只有揭示与阐发民族时尚创意与文化认同的生成性关联，以及推进时尚创意及其民族文化认同的当代建构，才能为时尚创意与文化产业提供理论支持和实践启示。在民族性与世界性的审美及文化张力中，促成民族服饰与时尚的当代建构和世界性的艺术与文化传播。

陈奇敏
2023年3月

Introduction

In the daily life of contemporary people, fashion not only manifests a popular style of clothing-life, but also acquires increasing social and cultural significance, because the world in which people live is inevitably becoming more and more fashionable, no matter they care about their dressing or not. In fact, expressive styles of various fashion arts are attracting people to learn about fashion, to construct their own sense of fashion, as well as to understand clothing lifestyle. At the same time, the design and aesthetic expression of contemporary fashion have to deal with issues like the exploration, reconstruction and interpretation of ethnic elements. In fact, all fashion designs, or even all creatives of the fashion industry, could hardly be separated from ethnic element and traditional culture, despite the fact that they are extremely concerned with the shaping and generation of modernity.

No doubt, creative is the fundamental appeal of fashion art, while aesthetic expression is the key to realizing creative. Creative is concerned with: firstly, the way that new ideas occur; then, the visual expression and realization of those new ideas; and thirdly, the possibility that these new ideas could generate a sense of fashion through visualization. Therefore, besides artistic design and expression, fashion creative involves people's aesthetic acceptance and identity, which, then, is closely related to specific ethnic culture. Accordingly, only by returning to anthropology and daily life, and aesthetically reconstructing the creative possibility of ethnic element, can we place the base of contemporary fashion creative in the context of history and traditional culture.

Moreover, fashion art and aesthetics are related not only to the taste of individual person, but also to that of race or ethnic group, so they could raise issues of art, aesthetics and cultural anthropology. For example, what kind of fashion art is beautiful? What is the nature of fashion beauty? And can we accept certain fashion type or style? These questions are not only important for artistic expression and aesthetics, but also relevant to ethnic group and human culture. In contemporary times, issues concerning the cultural identity on ethnic fashion creative have come to prominence, arousing widespread attention and becoming a hot topic in the art and fashion circle, which calls for the exploration, sorting out and contemporary reconstruction of ethnic element and traditional culture.

In today's international fashion industry, fashions and styles of different ethnic groups are being widely adopted and reconstructed, and these ethnic fashion trends are constructing the pluralism of world fashion. Here, fashion is not only a unique art of body beautification, but also a technical way of self-construction and identification. In the creative expression and design of fashion, art and technique are closely linked, and often infiltrated and attached to each other. At the same time, the artistic and technical means of fashion creative and design are associated with people's survival mode, body awareness and daily life.

According to the current situation of the visual expression on contemporary fashion creative, it is undoubtedly an important issue in the research of ethnic fashion creative and cultural identity to analyze the problems and constraints faced by creative in its further development. At the same time, how to deal with the close relationship between ethnic fashion art and culture on the basis of ethnic cultural diversity, is an art and cultural topic to be noted and explored. In fact, we should place ethnic element and fashion creative in the context of globalization, and then communicate with different ethnic groups or countries on fashion culture, so as to help contemporary fashion creative to gain self-awareness and cultural identity in diversified cultural tradition.

If we start from the visual expression of fashion creative, and take as the fundamental appeal the research on the cultural connotation and visual expression of ethnic element, as well as the contemporary construction of ethnic cultural identity, we will promote the contemporary development of ethnic fashion creative design, and facilitate the aestheticization of people's daily life. Therefore, revealing and interpreting the cultural connotation of ethnic element has become an indispensable foundation for ethnic fashion creative design and expression. To this end, the possibility and unique ways of visualizing ethnic creative and costume culture should also be explored. Although most anthropologists advocate cultural diversity, they often reveal and interpret the nature of culture just from a specific perspective. Therefore, it is very necessary to communicate and exchange different viewpoints and ideas while we research on the relevance between fashion creative and ethnic culture.

Of course, various elements related to contemporary art and daily life, as well as the association of these elements with their social, historical, and cultural contexts, are also designing issues worthy of attention and exploration. In terms of fashion art and culture, the reasons why many designers lack of innovation may be various, of which one most important and unignorable is, however, the shortage of cultural heritage in their fashion creative. This book, through in-depth study of ethnic elements and their cultural meanings, aims to provide reference of conceptual guidance, cultural context and theory construction for the contemporary development of fashion creative and ethnic culture, as well as for the penetration of ethnic fashion into daily life. Meanwhile, by analyzing and researching the existing problems of fashion creative, it tries to reveal the mechanism of exploring ethnic elements and generating meanings in fashion creative. Only by revealing and interpreting the generative relationship between ethnic fashion creative and cultural identity, and promoting the contemporary construction of ethnic cultural identity on fashion creative, can we provide theoretical support and practical enlightenment for fashion creative and cultural industry. And only in the aesthetic and cultural tension between ethnicity and globality, can we promote the contemporary construction of ethnic clothing and fashion, and the worldwide communication of art and culture.

Chen Qimin
March, 2023

目录

第一章　民族元素及时尚创意的生成

　　第一节　民族元素的构成、关联与特性 / 002

　　第二节　民族元素及其时尚化方式 / 014

　　第三节　民族元素时尚创意的生成 / 031

第二章　民族时尚创意的生成与视觉表现

　　第一节　创意的视觉转换与图式化 / 108

　　第二节　民族时尚创意及其视觉文化 / 120

　　第三节　民族性的生成与时尚的视觉表现 / 132

第三章　全球化语境里的民族时尚与文化认同

　　第一节　时尚创意的民族性与世界性 / 202

　　第二节　全球化与民族间时尚文化的对话 / 215

结语 / 263

参考文献 / 269

Contents

CHAPTER 1　Ethnic Elements and Generation of Fashion Creative

　　Section 1　Composition, Relevance and Characteristics of Ethnic Elements　/ 048

　　Section 2　Fashionizing Methods of Ethnic Elements　/ 064

　　Section 3　Generation of Fashion Creative on Ethnic Elements　/ 087

CHAPTER 2　Generation and Visual Expression of Ethnic Fashion Creative

　　Section 1　Visual Transformation and Schematization of Creative　/ 148

　　Section 2　Visual Culture of Ethnic Fashion Creative　/ 164

　　Section 3　Generation of Ethnicity and Visual Expression of Fashion　/ 181

CHAPTER 3　Ethnic Fashion and Cultural Identity in the Context of Globalization

　　Section 1　Ethnicity and Globality of Fashion Creative　/ 228

　　Section 2　Globalization and Inter-ethnic Dialogue on Fashion Culture　/ 246

Conclusion / 265

Bibliography / 277

第一章

民族元素及时尚创意的生成

作为一种观念与想法的表达，时尚创意与设计的表现是新异的、美观的，往往发生在族群存在及其文化的语境里。时尚创意所关涉的民族元素无疑是历史性的，对民族元素的揭示及阐明不可能与民族文化分离开来。而且，时尚的创意、设计与审美表现，应成为文化认同与传播的一种可接受方式。在创意与设计过程中，文化认同还表明了时尚史的某种连续性，如近些年流行的新唐装，既是一种现代的中式服装，也是对传统中国服装的现代重构。对于不同民族的时尚艺术与文化，迫切需要不断地沟通、对话与相互理解，以实现不同民族文化的相互认同。在这里，各民族时尚元素及其构成的跨文化传播，是以人类共同居住在此大地上为基础的，并表征为文本上的彼此互文与相互交织，但这又是以各民族文化独特性的保持为前提的。就时尚艺术创意与设计而言，其实并不存在任何天生的与一成不变的民族元素，一切元素原则上都可以得到基于创意的视觉与艺术表现。当然，民族元素涉及的方面与类型也是异质的与多元的，它们为时尚创意与设计提供了素材、话语与文化语境。在艺术的表现与审美上，民族元素是通过不断演变得以生成的。特别是，当民族元素被借鉴到时尚创意与设计中时，也会发生审美重组与意义的历史性变化，并与当下的时尚观念、想法发生互文性交织和对话，进而使那些具有独特民族特质的创意与时尚设计成为可能。实际上，各民族原生态的审美倾向与独特的文化旨趣，已经成为当代时尚创意与设计不可或缺的灵感来源。时尚从来都不只是隶属于某一特定民族或族群，各民族都有属于自己的时尚样式与艺术风格，而时尚表现方式又在不同民族中发生交流与当代重构。

第一节 民族元素的构成、关联与特性

这里所说的元素，指一种内在于事物本身的、事物最初由之构成的，且不能再被分解为其他组成的基本单元。据此，民族元素可以理解为：民族艺术与文化沉淀其中的、极具象征性意味的基本单元。对于视觉艺术与表现来说，线条、色彩、形状与纹理等无疑都可看作元素。当然，不同的民族元素与文化既有所区分，也相互关联和彼此交织，共同构成民族生活方式与文化这一开放性整体。值得注意的是，这些民族元素并不是民族文化可以分割的部分，虽然它们在本性上都是从某一特定的层面与视角，对民族存在与生活方式的一种敞开与揭示，但其实都是对民族文化的整体性的一种阐明。正因如此，民族元素无不具有某种不可分离的整体性与生成性特征。在各种民族元素及其揭示与阐释之间，一种互文式的艺术与文化的对话是不可或缺的。

一、民族元素的规定与构成问题

一般来说，元素是一种文化的基本构成单元与成分，它存在于民族艺术与文化的生成过程中。作为民族艺术与文化的一种基本构成，民族元素是民族结构得以成为自身的必要因素。"由于各要素间具有可重叠的特性，所以不能用死板的界线来划分它们。"❶ 实际上，民族精神与文化特质是通过其构成中的元素得以彰显的，与此同时，不同的元素及其文化特质共同构成民族文化本身。在民族的生存与生活中，民族元素及其构成是关切于民族自身的结构性因素。

在民族时尚的创意、设计与表现中，元素的结构往往是由内在、浅层与表观等构成的，不同层次的可视化程度有所差异，它们在相互关联中共同生成民族元素与文化的整体性特质。与元素结构相对应的是，民族精神与文化所关联的信仰、仪式与器物，它们不仅在不同层面得到揭示与阐发，还在艺术、思想与文化语境得以回应。因此，可以从民族元素三种不同的构成层面，揭示民族元素的规定及其艺术、审美和文化含义。对于所有的民族元素及其文化特质来说，信仰、仪式与器物是彼此关联与相互影响的。实际上，元素的不同层面的意义与旨趣，往往又是由某种整体性结构所规定的。

民族元素及其存在样式是多元化的且无穷尽的。在民族精神与文化构成中，信仰、仪式与器物是对民族整体性特质的揭示。对于民族元素而言，信仰、仪式与器物是揭示和阐释民族精神与文化的根本路径。原初的、历史的宗教塑造了人们的感性。对民族的生存与文化来说，信仰既是一种精神寄托和根本信念，也是一种终极性的诉求与信赖。信仰旨在超越一切有限的东西。

只有可以超越现实局限性的无限，才能为弥补人类自身的有限性提供可能。各民族的元素与文化，既可能与某种共同的信仰相关联，也可能与不同的信仰相关联。应当注意到，这里所说的信仰与仪式、服饰分不开。信仰处于民族精神与文化结构的最高层，最低层是民族生活所依凭的器物，而仪式则介于信仰与器物之间。神话以寓言式的、想象性的叙事来表达，它在民族艺术与文化的传承过程中，曾经起着重要的符码象征与规定性作用。无论是信仰、宗教，还是古代艺术形式，都曾受到神话深刻与广泛的影响。神话不仅构成了传统民族元素与文化的底蕴，而且在服饰设计中不断地被借鉴。

作为一种原始的宗教信仰，图腾崇拜把某种动物或植物当成神灵。应当说，"神话作为一种复杂、混合的精神构成物，本身带有一些永恒性（人类生活的意义、功勋、幸福）的问题，它正是用艺术形式将其传给后代"。❷ 信仰往往带有情感体验色彩，这在许多宗教信仰上得到了体现与强调。但也要看到，信仰与所信仰的物件是否客观存在没有必然联系。为了表达对图腾的崇拜，以及与其他氏族部落的区分，原始先民会在自己的身体上描绘或

---

❶ 帕特里克·弗兰克.视觉艺术原理[M].陈玥蕾，俞钰，译.上海：上海人民美术出版社，2008：40.
❷ 雅科伏列夫.艺术与世界宗教[M].任光宣，李冬晗，译.北京：文化艺术出版社，1989：8-9.

雕刻图腾形象。

对于原始先民来说，作为一种图腾装饰的文身关切的正是身体外表。而且，不同氏族先民与族群装饰所用的图形也是有差异的。信仰过程必须是经过内在回应的，其中需通过个人的经历和对灵性的追寻，进而选择一种适合自己的宗教信仰。人类在创造自己的现实世界的同时，也建构了一个带有民族精神与特质的神秘世界。在这个神秘领域内，人们寄托着自己的信仰和希望。实际上，一个民族不可能完全没有自己的信仰与精神寄托，因为，只有依靠信仰才能拉近有限和无限的距离，进而构成民族元素与文化不可或缺的精神特质。在中国历史上，儒教与道教曾经是基本的信仰体系。应当说，民族的信仰深刻地建构着民族的心智、精神与文化。

在儒家的思想中，孔子强调仁，重视礼。孔子的仁学是儒家的核心思想，它是对先秦礼乐文化的创造性改造，即用仁来解释礼乐文化。以孔子思想为核心建构的儒教，无疑是中国传统精神与文化的重要构成部分。儒家比德说强调了衣与人的关切甚至合一。与孔子同时代的老子，重视"道"，强调"德"，崇尚"无为"与"清净"。而且，道家所理解的艺术是关于道即无的艺术，如大象无形、大音希声表达了无之境界。在这里，各种具有信仰旨趣的观念与思想，都构成了民族服饰艺术与文化的精神特质。

原始道家主要指老子和庄子的学说，魏晋的新道家也即魏晋玄学。道家的核心思想是道自身，即作为自然的道。作为道士的服装，道服是中国古代的一种释道之服，元代与明初流传于民间。作为佛教的重要派别，禅宗的核心思想是心灵的觉悟，其根本问题不是外在的，而是内在的，也就是对人自身的佛性即自性的发现。后来，禅还成为日本的佛教样式，它是经由中国传播到日本的。应当说，佛禅的题材成为艺术表现与服饰设计的重要构成部分。

毫无疑问，民族元素的规定与内涵的揭示，也是离不开信仰与民族宗教及其文化特质的。一般来说，仪式是对具有宗教或传统象征意义的活动的总称。"仪式"一词来自英文的"ritual"，其原意是指手段与目的并非直接相关的一套标准化行为。在艺术史与美学史上，艺术与仪式的关联由来已久。与此同时，仪式往往具有一定的时段、特定的场合。在宗教里，仪式指在祈祷与礼拜中所奉行的某些固定程式的做法。

而且，仪式可以由个体、群体或团体组织主持和举行。也就是说，仪式中所表现的行为经常另有更深远的目的或企图。仪式既可以存在于任意场合或特定场合，也可以面向公众、私人场合或特定人群。作为信仰的主要载体，仪式不仅体现与表达着信仰旨趣，而且传递着符码象征的文化意义。民族地区的社会活动与日常生活，如交往、节庆、丧葬、嫁娶等，都是与特定的仪式、礼仪、着装相关联的，无疑也是民族风俗和习惯所特有的文化样式。在这里，礼仪是在交往中所体现出来的人们之间互相尊重的意愿，也就是与人交往的程序、方式以及实施交往行为时，人的外在方面的规范，包括服饰、仪态、语言与风度等。

随着人类社会与文化的变迁，仪式本身也会在不同的历史时期，表现出各不相同的形式及其社会与文化意义。"我们用仪式一词指代一种标准化的行为方式（习俗），其目标与手段的关系不是'直观的'，而是非理性的或无理性的。"❶ 仪式通常被视为象征性的、表演性的，以及由文化传统所规定的一套行为方式，经常被功能性地解释为：在特定群体或文化中，用以沟通、过渡、强化与整合社会的方式。譬如，过渡仪式就是指那些在人生特定时刻（出生、成年、结婚等）实行的典礼。

在中国西南、中南、东南等南方地区生活的少数民族，较为普遍地保持着基于"万物有灵"的原始宗教信仰。民族特色仪式就是指受少数民族风俗习惯，以及传统文化所支配的象征性活动，它能够使仪式参与者在内心与情感中，产生认同民族社会价值观念的直接效果。但可以说，民族的风俗与习惯一经形成就具有相对的独立性，成为民族灵魂深处的一种文化象征与价值取向。在这里，仪式成为一种与信仰相关的行为方式，这种行为的根本意义是具有精神指涉的象征性。在仪式发生的行为叙事里，特定的着装也有助于人们体验与理解精神旨趣，以及分享种族或族群集体的历史与文化记忆。

其实，民族艺术与文化及其对社会关系的整合，离不开习惯、惯例、禁忌与道德规范等。仪式及习惯与民族的价值观及文化特质相关，不同民族的仪式是其特有观念与精神的表现。当然，艺术不仅是一种有形的表现方式，更关切于族群的精神与文化诉求。因为"人们所观察到的艺术品是对一种文化的有形表现，因此，是依据该文化的视觉表征习惯建构和表达的一种精神"。❷ 值得注意的是，器物、工艺与服饰设计也是民族早期的艺术品样式，服饰设计与文化同样离不开各民族特定的视觉表征习惯与文化传统。

当然，民族风俗与习惯主要还是以文化、观念与思维模式，介入并渗透到民族生活中，进而影响着人们的行为。在民族信仰的基础上，独具特色的仪式使民族风俗与习惯，通过一套象征性体系外化为可视的行为与过程。在民族的生活世界中，传统的艺术与文化及其特质，其实无不与特有的风俗和习惯相关。对于创意来说，器物是理解与把握民族元素及其存在的载体，这里的器物不仅是艺术与文化印记的载体，而且其本身就是传统艺术与文化的历史性呈现。民间工艺的审美生成关切民族的历史性存在，民间工艺品则聚集了天地人与信仰旨趣。还要看到，器物及其实用性往往遮蔽了作品自身，因此对实用性的悬置是不可避免的。

只有在对一件器物的实用性做出必要的舍弃时，人们才能关注到它的存在本身，并使其打开和揭示生存世界成为可能。在哲学家马丁·海德格尔看来，人们虽然可以看到纯物，但它并不显现自己，而是封闭的，让人难以探究。与此同时，器物唾手可得的状态，恰恰使它从未受到过关注和打量。在海德格尔看来，作为某种物品或客观存在，艺术作品既不同于纯物，也不同于普通的器具，它以某种自足性独立地存在着。而且，一件艺术作品可

---

❶ 杰克·古迪.神话、仪式与口述[M].李源，译.北京：中国人民大学出版社，2014：33.
❷ 罗伯特·莱顿.艺术人类学[M].李东晔，王红，译.桂林：广西师范大学出版社，2009：31.

以向外界开放自己，而不受实用性的规制。

然而，对民族元素与文化来说，民间器物并不完全等同于海德格尔所说的器具，因为民族与传统生活方式中的器物更具有神秘性，而不仅仅局限于一般所说的工具性特征，它总是与民族的精神特质和地方性文化相关。"伊里巴强调的简洁、明亮色彩和异域风情的艺术风格，深深地吸引了波烈，波烈认为那些都是受客户欢迎的元素。"❶正因如此，不能把民族器物或工艺简单地归结为某种功能性实体。古代民间工艺的许多绣品，其图案主要是传统的与符号化的自然，但这些关于自然的传统图案的含义往往超出了自然本身。对器物命名与作出规定的问题，是与器物功能及文化等诸多元素和关系分不开的。

作为装饰与美化人身体的衣服，既是一种具有实际功用的器物，也是一种社会与文化象征符号。在艺术史与审美文化中，各种器物还成为视觉表现的原型或母题，并以图案的方式进入民族服饰与艺术的表现中。但一旦进入艺术表现与服饰审美里，那些器物就不再是一般的用具与实用品，而是已嵌入艺术、历史与文化语境里的文本存在。在这里，器物造型也称为"器形""形制"等，它与物质文化、仪式和日常生活密切相关。而且，这种生成性关联及其特质，还成为器形意义和信仰旨趣形成的语境，正是在这种语境里，器物与仪式、信仰的相互生成关系才得以建立。

应当意识到，不同民族的器物的造型与文化特质及其关联是有差异的。考古学对物质文化、仪式和日常生活关系的界定，传统上是以它们的特质及其区别为基础的。一般来说，仪式在特殊场所举行，并且运用较为特殊的手段。正因如此，仪式中的物质文化以其反常规性被彰显出来。从形式和语境及其关联来看，仪式所凭借的器物都与日常事项有着明显的区别。作为一种器物的服饰，既被用于人们的日常生活中，也被用于特殊的非日常性领域，比如节日着装与各种礼仪。

作为一种独特的器物样式，礼服往往出现于某些重大的场合，它是参与者穿着的既庄重又正式的服装。还要注意到，许多器物与工具都可能成为禁忌之物。正如弗雷泽所说："也许早在铁器还是新奇之物的上古社会就已经因迷信而不肯使用它了。"❷对服饰来说，禁忌主要指普通民众衣冠与着装行为有关信仰的禁忌。仪式与信仰的关联虽然与技道关系相似，但又不能仅仅归结和阐发为这种技道关系。在时尚创意与设计中，色彩元素无疑与各民族的文化特质密不可分。

毋庸置疑，技是揭示与通达道不可或缺的东西，而道又反过来规定与制约着技，但在生成论的思想语境里，任何关于技与道的二元论及其问题与困境都亟待得到解决。而且，道要规定技，技要服从、归于与通达道本身，但两者之间的相互生成与融为一体才是至境。任何对技的极端强调，往往容易导致技术主义，从而对道本身带来遮蔽。因此，要对技道

---

❶ 诺埃尔·帕洛莫·乐文斯基.世界上最具影响力的服装设计师[M].周梦,郑姗姗,译.北京：中国纺织出版社，2014：14.

❷ J.G.弗雷泽.金枝——巫术与宗教之研究[M].王培基,徐育新,张泽石,译.北京：商务印书馆,2013：375.

的传统问题与困境加以悬置与克服。与此同时，元素构成的分层与对分层的不断突破，正在成为一种基于互文的创意发生的可能基础。

二、民族元素意义的关联与互文

在这里，创意元素无不经由视觉转换来表达，从而将观念、想法传递到时尚艺术与服饰中。与此同时，民族元素意义的关联与传达不仅非常重要，而且无疑是一个极其复杂的生成过程。在"克洛德·列维-斯特劳斯看来，意义对于认知来讲，永远是不可公度的"。❶但还应看到，一切意义都处于不断解构与建构的交替过程中。在语言哲学里，意义相关于词语与事物的关联及其含义，因此离不开各种意义理论对词与句的理解及阐释。当然，民族元素不仅是一般性存在的，它还成为民族艺术与文化的重要构成。

民族元素及其构成的内在、浅层与表观，其实都是元素及其社会性、文化性关联所发生的不同层面。创意元素内在、浅层与表观之间的意义关联，也是经由信仰、仪式与器物的特定含义来理解的。当然，不同元素创意的视觉化方式与途径也是有所区别的。在内在、浅层与表观之间，以及在信仰、仪式与器物之间，存在着不可忽视的互文性关联，除此之外，在这两种互文性之间还存在着一种元互文。应当说，民族元素的意义建构能否得到民族文化的认同，是所有民族时尚创意与设计都要面对的问题。

任何民族元素的揭示与阐发，其实都离不开复杂的生成性互文。各民族都有其自身的精神与信仰的诉求，这些都表现为民族元素的内在性特质。笛卡尔提出的"我思故我在"的思想，把"从自身出发的思维"亦即"内在性"当作哲学的基本原则。

但只有到了黑格尔那里，思维内在性原则才真正成为近代哲学的基础。这里所说的内在的东西，显然是相对于外表而言的。但古典美学与哲学的认识论及其二元分立困境，难免又将民族元素规限在这种问题与困境里。还应当看到，仪式由个体或群体主持和组织进行，可发生在特定场合或任意地方。作为一种礼仪或表演性器物，脸谱往往具有神秘怪异与强烈的视觉效果，但不同民族又有其特定的造型样式与风格特征。

在仪式施行过程中，一般都有一套严格规定的程序与格式，并由此体现出人们的笃信和虔诚。维特根斯坦对仪式的某种独立性予以强调。"从维特根斯坦对詹姆斯·弗雷泽爵士所著《金枝》的注疏中可以清楚地看出，他主张行为模式、举止以及仪式这类词，应该与信念、解释、神话这类词有所区别，而拥有自主权。"❷就宗教人类学派的礼仪先行论而言，首先提出这个理论的是罗伯特·史密斯，其后，马雷特与普洛伊斯等也都提出了类似的主张。泰勒、弗雷泽等都认为，原始时代的宗教发生于原始哲学家头脑内萌生的某种宗教观念，如万物有灵观念、巫术观念等。

史密斯、马雷特等人反其道而行之，认为行动先于观念，先有宗教的行动，后来才在

---

❶ 若斯·吉莱姆·梅吉奥.列维-斯特劳斯的美学观[M].怀宇，译.天津：天津人民出版社，2003：137.
❷ 马里奥·佩尔尼奥拉.仪式思维[M].吕捷，译.北京：商务印书馆，2006：37.

此基础上产生比较明确的宗教观念。因此，这种宗教行动就是宗教礼仪。在大多数民族中，是从宗教礼仪中派生出神话，而不是从神话中派生出宗教礼仪。而且，礼仪本身就是由感受到同一宗教情绪的人们集体进行和完成的，各种祭祀活动的着装与仪式往往具有特定民族的精神与文化特质。在这里，社会集体赋予行动一定的规则，并依靠规则使行为活动固定下来，为以后仪式的实施提供了示范。当然，民族宗教礼仪的实施离不开器物的介入与凭借。

作为一种礼仪性的器物，服饰在许多具有神圣意味的活动中，彰显了一个人的审美情趣与文化素养。例如，印度传统风格服装一般以披挂围裹式纱丽为特征，加上带有神秘感的土红、深灰与褐色。人的服饰与着装既要自然得体及彰显个性，也要遵守某种约定俗成的规范或原则。在传统的傩文化里，无不涉及服饰、面具与歌舞等诸多方面，傩舞本身就是傩仪式的重要构成部分。目前，许多传统仪式正在变得世俗化与人性化。人类早已将其生活习俗、审美情趣与宗教观念，都积淀在日常生活的服饰穿戴方式中。此外，还必须关注生活环境与场合对人的着装的要求，也就是考虑与时间、地点和目的等的协调或呼应。

在戏剧表演中，道具、情节与场景对着装也有其特定诉求，这些传统都可以在现当代时装设计中得到表征。服饰文化的精神贯注与器物文明的内在特质，奠定与开启了民族衣生活与服饰文化及其建构。每个民族的创意元素都有其独特的、区别于其他民族元素的特质，所有特定元素及其文化特质也都是意义生成的基础。从工艺来看，民族服饰图案可以分为刺绣图案、织锦图案、蜡染图案、扎染图案、镶嵌图案等。一般来说，刺绣主要有苏绣、湘绣、蜀绣、粤绣与汉绣等。在众多少数民族刺绣中，苗族以刺绣精美细致与手法多样而著称。

在所有的器物或器具类型中，仪式型器物往往具有最高的精神性特质，而与一般器具的工具性与实用性相分离。仪式型器物往往只能出现于仪典性场合，在人与人或人与神的盟誓中扮演角色，这种器物在艺术与文化史上成为宗教性收藏品。比如，佛教要求仪式型器物必须经过"开光"程式，而后才能获得必要的神通。各民族都有其悠久的历史与文化，以及独特的民族元素与服饰传统。因此，揭示与研究各民族独特与不可替代的元素及其特质，以及这些民族元素在时尚创意里的表现方式，进而经由时尚创意来表征与彰显元素背后的民族文化，并由此彰显民族元素所隐含的精神意义是创意设计不可忽视的。

传统的民族服饰不仅涉及视觉性建构，还往往将信仰、仪式与器物特质相关联。在牯藏节上，苗族男子穿着牯藏头服饰举行祭祖大典，衣色鲜艳，纹样纯朴。在传统艺术表现与审美过程中，"通常每个部落都会使用一套族人都能看懂的基本符号，艺人可以按自己的意愿修改或组合这些符号"。❶ 在古代的交往仪式中，鞠躬是对他人敬佩的一种礼节方式。在传统的鞠躬礼仪中，人们必须立正、脱帽。其实，人们日常生活里的许多行为，都与特

---

❶ 帕特里克·弗兰克.视觉艺术原理[M].陈玥蕾，俞钰，译.上海：上海人民美术出版社，2008：23.

定的服饰、着装和文化相关。在仪式、宗教文化等行为与器物传承中，同样涉及深层的民族心理与文化特质，而且，各种行为与器物往往只有象征意义。

其实，仪式型器物本身就是仪式与器物的密切结合。值得注意的是，器物不仅能够在宗教仪式中通达神圣，而且它本身就被赋予了某种神圣性特质。除了仪式型器物外，还有功能型器物、身份型器物与精神型器物等。实际上，器物还往往成为时尚创意的构图元素，广泛地存在于民族的日常衣生活方式中。不少传统的时尚风俗如缠足等，无疑是对女子身体的一种塑形与重构，这种行为与器物、仪式密切相关，但这种做法由于贬损身体与缺乏人性，在现代的生活方式里已不再使用。

西周的祭服表明了冕服制度的形成与建构，此后礼就成为中国服饰文化的根本性规定。在日常生活中，人们往往采用招手致意、欠身致意、脱帽致意等形式来表达友善之意。其实，器物并不仅属于形而下的东西，它还被赋予了形而上的精神层面的意味。形而上指的是可感世界的根本性规定，它往往是抽象的与难以感知的，并且是作为可感世界的根据而存在的。英伽登认为，"形而上学质"是文艺作品的至高诉求。但是，这种质又离不开审美经验与审美价值关涉。其实，本体论就是探讨形而下世界的形而上根据的。但在东方文化里，并没有预设西方那样的本体论的存在。

但是，东西方在精神诉求与旨趣上又密切相关。其实，中国自古就不乏宇宙生成论的思想与文化特质。不同于一般日常生活的必需品，仪式中的器物常常具有装饰、情调、怀旧、道德化与趋利辟邪的属性。应意识到，"和对象物一样，意指作用的支撑物总是由物体、衣服、衣服的某些部件或饰品构成的"。❶ 还可以说，礼仪型器物既与民族精神图式和文化特质相关，同时又经由创意的视觉化及其表象得以彰显。除功能与实用之外，服饰等造物的社会与文化意义和旨趣还有待于揭示与阐发。而且，各种民族服饰及其元素一旦佩戴或装饰在身，无不散发出象征性而非功利性的意义。

例如，五行与五色就是象征民族内在精神的色彩元素，它们由于被纳入"礼治"而成为仪式的表现方式。鲍德里亚认为，现代性是以工业资本主义和资产阶级霸权上升为特征的生产的时代，而后现代则是一个由符号、代码和模型控制的模拟的时代。民族元素及其意义也难免在当代发生重构，而这种重构还与形形色色的殖民主义，以及后（新）殖民主义相关联。所有民族元素不仅具有自身独特的价值诉求，而且在与其他元素的相互生成中形成意义，这与从器物、仪式到信仰的发展过程相关，展现于不同层面与维度。

随着"民族风"在时尚界的流行，各类民族服饰的特有元素越来越为设计师们所青睐。挖掘、整理与运用民族服饰元素，对保护与传承民族艺术及时尚文化意义重大。但是，还要注意到服饰元素与图案的历史性变化。比如，"历朝历代对龙的形象进行了演化与发展，或爬行、或卷曲交缠，变化无穷，极具装饰感"。❷ 对民族元素及其意义的关注与强调，虽

---

❶ 罗兰·巴特.流行体系——符号学与服饰符码[M].敖军，译.上海：上海人民出版社，2000：73.
❷ 汪芳.中国传统服饰图案解读[M].上海：东华大学出版社，2014：22.

然是民族文化多样性的根本诉求与回归，但这往往又是以西方强势民族优越的文化心理为语境的。对西方殖民主义的文化批判，显然是民族时尚艺术建构与不断重构的前提。在创意与设计过程中，民族性不仅贯注于内在的精神图式中，而且在视觉审美中得到揭示与阐释。

三、元素的民族性与文化特质

一切艺术与时尚的创意与设计过程，其实都需要各种相关元素的介入与参与，而这些元素都有其特定的民族性与文化特质。民族性特质往往经由艺术创作及其文本得以体现，同时民族艺术又是与民族的人类学存在密切相关的。毫无疑问，这种民族性是艺术、时尚与文化不可忽视的人类学问题，它旨在将不同的时尚风格与文化区分开。实际上，民族的生存及其所关联的民族性特质，既是民族文化不可或缺的内在精神基础，也是民族时尚观念与思想得以生成的存在论前提。就服装与时尚设计而言，款式、色彩与材料其实都与民族性或地方性难以分开。

但这并不是说，民族性简单与直观地规定着时尚创意表现，以至于所有的时装作品都充斥着外显的民族元素，而旨在表明，民族性渗透在民族创意及其文化的根基里，并以各种或隐或显的独特方式得以表征，甚至在变形或抽象的当代艺术里得到重构。当然，时尚创意所涉及的元素无疑是多种多样的，各种元素及其关联揭示与彰显了创意的文化特质，这同时也在很大程度上，规定与影响着创意的艺术品位与独特生活情趣。具体来说，由于长期受佛教文化的影响，藏族具有独特的僧侣服制，因此，黄色就成为可重构的时尚元素。不仅如此，黄色还是历代帝王的专用色。

但在不同民族生活方式与文化里，黄色所表征的象征意味与趣味并不一致。因此，这里存在着一个民族元素有何独特的意味与特质，以及元素又是如何对时尚加以审美表现的问题。这些问题不仅表现在当代艺术语境里的视觉文化中，还关联到如何借鉴民族艺术及其在造型、色彩等方面的独特表现。揭示时尚所关联的元素及其文化特质，也是时尚创意得以生成与建构的重要前提。如何揭示视觉表现及其与民族特质的关联，以及民族元素的创意重构离不开当下生活方式的问题，也与不同时期民族元素的历史性发生的社会语境分不开。

对于民族时尚来说，元素及其风格还涉及民族文化特质问题，这种民族文化也关联着时代、生活与社会的诸多方面。应当注意到，"长期以来，艺术史学家也在思考艺术风格与场合、时代或与个人之间的关系"。❶ 民族元素及其向时尚艺术与设计的渗透，其实也是一个民族与传统文化在当代获得重构的过程。譬如，维多利亚装束多呈S形，内穿紧身胸衣与裙撑，这种传统元素与风格还在英国当代设计师薇薇安·韦斯特伍德的新款时尚里得到了重构。与此同时，还必须考虑究竟如何实现时尚化的表现，以及怎样才能建构富有文化

---

❶ 彼得·伯克.什么是文化史[M].蔡玉辉，译.北京：北京大学出版社，2009：113.

特质的时尚感的问题。

在艺术与文化的语境里，民族性及其元素得以在创造性的当下重构，无疑是激活民族创意与设计灵感的重要方式。当然，民族性特质也是民族衣生活时尚感赖以建构的精神与文化基础。如何在视觉化中表现民族意识与文化，也是民族时尚创意与设计应该加以探究的问题。与之相关，艺术的世界性特质表明，某一民族的艺术获得了世界性的文化认同。但只有充分注重民族性与世界性的生成性关联，才能促使民族的时尚融入并成为世界性的时尚。还可以说，艺术总是与一定民族的生活、文化相关切，并将对民族元素文化特质的揭示与民族精神的建构关联起来。

无论就创作者、接受者而言，还是考虑到艺术活动的发生，元素与民族生活的关切都是不可避免的，这无疑是艺术民族性存在的生成论基础。与此同时，无论是一般的自由艺术表现样式，还是具有实用诉求的时尚设计，它们都是人类生活史与文化得以建构的重要方式，而这些建构在社会与历史语境中表征出独特的文化特质。在17世纪，"对西欧的上等阶层来说，佩戴某些款式的假发是完全必需的，因此这种时尚得以持续存在了近一个世纪"。❶ 实际上，时尚创意总是与一定民族、群体的生存、生活相关的，这种创意尤其关切于特定族群的存在及其文化语境。

在结构与同构层面，文化特质的揭示与民族元素的重构是相互呼应的。在这里，民族性甚至成为时尚文化创意的重要来源，它也是地方艺术与文化特质揭示的精神关涉。在创意方面，由于涉及的因素众多，而且有无所不在的文化语境，元素的民族性及其文化特质的挖掘与阐发，无疑成为时尚创意与设计的重要诉求。元素的民族性与文化特质的揭示，无不与时尚创意的生成密切关联。正因如此，时尚等文化创意如何与民族元素发生关联，显然是应给予认真关注与深入探究的问题。在让·鲍德里亚看来，媒介在当代社会中的加速作用，相当于从现代生产领域堕落到后现代模拟社会。

与此同时，时尚创意的产生与表现，还关切于一切观念、想法的视觉化问题，因为时尚艺术其实主要是经由视觉化来表现的，但这种视觉化表现还关涉难以直接加以视觉表现的诸多因素。针对不同民族服装与色彩的象征意义，"列维-斯特劳斯试图强调自己观点适用的普遍性，而利奇则强调观点的相对性和文化的特殊性"。❷ 在不同民族的艺术表现与传播上，应以关联于内在精神图式的视觉化加以回应。一个民族的文化是该民族的灵魂与精神所在，显然是应加以挖掘、整理与当代传承的，否则一个民族的精神、观念与思想，就会式微并失去根本性的文化底蕴。

就民族元素的创意而言，涉及与视觉表现密切相关的文化重构，但这些都是以民族精神的文化特质为基础的。不同民族元素的创意视觉化方式，当然也是有所不同并应给予区别对待的。一种关于民族的时尚表现与创意设计，总是在不同层面对这种文化特质予以揭

---

❶ 詹姆斯·拉韦尔.服装和时尚简史[M].林蔚然，译.杭州：浙江摄影出版社，2016：112.
❷ 艾伦·巴纳德.人类学历史与理论[M].王建民，刘源，许丹，译.北京：华夏出版社，2006：142.

示与阐发。但绝不能采取简单的与非历史的文化执态,将民族艺术与文化遗存作出好坏与优劣的区分。应当说,民族的生存及其文化的民族性根基,既是民族艺术与服饰不可分离的人类学前提,也是民族时尚创意与设计的观念及思想之源。

作为一种历史性沉淀,文化既是经过漫长历史积累的产物,也是一种具有内在精神特质的东西,而且,文化是一个民族成为自身的标识与象征。"文化"一词源于拉丁文"cultura",意为栽培、种植与耕作等,它相关于人的一种生成性过程。在19世纪晚期,"文化"一词进入了诸多社会科学领域,并成为这些学科不可或缺的观念与思想构成。不同民族在艺术与衣生活上的关联和交往,以及时尚创意的跨文化传播都是不可避免的。这是因为任何民族都不可能绝对孤立地在世存在,正因如此,民族服饰与传统文化的复合性与混杂性,也成为民族生活不可忽视的精神与文化特质。

如果说,只有一些要么正确要么错误的东西存在于文化之中,那么,这种文化显然是被概念化的、抽干精髓的,甚至只是一种脸谱化的文化定格,无疑是没有内在精神与创造性可言的。对于民族艺术与文化来说,传承是不可或缺的历史使命与思想任务。应当看到,"对于审美反思的研究,不能局限于孤立的思想领域,而要结合各种审美现象以及具体的美感,还要关注审美观所隐含的社会文化寓意"。❶ 在民族服饰与文化的传承上,民族文化内在精神的挖掘与重构是至关重要的。但这并不意味着,人们可以简单地肯定好的与抛弃坏的东西,而是需要加以细心的分析与辨别,以及深入的解读与研究。

对待民族元素与文化的问题,任何粗鄙与草率的态度都是有害且不可取的。在民族元素与时尚创意里,民族文化特质的表征与视觉在各种层面相关。之所以如此,乃是因为文化本身就是一种结构性整体,但它又总是经由自身的开放性,而与其他民族甚至异质文化相关联。但应注意到,没有一个单一的与固定不变的民族性元素在那里,而它规定着时尚创意的发生与表现及其文化关联。民族文化渗透在民族时尚创意的根基与精神深处,以及一切与时尚相关的诸多元素及其关联与表现中。

在各民族的时尚创意中,要充分注重各民族元素及其文化特质的揭示,只有这样的时尚创意才会有民族文化的底蕴。同时,民族元素及其向时尚艺术的渗透与嵌入,还得考虑究竟如何实现时尚化表现,以及怎样才能获得当下时尚感的问题。而且,"把原始艺术或土著艺术看作是超越它自己的文化和语境并用一种普遍美学的声音与我们对话,会减少甚至否定它的原初意义和目的的重要性"。❷ 对于不同民族来说,视觉思维与心理习惯显然也是有所差异的,这些差异共同构成了民族元素与文化的生成性语境。

因此,元素的视觉化表现要考虑到不同民族间的差异,以及这些差异所关联的社会、历史与文化的意义。如带有浓郁吉卜赛风格的民族风情时装,就是以吉卜赛的民族元素为服饰文化特质的。在这里,民族与文化所具有的密切关联性是不可忽视的,民族文化本身

---

❶ 范丹姆.审美人类学:视野与方法[M].李修建,向丹,译.北京:中国文联出版社,2015:153.
❷ 温尼·海德·米奈.艺术史的历史[M].李建群,等译.上海:上海人民出版社,2007:266.

其实就是文化的重要样式。甚至可以说，任何民族的时尚创意都是以民族及其文化为底蕴的，并将这种文化特质作为时尚感生成不可分离的构成部分。还要看到，文化认同无不涉及文化针对性与适应性的问题。能否对民族文化特质加以充分的表现，这既取决于设计师独到的理解，也相关于如何对特定的元素进行对话式重构。

其实，艺术与文化的相互生成，无疑是以民族存在为基础的，民族的生存与生活甚至融入这种相互生成中。与此同时，民族文化通过各种变迁回应着民族的生活方式。一个民族最基本的社会实践活动，就是物质生产活动和精神生产活动，这是民族为了生存和生活所采取的重要活动方式。正是这一基本活动的存在与展开，建构了民族自己的物质文化和精神文化。甚至可以说，文化在本性上就是人化，一切文化都以人为根本的旨归与诉求。那些经过人加工改造及人化的非自然物，其实都可以涵括在文化领域。

对自然与生活的审美照观所积累的经验，无疑也成为民族艺术与文化的重要构成。如果只是对民族文化特质加以外在的、毫无内在精神关联的表征，就会贬损民族元素及其在当代重构所表现出来的艺术底蕴。实际上，民族共同的语言、地域与生活，以及表现于共同文化特质上的共同心理素质，显然是一个民族生存与认同的重要前提与基础。但应当注意到，在存在论上，这种不同民族的共存，也可能导致特定民族独特性的式微甚至消失。在同一个民族内部，各个成员的心理与文化气质其实也是有差异的，但这些差异又往往消弭在群体生活的共同存在中。

与此同时，无论是信仰、仪式，还是器物，它们的存在都有其不可分割的民族性与文化特质，以及它们与原始艺术和文化密切的生成性关联。因此，强调原始与民族的艺术和文化的独特性无疑是重要的。同时，"一切艺术的表现，都应当是由艺术家的精神中涌现而出，所以能'自然布列于心中'，然后能'不觉见之于笔下'"。❶ 而且，这种与民族生存相关切的文化特质及其揭示，是一个民族生活方式的根本性精神诉求之所在，这其实也是阐释民族时尚创意与设计的文化前提。

实际上，民族生活与文化不乏自己的信仰旨趣，包容的文化心态与开放的思想对话，之于民族时尚的创意与设计是必不可少的。作为多民族的融合体，汉族在文化上往往较为宽容开放，信仰上也呈现出多元性的特质。与其他民族相比，汉族的民族性与宗教性似乎显得并不那么直观与鲜明。实际上，仪式的参加者通常是某个社会群体，当然也可以是某个族群的一个家族，还可以是一个家庭或临时集约的社众。民间仪式是依靠"规仪"而传承的文化存在，它通常约束着人们的思维和生活方式。当然，民族特定的生存状况与处境，也可能导致原生态民族文化的相对封闭性。

服饰所承载的精神关涉与传统文化特质，可能远远超出了设计原初设定的各种实用功能，这种超越的意义在于社会与生活的视觉象征。应当说，民族元素的文化特质是与地域

---

❶ 徐复观.中国艺术精神[M].北京：商务印书馆，2010：307.

分不开的，譬如说，北方民族传统服饰裁剪精细、做工考究，南方民族服饰的裁剪就相对简单一些，但装饰的风格与意味更加强烈。其实，民间仪式往往具有显著的民间信仰色彩，以及浓郁的民族性与乡土文化特质。

在这里，乡村田园风格的服饰设计所强调的就是这种地方性与本土文化。而且，这些乡土风格还可分为英式乡土风格、法式乡土风格与美式乡土风格等。毫无疑问，独特的社会关涉与文化语境促成了艺术与文化元素独特性的生成与建构。在时尚的跨文化传播中，不同民族的文化特质也引起了关注。譬如，"欧洲人穿惯了招摇的宫廷服饰，惊讶于美洲妇女服饰的多样性"。❶因此可以说，民族元素所具有的社会与文化意义往往是不可替代的。在本土与民俗文化中，艺术与审美经验融会于人们的生存状态，它们本身甚至成为民族生活方式的重要构成。

艺术与服饰的社会和文化旨趣是多元的与复杂的，而元素的民族性与文化特质却关联到社会意义的生成。在创意与设计过程中，任何简单的复制与拿来都不可能从民族性文化特质中重构出独特的当代时尚。实际上，民族元素及其特质无不具有显著的时代、文化等特征。而且，民族的题材与装饰、造型艺术与表现方式，都会映射出各民族的生存环境、文化风俗等。作为一种人造物，传统服饰是民族精神及其独特贯注的生成物，也是对民族性元素及其社会与文化意义的揭示与彰显。

第二节　民族元素及其时尚化方式

虽然民族元素是时尚创意重要的基础与前提，但民族元素本身其实还不是时尚本身，它不会自动地、不加建构地进入时尚，更不能人为地或任意地将元素置入时尚创意中。其实，并不存在所谓绝对的与僵化的民族元素，一切与民族存在及其文化相关的元素或因素，实际上都可以成为潜在与可能的时尚创意元素，以及时尚当下感生成与建构的艺术、审美与文化前提。与此同时，民族元素及其艺术与文化在本质上都是生成性的，都有待于在当代进行创造性的审美建构与重构。只有基于建构与重构，原始的民族元素才能成为可能的甚至现实的时尚元素。虽然民族元素进入时尚的方式与路径是多种多样的，但是，这些创意思路与方法并不是固定不变与彼此无关的，它们是相互关联的与互文性的。还应当注意到，民族元素的时尚化并不是把元素简单纳入服饰文本，而是在表明与强调民族元素与各种语境相互关联的当下生成的。

一、作为时尚化的延异与顺应

民族元素在服饰中的借鉴离不开时尚化建构。之所以在此提及时尚化，旨在表明时尚

---

❶ 玛尼·弗格.时尚通史[M].陈磊，译.北京：中信出版社，2016：139.

的创意与设计是一种生成性过程，没有一种艺术表现形式可以离开该过程而成为时尚。一般来说，时新、新奇甚至陌生感，往往是一种时尚得以生成的感性特质。在服饰创意与设计过程中，如何充分借鉴民族元素并实现其在当代的重构，显然是民族乃至世界时尚艺术与文化的重要课题。考虑到时尚艺术与文化强调的是流变与独特的当下感，一切时装设计都把当下感的生成作为根本性诉求。民族元素的借鉴及其向时尚感的转化，实际上是一个不断生成与重构的过程。与时尚化相关联的创意方式不少，但每一种方式都是独特而不可替代的。

当然，从来就没有一个民族的时尚感是自动产生的，一个民族的元素也不能被时尚的建构。其实，艺术、时尚与美感从来都不是一成不变的。毫无疑问，艺术与时尚之美还会随时代而变，"在一个时代，它可能意味着美、感性的完美或技能的完善，在另一个时代，人们则认为、希望但又害怕它意味着意义的最彻底的不确定性和无意义的多形态的开放性"。❶ 建构是民族元素成为某种时尚元素的生成论基础，其与艺术及文化上的解构相关联。在时尚感的生成过程中，建构的发生往往是基于解构而存在的。

在生成论的语境里，民族元素的建构与解构还处于相互生成中。在艺术创意与设计中，建构所强调的是艺术表现与审美生成的过程，以及对这种过程的揭示与生成论表达。但实际上，建构还要首先拆解元素文本里既有的观念与意义模式，以及各种各样的理性哲学与形而上学预设。建构既不是一劳永逸的简单肯定与直接因循，也不是无中生有的所谓虚构或杜撰，而是一种对元素与文本的重新敞开及激活，以生成新的话语体系、意义与文化旨趣。民族元素及其向时尚艺术的介入，其实是将元素自身置入时尚文本，也就是元素时尚化的生成过程。

与建构相对的是解构，解构着重对文本及其意义加以解体与破坏。在解构的基础上，重构往往被理解与阐发为一种再建构，也就是说，重构将建构指向了已经构造起来的话语与意义。针对那些历史性存在与生成的民族元素，延异与顺应无疑是一种重要的时尚化手法。具体说来，"延"指延缓，"异"指差异，"延异"（分延）即由"区分"（differ）与"推延"（defer）两个词合成，它因此代表着原初意义被不断地放逐与消解。甚至还可以说，彻底的解构本身就离不开建构，建构与解构在本性上是相互生成的。其实，海德格尔的"拆解"（德文为 Abbau，英文为 unbuilding）被雅克·德里达借用与改造为"解构"。

在本性上，时间性使形而上学失去了最终的根基，而时间在时间化中成为虚无之源。正因如此，与时间性相关切的历史性特质，为民族元素重构出当下时尚感提供了根本性可能，虽然那些过时的样式也是时尚要解构的文本。还要意识到，一切既有的艺术表现与审美活动，都难以摆脱理性形而上学的规定与影响，这就亟待在解构中获得当下时尚感。随着人类生活方式的历史性变化，民族元素及其在服饰与时尚中的重构，也就是对民族元素

---

❶ 蒂埃里·德·迪弗.艺术之名：为了一种现代性的考古学[M].秦海鹰，译.长沙：湖南美术出版社，2001：66.

加以挖掘与表现的过程。

但西方近代以来，人的本性被固定化，与人相关切的生存状态，往往被归结为某种现成存在物。同时，理性难免成为探究艺术和审美的出发点，因此也遮蔽了生存与存在的生成本性。与此不同，海德格尔把此在的本性规定为去存在，由此作为探讨艺术和美的问题的根基。出于对反形而上学的彻底性诉求的回应，德里达提出并解释了延异并用于艺术与审美的研究之中。其实，延异往往表示一个词的意义，不仅取决于它与其他词的区别，而且存在于它在时间的流动中。

在这种流变中，一个词语与其他词语发生交叠、贯穿，从而推延了它的意义的出现。在时尚化的过程中，延异既对民族元素重构中的差异与延缓加以强调，同时重构所生成的这种别致与另类感似乎又似曾相识。如新维多利亚式套装，它虽在造型上留有19世纪宫廷女装的痕迹，但又不衬紧身胸衣。"自然，'延异'的这种始终都已经优先于'在'，不可能根据任何传统的时间上的或先验的优先来思考。"❶ 传统西方哲学及其逻各斯中心主义假设了一种固定不变的意义的存在，并坚持与强调对某种一致性的诉求。作为空间的隔离与时间的推延的关联，延异使静止的区分流动起来，而不是停留在任何固定的状态上。

作为一种延缓的踪迹，延异对意义的不断消解与逻各斯中心主义，在本性上是有所不同甚至针锋相对的。在这里，踪迹是在场的不在场，以及不在场的在场。在延异与顺应之间，起连接作用的无疑是展开。应当说，展开就是在延异的基础上，对民族元素及其意义的敞开与揭示。在时尚设计对民族元素的借鉴中，还需要发现元素可能被遮蔽的意义。也就是说，以延异为基础，展开将设计向着意义的生成与再建构拓展，它既能对民族元素的既有遮蔽物加以祛蔽，又能回到民族元素的原初意义来重构。

其实，没有任何时尚只是简单地复制和搬用以往的民族元素及艺术风格，当下时尚与审美风格的建构，仍然相关于对以往元素与风格的延异及展开。虽然迪奥的新风貌曾经获得世界范围的空前关注，但是，"事实上，新风貌一点也不新，它其实是一个20世纪30年代晚期和被占领时期的夸张风格的简化版本，并与英国和美国战时的服装出品呈现出完全相反的一面"。❷ 又如，源于20世纪70年代伦敦的朋克装，后来又跨文化传播并影响了欧美各国服饰风尚。20世纪90年代以后，时装界还出现了以鲜艳、破烂、简洁、金属与街头等为表征的后朋克风潮。

海德格尔认为，世界的本性是敞开的、开放的，大地的本性则是幽闭的，艺术作品正是世界与大地争执的结果。与此同时，作品不仅是自足的世界，还以其特有的开放性向艺术通达。在本性上，作品就是这种抗争的承担者，而真理就发生在这种争执中。在世界与大地的争执中，存在者整体显现出来，这种显现就是美，也就是真理的根本性发生。由于艺术具有建立世界和显现大地两大特质，因此其具有揭示世界的意义和存在的真理的价值，

---

❶ 埃克伯特·法阿斯.美学谱系学[M].阎嘉，译.北京：商务印书馆，2011：446-447.
❷ 詹姆斯·拉韦尔.服装和时尚简史[M].林蔚然，译.杭州：浙江摄影出版社，2016：245.

当然也指向浓郁民族特质与风情的传统元素。

应当说，关切于民族性的艺术表现与时尚创意，也是经由延异从地方性拓展而来的艺术世界，而在当下建构的艺术世界又反过来构成与大地的呼应。在这里，生成论是对艺术传统本体论及其形而上学的反动。在生存论那里，美的形而上学的本质与基础得以消解和解构，美的存在问题不再需要形而上学的设立。虽然海德格尔的思想主要是现代时期的，但他具有对现代性及其问题的深刻反思。同时正是海德格尔使德里达将解构作出了更彻底的推进。即使在解构主义与后现代语境里，重建与消解也是彼此关联、难以分离的，它们可以同时应用于创意的时尚化过程中。

例如，川久保玲时尚创意独创的前卫风格，显然并不全是纯民族性的元素与样式，而是把东西方元素纳入当代加以对话与重构。在存在论的语境里，存在的生成本性是应给予关注的根本问题，正是这种生成性使传统元素与文化的延异，在当代重构获得了一种历史性的特质。也就是说，存在即虚无表明没有任何根据，或者说自身就是自身的根据，这其实正是艺术与美的本性之所在。海德格尔为艺术与美的问题，构建了一个存在论的基础，此基础已不同于传统的形而上学，进而成为他中、晚期美学思想展开的前提。

对于一切时尚创意与设计来说，消解民族元素所固有的限定与各种内外遮蔽，无疑是将民族元素的本性加以揭示与延异的基础。而且，延异发生在一切作品或文本中，它使创意与设计的时尚化成为可能。甚至可以说，一切创新与时尚化无不源自或相关于延异。实际上，"解构的目的是重组，解构使很多看似不可能的造型因素，随着审美的变化变得可行和时尚"。❶ 当然，任何当下的创意、设计与时尚化的意义，又通过历史性与传统文化构成了回应与对话。在延异的基础上，顺应将传统的解构与当下语境发生勾连，这也是创意与设计的时尚化不可分离的构成。

顺着某种趋势适应时代的潮流，也是认知结构性质的改变。在对传统元素加以延异的前提下，形状、色彩、花纹与面料都涉及调和与顺应的问题。也就是说，顺应就是认知结构受被同化刺激的影响而发生变化。但这并不是说，顺应与时代所发生的变化简单地同化。可以说，顺应式结构是一个有足够柔性的开放式结构。在顺应的过程中，民族元素传统的意义既有所保留，又会发生相应的变化，然后传递到新的时尚文本与语境中。在这种开放与变化的结构中，民族的创意元素也发生着历史性的生成与互文。

这种顺应还涉及元素之间的关切与共同存在，以及不同元素的交织与对话及其在当代的重构。在创意与设计过程中，发生的正是诸多元素的相互呼应与彼此间的文化适应，以及各个元素与社会、历史和文化语境的调适，这样才能与元素的那些原初含义、旨趣发生历史性的生成性关联。除原有语境之外，这一过程还涉及民族元素在新的文本中的一致性问题。一切设计都是将创意观念加以视觉化表现，通过视觉把观念与精神转化为象征符码，

---

❶ 苏永刚.服装时尚元素的提炼与运用[M].重庆：重庆大学出版社，2007：67.

再经由接受者的解码而获得关于民族时尚的意义。因此，一切理念、观念都向创意发生视觉化转换，并将视觉符码予以揭示与拓展，以顺应着装者对时尚观念与表现的身份与文化认同。

但是，这种顺应并不能理解与把握为一种同化，因为它还须将不一致性控制在一定程度。其实，设计之所以能够成为一种艺术样式，显然是离不开理念或创意的视觉化的。蔡元培认为，"被服之装饰，如冠、服、带、佩及一切金、钻、珠、玉之饰皆是。近世文明民族，已日趋简素；惟帝王、贵族及军人，犹有特别之制服；而妇女冠服，尚喜翻新"。❶ 就时尚化的表达而言，即揭示与彰显民族元素的精神负载与文化意味。顺应一般体现为语言的语境和语言结构选择之间的相互适应，这也涉及与美化的社会和文化语境的呼应。

与此同时，顺应还关涉变异性、协商性与适合性等问题。在民族元素时尚化的过程中，顺应还要考虑到移译或借鉴本身所涉及的审美与文化语境。应当说，时尚感是既在某种传统的连续性中，又在这种连续的中断中来建构自身的。还要注意到，任何设计的创意所关联的问题与语境，实质上都是开放性的、生成性的，创意的过程往往是不确定的，因此需要不断地加以协商与顺应。比如，流行的分析与预测就是基于信息与市场，以及社会生活方式的变化与近期动态，对即将流行的色彩、款式与风格作出推断。甚至可以说，这种流行预测就是综合各方面资讯所协商的结果。

因此，设计的顺应性使人们得以从一系列不确定的可能性中，来建构那些当下颇具新意的元素意味与所在社会和文化语境的关涉性。在时尚化过程中，应尽可能选择可协商的时尚语言、设计符码与市场策略，以便达到对艺术与文化的交流、传播的理解和接受。但能否协商并没有一个明确的边界与严格的标准，而是取决于对何谓协商性本身的理解与不断重构。变异性和协商性的审美张力是时尚化的基础，因为它们为顺应提供了切实的可能性。应当说，顺应性是符码与话语表意功能的表征及其适应性体现。对各种相互冲突与对立的元素或因素加以渐变处理，旨在生成一种和解的张力，这也是一种与延异相对冲的顺应性手法。

作为一种艺术、审美与文化样式，时尚设计是不断地选择和顺应的生成性过程，但这离不开基于解构而发生的创意与表达的延异及其拓展。与此同时，时尚化的创意与设计表现本身，其实也是对先前的各类元素及其含义，尤其是既有审美方式与文化的一种挑战与疏离。但是，"从时尚的角度看，在反文化与现存文化之间不存在真正的对立"。❷ 因为，一切为了变化而作出的反离与质疑，无疑都难免成为一种新的既成文化样式，以及由此而受到后来艺术与文化的疏离与挑战。应当说，文化原型是文化的根本性源头或模式，但它又是形而上学预设的生成之物。

作为服装基础纸样的原型，显然是基于身体而相关于人体与服装的同构的。在新的质

---

❶ 奚传绩.设计艺术经典论著选读[M].南京：东南大学出版社，2002：79.
❷ 拉斯·史文德森.时尚的哲学[M].李漫，译.北京：北京大学出版社，2010：130.

疑与挑战的语境里，新的既成文化可能向它曾经反对的文化回归，这当然还涉及究竟何谓原型这一根本性问题。因此，人们对时尚作品或产品的设计与使用，也是一个根据生活处境和交往的变化，而不断作出选择与接受的审美与文化认同的过程。为此，就要从认知、社会与文化等层面，了解和把握设计究竟是如何顺应消费者的。首先，顺应须考虑认知方面的关涉因素，因为这种认知是社会与文化接受的理性基础。

一个时尚化的创意与设计表达，是否能够得到消费者认知上的理解与肯定，无疑是时尚设计能否被认同的前提。其实，人们对新的衣生活风格的适应，相关于设计对生活者的社会语境的顺应，以及对不同生活方式的包容与尊重。让·皮亚杰认为，顺应指人的主观图式不能容纳外界刺激，便改变原来图式以适应外来刺激的要求。但与之不同的是，"德里达在顺应这种新局势的时候，逐渐通过访谈变得让人更容易理解"。❶而且，时尚化不得不涉及文化间的相似与差异，以及各种新旧元素在时装中的相互关联。在审美与文化的顺应过程中，人们的主观图式也必须发生相应的改变，进而调整原有图式或建构新的图式，以适应生活方式与文化语境的当下变化。

在这里，任何民族元素与文化都难免经由延异而与当下语境发生顺应。任何一种时尚设计策略或手段，只要能够达到预期的目的与诉求，实际上就可以说都有其一定的可取之处。如果要使设计不仅满足功能性诉求，还要表现出某种独特的当下时尚感，对传统元素与既有技法的突破就必不可少。延异与顺应对于创意的时尚化表达，以及使这种表达适切于接受者，在此显然具有独特的审美与社会意义。毫无疑问，延异与顺应还要考虑着装者的文化及其社会语境的问题。时尚化既涉及何谓文化原型的问题，又关联对原型的拓展与重构。

只有得到充分的审美理解与文化认同，民族元素的创意与时尚化重构才具有可行性。在时尚创意中，延异与顺应及其生成性关联也是不可或缺的，因为一个完整的时尚化表达是基于这种关联的。延异是民族元素时尚化表现的基础，顺应则使设计的接受有了切实的可能性。其实，一切优良的时尚创意与设计都离不开延异，而不只是将民族元素简单地搬抄或移植。与此同时，顺应也相关于各种元素的互动，以及与人们心理预期的暗合，而不是简单迎合人们现有的趣味。一切基于民族元素重构的当代时尚，在引领衣生活趋势中依然是不可缺少的。延异是在民族元素原有含义的基础上，加以传承与解构的引申性创意活动。

这种延异还有待于顺应将其运用于新的文本，以及与这种文本相关联的生活与社会语境中。在创意与设计问题上，"我们可以将其他因受宗教和当地习俗影响而更有文化韵味的特征，添加到这些实际元素中，比如一些随时间推移而形成的对装饰元素或绘画色彩的审美偏好"。❷然而，什么元素可以延异与如何延异的问题，并不仅仅相关于原来民族元素的

---

❶ K.马尔科姆·理查兹.德里达眼中的艺术[M].陈思，译.重庆：重庆大学出版社，2016：169.
❷ 罗伯特·克雷.设计之美[M].尹弢，译.济南：山东画报出版社，2010：59.

存在，还要考虑到，怎样顺应所应关切的认知、社会与文化等因素。就服装构成而言，各种元素既相互区分，但又在形式上发生渐变，从而生成有差异的和谐之美。

作为一种时尚化方式，延异与顺应是传统元素在当代的重构，但这种重构既非简单的接受与沿袭，也不是非此即彼的中断与割裂，而是既关联又反离的似是而非与似非而是。其实，复古与怀旧的时尚风格也可看成由延异与顺应所建构。艺术与服饰的继承与文化传播，并不是原封不动地承袭既有的传统文化，而是在整理与研究基础上的当代重构。在时尚创意与设计过程中，延异与顺应是同一个过程的两个构成方面，它们不仅生成着自身，还处于相互的生成中。也就是说，从民族元素及其原初的艺术与文化含义，通过延异揭示基于历史性的新的意义，并将之拓展与顺应到创意设计与制作的全过程。

应当说，与设计所涉及的文化语境展开顺应式的对话，其实旨在延异拓展所应达致的艺术、审美与文化预期的实现。从来没有任何一个固定不变的元素，可以不经由延异与顺应及其相互关联，而简单与随意地搬抄到新的时尚设计中去。所有原封不动、画地为牢式的保留，对民族艺术与时尚文化都是有害无益的。因此，亟待抢在那些已丧失生存环境的古老文化消亡之前，对它们进行大量的收集、整理、记录、保存与重构工作。在时尚化过程中，传承与重构对于民族元素的创意与设计是必不可少的。

虽然日本的和服曾受到中国唐装的深刻影响，但它无疑又经历了在地性或异国性的延异，并与日本的生活方式和文化密切关联。例如，牛仔服虽然源于美国的西部地区，但它后来又延展与传播到社会各阶层与日常生活中，还成为一种相对确定甚至模式化的时装样式。在延异的基础上，还要不断回应各种不同的审美经验与服饰文化。创意与设计亟待对民族元素加以整理、揭示与阐发，从而促成少数民族传统元素的时尚化转换。在民族的生活方式中，设计所涉及的社会、历史与文化语境，无不相关于世代传承、相沿成习的心理习惯。与此同时，延异与顺应都必须考虑各种语境的生成与变化，以及这些变化所关联的艺术表现特质与审美旨趣。

二、挪用、拼贴与时尚的生成

虽然民族时尚的发生、建构与传统元素、文化密切相关，但这种建构依然是经由消解来重构当下时尚感的，因此对解构主义风格与手法的借鉴具有不可忽视的意义。作为一种解构手法，挪用与拼贴不仅在后现代艺术与文化中得到了强调，而且在当代民族时尚创意与设计中具有重要价值。从词源学的角度来看，"挪用"几乎不能再简单或更直接了，它来源于拉丁文"ad"，意思为"向、往……（to）"，具有"参照（referring to）"的含义。挪用（appropriate）含有"模仿与复制"的意思，往往指将某事物从原来的地方搬到另一个地方，从原来的语境移到另一个语境。

应该说，作为后现代主义艺术最重要的创作方法之一，挪用体现了当代艺术与现代艺术的区别及断裂，尤其是对艺术提倡的"原创性"的颠覆与挑战。还可以说，"后现代艺术在将来自各流派、各民族、各地区的样式堆砌到一起的时候，艺术家做的就是一个折中的工作"。❶ 在这种挪用过程中，由于语境的历史性变化，可能导致元素或文本原初含义的改变，从而使符码的解码出现新的意义。在当代艺术表现与创作中，挪用的方法得到了反复的使用与广泛的借鉴，甚至成为最为流行的艺术表现与创作手段。

在对挪用的借鉴与使用中，往往会产生意想不到的特别效果与意义。在广义上，挪用既指对自然的客观对象的挪用，也包括对艺术品本身的挪用。如果挪用涵盖了对自然的模仿，那么挪用就成了艺术本身。在狭义上，挪用仅指对艺术品的挪用。其实，挪用还暗指不正当占有某物甚至绑架或偷窃。但应看到，挪用并不是被动的、客观的、漠然的，而是积极的、主观的、充满目的的。根据挪用的对象和内容的不同，可以将挪用分为表现手法上的挪用、观念与思想的挪用，以及视觉与图像的挪用等。正是这些不同的挪用手法，构成了民族时尚美的诸多理解维度。

还可以说，挪用是使每一个自我发生断裂和错位的策略，它所产生的间离效果不乏消解与重构的特质。与挪用相关，拼贴打破了传统元素的组合与构成方式，以及艺术风格与手法的既有边界，从而使所呈现的感觉独特而别致。如果仅仅从"拼贴"（collage）这个词来讲，它是文本创作的一种技巧，其特征在于从整体上审视它是全新的，但组成它的每个部分都是原有的。也就是说，拼贴将这些原有的不同部分巧妙地整合在文本中，就可以使其呈现出与原来面貌大不相同的特质。

但应看到，拼贴手法不同于传统的拼贴图案。如果说，传统的拼贴图案更多地强调了材料本身的质地与自然纹理，那么，作为解构的拼贴手法诉诸的则是一种非传统与反惯常的组合方式。在艺术与文化研究中，虽然挪用、拼贴是后现代主义采用的重要手法，但这些手法并没有局限在后现代主义思想领域，而是被广泛地运用在艺术与时尚的创意设计中。应意识到，挪用、拼贴是对具有当代意味的后现代主义设计观念的借鉴和延伸。对以解构主义为根本的后现代主义手法的借鉴与运用，对民族元素与艺术表现在当代的重构具有别致的意趣与情调。而将不同民族文化的异质性通过挪用与拼贴，更会产生一种复杂的异质文化情调与趣味。

后现代主义对元解释和文本固定不变意义的反对予以强调。在保持原图式不变的前提下，挪用通常将文本进行置换与解构。当然，由于挪用概念相对宽泛，往往都是先从定义挪用入手，通过与模仿、复制等概念进行深入与细致的比较，分析和阐明艺术与设计及其挪用所具备的特有功能。后现代主义者认为，对给定的一个文本、表征和符号，都有无限多层面的解释可能性。在民族时尚的创意与设计过程中，挪用与拼贴就是对那些固定不变的传统解释的突破，旨在为解释提供不确定性与多元化特质。

正因如此，一般的字面意思和传统解释，就不得不让位给作者意图和读者反映。随着

---

❶ 包铭新，曹喆.国外后现代服饰[M].南京：江苏美术出版社，2001：83.

艺术、审美与文化全球化进程的不断加剧，时尚设计经历了从传统到现代乃至后现代的更迭。因此应看到，"后现代主义改变了关注的方式，不再像符号学家那样只对个别对象凝神细察，而是要求代之以一种多样化的破碎的而且常常是断续的'观看'"。❶但在时尚创意过程中，简单挪用与拼贴的设计风格，其实已不再是民族设计的根本出路。而且，直接借鉴与不加改造地移植传统的东西已无济于事，破碎对整体性加以解构并为拼贴式重构奠定了基础。

在民族时尚的表现中，挪用与拼贴及其相互生成涉及对传统的解构，以及在与既有风格的对话中重构当下时尚感。这种对话既发生在不同元素、文本之间，又发生在文本与各种语境之间。德里达首先提倡的是，在文本的能指与所指之间建立非必然的联系，其目的在于凸显能指与所指搭配的任意性，以及它们之间的差异性与非简单对应性，使所指脱离和摆脱对既定能指的依附，从而扰乱与解构已经固化的结构主义思想。广义的拼贴其实正是拼贴的核心理念之所在，也就是多元、并存、随意、借用等的广泛借鉴。

还要注意到，拼贴的自动构想原则与主题的非理性并置，以及所引起的变形与新意的可能性。应当说，挪用与拼贴并未彻底抛弃传统元素的意义，发生的只是意义与语境及其关系的变化。在本性上，一切现代时尚创意都与解构和后现代主义密切相关。"当然，时装的历史并没有明显的、得到充分证明的现代主义阶段。"❷而且，拼贴还生成了某些在原先的框架与语境中难得一见的陌生感与奇异感。与此同时，拼贴广泛地应用于时尚创意与设计中，尤其是当下时尚感的生成过程中。毫无疑问，拼贴还可以应用于摄影、建筑、文学、音乐等诸多领域。

在这里，狭义的拼贴是一种作画技法，将剪下来的纸张、布片或其他材料，粘贴在画布或其他底面上，从而形成特定的构图效果或画面布局。从理论与方法的视角来看，拼贴是具有后现代意味与思想特质的话语建构方式，它在时尚感的生成上产生了一种与先前元素及其传统组合不同的印象。譬如，朋克激进的"拼贴美学"及其表达，将都市生活的别针等碎屑与肮脏的服装碎片加以再生利用。虽然拼贴往往带有偶然性、随意性，但仍然存在一个究竟如何才能产生时尚感的问题。

同时也可以说，拼贴就是将不同作品、段落、词语、句子掺杂在一起，从而产生一种新的、陌生的和非日常的感觉与审美经验。在这个多元化的时代，确信无疑地谈论艺术与审美的规定，实际上早已成为一件异常困难的事情。还要看到，一切既有的元素及其构成都面临着来自时尚化的挑战。现代艺术不仅失去了传统艺术所赖以建立的根据，而且在其自身的流变与生成过程中，衍生出了关于自身的难以理喻的把握。其实，拼贴在服饰设计中的应用由来已久，例如，服装面料中的补丁图案就是传统拼贴图案的典型样式。当代艺术又拓展出难以穷尽的拼贴手法与方式，为时尚的表现与质感的发生提供了诸多可能性。

---

❶ 安吉拉·默克罗比.后现代主义与大众文化[M].田晓菲，译.北京：中央编译出版社，2001：18.
❷ 史蒂文·康纳.后现代主义文化——当代理论导引[M].严忠志，译.北京：商务印书馆，2002：293.

究竟是在其存在中领会艺术所关联的意义，还是在话语中敞开艺术的存在及其遮蔽，都是有待于在后现代主义思想语境中加以回应的问题。在时尚的创意与设计中，还要充分考虑艺术表现的重构与各种冲突因素的协调，以及如何在解构中重构关于艺术与时尚表现的新奇感。即使在当代艺术与时尚创意的语境中，拼贴仍然有一个怎样才能达到别致美感的问题。与胸前及背后缀有补子的补服的传统拼贴相比，具有当代时尚化特性的拼贴更强调对既有规则与传统秩序的改变和重构，而非维系某种品级与阶层严格的社会标识与文化符码。

实际上，拼贴法的基本构想并无特别创新之处，它只是使似乎并不相关的事物及形象产生关联与组接，旨在改变艺术元素在传统表现手法中的关系与构成。"协调是服装中不可缺少的形式美法则，服装是由多个元素组合而成的，其款式的风格、色彩的运用、面料的组合、装饰的添加、配饰的搭配等都应符合整体设计要求。"❶ 应当看到，服饰各元素的协调与统一是对变化的一种回应，但这绝不是对变化与差异的彻底取消或消解。拼贴完全颠覆了传统艺术的连贯性和一致性，使艺术文本曾有的连续脉络和纵深变化消失殆尽。当然，所有前卫与先锋的时尚化观念与技法，其实都依然离不开与传统文化的思想对话。

这里的问题在于，由于根据与基础的日趋式微甚至根本失却，时尚等艺术表现往往在自律中自说自话。因此出现的联动式情形似乎是，一方面，艺术与自然、生活的边界在迅速地消失；另一方面，艺术与大众文化之间的区分也正在模糊。对于这些变化与趋势，服饰与时尚亟待在走近与远离大众生活之间寻求审美与文化张力。在当代，时尚产业界力图把颇具新锐感的作品推向日常生活，这就难免在打破艺术与生活、大众文化原初界限的同时，又必须在新的视域里促成它们之间的关联、交织与融合。

在这里，拼贴为人们重新理解与把握传统元素及其生成性特质，以及与之相关的文本建构与解构提供了独特的视角。在现代艺术诞生之后，拼贴就开始成为具有特别意义的时尚表达方式。在对固有的理论与思想加以消解之后，后现代主义其实并未导致艺术与审美的真正终结，而是极大地改变了人们对艺术、时尚及其文本的话语解构的理解。而且，后现代主义还为时尚创意的表现与审美，提供了更为宏阔与未曾预想的视域与可能性。因此，艺术与美的问题将在多元视角下，得到重新的思考、解构，并加以时尚化的审美重建。在当代艺术表现与时尚设计中，挪用、拼贴的应用往往具有独特与别样的意趣。

应当说，这种解构与重建总是相互生成的，从来就没有简单甚至绝对意义上的解构，解构本身就是新思想的生成过程，而任何新的建构或重构又将导致新的解构。而且，时尚的重建与解构既相互区分，又彼此互动与交织。在后现代主义语境中的重建，并不是一种观念与思想的再体系化，也不是一种新形而上学的致思模式。这里旨在表明的是，新的艺术与思想在永恒的流变与生成中，以一种挪用与拼贴的手法回应既有传统，显然这也是时

---

❶ 马蓉.民族服饰语言的时尚运用[M].重庆：重庆大学出版社，2009：54.

尚的这种生成性特质的重要构成方式。

　　作为一种创意与设计技法，挪用、拼贴与原初的质料、元素并非毫无关系，而是在新的审美、文化与理论视域中，对先前的质料与元素加以重构以实现表现上的创新。无论是什么样式的艺术，还是艺术自身的本性与特质，其实都是历史性的与生成性的，并无确定不变的规定与法则。先前的元素与曾经的问题也会以不同的方式，出现在经由挪用与拼贴所表达的创意与设计中。在挪用与拼贴中，关于元素及其组合非此即彼的分类，显然不再具有原初的根本性意义与价值，但这种解构又是对民族元素与文化的当代重构。正是在规则与手法的历史性生成中，当下时尚感及其文化意义的重构才是可能的。

　　实际上，挪用与拼贴的艺术表现手法并非现在才有。在广为流传的剪纸、刺绣、壁画、布贴等民间艺术中，从创意、造型、构图等方面都能够看到对挪用、拼贴的使用。因此，挪用、拼贴既可以借鉴到传统民间工艺中，同时也可用于具有解构主义特质的当代时尚创意与设计的表现与传达中。当然，挪用、拼贴的应用还关涉艺术表现样式，以及与特定样式相关的审美与文化语境，并以其特有的解构性来重构民族元素的当代意义。通过挪用与拼贴的使用，可以对各种艺术质料与手法的传统界限加以超越，甚至能够生成另类的颇具时尚感的艺术效果与审美经验。

　　在此基础上生成的民族时尚感，既是传统的、富有历史性特质的，同时更具有当下独特的新奇感与陌生性。"这样，时尚一方面意味着相同阶层的联合，意味着一个以它为特征的社会圈子的共同性；另一方面，在这样的行为中，不同阶层、群体之间的界限不断地被突破。"❶ 在突破与消解时尚固有阶层性的问题上，挪用与拼贴等方式往往产生意想不到的弥合作用。在时尚创意与设计中，挪用与拼贴等手法、方式的借鉴与运用，又不乏对某一民族元素与文化的充分强调。

　　当然，任何经由创意设计与艺术表现，而对民族元素与文化的阐发都离不开时尚化的问题。在挪用与拼贴手法的应用中，那些看似毫不相干的碎片所构成的独特关联，打破了传统艺术的叙事与表现方式及其理解。经过挪用与拼贴的消解，就可以生成具有陌生与新奇感的艺术与审美效果，从而让人们产生较为强烈的感触甚至心理震撼。一切元素与文化的生成性关联，都与人们如何进行审美与文化建构分不开。还可以说，挪用与拼贴指的是在文本的创作与生成阶段，艺术家与设计师所使用的一种技巧或策略，这种技巧的特征在于从整体上加以重新审视与再构。

　　具体说来，民族服饰的时尚化既离不开对神话传说、图腾信仰的发掘，还可以借助挪用与拼贴等手法加以当代重构。对时尚创意与表现来说，虽然所组成的每个部分都是原有的，但设计将这些原有的不同部分巧妙地整合在一起。当然，这种整合不一定是各个原来文本的简单堆砌，因为这种堆砌往往会使文本呈现出粗糙的感觉。应当看到，挪用与拼贴

---

❶ 齐奥尔格·西美尔.时尚的哲学[M].费勇，吴蓉，译.北京：文化艺术出版社，2001：73.

手法的多元化表现与应用，不仅在创作的颜色、肌理和质感上产生变化，而且呈现出游戏的风格与反讽等后现代旨趣。

鲍德里亚认为，时尚是一种能指的简单游戏，除了符码，它不产生任何别的东西，而且无涉价值与道德。应当说，从立体主义艺术开始，达达主义、未来主义、超现实主义等都充分借鉴与推进了挪用与拼贴的艺术手法。"鉴于所有这些特征，会很清楚地看到时尚是后现代世界的一部分。"❶ 与此同时，非现实与超现实的观念及其技法与手段，成为时尚创意与艺术表现的重要方式。挪用与拼贴的艺术沿袭至今，一直散发着独特与别致的时尚意趣与魅力，并且在艺术家与设计师的探索下不断改进、创新。对于超现实主义艺术家来说，挪用与拼贴是一种用来表现真实的内在自我和潜在意识的手段。

在民族元素与艺术的审美及文化重构中，挪用与拼贴还会生成一种既传统又奇异的意味。在朋克风格的时装里，构成图案涉及怪诞、黑色幽默与各种冲突元素的组合。当然，挪用与拼贴并不只是一种创作的技巧或方法，由于关涉艺术品生产方式所寄寓的意识形态因素，它们还成为一种对当代艺术、审美与文化的回应和对话方式。在全球化时代，时尚创意与设计的一致性与同质化趋势，不仅消弭与解构了时尚艺术独特的文化旨趣，同时也忽视了各种民族与地方的文化差异性。

作为一种反传统的时尚话语，挪用与拼贴同时构成了新的时尚文本。在对挪用与拼贴的借鉴中，显然要注意对民族元素与文化的挖掘与当代重建，而庸俗、平庸与简单拿来所导致的同质化是应加以克服的。"拼贴的方式可以将不同风格、不同年代的材料进行组合，表现一种看似随意却独特的新境界。"❷ 作为一种解构的时尚化，无不涉及对传统与既有风格的反离与重构。还要注意到，如果时装设计只是将原有意义抽空、移植，甚至剔除原有的民族性，无疑会导致支离破碎，从而使当代时尚设计中的民族元素失去文化重构的语境。

除马塞尔·杜尚的达达主义之外，罗伯特·劳森伯格把所有可以找到的东西与材料，甚至喂饱的山羊、剪碎的报纸、布料、时钟、摄影、绘画等，都塞进自己的作品中，并以颜色加以拼合。劳森伯格打破了传统的绘画、雕塑与工艺的界限，从而形成了自己独特的艺术表达方式与审美经验。实际上，挪用与拼贴既相互关联又彼此生成，共同构成了对原初文本的一种回应方式，也就是说，它们既基于原来的元素与文本，又对这些元素与文本加以解构。在时尚创意中，挪用为拼贴提供了一个文本的可能基础与前提，而拼贴又将挪用而来的元素与文本进行重构。随着传统与现代的交织日趋密切与复杂，如何打破既成框架与体系以实现当下创新，无疑也是一个亟待探究的艺术、审美与文化问题。

三、基于拆解与重组的时尚意味

如果说，现代主义注重的是形式的自律与一致的诉求，那么，后现代主义时尚的设计

---

❶ George Ritzer. Postmodern Social Theory[M]. New York: The McGraw-Hill Companies, Inc, 1997:94.
❷ 苏永刚.服装时尚元素的提炼与运用[M].重庆：重庆大学出版社，2007：75.

手法旨在打破以往的统一、平衡、和谐,以及对整体感等设计原则的借鉴与强调,从而展现出设计手法的多元性和可变通性特质。譬如说,"通过纽扣、拉链、按扣、钩扣或尼龙搭扣的运用,可以增加或减少服装上的元素,从而对服装进行重组"。❶ 甚至可以说,某种时尚意味的生成与审美建构,正是基于拆解与重组等带有解构风格的技法来实现的。在结构主义中,关系得到了充分的认同并被作为实体的替代。结构主义之所以如此,是因为它旨在克服认识论与实体论的困境。

但这种对关系与结构的强调,后来又受到了后结构主义与解构主义的反对。根据德里达"拆解所指向的其实是对结构中心的绝对服从"这一法则,这种破坏也是针对现代主义的同一性、中心性与整体性而言的。与薇薇安·韦斯特伍德一样,艾尔莎·夏帕瑞丽也以荒谬的玩闹拆解了所谓的主流设计,从而引起了设计师们与时尚界对美的重新思考。一切既有的现代时尚文本及其意义,往往难免基于业已形成的关系或结构。因此,时尚创意的不断生成与建构,就不得不涉及对既有时尚元素及其结构的拆解。在这里,拆解促成了对各本文的差异性特质的强调,并随着对外来差异与区分的引入与参照,进而对原本文的结构中心形成消解与解构的态势。

由于结构一般具有固定性和确定性,相反的结构往往会产生类似的意义,这其实也表明了建构与解构需要不断交替进行。还应当看到,现代艺术对深度感即独根的偏好与对解释的依赖,尤其是,现代主义强调在文本的解读与阐释中,那些起规定性作用的概念体系与知识系统。与之不同,后现代主义强调平面性、表面性即须根的特征,以及误读在艺术的理解与解释中的重要意义。如果说,现代主义还看重所指,强调能指与所指的一一对应,因此而具有形而上学的痕迹,并把这种模式用于艺术与美的阐释的话,那么后现代主义则是一种反讽,并表征为一种能指❷的游戏。

值得注意的是,德里达的解构主义针对的无疑是西方哲学与思想所涉及的一系列二元分立,如言语与文字、真理与谬误、自然与文化等。在当代,针对传统服饰的拆解与解构,表现在对内与外、细与粗等诸多二元分立的颠覆,如外套可以翻过来穿,粗糙的毛边与未完成的缝头,取代了精细与讲究的做工,这些其实都是有意为之的独特创意。其实,正是原始预设的二元分立构成了被人们所认同的等级秩序,同时也由此导致了诸多的认知问题与思想困境。在民族时尚的创意过程中,这种传统的二元分立还表征为男性与女性、优雅与粗俗等,但这些诸多的等级体系受到了来自消解的挑战。

在后现代的语境里,能指其实并不指向任何的所指,而能指与所指的对应性关联也不再具有什么实质性意义。在这个全球化时代,现代性及其所规定的对一致性的推崇与诉求,难免导致艺术、审美与文化的同质化问题出现。实际上,"当代后现代主义理论已经以这

---

❶ 杰伊·卡尔德林.时装设计100个创意关键词[M].曹帅,译.北京:中国青年出版社,2012:118.
❷ 能指和所指是语言学上的一对概念,能指意为语言文字的声音,形象;所指则是语言的意义本身。按语言学家或者哲学家们的划分,人们试图通过语言表达出来的东西叫"能指";而语言实际传达出来的东西叫"所指"。

种方式日益转向通俗文化实践，以便寻求文化多元性和抵抗性模式"。❶ 就创意与设计来说，许多赶时髦的时装既趋同又毫无个性，还往往流于庸俗化、浅薄化与低级趣味，更无内在精神贯注与审美文化特质可言。但与此同时，那些过于道德化的评价与处置也是应加以反对的。

如果说，现代主义仍然强调创作、叙述与宏大历史，而这里的宏大叙事又总是基于主体与理性的，那么，后现代主义尤其是解构主义则强调了审美接受，以及对宏大叙事的反叛、解构与放逐。在弗朗索瓦·利奥塔看来，正是启蒙运动促成了宏大叙事的产生。后现代关注对创作主体的消解与解构，强调作为反叙述的、关切于个人生存经验的个人语型。但在现代与后现代之间，并没有一个非此即彼的严格区分，它们是交织、渗透与相互生成的。其实，打破结构主义的整体感与同一性，也有助于培养受众的怀疑精神与多元的文化心态。

自波普艺术发生以来，拆解与重组就是对旧有元素、文本（含图像）等的处置，依然是后现代艺术家与设计师最常见的方法与技巧，而是否原创或真迹能否存在，在此全然并不重要。经过对传统元素及其结构的拆解，既为民族符号与文化在当代语境里的重组提供了可能，也为民族性与世界性、当代性之间的生成性关联作出了审美与文化奠基。应当说，拆解是不断地打破旧结构，进而组成新结构的过程。拆解颠覆了传统时装的一般概念与传统意义，在不断的解构中寻找艺术与时尚创意表现的方式。

在解构主义中，存在不断被否定，中心不断被转移，其空缺则由不在场的共存来补充。在德里达看来，作品是永远开放的，读者的阅读也是创造过程。甚至可以说，着装者对服饰文本的解读总是未完成的、不确定的，任何解读视角在敞开文本的同时，又难免对文本造成了新的遮蔽。"在《一个Z和两个O》当中，这位英国电影人彼得·格林纳威拆解的是从启蒙运动文化当中生长起来的分类学传统。"❷ 其实，拆解不仅针对不同的问题，还可以指向各种艺术样式。在这个全球化时代，不同国家、地方与民族之间的时尚交流越来越频繁，服装原先的在地性特质也得到了世界性的艺术与文化回应与重构。

与此同时，解构与重组就涉及把对称的、规则的与格式化的东西，通过交叉、扭转、错位、颠倒等变化，使之呈现出某种不对称、无规则与非格式化的造型，进而从中生成与建构出意想不到的变幻与动感之美。在当代，时尚流行的速度、节奏与传播越来越快，巴黎时尚发布会各大秀场的流行时装发布，隔天就会出现在全球各个角落的时尚精品店中。在这种快速传播与消费的当代时尚趋势中，人们追求个性的潮流逐渐成为服装设计师设计作品的旨归，但这种努力又往往会被快速地仿效而失去其独特性。

从民族服装元素及其结构入手，以拆解的艺术表现理念与手法，打破原有元素的固有关系与格局，展现给穿着者与观看者不一样的感官体验。各民族的元素无疑为时尚创意提

---

❶ 史蒂文·康纳.后现代主义文化——当代理论导引[M].严忠志，译.北京：商务印书馆，2002：296.
❷ K.马尔科姆·理查兹.德里达眼中的艺术[M].陈思，译.重庆：重庆大学出版社，2016：174.

供了文化上的多样性。在德里达看来,"解构并不是诉毁或破坏,如果它是什么的话,……那它也是对于存在的一种思考,是对于形而上学的一种思考,因而表现为一种对存在的权威或本质的权威的讨论,而这样一种讨论或解释不可能简单地是一种否定性的破坏"。❶ 但不同民族的艺术特质与服饰文化,并不能自动地、简单地设置入时尚作品里,因此,不断地消解与重构对时尚而言是不可或缺的。

通过拆解与重组所生成的时尚意味,显然也离不开一定民族或族群的日常生活所赖以实现的生活世界。一切时尚,都是经由对先前元素及其关系的拆解而实现的一种重组来产生出某种陌生的时尚感的。自20世纪60年代以来,具有颓废风格与街头特质的乞丐服流行开来,山本耀司与川保久玲后来将之推向了T形台,而如今它仍然是大学生与青年广为看好的时髦着装。还要意识到,民族的生活世界(包括衣生活)又是与大众文化分不开的。大众文化往往具有某种特定的意识形态功能,它还解构了传统文化中许多原始的意义。而且,拆解与重组还可以指向既已形成的时尚。

作为反时尚的行为与文化,甲壳虫乐队、滚石乐队与鲍勃·迪伦等,往往以其独特的服饰表达着标新立异的诉求。当然,大众文化也为时尚的重构提供了艺术与思想上的可能。实际上,民族时尚的拆解与重组从来都是相辅相成的。与此同时,设计正是在拆解与重组的基础上来生成自身旨趣的。在这里,拆解与重组其实就是重新分析与整理代码或符码,使各种被解构的服饰符码发生重新编码。不同民族的服饰风格与审美文化,显然为民族文化作出了文化上的奠基,但如何去拆解与重组依然是当代时尚创意与设计的重要问题。

基于新的编码与不断解码,时装生成出创意所力图达致的旨趣与意味。一切民族元素无不具有艺术、审美与文化等特质,因此对经典与传统的任何当代拆解与重组,只有经由不断探究才能避免粗鄙的误读与破坏。这里的问题与困境在于,一切拆解与重组都不可能彻底摆脱误读或曲解。通过解构与重组所达成的解读究竟是何种意义上的误读,这相关于人们对这种设计的审美与文化上的理解。由于现时的观念总处于嬗变与更新中,民族元素的拆解与重组应该是一个历史性过程,而不是一种可以简单复制与移植的观念图景与视觉模式。也就是说,民族元素永远处于观念与视觉的生成中。

还可以说,拆解与重组是这些元素在时尚艺术中,通过建构而得以出现的一个重要方式与路径。这就要求在创意过程中,关注民族元素的开放性与可变性特质,以及充满了多义性的生成式文本样式。这种多样性特质为拆解与重组提供了可能,而拆解与重组反过来又构成了对文本多元意义的揭示与阐发。不同民族的元素与文化间的生成性关联,并非简单地并置在某一文本的视觉表象上,而是在深刻的对话里来生成出新的时尚意义。而且,民族元素与文本在符号中留下了大量的空白,通过设计师与之进行的思想对话与文化沟通,实现不同的民族与文化及其在当代衣生活领域的重建。

---

❶ 雅克·德里达.一种疯狂守护着思想——德里达访谈录[M].何佩群,译.上海:上海人民出版社,1997:18.

时尚为人们建构了一种更为宽泛的社会与文化语境，让时尚创意发生在民族性与世界性的关切之中。在时尚创意与设计过程中，还要打破历史所带来的固有审美倾向与文化定式，这是因为，"间离理论总是植根于日常生活的麻木和熟视无睹，必定总是把我们与日常生活间离开来……"❶ 也就是说，经由拆解与重组使民族元素与文化产生新的意义与旨趣，让不同时期的民族文化语汇相互对话与碰撞成为可能，进而生成出一种基于审美与文化区分的创意交织与互文。

在创意与设计中，民族元素往往生成与建构在开放性的审美与文化语境，并融入多元艺术与文化的建构与不断重构中。实际上，陌生感与间离效果是民族时尚设计所要考虑的问题，这既涉及各民族艺术与文化特质自身的独特性，还相关于借助各种拆解与重组手法所实现的表达。当拆解与重组被用于既定体系与架构时，这其实也是一个艺术、审美与文化再生的过程。为了时尚设计的新奇性与陌生感的生成，既有的关联与模式的解构就是必不可少的了，这难免导致与产生一定程度上的模糊性和多义性。民族原有的元素及其固有结构被拆解、重组，旨在产生一种不同于日常生活的新奇感。

但这里的陌生感与间离效果，其实并不一定是什么稀奇古怪的东西，也不能只是归结为人为的杜撰或臆想，或许是对业已被遮蔽的时尚感的祛蔽与再发现。应注意到，后现代主义对元解释、宏大叙事与形而上学的反叛，为民族元素及其在时尚创意中的重构提供了可能。反叛以强调非理性因素来达到一种设计中的轻松和宽容。后现代主义从来都不是一个具体、单一的风格，也不能仅仅因为作品的时代而界定为后现代风格。其实，更没有一个关于后现代主义的固有概念与僵化体系，因为一切形而上学都是后现代主义力图拆解与克服的。

还可以说，拆解打破了元素间原有的关系与结构，将之分解为诸多的构成要素加以重组，以生成别致与新颖的当下感与时尚意味，而且，这种意味往往还带有民族艺术特质与文化情调。在艺术人类学视域，各种不同民族都有其不可替代的独特性，但这些彼此区分的民族性特质又并非完全不同。在结构主义中，整体之于部分的优先重要性得到了强调。而且，任何事物都是复杂的与难以分割的生成性整体。任何一个组成部分的性质都不可能孤立地被理解，而只能把各部分放在一个整体的关系与语境里，即把各部分之间联系起来才能得到理解与阐发。在结构主义看来，部分之间的关系相关于整体与部分的关系。

但对既有结构的解构与不断再建构，却成为从日常性揭示时尚特质的重要方式。结构主义方法的本质和首要原则在于，力图揭示与研究联结和结合诸要素的复杂关系，而不是致力于诸单一要素支离破碎的分析。民族时尚创意的发生与当下建构，相关于各民族元素及其既有结构的拆解。当然，这种拆解与解构，并不是简单否定与破坏先前的传统与思想，而是旨在激活诸多传统元素与文化及其关联，以重组、建构与生成出当下的特别时尚意味。

---

❶ 弗雷德里克·詹姆逊.布莱希特与方法[M].陈永国，译.北京：中国社会科学出版社，1998：97.

源于西方的西装，在现代则成为各种礼仪服装，并作为当代国际服装而普及全球。

当然，在不同的地域与历史时期，西服的款式与风格显然又有所变化。在实质意义上，解构主义的根本策略就是消解元素原有的结构与秩序。对服饰与时尚设计而言，被拆解的东西主要是既有的关系与结构，以及由此形成的视觉与审美表现方式与习惯。譬如，"这种时尚所采用的色彩因文化而异，比如在非洲是红色、绿色和金色，在美国是红色、绿色和黑色"。❶ 当然，原有的结构与秩序不仅相关于艺术与文化，往往还涉及社会与人类生活方式的各个方面。拆解也涉及那些打破常规印象的设计思路，从而带来别致、新奇的创意观念与艺术效果。应意识到，不同民族对元素的理解与喜好也有所不同。

在这里，民族时尚的轮回并非简单的回归与还原，而是在回溯里对原有意味与旨趣加以重构。拆解与重组广泛地存在于时尚设计领域，它所带来的特别效果在时尚艺术中显得别出心裁。正是这种拆解打破了民族元素已有的秩序与结构，然后创造出相关于民族文化的、更为新颖与别致的时尚感。在日趋注重与追求个性的时代，复古风格的重新出现与当代流行，使得人们更加关注传统元素的拆解与重组。在拆解与重组中，不同地域与时代的特质无不嵌入新的时尚文本样式里。在时尚感的生成中，任何非此即彼的做法都会受到消解。但拆解与重组既不是对传统的抛弃与放逐，也不是简单地回到过去与传统中去。

这里旨在表明，通过对各种复古风格及其元素的分析与阐发，探讨如何拆解与提取经典服饰元素进行重组并加以运用。例如，一种称为非洲中心主义的时装样式，显然是与非洲的地域性及其传统文化相关的，但它又不乏与当代世界性时尚感的密切关联。在拆解与重组里，偏见与误读都是难以避免的解释学事件，但这可以通过不断的对话与讨论去克服。如果说，在艺术与服饰设计方面，现代主义关注的往往是语义，那么，后现代主义则关切于修辞与话语生成，旨在对服饰元素加以修辞学的当代重构。再如，现代主义主要涉及对范式、主从结构、隐喻的强调，那么，后现代主义则注重句法、并列结构与对转喻的借鉴。

应当说，现代主义强调的是本原与确定性，后现代主义则强调差异与非确定性。在拆解与重组的过程中，一切时尚与非时尚的东西都被纳入互文里。这里极端的情形在于，时尚甚至成为某种非时尚与反时尚的东西，也就是说，非时尚与反时尚介入了时尚领域，进而成为一种崭新的时尚样式与审美风格。"对于阿皮亚来说，后现代主义拒绝一切排外主义和普遍主义的主张。"❷ 在基于拆解与重组的时尚创意过程中，人们既要注重特定民族元素及其文化内涵的揭示，还应通达与实现时尚审美和文化的当代重构。实际上，在民族时尚的创意与设计中，运用拆解与重组手法无疑是一种新的创意思路。

---

❶ 杰·卡尔德林.形式·适合·时尚[M].周明瑞，译.济南：山东画报出版社，2011：83.
❷ 沃特伯格.什么是艺术[M].李奉栖，张云，胥全文，等译.重庆：重庆大学出版社，2011：323.

第三节 民族元素时尚创意的生成

从观念与思想的层面讲，拓展与发掘出创意的构思与当下建构，并把创意加以视觉化表现是设计的应有之意。对于服饰设计来说，观念与创意除了主张与强调新颖、别致外，还应以内在精神与文化特质作为根本性底蕴。实际上，设计在本性上可以理解为创意的视觉化表现与制作的实现，并在对视觉化的不断解构中去回应时尚观的变化。虽然说，创意具有不可替代与极其重要的意义与价值，但这并不意味着，创意越抽象、越深奥、越显得似乎有文化就越好，因为还要考虑到视觉化表现与实现的可能性，以及创意观念如何被日常生活与大众文化所接受的问题。尽管说，观念的可视化表现与传达往往是有限度的，但达到淋漓尽致与尽善尽美的密切关联与切合，却是时尚创意的审美表现与文化的根本性诉求。但还应注意到，任何创意都不可能是僵化与固定不变的，它总是处于不断的生成、建构与重构的过程中。

一、时尚意义的文化性与民族性

文化内在精神的不可分离性，无疑是一切艺术与设计的根本性特质，时尚艺术表现与创意设计当然也不例外。时尚以一种流行的趋势与潮流，进入了人们的生活世界与公共领域。毫无疑问，"时尚"是一个被广泛使用与耳熟能详的词汇，它频繁出现在报纸、媒体与人们的交流之中。其实，"时尚的本质存在于这样的事实中：时尚总是只被特定人群中的一部分人所运用，他们中的大多数只是在接受它的路上"。❶ 在大众文化的语境里，追求时尚早已蔚然成风，甚至令人趋之若鹜，时尚因此成为一种重要的生活方式。在对观念可视化的强调中，时尚创意与设计的民族性及其审美表现，无不具有独到与特别的意象与艺术韵味。

正因如此，那些富有个性化特征的创意与设计观念，以及独特与新奇的表现手法与制作技巧，显然是时尚艺术与文化不可或缺的根本性前提。在时尚创意里，人们所力图实现的所有回归与反叛，其实都不可能完全摆脱民族性特质，尽管这种民族性特质可能是以变形或抽象的方式介入的。也就是说，作为一种不可忽视的亚文化形式，时尚总是与一定的族群或民族分不开的，与此同时，时尚往往又力图超越民族性特质的限制。但在文化的分类上，时尚又总是在不断突破对亚文化的规限。时尚可以理解为，在特定时期内率先由少数人尝试与发起，后来为社会大众所仿效甚至推崇的衣生活样式。

显然，当下流行的独特性与新奇感是时尚不可或缺的。应当说，时尚的这种陌生感与新颖性特质，也是对民族服饰与传统文化的一种视角敞开，但在这种敞开与显现又难免造成对已有视角的遮蔽。在服饰与着装方面，这种时尚往往是通过时装的样式表现出来的。

---

❶ 西美尔.时尚的哲学[M].费勇，译.北京：文化艺术出版社，2001：76-77.

值得注意的是，时尚的发源并没有一个严格的时间界限。因此，时尚虽然强调的是当下感与即时性，但它也是一种历史性生成的文化样式。在中世纪，时尚无疑是与贵族阶层紧密相连的，并与这一阶层的群体和文化特质分不开。贵族出于对其阶层生活品位与格调的诉求，往往雇佣著名时装设计师为其定做与众不同的时装。

正是由于时尚的阶层性，规定了这种生活方式自身的分层性特征。在当今，时尚虽然依然具有阶层性的意味与象征，但这种阶层性并没有中世纪与近代的阶层性那么稳固。与此同时，时尚也在不同的社会群体、团体与个人之间发生区分。但还要注意的是，"直至今日，我们很难单从一个人的外表判断他的社会阶层、经济地位、职业或国籍"。❶ 即使如此，也并不意味着民族元素与服饰文化不重要。可以说，一切业已形成的文化传统都离不开历史性沉淀，当然也与人们的生活方式和文化自觉分不开。在传统的社会与文化语境中，如果人们想要过一种时尚与流行的生活方式，就必须了解自己身处的阶层的特质与文化品位。

一般来说，对本阶层的生活与文化语境的认知与理解，才能使自己的时尚风格不至于变得不伦不类，但时尚的这种阶层性关联甚至对应在当代受到了挑战。对时尚来说，意义及其关联不仅是结构性的，同时还是开放性与生成性的。在时尚意义的生成中，民族与文化的介入与生成性关联是不可或缺的。其实，时尚早已深入人类生活方式的诸多方面，如衣着、打扮、饮食、行为、居住、消费，以及情感的表达与思考方式等。与此同时，时尚常常被人们在与流行相提并论的意义上来把握，虽然说，时尚与流行的密切相关是无可置疑的，但它们其实并不能相互等同。

简单地说，时尚显然是可以流行的，同时往往也是流行性的，但如果一味地广为流行，甚至将这种流行无限外推，则难免会导致时尚的终结。在这里，"艺术的目的是使你对事物的感受如同你所见的视象那样，而不是如同你所认知的那样；艺术的手法是事物的'反常化'手法……"❷ 就时尚来说，陌生化的手法也往往得到了充分的借鉴与体现，即使向那些历史性传统的回归其实也会产生陌生感。一定程度与时间内的流行与趋势，无疑是时尚成为时尚必不可少的表征。

其实，时尚诉求也相关于生活的艺术与审美，但生活方式关注更多的是当下的时尚感，而不是这种服饰与着装的悠久的历史感。但一切时尚都不可能脱离其历史感而存在，民族的历史性与文化特质就嵌入在时尚样式中。作为一种衣生活方式，时尚与文化无疑是不可分离的，它本身就是一种重要的艺术与文化样式。当然，时装与时尚文化往往是一种及时性的亚文化，它们虽然通过对所谓主流文化的疏离与补充来表现，但这种时尚文化从来都不是一种可有可无的文化样式。对于服饰与时装而言，模仿、从众其实只是时尚生活的初级阶段，还应从时尚的流转与轮回过程中，揭示时尚流变所彰显出来的新的意义与趣味。

在着装与衣生活方式中，时尚风格与文化品位是一种被普遍关注的问题。然而，追求

---

❶ 丽塔·裴娜.流行预测[M].李宏伟，王倩梅，洪瑞璘，译.北京：中国纺织出版社，2000：91.
❷ 维克托·什克洛夫斯基，等.俄国形式主义文论选[M].方珊，等译.上海：三联书店，1989：6.

时尚不在于被动的追随与效仿,而在于建构切合自己的独特时尚感,以及对时尚生活方式与意义的特别理解。而对时尚的这种审美理解与文化阐发,总是相关于一定族群及其精神特质的。其实,时尚触角已深入与渗透人类生活的各个方面,同时也与一定民族或族群的生活方式密不可分。一般来说,时尚往往带给人的是一种愉悦与优雅的感觉,尤其是,时尚为人们日常与贫乏的生活提供了独特的经验与感悟。

应当可以说,时尚还可能赋予人们以不同的气质和品位,以及别致的生活情调与独特的个性。人类对时尚的喜好与对流行文化的诉求,无疑促成了人类生活的审美化与审美的生活化,但时尚的各种关联之物其实都离不开民族底蕴与文化特质。毫无疑问,时尚是一种循环变迁与不断更新的艺术与文化样式。应当看到,人们追逐细节点缀的时尚风格的行为依然风行,尤其是随着流行趋势的不断更替与加快,琳琅满目的时尚饰品与各种新潮时装,总会让人生成耳目一新甚至目不暇接的视觉感受。时尚与民族、文化的生成性关联仍是不可忽视的,但这又相关于在理解与阐发上对传统认识论的克服与突破。

在不少人眼中,时尚即是简单化,与其浪费与奢华,不如朴素与节俭。但与此不同,奢华往往还是被当成时尚与流行的代名词。在当代生活方式里,人们对时尚的理解是彼此不同的,但对人们日常生活的审美化来说,"如果是在一个极富艺术文化痕迹的环境中,那么对艺术有偏爱的时尚主顾就能理解并欣赏设计师的作品"。❶ 应当注意到,有时时尚只是为了标新立异、制造噱头,甚至哗众取宠,并没有什么实质性的审美价值与文化内涵可言,这样的时尚实际上也只是一种视觉表象而已。

在日常生活方式中,那些与流行趋势不同步的人或物象,往往还会被指为老土、落伍,但与流行趋势并不一致的着装未必没有时尚意味。不少时尚的反对者甚至认为,时尚是一种流俗与普泛的大众文化样式,它无非是以新奇、庸俗、无理性噱头,建构关于流行与时髦生活的幻觉与拟象,时尚因此被看作一种没有独立价值判断的从众生活方式。关于时尚的不同见解与看法,既相关于一定的群体与阶层及其差异,又构成了时尚评价的理论与思想多样性。其实,时尚虽然往往是一种当下的与时髦相关的生活方式,但它终究离不开人们生活方式所依凭的民族与文化语境。

与此同时,对历史感的遮蔽也是当下时尚的一种权宜之计。在这种看似浅表的遮蔽之中,却是时尚对基于时间性的历史感的一种悬置,而这种悬置又将时尚纳入即将到来的过去之中。应当可以说,时尚虽然基于当下、面向未来的生活意趣,但它从来就没有也不可能与过去生活样式彻底分离。在这里,不同的时尚创意往往也可看作对业已过去的艺术所作出的历史性、有差异的回应。作为一种艺术、美和文化的象征,传统服饰及其在当代的审美与时尚化,其实也是时尚意义的民族性与文化意义建构的重要构成。

从古至今,从西方到东方,人们的衣生活方式总是与族群、文化密切相关的。其实,

---

❶ 杰·卡尔德林.形式·适合·时尚[M].周明瑞,译.济南:山东画报出版社,2011:224.

给当代和下一代留下深刻印象和意义的象征，无疑是一种艺术、审美与文化生成的内在诉求。毫无疑问，所有民族的衣着与时尚都是审美与文化的建构物，同时它又反过来建构着人们的身体意识与审美经验。还应注意到，时尚艺术与文化融合了所在时代的价值观念与生活趣味。随着接受视觉冲击的阈限的不断提高，人们更加迫切地期待日益强烈的审美震撼。

虽然说，时尚一般典型地体现在人们的衣着样式之中，但它并非只存在于服装与日常生活领域，还可拓展到当代艺术、建筑设计与民间工艺等领域，它更是广泛地发生在人们的日常生活与精神世界中的文化事件。同时，时尚也是对日常生活及其意义的重新发现，尽管它在流行与变化多端里难免缺乏某种深刻性。时尚其实从来都不乏民族与文化特质的贯注与沉浸，但这些贯注与沉浸往往是以变形与修辞的方式进行的。在时尚的表现与设计过程中，民族与文化特质隐蔽在时尚视觉的表象中，并经由视觉表现与民族内在精神图式相回应。

而且，前卫与先锋时尚还常常是一种亚文化样式，但这种时尚又介入与渗透在各种艺术与文化样式中。应意识到，亚文化为文化的构成注入了与特定族群、阶层相关的异质性。实际上，一种亚文化不仅包含着与主文化相关的价值与观念，同时也有属于自身的独特价值、观念与生活方式。民族时尚对民族的历史记忆加以挖掘、整理与重构，旨在生成既有民族文化特质又不乏当下感的时尚样式。在生成论的语境中，文化是一个变成与成为文化本身的过程，即文化化或化为文化，正如民族化就是民族自身一样，但民族化并不等同于在不同民族间简单转换。

可以说，民族时尚之盛行于当代日常生活中，无疑是日常生活审美化的一个重要构成，但这种审美化也是与大众艺术和流行文化相关的。比如，曾经穿佐特套服的往往都是年轻的非裔和墨裔的美国人。"为了避免被误认为是西服，佐特套服不得不在原来的日常西服上加以更大的改变。"❶ 在日常生活审美化与民族时尚的相互促进中，既有对原有表现与意味的改变与消解，又不乏新旧的彼此交织与融合。可以说，民族性一直是时尚及其地方性文化的基础，而这种地方性又为民族性提供了某种在场性与大地之基础。

一般而言，民族文化往往具有地域性、多元性和原生态性等特质。那些富有民族性特质的衣着与时尚服装，不仅引领着时尚的异域风情与别致经验，还呈现出地方性和多元化的文化特点。虽然任何民族的文化均不必依附于其他文化而生成自身，但各个不同民族及其文化之间的关联却是无法否认的。各种民族文化之间并不存在优劣高下之分，甚至也没有什么先进和后进（落后）的简单区分。在人类的生存与衣生活方式中，任何民族都难免与其他民族发生民族间的关联，诸多民族的共生也由此被贯注某种混杂性。对于服饰艺术与审美而言，创意与设计的民族性与文化性又是不可分割的。

---

❶ 马尔科姆·巴纳德.艺术、设计与视觉文化[M].王升才，张爱东，卿上力，译.南京：江苏美术出版社，2006：149.

泰勒所提出的是关于狭义文化的早期经典学说。而后来的传播学派把文化传播现象推到极端，反对进化论对文化传播的揭示与阐发。各民族艺术与文化创意的生成，以及在不同民族之间的艺术、审美与文化交流，在日常生活审美化中的意义是不可忽视的，而且这种艺术交流与时尚的跨文化传播，又是以特定民族及其文化的在地性为依凭的，但同时又在不断突破某些地域性特质的制约与局限。还可以说，时尚的民族性特质与传统文化的关涉，无疑是民族自我认同及其当代建构所不可回避的。

随着经济社会的快速与极大发展，民族的风俗习惯与独特生活方式的式微，民族文化的多元性特质往往被规定在某种一致性中。应当说，"经过历代服饰文化的不断积累、融合、嬗变、创新，日趋精细缜密、丰美华赡，逐渐形成了我们中华民族独具民族个性和文化传统的中国服饰文化，充分体现了中华民族的精神和文化风貌"。❶ 在全球化时代，民族与地方的文化遭遇了严峻的挑战。因此，亟待从不同创意与设计的对话中，建构出独特性与一致性之间的审美与文化张力。各个民族都形成了独特的生活方式、信仰意识、礼仪习俗与风土人情等，而这些因素又建构了各民族不同的审美风格和文化特质。

与此同时，各民族也形成了独具特色和风格迥异的服饰文化。但在经济社会的变迁与发展中，民族服饰与传统文化也面临着式微甚至消失的危险，因此，对民族传统文化的尊重和保护问题就凸显出来。但这并不是说，挖掘民族元素就是向原始衣生活方式的简单回归，而是旨在强调民族元素与传统及其在当代文化语境里的重构。为使各少数民族的服饰与传统文化得到保护与传承，亟待对民族文化遗产有计划地进行搜集与整理等，旨在促使少数民族的历史文化遗产得以保存下来。

当然，对民族服饰艺术与文化的保护与传承，难免涉及与其他民族文化甚至外来文化的关联，并在当代的社会与文化语境里加以再创造与阐释。其实，民族特质的生成离不开一个共同体，以及特有的历史过程和共同的文化语境。作为古希腊与古罗马人穿着的一种连袖直线式宽大束腰长衣，后来又在袖型、衣长与装饰细节上有了显著变化，同时还影响了后世许多服饰与时尚的创意与设计。甚至可以说，时尚艺术与设计表现总是与一定的族群及其生活方式分不开的，但又不能只是将时尚艺术与文化归结为民族的与传统的。

还要看到，文化是对基本的民族生存方式的揭示与阐发，而民族的存在又是文化的此在与存在论基础。当然，时尚的这种基于传统文化根基的重构也是必不可少的。对拉克鲁瓦来说，创意灵感与民族文化密切相关，这是因为，"他的设计深受家乡阿尔斯的影响：那一地区有原始而又纯真的绘画、吉卜赛人、斗牛表演和民族服装"。❷ 但如果缺乏在当下语境的重构与再造，民族元素与传统都不可能自动发生时尚化的转化，这种时尚化无疑是一种视觉、审美与文化的建构与生成。

另外，时尚艺术与文化是传统文化的延伸、扩展和丰富，而不是脱离民族与传统文化

---

❶ 楼慧珍, 吴永, 郑彤. 中国传统服饰文化[M]. 上海: 东华大学出版社, 2004: 3.
❷ 邦尼·英格利希. 时尚: 50位最有影响力的世界时尚设计大师[M]. 黄慧, 译. 杭州: 浙江摄影出版社, 2012: 42.

的一种纯粹的虚构与臆测。通过与各种生活方式的历史性发生的关联，民族服饰艺术的保护与文化传统的不断传承，也成为一种关于民族生活意义的发现与揭示。而且，民族生活意义的发现其实也是与各种艺术表现分不开的，但还要经由对各个民族的人类学此在及其存在的揭示，去消解与解构这种人类学此在及其可能的主体论痕迹，以彰显民族性与文化性之间的互文与相互生成。在创意与设计过程中，揭示各种民族元素时尚意义的生成，无疑也是时尚艺术、审美与文化研究的重要课题。

二、民族元素及其时尚意义的生成

时尚不仅具有一般艺术与设计所应有的特征，还具备独特的、不可替代的审美与文化特质，这是因为，时尚与人们的生活、身体及其历史性的联系更加密切。当对各种各样的民族元素与文化进行重构，以生成出时尚的特别意味与旨趣时，无疑应弄清楚究竟什么是时尚的意义。实际上，这里所说的时尚除了具有浓郁的当下感外，它往往还与民族元素与传统文化及其特质相关联。通过陌生化将民族元素所潜在的意蕴揭示出来，是生成新颖与别致的时尚意义的根本之所在。

应当说，所谓陌生化就是对日常与常规的偏离，从而造成语言理解与感受上的陌生感。在指称上，陌生化使现实生活中为人们习以为常的东西化为一种具有新的意义与旨趣的事物。在1995年秋冬系列中，韦斯特伍德运用苏格兰格子呢打造与重构19世纪式样的廓型，面料、线条与配饰渲染着浓郁的英伦风。在语言结构上，人们司空见惯的语法规则，被化为具有新的形态与审美价值的语言艺术。陌生化的基本构成原则，是表面互不相关而内在又不乏联系的因素间的对立和冲突，并由此形成了一种非日常与不一般的感觉与新奇印象。

当然，陌生化的时尚感及其表现并不只是解构性的，一切艺术表现手法其实都是时尚表达可凭借的。也许正是对立和冲突，造成了陌生化的表象或表象的陌生化，从而给人以感官的刺激或情感的震动。毫无疑问，这种陌生化往往是相对于日常性而言的。比如说，"传统的艺术致力于产生美好的事物，而不是新奇的东西，当今的艺术则反其道而行之"。[1]一般来说，人们对外界的刺激往往具有趋新与好奇的心理效应，而那些毫无新奇与熟视无睹的事物或情境，常常难以引起或维持人们的兴趣与关切。只有新异与别致的创意设计，才能唤起人们独特的艺术经验与审美情趣，从而生成为人们所期盼或青睐的时尚感。

在疏离的基础上，人们发掘出对自我本性新的意识与认同，而陌生化正是化熟悉为新奇的重要方式。"陌生化"一词，其实可以追溯到亚里士多德那里。当然，亚里士多德并没有正式提出"陌生化"概念，而用的是"惊奇""奇异""不平常"等说法。人们往往会对身边与眼前事物习以为常，甚至视而不见、充耳不闻。可以说，广泛的流行也就是时尚终结的开始，并为以后时尚与流行作出了历史性奠基。在时尚的轮回中，意义的遮蔽与显现

---

[1] 瓦迪斯瓦夫·塔塔尔凯维奇.西方六大美学观念史[M].刘文潭，译.上海：上海译文出版社，2006：46.

既相互区分，又彼此交织在一起。陌生化把平淡无奇的事物变得不寻常，从而增加了艺术与设计的别致感与新鲜感。

与此同时，陌生化其实也是为了保证审美距离的需要，以满足人们对新奇事物的心理诉求及其实现。布洛的审美距离说指出，在艺术、设计与审美过程中，人们应在心理上保持一定的审美"距离"。民族元素与文化特质及其建构，不仅为时尚独特意义的生成提供了文化上的可能性，同时又为同质化及其问题的克服奠定了基础。应当说，透过距离观看事物的方式是特殊的观物方式。由于一般人往往缺乏保持距离的能力，极易达到距离的极限而产生失距的现象，所以他们每每不能像艺术家那样思考与操作，更难以用天真无邪的艺术与审美眼光观赏事物。

对时尚感的生成与建构而言，民族元素及其文化不可替代的独特性，无疑为审美距离提供了切实的可能性基础。一旦艺术与审美进入了社会与现实生活，就容易导致生活的琐碎、奢侈与媚俗化。如缺乏恰当的审美距离，就会导致人们审美疲劳与倦息，从而陷入一种平均化与了无新意的日常性里。由于功利与实用的关涉，人们往往会减弱对艺术与审美的兴奋，难以生成新奇与愉悦的美感与经验，甚至还会产生疲倦与厌弃的情绪。如果人与物、人与人之间缺乏审美距离，人们难免会对其他人或物失去兴趣。对时尚创意与设计来说，审美距离的缺失导致了审美疲劳，而美感的式微来得更为快捷与特别明显。

还要注意到，民族元素的时尚感及其文化意义，既可通过特定的款式与造型加以表现，当然也能经由对色彩的独特强调来达到。民族元素与文化的陌生化与时尚感，是经由民族的独特性来加以揭示与表现的。在中国服装设计师吴海燕的时尚设计中，其对民族元素与传统文化情有独钟，但她所主张与强调的不只是中国红，而是一种更为广泛与包容的大东方美。应当看到，没有民族性特质的时尚可能失之于同质化，但如果仅仅将时尚归结为民族性也是不可取的。虽然文化的保守性是民族文化所固有的特质，但保守的方式与程度在各民族间又有所不同。一个民族的文化之所以延续相当长的时间，其实也是与文化的这种保守性分不开的。

值得注意的是，每一种文化中的民族性特质都是传承下来的，曾经历过不少朝代的更替与文化的历史性沉淀，但无不经历着后来一切时代的解构与重构。民族艺术与文化的特质是相对稳定、凝固与完整的，如伦理道德、价值观念、生活习惯、社会礼俗、语言文字等，它们都会在时尚里经由视觉而得到直观的表现与传达。在这里，"艺术家们所致力于或展望的一些哲学观点会有助于产生一定的视觉效果，不论这些观点多么有局限性，这些艺术效果可以超越作品特定的历史环境"。❶ 因此，时尚的视觉效果又总是与特定的历史性相关联。当然，民族与传统文化自身也在发生变化，并呈现出不同的历史性痕迹与文化特质。

实际上，作为时尚感的一种生成方式，陌生化可以分为几个不同的层面或维度，这些

---

❶ 保罗·克劳瑟.20世纪艺术的语言：观念史[M].刘一平，译.长春：吉林人民出版社，2007：168.

层面或维度彼此关联并生成时尚意义。首先，强调时尚与日常生活着装的区分与分离。其次，通过前卫或先锋艺术表现给时尚带来新奇感。最后，经由向日常生活与常规艺术的回归，重新发现时尚元素与表现被遮蔽的意义与旨趣。在这里，日常生活其实就是人们每天过的生活。在不同的社会与时代，日常生活方式当然也有所改变或变迁。在现代生活方式中，不同的材质所提供的时尚感也是有差异的，这些差异需要在特定族群或阶层进行相应的理解与阐释。

在民族元素时尚感的建构中，人们往往会依照目的或旨趣的不同，选用特定质料加以表现与当代重构，以生成别致有趣的新奇意味与独特感觉。但由于环境、气候、风俗、文化等差异，各个民族经过长期的生存与生活，形成了彼此不同、五彩缤纷的民族风格。但即使是在民族的生活方式里，仍然难以摆脱平均化的、常规化的模式与习俗，因此对新奇感的诉求有助于生活的审美化。对一切民族生活方式来说，时尚感的生成也同样意味着其与日常生活的区分。

甚至还可以说，正是在与日常生活的区分里，时尚成为一种富有新意的生活方式。作为民族日常生活的重要构成，民族的时尚艺术与衣生活方式，也同样构成了对民族生活日常性的挑战。在民族时尚艺术里，民族的性格与文化得到了独特的体现，同时也给民族的日常生活方式带来了新意。民族性格相关于表现在民族文化上的心理状态，也与民族共同认同的心理与文化特征分不开。实际上，民族性格的生成是一个长期积淀与建构的过程，同时又不得不受到许多因素的影响与制约，其中最重要的因素就是该民族的精神与文化。时装并不只是被理解为不同于常服的服装，它的时尚性有时并没有与日常性严格区分开。

如何与异质文化对话与交流，显然也是所有时尚所应回应的创意问题。关注与尊重民族元素与文化的内在规定性，对于民族艺术与时尚文化的建构都是不可或缺的。在雷蒙德自己的研究文章之中，他赞扬了法国的时尚产业。譬如，"雷蒙德将时尚巴黎女郎的优越性与法国时尚、法国民族联系起来，这证实了时尚巴黎女郎话语在国际环境中是如何推动法国时尚产业的"。[1] 而且，民族性文化有时还具有较强的排他性，尤其是可能会将异质文化拒之门外。正因如此，不同异质文化之间的沟通与交流，对各个民族时尚的生成也是不可或缺的。

由于所有文化内在的凝聚力，同质文化内部个体间的理解显得较为容易。作为一种符码，时尚意义不仅关切到艺术文本，还经由这些文本而涉及社会、历史与文化。对民族元素时尚意义的当代揭示与阐发，必将涉及诸多学科与文化的观点。民族性体现了一个民族自身的、不可替代的独特性，表征着一定民族文化的传承、积淀与特定地域文明的特点，而且密切相关于民族的特定精神和文化特质。因此，民族时尚应既从内部坚守民族文化的个性与特质，同时又从外部关联于全球文化的某种一般性。在不同民族的交往与生活方式

---

[1] 露丝·E.爱斯金.印象派绘画中的时尚女性与巴黎消费文化[M].孟春艳，译.南京：江苏美术出版社，2010：229.

的交流中，文化的适应性也是一个与时尚意义相关的问题。

其实，还可以通过对前卫或先锋艺术表现手法的借鉴，为民族时尚艺术与审美文化带来独特的新奇感。作为现代艺术流派之一，先锋艺术泛指新的艺术表现方式与风格，它往往具有对传统的反叛性与颠覆性。作为对既有艺术体制的反动，先锋艺术的先锋性本身就是历史性的，并不可避免地经历着不断的解构与消解。但是，后现代主义并非一味地反叛艺术传统，也涉及通过艺术与设计来重构传统元素，并使之生成与建构当下的衣生活时尚感。但既不能把时尚仅仅归结为某种先锋艺术，也不应否定许多先锋艺术往往具有时尚特质。

在这里，先锋艺术出现在西方现代性应有之意中，它是西方现代提出的、与后现代相关的概念。先锋时尚就是将先锋的艺术手法与技巧，运用在时尚（包括民族时尚）的创意与设计之中，从而形成具有先锋意识与感觉的当代民族时尚。把先锋风格与民族元素加以生成性关联，所形成的其实就是民族的先锋性时装。还要注意，各个民族的艺术与文化之间发生着交织与互文。比如，中原华夏文化与带有区域特征的吴越、巴蜀、荆楚、齐鲁、燕赵、岭南等文化并存，同时又是与蒙、藏、回、壮等多个民族文化彼此共生的。正因如此，不同民族的精神图式与视觉习惯，往往难以分离地、历史性地交织在一起。

与其他地区相比，少数民族的特殊性与特定的地域和民族精神图式分不开。在全球化的今天，中国的民族文化与世界所有民族文化一样，无不面临着新的挑战与文化选择的困境。无论是固守民族本位的民族主义，还是全面走向西化的民族虚无主义，其实都不可能使民族文化在世界文化之林占有应有之地。实际上，特定民族元素及其时尚意义的生成，也是在与其他民族的对话和文化回应里实现的。基于独特性的民族时尚陌生化的生成与建构，是民族艺术与时尚创意至关重要的表征特质，也由此构成了时尚意义发生的感觉基础。

在时尚趋势的流行与预测中，虽然说不必对各个具体种族起源加以追溯，但起源也是民族元素意义生成不可分离的历史语境。应看到，文化的异质性生成与存在于不同民族的文化之间，这或许是时尚感生成的族群与文化的生成论前提。"然而，所有投身流行预测工作的人员都必须了解，这个族群的品位将是引导整个服装市场需求的主要动力。"[1] 与异质文化相对应的就是同质文化，它指在那些不同的种族与文化的特质中，人们所拥有的相同或相似的共有文化特质。还可以说，现代艺术与文化正是多种异质文化的组合与交融。

因此，各种不同的艺术与文化的共在，成为时尚创意不可或缺的生活、历史与文化语境。与此同时，各个不同地域的异质艺术与文化的存在，其实也难免融入艺术与审美的异质性关联里，并在彼此文化的共在中彰显出陌生感。同质的艺术与文化是世界文化整体中较稳定的部分，它使世界范围内的艺术与文化对话成为可能。但由于人类的生存环境与民俗仪式、生活趣味等差异，民族元素与文化在表达时也呈现出各自的独特性。这是因为任

---

[1] 丽塔·裴娜.流行预测[M].李宏伟，王倩梅，洪瑞璘，译.北京：中国纺织出版社，2000：118.

何民族元素及其意义与旨趣的解读，其实都离不开相关于地方与历史的文化语境。

人类与自然发生关联而获取生存机会的方式、手段，乃至长期积淀的民族心理也随不同的地域、种族而有所差异。还要看到，这种地域性不仅是相关于实体及其空间的，它更是特定民族生活世界生成与建构的基础，同时也是该民族记忆与集体无意识的发生之所。正因为如此，人们的时尚生活方式也彰显出了地方性与异质性。而且，由此形成了具有强烈个性色彩的文化体系，这种文化体系当然也是文化整体的重要构成。但在不同的地域与民族文化之间，甚至还可以在相对的意义上成为异质文化。在服饰与时尚的创意设计中，通过各自的特性来相互区分开，并生成彼此不同的独特时尚感。

显而易见，时尚创意旨在揭示设计及其自由的本性。当然，一切民族文化及其差异只能是相对的，在不同的艺术样式与服饰文化之间，存在的往往只是符码及其自身的差异，而非简单的对立、一致与非此即彼。对于艺术、审美与文化的评价来说，创意总是在某些文化的价值体系中完成的，因为每个个体都具有各自的阅历和经验，这就导致了对设计的文化差异性形成了不同理解。但在跨文化的时尚传播中，各种文化特质交织而生成出时尚意味。时尚意义及其生成的相对性与历史特征，在异质的时尚与文化中显得极为突出。

这里所说的异质性与同质性，往往是相比较而存在的，它们共同构成艺术与设计的文化特质。除此之外，开放的创意与设计文本及其生成，又为异质与同质的彼此生成提供了可能性。应当说，不同族群或个人的美感其实并不相同，"虽然它是所有艺术创作的基础，但并不是说美感是装饰创作的唯一理由"。❶ 而且，任何一种设计都不能只有异质性或同质性。在某种一致性或同质化中，寻求民族独特的创意是至关重要的审美与文化诉求。任何时尚创意与意义的生成与阐释，都离不开各种民族文化之间的交流与互文。

然而，具有不同文化内涵与特质的民族元素，并非单一与纯粹地出现在时尚创意设计中，而是在多种民族文化的勾连与交融里，生成与实现自身在当下的独特时尚意义。在全球化的过程中，民族时尚文化的生成与历史性发生，总是呈现出两种看似相互冲突的态势，即同质性文化与异质性文化的悖论，而一切时尚创意与设计是不可能彻底游离在此悖论之外的。在时尚创意与设计中，人们越来越关注对不同民族元素与文化的吸纳，并力图在民族间的艺术与文化对话里构建独特时尚。

各个异质文化之间的关联，经由相互的适应、互补与融合，生成为一种新的异质文化感。在这里，人类及其各个民族、族群的时尚衣生活，无不面临着同一性与差异性之间的审美与文化冲突。尤其是，各个不同民族的时尚文化的根基与基础，往往都具有自身的延续性、稳定性与差异性，这就使得非西方国家的民族文化意识超乎寻常地得到了关注与强化，这其实也是在全球化时代对现代性及其一致性诉求的反应。但各种样式的殖民主义与极端的民族主义，都是当代民族时尚创意与设计应加以警惕与批判的，而民族间的文化交

---

❶ 阿尔弗雷德·C.哈登.艺术的进化：图案的生命史解析[M].阿嘎佐诗，译.桂林：广西师范大学出版社，2010：171.

流与彼此认同则是民族时尚创意不可或缺的人类学基础。

三、民族时尚创意的生成及其方式

一切民族或族群元素的时尚化过程，以及这些民族元素在时尚设计里的表达，都有待于特定艺术表现方式来加以揭示与探究。民族时尚创意的生成方式与路径，既相关于各种艺术表现与工艺流程，还涉及民族的心理、社会与文化。这里应强调的是，"艺术和设计是开放的学科：对于某一既定的问题或情况没有所谓正确的答案，这也是此学科之所以会对许多设计师产生无穷魅力的根本所在"。❶ 在此可以说，设计在形式与质料及其关系上的创意，在根本意义上相关于时尚的创意与设计，这有助于不断地突破形式与质料及其概念框架的传统规限。

当然，时尚创意与设计也有不少区别于一般设计之处，这是因为，时尚不得不回应其与身体及其存在的独特关联，以及艺术与审美如何建构当下时尚感的问题。在艺术与设计中，形式、质料及其生成性关联，从来都是必须加以认真考虑与揭示的问题。在亚里士多德看来，形式、质料与具体事物都是实体性的。设计虽然不同于无功利的自由（纯粹）艺术，但无疑又离不开艺术表现与审美经验。虽然说，器物制作有时也可以与设计创意本身适当分离，但设计应为制作提供一种审美的考虑与切实的可能性。

还应注意到，设计同样涉及祛功利化与审美生成，这样设计出来的产品才会具备超越性的美感。康德对依存美（附庸美）与自由美（纯粹美）的区分，虽然为设计艺术与自由艺术的区分奠定了基础，但这种区分及其边界难免受到不断消解与重建。特别是，随着唯美主义所遭遇的问题与困境，设计艺术与自由艺术的传统区分日趋模糊。在中外时尚史上，各民族都有其风格不同的裙装，如苏格兰短裙、俄罗斯长裙等，这些时尚风格在不同的历史时期，又表现出各不相同的款式、长短与特质。作为一种基于目的与创意的造型活动，艺术设计显然并不只是技术与实施的过程，还是一种相关于视觉与审美的文化建构。

就服饰与时装来说，创意是一切设计都不可或缺的首要与根本之所在，同时也是时尚感得以生成与建构的观念与思想性基础。一切创意与设计都离不开视觉化的过程，并在这种视觉化过程中建构独特的时尚感与审美趣味。在这里，视觉化旨在激活设计师与受众的形象思维，使其头脑里呈现出视觉可接受的图像样式，从而生成与传播艺术表现与审美经验。虽然说，设计的美主要包括功能美、形式美、材质美等方面，但一切关于美与审美经验如此简单的划分，其实无不是无可奈何的权宜之计而已。

在传统的服饰与设计中，各种艺术表现方式与审美视角，都是特定族群精神图式自身的呈现。在设计之美的表现中，功能美与人的生理需要满足后而产生的感悟、情感与审美经验相关。与此同时，形式美涉及的一般是产品所具有的形、声、色及其关系与结构。在

---

❶ 罗伯特·克雷.设计之美[M].尹弢,译.济南：山东画报出版社,2010：17.

克莱夫·贝尔看来,"我把线条和颜色的这些组合和关系,以及这些在审美上打动人的形式称作'有意味的形式',它就是所有视觉艺术作品所具有的那种共性"。❶ 通常来说,形式美的构成因素涉及感性质料及其组合或构成,也关联不同民族或族群的时尚风格及其审美情感。在这里,构成形式美的感性质料的关系与构成,其实也就是关联于设计品的形式美的法则。

在创意与设计中,相关于形式美的主要法则有:齐一与参差、对称与平衡、比例与尺度、黄金分割律、过渡与照应、稳定与轻巧、节奏与韵律、渗透与层次、质感与肌理、调和与对比、多样与统一等。但对任何规则的简单套用与直接搬抄,都难以产生真正的时尚感及其不可替代性特质。实际上,任何民族创意与设计及其发生,都是对既有规则的独特回应甚至突破。还可以说,这些形式法则是人类从造物与审美中揭示出来的,并对创意设计具有某种规定性的理想标准与诉求。在康德看来,形式美具有独立于质料与功用的纯粹性,但在现当代时期,这种形式美又不可分割地与质料、功用发生着关联与互生。

由此,时尚创意既离不开视觉与审美表现,同时也与人们的日常生活分不开。在唯美主义与形式主义中,艺术形式的纯粹性得到了充分的强调。对于形式主义而言,艺术、审美的独立性与形式的绝对化是极其重要的。形式主义还强调了艺术形式的独立审美意义。在生成论现象学的语境中,民族时尚意义的发生总是在与其他民族的区分中实现的。唯美主义极大地影响了抽象的与非再现性的现代艺术运动,进而推动了结构主义和符号学的产生和发展。而且,现代建筑追求空白与中性的形式结构的倾向,也受到过唯美主义与形式主义的深刻影响。

应当强调的是,唯美主义与形式主义对民族时尚也具有重要意义,因为对于各种不同的民族或族群来说,除了强调设计与民族生活的功能性关联外,还把各具特色又彼此不同的唯美效果表现出来。就美本身及其多样性而言,"为了这个缘故与其将之称为美的种类,还不如将之称为美的变相来得合适些"。❷ 因此,唯美的时尚文本样式又以其开放性,回应着社会、历史与文化语境所涉及的问题。其实,民族元素及其时尚感,是在独特与别致的美的建构中产生的。而且,时尚美的建构并不局限于优美与美的传统分类。

从柏拉图到黑格尔,西方哲学把质料看作黑暗的、混沌的与惰性的,往往从形式上探讨艺术表现与审美经验的问题。在这里,纯形式虽然似乎介于质料与理念之间,但接受的却是理念自身的根本规定。在古希腊,理念本身往往内含视觉与形式的意义。在民族的服饰文化中,各种色彩都具有彼此相异的意味与情感关联,并发生着历史性的变化与不断的意义重构。在质料方面,时尚的创意与表现一般经由面料等来实现。基于质料的性状与质感,如何对民族元素加以表现是时尚设计的重要问题。在亚里士多德那里,世界乃是由各种形式与质料和谐一致的事物构成的。

---

❶ 克莱夫·贝尔.艺术[M].薛华,译.南京:江苏教育出版社,2005:4.
❷ 瓦迪斯瓦夫·塔塔尔凯维奇.西方六大美学观念史[M].刘文潭,译.上海:上海译文出版社,2006:159.

亚里士多德从结合的角度探讨事物的生成与变化，质料与形式原初主要限于对器具与设计的揭示与描述，但后来被沿用到自由艺术的表现与评价中。在亚里士多德看来，因主要有四种基本的类型或样式，第一种是质料因，即形成物体的主要物质。当然，这也涉及服饰与时装所用到的各种材料。如果说，面料为服饰与时装提供了质料因，那么，服饰与时装的款式就是形式因，手的使用与制作工具是动力因，而服饰与时装的功能与用途则是目的因。亚里士多德认为既没有无质料的形式，也没有无形式的质料，因此他强调质料与形式的密切关系。

但是，质料与形式仍然面临着不可回避的二元分立的困境。虽然美学曾被规定与把握为感性学，原初主要研究自由艺术与审美经验，但仍然不得不回应设计与功能问题，同时也不可能摆脱技术及其关涉。这也就是说，"美是在一种与对象有时是更为智力性的、有时是更加肉体性的接触中给我们显示的。就是在这样的经验之中，技术对象才能为我们审美化"。❶ 这里的质料美指设计所涉及材料本身的质地，以及与之相关的艺术表现展现出来的美感。例如，古朴、神秘的服装相关于尘封的历史；明亮、瑰丽的金属装饰，让我们想到了未来的科技；而那些柔和与含蓄的纤维面料，无疑使我们想到温馨的家庭气氛。

一般来说，流动、飘逸的曲线与配饰，使人们联想到喧嚣的都市与浪漫的情感，坚韧的面料则让人想到宁静的乡村等。时尚意义的生成也同样离不开审美化的过程，以及这种审美化对民族元素的揭示与重构。应当说，面料不仅可以揭示与诠释服装的风格和特性，还直接影响着服装的色彩、造型及其表现效果。在民族服装与时尚设计中，面料各式各样、五花八门，令人目不暇接。实际上，各种不同的质料及其肌理与质感，无疑都为创意与时尚感的生成注入了独特的审美旨趣。

从总体上来讲，优质面料具有舒适、吸汗透气、悬垂挺括、视觉高贵、触觉柔美等特点。因此，设计与制作在正式社交场合穿着的服装，一般宜选用纯棉、纯毛、纯丝、纯麻制品。不同于一般的自由艺术，服饰还要充分考虑着装者的功能诉求，而对衣着的审美预期也与这种功能性分不开。在康德那里，不同的感觉与经验及其共通性关系受到了关注。时尚感及其意义的生成与建构，也是与这种审美通感密切相关的，但又并不局限在唯美主义的文本中。自由美就是不以对象的概念（例如，客观的目的性）为前提，而依存美则以这样一个概念并以按照这概念的对象的完满性为前提。

在康德看来，当我们被一个对象所刺激时，它在表象能力上所产生的结果就是感觉。因此，那种经过感觉与对象相关的直观就叫作经验性的直观，而一个经验性的直观的未被规定的对象就叫作现象。应当看到，时尚美虽然具有某种关涉功用与实际的依存性，但它也受到自由艺术及其审美风格的影响。在现象中，与感觉相应的物品被称为现象的质料。根据康德的观点，一切现象的质料都只是后天被给予的，但其形式却必须全都天生地在内

---

❶ 米·杜夫海纳.美学与哲学[M].孙非，译.北京：中国社会科学出版社，1985：214.

心中为这些现象准备好的。

唯美主义、"为艺术而艺术"、形式主义美学的思想来源，其实就是康德所说的这种自由美，显然也就是纯粹的、无功利的形式美。从这个意义上来说，"康德也许是第一个强调新是时尚的本质特质，同时也是真正具有声望的时尚理论家……"❶ 在这里，康德也由此否定了时尚与唯美的简单关联。但是，时尚设计被视为一种艺术活动，也就是艺术生产的重要构成方式，创意对美的表现离不开一定的质料。就民族时尚而言，创意的生成既离不开一般所说的观念的创新，更不可能没有特定的精神与文化特质贯注其中，以及由此而生成的相关于特定人群的独特意味与魅惑。

实际上，独特创意是走向民族精神与文化魅惑的一种回归，这种回归即返回到与民族生存和文化相关的特定精神领域和语境中。而且，只有从民族精神及其图式的重构出发，才能充分表现与阐发当下的时尚创意与趣味，以及与之相关的独特的艺术与审美经验。譬如，不对称特质由于具有奇特与别样的意味，而得到过不少设计师的广泛借鉴与运用。与此同时，这种返魅其实也是对民族魅惑的一种重构，并在不同民族创意样式之间显示出差异。在民族时尚的创意中，特定服饰是与时尚设计的目的或功用不可分的，它们依然具有某种难以断裂的连续性特质。

毫无疑问，创意与设计的生成与存在，都相关于形式和质料及其生成性关联，并以此克服形式与质料关系的传统模式及其问题。如曾经象征着地位、权利与荣誉的冠，至今仍在一些君主制国家的加冕仪式里使用着。在对"新原始风格"符号的自由性的揭示上，雅克·布兰齐认为，"设计师寻求他们自身识别的创意点，他们自身语言编码的构建使他们可能就像是部落首领一般"。❷ 对质料的审美心理与感受，还涉及不同感觉之间的关联与融通。也就是说，时尚的创意及其审美需要多种感官共同介入而实现，而审美通感在质料的审美观照中具有不可替代的作用。

在亚里士多德看来，柏拉图的理念论不能说明事物的存在，因为柏拉图的理念与个别事物是相分离的。所谓的"质料因"就是事物的"最初基质"，即构成每一事物的原始质料。与此同时，"形式因"则指事物的"本质规定"。任何设计与造物都摆脱不了质料与形式的概念图式，但又无不涉及对这种图式加以独特的回应与重构。在亚里士多德看来，质料是潜能，形式是现实，二者的关系就是潜能与现实的关系。形式作为主动的、积极的成因，在质料的形式化过程中，给质料以规定，使质料成为现实个体。

质料则有待于形式的赋形，而形式在创意与表现中，总是关乎精神的。形式作为事物之本质、定义、存在和现实，是与事物的潜能的质料相区别的，但形式又不可能脱离质料而存在。在亚里士多德那里，目的论事先预设了某种目的，然后分析如何去实现这种目的。如何在创意与设计中，将质料与形式作出独特的关联与回应，成为时尚意义生成不可回避

---

❶ 拉斯·史文德森.时尚的哲学[M].李漫，译.北京：北京大学出版社，2010：21.
❷ 维克多·马格林.设计问题：历史·理论·批评[M].柳沙，张朵朵，等译.北京：中国建筑工业出版社，2010：35.

的问题。在视觉艺术的质地美中，形式与质料实现了密切的生成性关联。实际上，形式与质料的简单二分，限定了对形式与质料的充分揭示与表现。

虽然杜夫海纳认为，在逻辑中，形式不是一个对象的形式，不再与质料密切相关。但是，审美的形式却应使质料具有形式。但进入现代以后，形式不再由内容所简单决定，而内容与形式的传统关联难免被解构。对创意而言，"时装的本质即在于此，它感受到了言语难以表达的，感触到了一种'精神'，并且由于它综合归纳了分散的要素，而成为至高无上的，它是抽象化的过程"。❶ 那么，形式及其在当代时尚创意里的表现与建构，不再受制于质料与形式的传统关系及其困境。

只有克服与走出质料与形式的传统关系及其问题，才能显现出形式所蕴含的生成论意味与旨趣。除了对特定民族文化意味加以关注外，时尚创意的形式感也是极其重要的表现诉求。由现代转向后现代，西方思想的规定性由存在变成了语言或话语。时尚的创意与设计方式，都是视角性与多元化的，同时又是对传统的回应与当下重构。后现代消解了近现代的艺术理念与审美观念，其思想的根本特质就是解构性的，表现为不确定性、零散性、非原则性与无深度性等。如果说，现代美学在存在的境域中仍然关注形式的话，那么，后现代主义则坚持强烈的反形式倾向。与此同时，这也为民族时尚创意及其当代生成与表现提供了重要契机。

---

❶ 罗兰·巴特.流行体系——符号学与服饰符码[M].敖军，译.上海：上海人民出版社，2000：123.

CHAPTER 1

Ethnic Elements and Generation of Fashion Creative

As expressions of concepts and ideas, fashion creative and designs are often new and aesthetic, occurring in the context of ethnic and culture existence. The ethnic elements involved in fashion creative are undoubtedly historical, and the revelation and expression of ethnic elements cannot be separated from ethnic culture. Moreover, fashion creative, design and aesthetic expression should become an acceptable way of cultural identification and communication. In fashion creative and design, cultural identification shows a certain continuity of fashion history. For example, the newly popular Chinese Tang suit is actually a modern reconstruction of traditional Chinese clothing. However, among fashion arts and cultures of different ethnicities, there is an urgent need for continuous communication and mutual understanding in order to promote their mutual cultural identification. Here, the cross-cultural communication of fashion elements, characterized by the intertextuality and intertwining of texts, is based on the fact that human beings live together on this earth, while with the uniqueness in ethnic culture as the prerequisite. As far as fashion creative and design is concerned, ethnic elements involved are never changeless and immutable, and in principle they can all get creative visual and artistic expressions. Ethnic elements are also heterogeneous and diverse in aspects and types involved, providing materials, discourses and cultural contexts for fashion creative and design. In terms of artistic expression and aesthetics, ethnic elements acquire their identity through constant appearances and evolvements. In particular when ethnic elements are borrowed into fashion creative and design, they would experience historical changes in aesthetic reorganization and meaning, and have intertextual interweaving and dialogues with current fashion concepts and ideas, thus making possible those fashion creative and designs with special ethnicities. In fact, the indigenous aesthetic tendencies and unique cultural interests of different ethnic groups have become an indispensable source of inspiration for contemporary fashion creative and design. Fashion never belongs to a particular ethnic group, as each ethnic group has its own fashion and art styles, and fashion expressions get constant exchanges and contemporary reconstructions among different ethnic groups.

Section 1 Composition, Relevance and Characteristics of Ethnic Elements

Here, element refers to a kind of basic unit that is an inherent component of a thing and cannot be decomposed further. Accordingly, ethnic element can be understood as: the basic unit that is highly symbolic with ethnic art and culture deposits. Lines, colors, shapes, and textures could all be considered elements of visual art and expressions. Different ethnic elements and cultures are both distinguished from each other and interrelated to each other, forming an open whole of ethnic lifestyles and cultures. And it is worth noting that ethnic elements are an indivisible part of an ethnic culture, and a clarification of the integrity of ethnic culture, although they disclose and manifest ethnic existence and lifestyle just from a specific level or perspective. Therefore, ethnic elements are characteristic of both integrity and generativity. An intertextual dialogue of art and culture is indispensable for the revelation and interpretation of various ethnic elements.

1. Definition and Composition of Ethnic Elements

In general, ethnic element is the basic building block and component of a culture, existing in the generating process of ethnic art and culture. As a basic component of ethnic art and culture, ethnic element is the essential factor for the forming of ethnic structure. "Due to their overlapping nature, elements cannot be classified by rigid standards."❶ In fact, ethnic spirit and cultural characteristics are manifested through elements in their composition, while various elements with special cultural characteristics constitute the ethnic culture in turn. In the existence of an ethnic group, ethnic elements and their composition are the structural factors concerning the identity of the ethnic group.

In ethnic fashion creative and design, the structure of elements is often composed of deep, shallow, and surface levels, which are different in the degree of visualization but interrelated to generate the integral characteristic between ethnic elements and culture. Corresponding to the structure of elements are beliefs, rituals, and artifacts endowed with ethnic spirit and culture. They are not only revealed and elaborated at different levels, but also responded to in the context of art, thought, and culture. Therefore, from the three constitutional levels of ethnic elements, it is possible to reveal their contents as well as their artistic, aesthetic, and cultural meanings. For all ethnic elements with special cultural characteristics, beliefs, rituals, and artifacts are related and influential to each other. In fact, the meaning and purport of an element on different levels are often defined by some integral structure.

Ethnic elements exist in plural modes and endless forms. In ethnic spirit and cultural composition, beliefs, rituals and artifacts reveal the integral ethnic character. In terms of ethnic elements, beliefs, rituals and artifacts are fundamental ways of manifesting and interpreting ethnic spirit and culture. Primordial and historical religion has shaped people's sensitivity. For the existence and culture of an ethnic group, belief is a spiritual sustenance, a fundamental faith, as

---

❶ Frank P. The Principle of Visual Art [M]. Chen Yuelei, Yu Yu (tr). Shanghai: Shanghai People's Fine Arts Publishing House, 2008:40.

well as an appeal to ultimacy. Belief is aimed at transcending everything that is limited.

Only the infinity that can transcend the limitations of reality can provide the possibility to make up for one's own limitations. The elements and cultures of various ethnic groups may be related to a common belief or to different beliefs. And beliefs are also inseparable from rituals and costumes. Beliefs are at the highest level of ethnic spirit and cultural structure, artifacts on which ethnic life depends are at the lowest level, while rituals are in between. Myth is expressed in allegorical and imaginative narratives, playing an important symbolic and stipulative role in the inheritance of ethnic art and culture. Beliefs, religions, and ancient arts have all been deeply affected by myth. Myth not only constitutes the heritage of traditional ethnic elements and culture, but also offers continuous reference for clothing design.

As a primitive religion, totemism treats certain animals or plants as deities. It is true that "myth, as a complex and compounded spiritual constitution, contains some eternal topics (like meaning of human life, merits, happiness, etc.), and passes them to future generations in artistic forms."[1] Beliefs are often colored with emotional experience, which is reflected and emphasized in many religions. However, belief does not necessarily mean the objective existence of the things worshiped. In order to express the worship of their totems and to distinguish themselves from other clans, primitive ancestors usually painted or carved totem images on their own bodies.

For primitive ancestors, tattoo as a totem decoration reflected their concern over body appearance. And the graphics used by different clans and ethnic groups were different. A person's belief must involve a process of internal response, and he would choose a religion that suits himself through personal experiences and spiritual pursuits. When human beings created a real world, they meanwhile constructed a mysterious world with ethnic spirit and characteristics, and pinned their beliefs and hopes on it. In fact, an ethnic group cannot be devoid of beliefs and spiritual sustenance, because only by holding faith can it draw near the distance between the finite and the infinite, and then constitutes the spiritual character indispensable for ethnic elements and culture. In Chinese history, Confucianism and Taoism used to be basic belief systems. The belief of an ethnic group in a profound sense would construct the mind, spirit and culture of the ethnic group.

Chinese Confucianism emphasizes benevolence and rites. Confucian benevolence, the core idea of Confucianism, is a creative transformation of rite and music culture in the pre-Qin period, or, a special way to interpret the rite and music culture. Confucianism, with thoughts of Confucius as its core, is undoubtedly an important component of Chinese traditional spirit and culture. In

---

[1] Yakovlev E. Art and World Religions [M]. Ren Guangxuan, Li Donghan (tr). Beijing: Culture and Art Publishing House, 1989: 8-9.

Confucianism, views on merits of men emphasize the close relationship or even the integration between clothing and men. Laozi, a contemporary of Confucius, attached importance to concepts of Dao (the Way) and De (the Virtue), and advocated inaction and purity in behavior. Moreover, the art understood by Taoism is the art of not being, for example, the great sound seems soundless, and the great image seems formless expresses the realm of not being. Here, all kinds of thoughts concerning beliefs constitute the spiritual characters of ethnic costume art and culture.

Original Taoism mainly refers to the doctrines of Laozi and Zhuangzi, and the neo-Taoism in the Wei and Jin Dynasties is also called the Wei-Jin Metaphysics. The core idea of Taoism is Dao (the Way) itself, or, the Way as nature. The Taoist costume, popular in folk life during the Yuan Dynasty and the early Ming Dynasty, was a kind of clothing manifesting the ideas of Taoism in ancient China. The Zen, an important school of Buddhism, mainly advocated the enlightenment of the mind, as the fundamental problem was internal rather than external, namely, the discovery of one's own Buddha nature, or of one's self. Later, Zen got spread from China to Japan and became the Buddhist style of Japan. And the theme of Buddhism and Zen has become an important part of artistic expression and costume design.

The disclosure of the contents and connotations of ethnic elements is inseparable from ethnic beliefs, religions, and cultural characteristics. In general, ritual is a general term for activities that have symbolic religious or traditional meaning. The English word ritual originally refers to a standardized set of actions, whose means and ends are not directly related to each other. In art history and aesthetic history, art and ritual have long been connected. At the same time, a ritual is often conducted in a certain period and on a specific occasion. In religion, ritual refers to certain fixed procedure practiced in prayer and worship.

A ritual can be hosted and organized by an individual, a group or an organization, and the behaviors accompanying it often show further purpose or attempt. A ritual can be performed on a general occasion or a specific occasion, to the public, the private, or the specific group. As the main carrier of belief, ritual not only reflects the purport of belief, but also conveys the cultural significance of sign and symbol. Social activities and daily life in ethnic areas, such as communication activities, festivals, funerals, marriages, etc., are all associated with specific rites, etiquettes, and clothing, reflecting unique cultural styles of ethnic customs and habits. Rites and etiquettes show the willingness of people to respect each other in communication, that is, they are the procedures and methods of interacting with people, as well as the external communicative norms for people's clothes, languages, manners, etc..

With the shift of human society and culture, the ritual itself will change in form and cultural significance during different historical periods. In short, we use the word ritual to refer to "a standardized behavior mode (custom), with the relationship between its goals and means being not intrinsic, but non-rational or irrational." ❶ Ritual is often regarded as symbolic, performing, and a set of behaviors defined by cultural traditions. It is functionally defined as: the mode for communication, transition, strengthening and integrating society by a particular group or culture. For example, transition rituals are those performed at a specific point in one's life (birth, adulthood, marriage, etc.).

Minorities living in the southern regions of China generally maintain their primitive religious beliefs based on animism. The ritual with ethnic characteristics refers to the symbolic activities governed by the customs and traditional culture of ethnic minorities, and it can make the participants identify their social values directly in heart. Once ethnic customs and habits are formed, they would gain relative independence and become a cultural symbol and value orientation deep in the soul of the ethnic group. Here, rituals have become a mode of behavior in connection with beliefs, and the fundamental meaning of such behaviors is symbolic of spiritual reference. In behavior narratives of rituals, specific costumes help people experience and understand spiritual interests, as well as share historical and cultural memories of a race or ethnic group.

In fact, the integration of ethnic art and culture with society is inseparable from habits, conventions, taboos and moral norms. Rituals and habits are related to ethnic values and cultural character, so rituals of different ethnic groups can manifest their unique concepts and spirits. More than a tangible way of expression, art is also concerned with the spiritual and cultural appeals of ethnic groups. "Artworks that people can observe are a tangible expression of a culture, hence, a spirit that is constructed in accordance with the visual expression habits of that culture." ❷ Artifacts, handicrafts and clothing designs are also art styles in the early days of an ethnic group, inseparable from the specific visual expression habits and cultural traditions of the ethnic group.

Of course, ethnic customs and habits are mainly based on culture, concepts, and thinking patterns, which penetrate into ethnic life and affect people's behavior. Based on ethnic beliefs, unique rituals make ethnic customs and habits externalized into visible actions and processes through a symbolic system. In the world of ethnic life, the characteristics of traditional art and culture are essentially related to special customs and habits. For creative ideas, an artifact is the being that grasps the existence of ethnic elements. It is not only the carrier of art and cultural imprint, but also the historical presentation of traditional art and culture. The aesthetic generation of folk arts concerns the historical there-being of the ethnic group, and folk crafts embody the relations between nature and human beliefs. As the practicality of artifact often obscure the work

---

❶ Goody J. Myth, Ritual and the Oral [M]. Li Yuan (tr). Beijing: China Renmin University Press, 2014:33.
❷ Layton R. The Anthropology of Art [M]. Li Dongye, Wang Hong (tr). Guilin: Guangxi Normal University Press, 2009: 31.

itself, the suspension of its practicality is necessary sometimes.

Only by overcoming its practicability, an artifact can concern the being itself, and make it possible to open and reveal the living world. In Heidegger's view, although the pure object is able to be seen, it does not reveal itself. It is closed and blocked, open to nothing and difficult for people to explore. At the same time, the ready-to-hand state of artifact is the very reason that it has never been noticed or examined as itself. According to Heidegger, as an object or a being, a work of art is different from both pure object and ordinary appliance, because it exists on its own with some kind of self-sufficiency. Moreover, a work of art can open itself to outside without being subject to regulations of utility.

However, for ethnic elements and culture, folk artifacts are not exactly the same as Heidegger's concept of objects, because the artifacts in the ethnic and traditional lifestyles are more mysterious, not limited to instrumental feature, but related to ethnic spiritual character and local culture. "The simple, bright colors and exotic artistic styles emphasized in Iriba deeply attracted Pall, who considered those elements to be popular with customers."❶ Therefore, ethnic artifacts or crafts cannot be simply classified into functional objects. The patterns of ancient folk embroideries are mainly about nature in a traditionalized and signified way, but with meanings going beyond nature itself. The way to name and define artifact is closely related with its function and other cultural elements.

Clothes, as a means of decorating and beautifying human body, are not only artifacts with practical functions, but also symbols of society and culture. In the art history and aesthetic culture, various artifacts have become prototypes or motifs of visual expressions, and have entered ethnic costumes and art expressions in the form of patterns. But once that happens, those artifacts are no longer ordinary objects with practicality, but texts embedded in the context of art, history and culture. Here, shapes of artifacts are closely connected with material culture, rituals, and daily life, and this generative association and its characteristics have become the context for the forming of shape meanings and belief purports. It is in this context that the mutual generation of artifacts, rituals and beliefs can take place.

Artifacts of different ethnic groups are different in their shapes and cultural characteristics. Archaeology has traditionally defined the relationship among material culture, rituals, and daily life on the basis of their characteristics and differences. Generally, ritual is held in a special place by a special means. Because of this, the material culture in ritual is manifested with its unconventional nature. Judging from the relationship between form and context, the artifact used in

---

❶ Lovinski N P. The World's Most Influential Fashion Designers [M]. Zhou Meng, Zheng Shanshan (tr). Beijing: China Textile Publishing House, 2014:14.

a ritual is clearly different from that for daily occasions. As a kind of artifact, costume is used not only in people's daily life, but also in special non-routine fields, such as festivals and ceremonial occasions.

As an artifact of unique style, ceremonial dress is often used on some important occasions, appearing solemn and formal on the wearer. Many artifacts and tools may become things of taboo. For example, "maybe in the ancient society when iron wares were still novelties, people already refused to use them out of superstition." [1] In terms of clothes, taboo is mainly on people's dress that may be associated with some beliefs. Although the relationship between ritual and belief is similar to that between technique and way, it is more complex in interpretation. In fashion creative and design, element of color is closed related to cultural characteristics of various ethnic groups.

The technique is indispensable for revealing and accessing the way, and the way in turn regulates and constrains the technique. And in the context of generative theory, any problems and dilemmas brought by the dualism about technique and way are in an urgent need to be overcome. The way should stipulate the technique, and at the same time, the technique should obey and access the way, hence the ultimate realm is the mutual formation and integration of the two. Extreme emphasis on technique often leads to technicism, covering the way in itself. Therefore, it is necessary to suspend and overcome the traditional problems and dilemmas on technique and way. Meanwhile, the stratification of elements and continuous breakthrough of present stratification are providing the possibility for the occurrence of intertext-based creative ideas.

2. Relevance and Intertextuality between Meanings of Ethnic Elements

Creative elements are always expressed through visual transformation, so that concepts and ideas are conveyed into fashion art and clothing. And the interconnection between meanings of ethnic elements is not only of great importance, but also a generative process extremely complex, according to Claude Levy-Strauss, meaning is always incommensurable to cognition.[2] But we should also see that all meanings are in the alternating process of deconstruction and construction. In the philosophy of language, meaning is related to the relationship between words and objects, so various meaning theories are inseparable from the understanding and interpretation of words and sentences. Of course, ethnic elements are not only a general existence, but also an important component of ethnic art and culture.

Moreover, the deep, shallow and surface levels in the structure of ethnic elements are actually

---

[1] Frazer J G. The Golden Bough: A Study in Magic and Religion [M]. Wang Peiji, Xu Yuxin, Zhang Zeshi (tr). Beijing: Commercial Press, 2013: 375.

[2] Merquior J G. L'Esthtique de Lévi-Strauss [M]. Huai Yu (tr). Tianjin: Tianjin People's Publishing House, 2003:137.

places where the social and cultural associations of elements occur. The meaning connections between creative elements at deep, shallow, and surface levels are understood through specific connotation of beliefs, rituals and artifacts. Of course, creative ideas on elements are different in their visualization methods. There is a non-negligible intertextual connection between element's deep, shallow and surface levels, as well as between belief, ritual and artifact. In addition, between these two types of intertextual connections, there is a kind of meta-intertextuality. Whether or not the meaning construction of ethnic elements can be identified by ethnic culture is a question that all ethnic fashion designs must face.

The revelation and interpretation of any ethnic element can't be separated from complex generative intertextuality. Different ethnic groups have their own spiritual appeals and beliefs, manifesting the inherent characteristics of ethnic elements. "The idea of I think," therefore I am put forward by Descartes regards "thinking from oneself," namely, "internality" as the basic principle of philosophy.

But not until the time of Hegel did the internality of thinking really become the real basis of modern philosophy. The internality here is obviously opposite to externality, but this epistemology of classical aesthetics and philosophy inevitably restrict ethnic elements to the dilemma of such dualism. It should also be seen that rituals are hosted and organized by individuals or groups, on specific or general occasions. As a ritual or performing artifact, facial makeup often produces a mysterious and strong visual effect, with different ethnic groups having different modeling styles and characteristics.

In the process of performing a ritual, there is generally a set of strictly prescribed procedures, reflecting people's belief and piety. In Wittgenstein's works, a certain independence of ritual is emphasized. "It is clear from his comments on Sir James Fraser's *Golden Branch* that he argues that words such as patterns of conduct, manners, and rituals should be distinguished from words such as beliefs, explanations, and myths, thus gaining their autonomy." ❶ The first who proposed etiquette antecedent theory in the school of religious anthropology was Robert Smith. Later, Maret and Pluyce also made similar claims. Scholars like Taylor and Fraser believed that primitive religions came from certain religious ideas in the minds of primitive philosophers, such as ideas of animism and witchcraft.

But Smith, Maret and some other scholars held opposite opinions, thinking that action preceded ideas, and that religious activities were the basis for the generation of clearer religious concepts. Therefore, such religious activities were religious rituals actually. In most ethnic groups,

---

❶ Perniola M. Ritual Thinking [M]. Lv Jie (tr). Beijing: Commercial Press, 2006:37.

myths were derived from religious rituals, not vice versa. Moreover, ritual is performed and completed collectively by people who experience the same religious emotions, and the costumes and ceremonies of sacrifice activities often have specific spiritual and cultural characteristics of an ethnic group. Here, the social groups assign certain rules to actions and fix activity routines with those rules, providing a demonstration for the implementation of later rituals. Of course, the implementation of ethnic religious rituals must rely on the intervention of artifacts.

As a kind of ritual artifact, costumes of some sacred activities show a person's aesthetic taste and cultural accomplishments. For example, sari, a traditional wrap-style costume of Indian, is usually made in mysterious colors as ochre red, dark gray and brown. People should dress not only in a natural and decent way, but also in accordance with certain conventional norms. For instance, in Chinese traditional Nuo culture, Nuo dance is an important part of Nuo ritual, which involves costumes, masks, songs, dances and many other aspects. At present many traditional rituals are turning to a mundane and humane direction. Human beings have long deposited their living customs, aesthetic tastes and religious concepts into the dressing ways in daily life. In addition, the requirement of living environment on people's dress should be noted, that is, the coordination between clothes with time, place and purpose should be considered.

In theatrical performances, props, plots and scenes also have specific requirements for costumes. These traditions can be represented in modern and contemporary fashion design. The spirit of clothing culture and the inherent character of artifact civilization have started the ethnic clothing life and the construction of clothing culture. The creative elements of each ethnic group have their unique characteristics, forming the basis for meaning generation. For example, according to their craftsmanship, Chinese ethnic costume patterns can be divided into embroidery patterns, brocade patterns, batik patterns, tie-dye patterns, and mosaic patterns. And Chinese embroidery mainly includes Suzhou embroidery, Hunan embroidery, Sichuan embroidery, Guangdong embroidery and Wuhan embroidery. While among the embroidery of Chinese ethnic minorities, the Miao ethnicity is famous for its exquisite embroidery and diverse techniques.

Of all the types of artifacts, ritual artifacts often have the highest spiritual qualities, which are separated from the utility and practicality of general objects. Ritual artifacts often appear only on ceremonial occasions and play roles in people-to-people or people-to-god pledges, thus becoming religious collections in the history of art and culture. For example, Buddhism claims that ritual artifacts must go through a "consecration" procedure before they obtain necessary magical powers. Each ethnic group has its own history and culture, as well as unique ethnic elements and costume traditions, therefore, it is of great necessity to study and reveal the unique characteristics of ethnic group elements, as well as their expression modes in fashion creative, and then to manifest the ethnic culture and spiritual significance embedded in those elements through fashion creative and design.

Traditional ethnic costumes not only involve visual construction, but also arouse the interconnection among beliefs, rituals and artifacts. On the Guzang Festival of the Miao people, a chosen man would host the ancestor-worship ceremony, dressed in the festival-chief costume of bright clothes and simple patterns. In traditional aesthetic process and artistic expression, "Every tribe usually uses a set of basic signs intelligible to its members, and artists can modify or combine these signs as they wish."[1] In ancient Chinese etiquette, bowing was a manner of showing respect, and to perform traditional bowing etiquette, one must first stand up straight, and then take off their hats. In fact, many behaviors in people's daily life are related to specific clothing custom and culture. In their inheritance, ritual behaviors and artifacts passed down their symbolic meanings, and this process also involves deep ethnic psychology and cultural character.

In fact, ritual artifact is a close combination of ritual and artifact. Not only can the artifact reach sacredness in religious rituals, but it is endowed with a certain sacred quality in itself. In addition to ritual artifacts, there are also functional artifacts, identity artifacts, and spiritual artifacts. Artifacts often become the composition elements of fashion creative, widely present in the clothing life of an ethnic group. Some traditional fashion customs, such as foot binding in ancient China, which reshaped a woman's body, are closely related to artifacts and rituals, but they are abandoned in modern clothing life due to harm to the body and lack of humanity.

The sacrificial costumes in the Western Zhou Dynasty of ancient China showed that the system of sacrificial costume for kings had established, and since then being ritually proper has become the fundamental stipulation in Chinese costume culture. In daily life, people often use rite forms like waving, bowing, and taking off hat to express friendliness. In fact, being more than a physical thing, artifact is also given a metaphysical and spiritual meaning. Metaphysics, abstract and difficult to perceive, refers to the fundamental provisions of the sensible world, or the basis of the sensible world. According to Ingarden, "metaphysical quality" is the supreme appeal of literary and artistic works. However, this quality is inseparable from aesthetic experience and aesthetic value. In fact, ontology discusses the metaphysical basis of the physical world. But in Chinese and eastern cultures, there is no such presupposition of the ontological existence as in the West.

On the other hand, the spiritual appeals and interests of the East and the West are closely related. In fact, China has developed the cultural ideology on cosmogenesis since ancient times. Different from objects in daily life, ritual artifacts often have the attributes of decorating,

---

[1] Frank P. The Principle of Visual Art [M]. Chen Yuelei, Yu Yu (tr). Shanghai: Shanghai People's Fine Arts Publishing House, 2008: 23.

expressing, memorizing, moralizing and blessing. It should be realized that "like the signified, the signifier is always made up of objects, clothes, certain parts of clothes or accessories." [1] Ritual artifact is related to ethnic mental schema and cultural character, manifested and highlighted through the visualization of creative ideas. In addition to their functions and practicality, artifacts like clothes wait to be disclosed and elucidated on their social and cultural meaning. Once various ethnic costumes and elements are worn on human bodies, they always send out symbolic rather than utilitarian meaning.

For example, the Five Elements and the Five Colors are the color elements that symbolize the inner spirit of Chinese ethnic group, becoming ritual expressions when they are incorporated into the system of "rule of rite". In Baudrillard's opinion, modernity means an era of production characterized by industrial capitalism and the rising hegemony of bourgeois, while post-modernity an era of simulation controlled by signs, codes, and models. Contemporary era inevitably brings the reconstruction of ethnic elements, and the process is also associated with various phenomena of colonialism and post (new) colonialism. Any ethnic element not only has its own unique value appeal, but also forms meaning through its mutual generation with other elements, which is displayed on various levels and dimensions, such as in the process from artifacts, rituals to beliefs.

With the popularity of "ethnic style" in the fashion industry, the unique elements of various ethnic costumes are becoming more and more popular with designers. The exploration, arrangement and use of ethnic costume elements are of great significance to the protection and inheritance of ethnic art and fashion culture. However, the historical changes in clothing elements and patterns should be noted. For example, "Chinese dragon has got evolved and developed in its image through dynasties, and it holds various postures – crawling, curling or intertwining, full of change and highly decorative."[2] The attention to ethnic elements and their meanings is the fundamental appeal of ethnic culture diversity, which, however, often occurs in the context of west-centered superior cultural psychology. The cultural criticism on Western colonialism is obviously the prerequisite for the construction and reconstructions of ethnic fashion art. In fashion creative and design, ethnicity not only gets infused into the inner mental schema, but also receives revelation and interpretation in the visual aesthetics.

3. Ethnic and Cultural Characters of Elements

All art and fashion creative and designing require the involvement and participation of various related elements, which have their own ethnic qualities and cultural characteristics. Ethnicity is

---

[1] Barthes R. Système de la Mode [M]. Ao Jun (tr). Shanghai: Shanghai People's Publishing House, 2000:73.

[2] Wang Fang. Interpretation of Chinese Traditional Costume Patterns [M]. Shanghai: Donghua University Press, 2014:22.

often manifested through artistic creations and texts, and ethnic art is closely associated with the anthropologic existence of an ethnic group. This ethnicity presents an anthropological issue not be ignored in art, fashion and culture, aiming to distinguish fashion styles and cultures from each other. The existence of an ethnic group with its ethnic characteristics is not only the indispensable spiritual foundation of its ethnic culture, but also the existential premise for the ideological generation on its ethnic fashion. As far as clothing and fashion design are concerned, styles, colors and fabrics are never separable from ethnicity or local characters.

But ethnicity does not regulate in a simple and intuitive way that all expressions of fashion creative should be full of explicit ethnic elements. Actually, ethnicity penetrates into the foundation of ethnic creative and culture, represented in visible or hidden ways, even reconstructed in deformed and abstract contemporary art. Of course, fashion creative involves diverse elements, whose interconnection reveals the cultural characteristics of creative, and influences the artistic taste and style of designing. For example, due to the long-term influence of Buddhist culture, the Tibetans have a unique monk costume, whose yellow color has become a reconstructible fashion element. After all, yellow used to be the exclusive color for Chinese emperors.

However, the symbolic meaning of yellow varies in different ethnic lifestyles and cultures. Therefore, there appear questions of what are the unique meanings and characteristics of ethnic elements, and how they could get aesthetical expressions in fashion. These questions not only confront the visual culture in the contemporary art context, but also concern how to draw on ethnic art and its unique expressions in aspects of shaping, color, etc.. Revealing the elements associated with fashion and their cultural characteristics is an important prerequisite for the generation of fashion creative. In order to uncover the connection between visual expressions and ethnic characteristics, and between creative reconstruction of ethnic elements and current lifestyles, one should give full attention to the social contexts generating ethnic elements in different historical periods.

For ethnic fashion, elements and their styles reflect characteristics of ethnic culture, which is related to many aspects of the times, the life and the society. Therefore, "for a long time, art historians have been thinking about the relationship between artistic styles and occasions, times or individuals." [1] The penetration of ethnic element into fashion art and design is also a process of reconstructing ethnic and traditional culture in the contemporary era. For example, Victorian dress is usually S-shaped, with close-fitting corset and bustle worn inside, and this traditional style has been reconstructed in the new fashions of British contemporary designer Vivian Westwood. At the

---

[1] Burke P. What is Cultural History [M]. Cai Yuhui (tr). Beijing: Peking University Press, 2009:113.

same time, we must also consider how to realize fashion-oriented expressions and how to construct a fashion sense rich in cultural characteristics.

In the context of art and culture, the creative reconstruction of ethnic elements is undoubtedly an important way to inspire ethnic creative and design. Of course, ethnicity is the spiritual and cultural foundation of constructing the fashion sense in ethnic clothing life. And how to express ethnic ideology and culture in visualization is also a question that should be explored in fashion creative and design. At the same time, the cosmopolitan nature of art shows that the art of a certain ethnic group could gain worldwide cultural identification. Only by realizing fully the generative connection between ethnicity and the world can we promote the integration of ethnic fashion to global fashion. Art is always relevant to the life and culture of a certain ethnic group, hence to revealing cultural characteristics of ethnic elements and constructing ethnic spirit.

Considering the creator, the recipient, and the occurrence of artistic activities, the connection between elements and ethnic life are ubiquitous, which forms the generative basis for the ethnicity of art. Whether free art expressions, or practical fashion designs, they are all important ways for the construction of human life history and culture, manifesting unique cultural characteristics in the context of society and history. For example, in the seventeenth century, "it was absolutely necessary for the upper classes in Western Europe to wear certain styles of wigs, so this fashion continued for almost a century." ❶ In fact, fashion creative is always related to the life of certain ethnic group, particularly to the cultural context for the existence of that ethnic group.

In terms of structure and isomorphism, the revelation of cultural characteristics and the reconstruction of ethnic elements echo to each other. Ethnicity has even become an important source of fashion creative, and it is also the spiritual concern in the disclosure of local art and cultural characteristics. As fashion creative always occurs in a cultural context and involves many factors, the exploration and interpretation of the ethnicity and cultural characteristics of elements have become the important appeals of fashion creative and design. So, the question how cultural creative of fashion is related to ethnic elements should be given full attention and in-depth exploration. According to Jean Baudrillard, the accelerating function of media in contemporary society is equivalent to that causing the decline from modern production to postmodern simulation.

At the same time, the generation and expression of fashion creative concerns the visualization of all concepts and ideas, because fashion art is mainly expressed through visualization, which, however, involves many factors refusing its direct presentation. On the symbolic meanings of different ethnic costumes and colors, "Levi-Strauss tries to emphasize the universality of his

---

❶ Lavel J. Costume and Fashion: A Concise History [M]. Lin Weiran (tr). Hangzhou: Zhejiang Photography Publishing House, 2016:112.

viewpoint, while Leach stresses the relativity of perspective and the specificity of culture." ❶ Artistic expression and communication should be responded with visualization related to the inner mental schema. The culture of an ethnic group is where the spirit of the ethnic group lies, which should be explored, sorted out and inherited in the contemporary era. Otherwise, the spirit, concepts, and thoughts of an ethnic group will fade away and lose its fundamental cultural heritage.

The creative of ethnic elements involves cultural reconstruction that is linked to visual expression and based on ethnic spirit with cultural characteristics. Different ethnic elements should be treated with different methods of creative visualization. The fashion expression and creative design about an ethnic group always reveals and elucidates its cultural characteristic at different levels. However, we must not label ethnic art and cultural relics as superior or inferior from a simple and non-historical cultural attitude. The existence of an ethnic group and its ethnic root of culture are not only the anthropological premise necessary for ethnic art and clothing, but also the ideological source of ethnic fashion creative and design.

As a historical heritage, culture is generated through accumulation of a long history. With inherent spiritual characteristics, culture is also the logo and symbol of an ethnic group's identity. The word culture is derived from the Latin word "cultura", which means cultivation, planting, farming, etc., implying a generative process related to humans. In the late nineteenth century, the word culture entered many fields of social science and became an integral part of the concepts and ideas in those disciplines. Because no ethnic group can exist in the world in absolute isolation, different ethnic groups naturally associate with each other in art and clothing life, and cross-cultural communications of fashion creative become inevitable. As a result, the complexity and hybridity in ethnic costumes and traditional culture has become the spiritual and cultural traits of ethnic life that cannot be ignored.

As long as something existing in the culture is thought as either right or wrong, this culture would become conceptualized, drained out of essence, or even a stereotyped frozen culture, without inherent spirit and creative at all. For ethnic art and culture, inheritance is an essential historical mission and ideological task. It should be seen that "The study on aesthetic reflection cannot be confined to isolated areas of thought, but be combined with specific aesthetic phenomena and feelings. Besides, the social and cultural implications implied by aesthetics must also be

---

❶ Barnard A. History and Theory in Anthropology [M]. Wang Jianmin, Liu Yuan, Xu Dan (tr). Beijing: Huaxia Publishing House, 2006:142.

paid attention to."❶ To the inheritance of ethnic costumes and culture, the exploration and reconstruction of the inner spirit of ethnic culture is very crucial. This does not mean that people can simply affirm good things and discard bad ones, but instead, they should make careful analysis and discrimination, as well as in-depth interpretation and research.

Any crude and hasty attitude to issues concerning ethnic elements and culture is harmful and undesirable. In fashion creative involving ethnic elements, representations and visualizations of ethnic cultural characteristics interact with each other at various levels. That is because despite its own integrated structure, culture is always associated with other ethnic groups and heterogeneous cultures through its openness. There is no such isolated and fixed ethnic element, which stipulates the expression of fashion creative and its cultural connection. In fact, ethnic culture permeates into the roots and inner spirit of ethnic fashion creative, as well as the connections and expressions of numerous fashion elements.

The fashion creative of an ethnic group can obtain the heritage of its ethnic culture only when the interpretation of its ethnic elements and cultural characteristics is emphasized. At the same time, to infiltrate and embed ethnic elements into fashion art, one must consider how to realize fashion expression and how to obtain the sense of current fashion. "If we pull primitive or indigenous art out of its own culture and context, and make it speak to us in a universal aesthetic voice, the importance of its original meaning and purpose will be reduced or even negated."❷ Different ethnic groups are obviously different in visual thinking and psychological habits, and these differences together constitute a generative context of ethnic elements and cultures.

Therefore, visualization of elements must take into account differences between ethnic groups and the social, historical, and cultural meanings accompanying those differences. For example, the ethnic fashions with strong Gypsy styles take the ethnic elements of Gypsy as their cultural characteristics. Here, the close relationship between ethnic group and culture cannot be ignored, and ethnic culture itself is actually an important style of culture. It can even be said that the fashion creative of any ethnic group contains characteristics of its ethnic culture, which is an inseparable component of fashion sense. As cultural identification always involves cultural pertinence and adaptability, whether ethnic cultural characteristics can be fully expressed depends not only on the designer's unique understanding, but also on how to reconstruct specific elements in a dialogue manner.

In fact, the mutual generation of art and culture is undoubtedly based on the existence of an

---

❶ Van Damme W. Anthropology of Aesthetics: Perspective and Methods [M]. Li Xiujian, Xiang Dan (tr). Beijing: China Federation of Literary and Art Circles Publishing house, 2015:153.

❷ Minor V H. Art History's History [M]. Li Jianqun. et al (tr). Shanghai: Shanghai People's Publishing House, 2007:266.

ethnic group and the latter has even melted into this mutual generation. At the same time, ethnic culture responds to the lifestyle of the ethnic group through various changes. The most basic social activities of an ethnic group are material and spiritual production activities, which are important ways for the ethnic group to survive. It is through these basic activities that the material and spiritual cultures of an ethnic group are constructed. In other words, culture means humanization in its nature, and all cultures regard humans as the fundamental purpose and appeal. All non-natural things processed and transformed by humans, namely, all humanized things, can actually be included into the field of culture.

Experiences accumulated from aesthetic observation of nature and life have also become an important part of ethnic art and culture. If the cultural characteristics of an ethnic group are represented without connection with its inner spirit, the artistic connotation expressed through the reconstruction of its ethnic elements will be impaired. In fact, the common language, region and life of an ethnic group, as well as the common psychology manifested in its common cultural traits, are important prerequisites and foundations for the existence and identification of this ethnic group. However, it is noteworthy that in terms of ontology, the coexistence of different ethnic groups may lead to the decline or even disappearance of certain ethnic uniqueness. Actually, even members within the same ethnic group are different in psychological and cultural temperament, but these differences are often obliterated in the common existence of community life.

At the same time, beliefs, rituals, or artifacts all exist in close association with ethnic and cultural characters, and they hold a generative connection with original art and culture. Therefore, it is important to emphasize the uniqueness of primitive and ethnic art and culture. "All artistic expressions should emerge from the artist's spirit, so they can be 'naturally arranged in the mind', and then 'spontaneously written out of the pen'."[1] Revealing the cultural characteristics related to an ethnic group's existence is the fundamental spiritual appeal of its ethnic lifestyle, as well as the cultural premise for interpreting ethnic fashion creative and design.

An ethnic group doesn't lack unique beliefs and interests in its life and culture, but an inclusive cultural mentality and open-minded dialogue are essential to ethnic fashion creative and design of. For example, as a multi-ethnic fusion, the Han ethnicity tends to be more tolerant and open in culture, presenting a diversity of characteristics in beliefs. So compared with other ethnic groups, the ethnicity and religion of the Han people seem less clear and distinct. As for a ritual, its participants are usually a social group, sometimes a clan of a certain ethnic group, a family or a temporarily collected crowd. Folk rituals are cultural existences inherited through observances,

---

[1] Xu Fuguan. Chinese Art Spirit [M]. Beijing: Commercial Press, 2010:307.

usually restricting people's thinking and lifestyle. Sometimes, specific living conditions and circumstances of an ethnic group may lead to the relative closure of original ethnic culture.

The spiritual concern and traditional cultural characteristics carried by a dress may far exceed the practical functions of original design. The significance of this transcendence lies in the visual symbol of society and life. Cultural characteristics of ethnic elements are inseparable from their regions. For example, traditional clothing of Chinese northern ethnicities is usually carefully-tailored and delicately-made, while that of southern ethnicities is relatively simple-tailored yet highly-decorative. In fact, folk rituals are often distinctively colored with folk beliefs, as well as strong ethnic and local cultural characteristics.

Clothing designs of rural style highlight local cultures, which include British local style, French local style, American local style, etc.. No doubt, unique social concerns and cultural context have contributed to the generation of the uniqueness of art and cultural elements. In the cross-cultural communication of fashion, cultural characteristics of different ethnic groups have attracted attention. For example, "Europeans, who are accustomed to fancy court costumes, are surprised at the diversity of American women's clothing."[1] Therefore, the social and cultural significance of ethnic elements is often irreplaceable. In native and folk cultures, artistic and aesthetic experiences are integrated into people's lives and become an important part of ethnic lifestyle.

The social and cultural purports of art and clothing are multifold and complex, and the ethnic and cultural characters of elements are related to the generation of social meaning. In fashion creative and design, any simplified copying and borrowing cannot reconstruct the unique contemporary fashion from ethnic cultural characteristics. In fact, all ethnic elements and their characteristics are obviously marked by times and culture. Moreover, ethnic themes, decorations, plastic arts and expressions all reflect living environments and cultural customs of various ethnic groups. As a man-made artifact, traditional clothing is filled with unique ethnic spirit in its production, manifesting the social and cultural significance of ethnic elements.

Section 2   Fashionizing Methods of Ethnic Elements

Although being an important foundation and premise of fashion creative, ethnic element is not yet the fashion itself. Ethnic element cannot enter fashion automatically without being constructed, and be placed into fashion creative factitiously and randomly. In fact, there is no so-called absolute and fixed ethnic element. All the factors related to ethnic existence and culture can become

---

[1] Fogg M. (ed). Fashion: The Whole History [M]. Chen Lei (tr). Beijing: China CITIC Press, 2016:139.

potential elements of fashion creative, as well as the artistic, aesthetic and cultural premise for the construction of the current sense of fashion. At the same time, ethnic element, art and culture are all generative in nature, need to be creatively constructed and reconstructed in contemporary times. Only through construction and reconstruction, can original ethnic element become potential or even realistic fashion element. Ethnic element can enter fashion in various ways, which, however, are not fixed and irrelevant, but associated and intertextual with each other. It should also be noted that the modernization of ethnic elements does not mean simply integrating the elements to fashion texts, but emphasizes the current generation of the correlation between ethnic elements and various contexts.

1. Différance and Conformity as Fashioning Methods

The borrowing of ethnic elements in clothing cannot be separated from the fashionization. Fashionization means that fashion creative and design is a generative process, and no artistic expression can become a fashion without this process. Generally speaking, newness, novelty, and even strangeness are the perceptual qualities for the generation of fashion. In costume creative and design, how to fully draw on ethnic elements and realize their contemporary reconstruction is indeed an important issue for ethnic (or global) fashion art and culture. Considering that fashion art and culture emphasize changes and the unique current sense, all fashion designs take the generation of this sense as a fundamental demand. The borrowing of ethnic elements and its obtaining of the fashion sense are actually in a process of continuous generation and reconstruction. There are many creative modes associated with fashionization but each one is unique and irreplaceable.

Of course, the fashion sense of an ethnic group has never been generated automatically, and it is impossible that the elements of an ethnic group cannot be fashionably constructed. In fact, art, fashion and sense of beauty never remain still, but change over time. " In one era, it might mean the perfection of beauty or the maturity of skill; while in another, people might think, hope or fear that it signifies the absolute uncertainty of meaning and the meaningless polymorphic openness."[1] Construction is the generative basis for the fashionization of ethnic elements, and related to the deconstruction of art and culture. In the generation of fashion sense, the occurrence of construction is often based on deconstruction.

In the context of generative theory, the construction and deconstruction of ethnic elements are in mutual generation of each other. In artistic creative and design, construction emphasizes the process of artistic expression and aesthetic generation, as well as the revelation and generative

---

[1] Duve T D. Au Nom de L'art: Pour une Archéologie de la Modenité [M]. Qin Haiying (tr). Changsha: Hunan Fine Arts Publishing House, 2001:66.

expression on this process. But the construction must first dispel the existing concepts and meaning patterns in the text of elements, as well as various rational philosophy and metaphysical presuppositions. Construction is neither simple affirmation and direct acceptance once and for all, nor fiction or fabrication made out of nothing, but a reopening and activation of elements and texts to generate a new discourse, meaning and cultural purport. The involvement of ethnic elements into fashion art actually means setting elements into the text of fashion, that is, the generating process of element fashionization.

The opposite of construction is deconstruction, which focuses on the disintegration and destruction of text and its meaning. On the basis of deconstruction, reconstruction is often understood as a second construction, that is, reconstruction points to the discourses and meanings having been constructed. For those ethnic elements generated in history, différance and conformity are undoubtedly important fashionizing methods. Specifically, différance is a combination of the words differ and defer, signifying a constant exiling and dispelling of original meaning. It may be said that, thorough deconstruction is inseparable from construction, as they are inherently generated from each other. Jacques Derrida borrowed Heidegger's German word Abbau (which literally mean unbuilding), and transformed it into the concept deconstruction.

In nature, temporality has made metaphysics lose its ultimate foundation, and time has become the source of nothingness in temporalization. Accordingly, the historical character linked with temporality has provided a fundamental possibility for ethnic elements to reconstruct a sense of current fashion, although those outdated styles are also the texts to be deconstructed by fashion. As existing artistic expressions and aesthetic activities are difficult to escape the stipulation and influence of rational metaphysics, it is urgent to acquire a sense of current fashion in deconstruction. With the historical change of human lifestyle, the reconstruction of ethnic elements in clothing and fashion is the process of exploring and expressing ethnic elements.

But since modern times, human nature has been immobilized in the West, and the existing state of human beings is often attributed to some kind of ready-made being. At the same time, rationality is usually the starting point for exploring art and aesthetics, which in a degree obscures the generative nature of existence. In contrast, Heidegger defined the nature of there-being as de-existence, which forms the basis for exploring issues of art and beauty. In response to the radical appeal of anti-metaphysics, Derrida proposed and explained différance and used the concept in the study of art and aesthetics. In fact, différance indicates that the meaning of a word not only depends on its difference from other words, but also exists in its flowing in time.

In this evolution, one word overlaps and permeates other words, thus delaying the emergence of its meaning. In the process of fashionization, différance emphasizes the differences and delays in the reconstruction of ethnic elements on one hand, and the familiarity with the novel and alienated feelings brought by the reconstruction on the other hand. For example, the new Victorian suit keeps the trace of 19th-century court women's clothing in is shape, it does not line it with corset. "Naturally, 'différance' has always taken precedence over 'being'. One cannot think about it in terms of any traditional temporal or transcendental priority."[1] Traditional Western philosophy and its logocentrism assume the existence of a fixed meaning, and insist on the appeal for a certain consistency. As the connection between the isolation of space and the deferral of time, différance makes the static distinction flow rather than stay in any fixed state.

As a trace of delay, différance dissolves meaning continuously, being different from or even opposite to logocentrism in nature Here, the trace refers to the absence of presence, or the presence of absence. Différance is undoubtedly connected with conformity by unfolding, which means to disclose and reveal meanings of ethnic elements on the basis of différance. In integrating ethnic elements to fashion design, it is necessary to discover the meanings of elements that may be obscured. In other words, based on différance, unfolding process leads design into the generation and reconstruction of meaning, not only removing the existing cover of ethnic elements, but also reconstructing the original meaning of ethnic elements.

Actually, there is no fashion that simply copies and adopts past ethnic elements and artistic styles, and the construction of current fashion and aesthetic styles is still related to the différance and unfolding of previous elements and styles. For example, although Dior's new look has received unprecedented worldwide attention, in fact, the new look is nothing new. "It is actually a simplified version of the exaggerated style of the late 1930s and the Occupied Period, being completely opposite to that of wartime clothing in the United Kingdom and the United States."[2] Another example is punk-style clothing, which originated in London in the 1970s, and later spread across cultures and influenced European and American fashion trends. After the 1990s, the post-punk trend, with bright, tattered, simple, metal and street-style characteristics, appeared in the fashion industry.

Heidegger believes that the nature of the world is open, of the earth is closed, while art works are exactly where the world and the earth come into conflict. A work not only is a self-sufficient world, but also has access to art with its unique openness. In nature, art work is the bearer of this kind of conflict, and truth comes out of this dispute. In the struggle between the world and the earth, the beings manifest themselves as a whole, and this manifestation is the fundamental

---

[1] Faas E. The Genealogy of Aesthetics [M]. Yan Jia (tr). Beijing: Commercial Press, 2011:446-447.
[2] Lavel J. Costume and Fashion: A Concise History [M]. Lin Weiran (tr). Hangzhou: Zhejiang Photography Publishing House, 2016:245.

occurrence of beauty, or, of truth. As art is characterized with double functions – building the world and showing the earth, it has the value of revealing the meaning of the world and the truth of existence, and is oriented to traditional elements with strong ethnic characteristics.

Art expressions and fashion creative connected with ethnicity extend their local characters to the art world through différance, and the art world that is currently constructed in turn constitutes a response to the earth. Here, the generative theory is a reaction to the traditional ontology and metaphysics of art. In the generative theory, the metaphysical essence and foundation of beauty are dispelled and deconstructed. The existence of beauty no longer requires the premise of metaphysics. Although Heidegger's thought is mainly about modern times, he has a deep reflection on modernity and its problems. At the same time, it was Heidegger that enlightened Derrida to promote deconstruction more thoroughly. Even in the context of deconstruction and postmodernism, reconstruction and dissolution are interrelated and inseparable, able to be applied simultaneously in the fashionization of creative ideas.

For example, the original and avant-garde fashion of Rei Kawakubo doesn't make pure use of ethnic elements and styles, but integrates eastern and Western elements into the contemporary world for communication and reconstruction. In the context of ontology, the generative nature of existence is a fundamental issue to be concerned with. It is this generative nature that makes the différance of traditional elements and cultures acquire a historical trait in contemporary reconstruction. In other words, being is nothing is baseless and being is self-evident, which is the very nature of art and beauty. For the issue of art and beauty Heidegger built an ontological foundation, which was different from traditional metaphysics and became the premise of his aesthetic thoughts in middle and late stages.

In fashion creative and design, dissolving inherent limitations and various coverings of ethnic elements is the basis for the revelation and différance of their nature. Différance occurs in all works or texts, making possible the fashionization of creative and design. It can even be said that all innovations and fashions are originated from or linked with différance. In fact, the purpose of deconstruction is to recombine. "Deconstruction has made many factors seemingly impossible for modeling become feasible and fashionable with aesthetics changing."❶ Of course, the current meaning of any creative, design and fashion could constitute response to traditional culture through historical character. On the basis of différance, conformity links the deconstruction of tradition with the current context, which is also an inseparable part of the fashionization of creative and design.

---

❶ Su Yonggang (ed). The Refinement and Application of Fashion Elements [M]. Chongqing: Chongqing University Press, 2007:67.

Following certain trend to adapt to the times can be seen as a change in the cognitive structure. On the premise of difference of traditional elements, shape, color, pattern and fabric all involve issues of compromise and conformity. In other words, conformity is the change of cognitive structure affected by the stimulus of assimilation. But conformity doesn't mean a simple assimilation with the changes of the times, instead, the conforming structure is an open one with sufficient flexibility. In the process of conformity, the traditional meaning of ethnic elements is retained, and corresponding changes take place at the same time, which would be transferred to the new fashion text and context. In this open and changing structure, ethnic elements of creative experience historical generation and intertextuality.

This conformity also involves connections, coexistence and dialogues of different elements, as well as their contemporary reconstruction. In creative and design, just because elements echo and adapt culturally to each other, as well as to the social, historical, and cultural contexts, they can form historical generative associations with their original meanings and purports. In addition to original contexts, the process also involves the adjustment of ethnic elements in new texts. All designs transform ideas and spirit into symbolic codes through visualizing creative, and the meanings of ethnic fashion are revealed after recipients' decoding. Therefore, ideas and concepts are visualized into creative, and visual codes are revealed and developed to conform to the wearers' cultural identification for fashion concepts and expressions.

However, this conformity cannot be understood as an assimilation, because it must also control the inconsistency to a certain degree. In fact, the means that design becomes an artistic style is inseparable from the visualization of creative ideas. As Cai Yuanpei observed, "Apparel and accessories include crowns, suits, belts, pedants, and all ornaments of gold, diamonds, pearls, and jade. They have become increasingly simplified in ethnic groups of modern civilization, but emperors, nobles and soldiers still wear special uniforms, and women still pursue the update of fashion." ❶ Fashionized expression aims to reveal and highlight spiritual and cultural meanings of ethnic elements. Conformity is generally reflected in the mutual adaptation of choices between language context and language structure, which also concerns echoing to a beautified social and cultural context.

At the same time, conformity is related to issues such as variability, negotiability and suitability. In the fashionization of ethnic elements, conformity also involves how to translate or utilize relevant aesthetic and cultural contexts. The sense of fashion gets constructed not only in a continuity of tradition, but also in the interruption of this continuity. The problems and contexts

---

❶ Xi Chuanji (ed). Selected Classical Readings on Design Art [M]. Nanjing: Southeast University Press, 2002:79.

associated with any design creative are in nature open and generative, and the creative process is often uncertain, so constant negotiation and conformity are necessary. For example, based on messages and markets, as well as changes and developments in social lifestyles, analysis of fashion makes predication on upcoming colors, patterns, and styles. This kind of fashion prediction is a result of comprehensive negotiation on all kinds of information.

Therefore, the conformity of design allows people to construct, from a series of uncertain possibilities, the relevance between innovative meanings of elements and their social cultural context. In the process of fashionization, we had better choose negotiable fashion languages, design codes and marketing strategies, so as to achieve understanding and acceptance about the communication of art and culture. But it all depends on our understanding and continuous reconstruction of the concept negotiability, for which there is no clear boundary and strict standard. The aesthetic tension between variability and negotiability is the basis of fashionization, because they provide practical possibilities for conformity. It may be said that, conformity represents the ideographic function of codes and discourses and manifests their adaptability. Dealing with conflicting elements in gradually changing manner aims to generate a tension of reconciliation, which is a conforming method that counteracts différance.

As an artistic, aesthetic, and cultural style, fashion design is also a generative process of constant selection and conformity, which is, however, inseparable from the différance and development of creative and expression on the basis of deconstruction. At the same time, fashionized creative and design is actually a challenge to and an alienation from the previous meanings of elements, especially the existing aesthetic modes and culture. However, "in terms of fashion, there is no real opposition between counter-culture and the established culture"[1], because all challenges and alienations for the sake of change would become a new established cultural style, which may in turn be alienated and challenged by later art and culture. On one hand, cultural archetype is the fundamental source or pattern of culture, on the other hand, the product of metaphysical presupposition.

However, the prototype as the basic pattern of clothing is obviously based on human body and related to the isomorphism between human body and clothing. In the new context of challenging, the new established culture may return to the culture it once opposed, which also involves the fundamental question of what is archetype. Therefore, the designing and using of fashion works is also a process of aesthetic and cultural identification that people make constant choices and acceptance on the basis of changes in living situations and interactions. To this end, it is necessary

---

[1] Svendsen L. Fashion: A Philosophy [M]. Li Man (tr). Beijing: Peking University Press, 2010:130.

to make clear in which ways the design conforms to consumers from cognitive, social and cultural aspects. First of all, conformity must take into account factors concerning cognition, which is the rational basis for social and cultural acceptance.

Whether a fashionized creative and design can be understood and affirmed by consumers is undoubtedly the premise for its recognition. In fact, people's adaptation to new clothing lifestyle is related to two points of designing: its conformity to the social context, and its tolerance and respect for different lifestyles. According to Jean Piaget, conformity means that a person's subjective schema that cannot accommodate external stimuli is changed to meet the requirements of external stimuli. In contrast, "Derrida gradually became intelligible through interviews when conforming to the new situation."[1] Fashionization has to involve similarities and differences between cultures, as well as interrelation in fashion between old and new elements. In the process of aesthetic and cultural conformity, people's subjective schema must change accordingly, adjusting the original schema and constructing a new schema to adapt to the current changes in lifestyle and cultural context.

Any ethnic element and culture will inevitably conform to the current context through différance. Any fashion design strategy or method, as long as it can achieve the intended purpose, can be seen as having certain merits. If the design is made not only to meet functional requirements, but also to show a unique sense of fashion, the breakthrough of traditional elements and existing techniques will be essential. Différance and conformity have unique aesthetic and social significance to the fashionized expression of creative and to the acceptance of this expression. And in différance and conformity, the wearer's culture and social context also need to be considered. Fashionization involves not only the definition of cultural prototype, but also the extension and reconstruction of the concept.

Only by receiving thorough aesthetic understanding and cultural identification can fashionized reconstruction and creative of ethnic elements become feasible. In fashion creative, the generative connection between différance and conformity is also indispensable, because a complete fashionized expression is based on this connection. Différance is the basis for the fashionized expression of ethnic elements, while conformity makes the acceptance of designs practically possible. In fact, all good fashion creative and designs are related to différance, rather than simply copying or transplanting ethnic elements. At the same time, conformity is not simply catering to people's existing tastes, but related to the interaction of elements and the coincidence with people's psychological expectations. All contemporary fashions based on the reconstruction of ethnic

---

[1] Richards K M. Derrida Reframed [M]. Chen Si (tr). Chongqing: Chongqing University Press, 2016:169.

elements are indispensable forces leading the trend of clothing life. Différance is an extended creative activity on the basis of inheriting and deconstructing original meanings of ethnic elements.

Through conformity, this différance could be applied to the new text and to the social context associated with this text. "In creative and design, we can add to realistic elements some cultural features influenced by religion and local customs, such as time-honored aesthetic preference to decorative elements or painting colors."[1] However, the questions of in which ways which elements can be involved in différance concerns not only the existence of original ethnic elements, but also approaches of conforming to relevant cognitive, social, and cultural factors. In terms of clothing composition, on one hand various elements are distinguished from each other, one the other hand they change gradually in form, thus generating a harmonious beauty based on differences.

As a fashionizing way, différance and conformity bring about the contemporary reconstruction of traditional elements, which is neither a simple acceptance and inheritance, nor an absolute discontinuity and fragmentation, but a paradox of interdependency and antagonism. In fact, the retro and nostalgic fashion style can also be seen as constructed by différance and conformity. The inheritance and cultural dissemination of art and clothing does not mean the whole acceptance of the existing traditional culture completely, but a contemporary reconstruction on the basis of reorganization and research. In fashion creative and design, différance and conformity are two components of the same process, generating each other in self-generation. In other words, it is a process that the original artistic and cultural meaning of ethnic elements is endowed with a new historical meaning through différance, and then applied into creative design and production through conformity.

Actually, a dialogue conforming with the cultural context involved in design is intended to bring original artistic, aesthetic and cultural expectations into différance and development. There has never been any fixed element that could be simply copied into new fashion designs without experiencing the interactions between différance and conformity. All reservations without any change or breakthrough are also harmful to ethnic art and fashion culture. Therefore, it is urgent to carry out work of collecting, sorting, recording, preserving and reconstructing before the ancient cultures having lost their living environments die. In the process of fashionization, inheritance and reconstruction are essential for the creative and design of ethnic elements.

Although Japanese kimono was once profoundly influenced by Chinese Tang costumes, it has undoubtedly experienced différance out of local characters or foreignness, and become closely

---

[1] Clay R. Beautiful Thing: An Introduction to Design [M]. Yin Tao (tr). Jinan: Shandong Pictorial Publishing House, 2010:59.

linked to Japanese lifestyle and culture. For another example, although jeans originated from the Western region of the United States, it has since been spread to all levels of society and daily life and become a relatively stable or even modeled fashion style. On the basis of différance, we should keep responding to different aesthetic experiences and clothing cultures. In creative and design, it is in urgent need to rearrange, reveal and interpret ethnic elements, so that traditional elements of ethnic minorities could be transformed to fashion. In ethnic lifestyles, the social, historical, and cultural contexts involved in design are all related to the psychological habits passed down through generations. At the same time, différance and conformity must take into account the generation and change of various contexts, as well as the artistic characteristics and aesthetic interests associated with these changes.

2. Appropriation, Collage and Generation of Fashion

The construction of ethnic fashion is closely related to traditional elements and culture, but because the sense of current fashion is reconstructed through dissolution, referring to deconstructive styles and techniques is of great significance. As common deconstructive techniques, appropriation and collage are not only emphasized in post-modern art and culture, but also highly valued in contemporary ethnic fashion designing. From etymological point of view, the meaning of the word appropriate is very clear and direct, with the Latin part "ad" meaning "referring to". "Appropriate" means "imitate and copy", which usually refers to moving something from one place or one context to another.

As one of the most important creating methods of postmodern art, appropriation reflects the difference and breaking between contemporary art and modern art, especially the subversion of the concept originality advocated by art. It can be said that "when post-modern art stacks together styles from various genres, ethnic groups and regions, what the artist is doing is an eclectic job."[1] In this process of appropriation, due to the historical change of contexts, original meanings of elements or texts may change and new meanings may be decoded. In contemporary art expression and creation, appropriation has been repeatedly used and widely referred to, and has even become the most popular technique of art expression.

In borrowing and using the technique appropriation, special effects and meanings may appear out of one's expectation. In a broad sense, appropriation is targeted to both objects of nature and works of art, while in a narrow sense, only to the latter. If appropriation covers the imitation of nature, then it is a form of art itself. Actually, appropriation also implies improper

---

[1] Bao Mingxin, Cao Zhe. Postmodern Costume Abroad [M]. Nanjing: Jiangsu Fine Arts Publishing House, 2001:83.

possession of something, or even abduction or theft. Anyhow, the method is not passive, objective, and indifferent, but active, subjective, and purposeful. According to its object and content, appropriation can be divided into that of expression techniques, of ideas, and of visual images. It is these different kinds of appropriation that constitute various dimensions of understanding the beauty of ethnic fashion.

Also, appropriation is a strategy to break and dislocate each self, and the alienation effect it produces has some characteristics of dissolution and reconstruction. Related to appropriation, collage breaks the combination of traditional elements, as well as the existing boundaries of artistic styles and techniques, thus presenting a unique and chic effect. The word "collage" refers to a technique of text creation, which gives the whole a new appearance though each part being old still. In other words, the technique collage integrates original different parts into the text tactfully, so that it can present a very different appearance from the original one.

But contemporary collage is different from the traditional one. If traditional collage emphasizes the material itself and the natural texture, then contemporary collage, being a deconstructive method, resorts to a non-traditional and anti-conventional combination. In the study of art and culture, although appropriation and collage are considered important methods of postmodernism, they are not limited to that field, but widely used in art and fashion creative designs. It should be realized that appropriation and collage are the borrowing and extension of postmodern design concepts with contemporary meanings. This borrowing and application of post-modern methods based on deconstructionism has a unique effect for the contemporary reconstruction of ethnic elements and artistic expressions. And the heterogeneity of different ethnic cultures will produce a complex and alienated cultural taste through appropriation and collage.

Postmodernism emphasizes opposition to the meta-interpretation and the fixed meaning of text. Appropriation usually replaces and deconstructs text without changing its original schema. Because the concept appropriation is relatively broad in sense, we often start from the common definition of appropriation, and end up with an analysis of the unique functions of appropriation in art and design through in-depth and detailed comparison of it with concepts like imitation and reproduction. Postmodernists believe that there are infinitely possibilities of interpretation to a given text, symbol and code. In the creative and design of ethnic fashion, appropriation and collage are breakthroughs of those fixed traditional interpretations, aiming to provide uncertainty and diversity for interpretation.

In this case, general literal meanings and traditional interpretations have to give way to the author's intention and the reader's reflection. With the globalization of art, aesthetics and culture intensifying, fashion design has undergone changes from traditional style to modernism and even postmodernism. Postmodernists have changed the way of attention. "Instead of focusing on individual objects like semiologists do, they 'watch' in a diversified, broken and often intermittent way."[1] But in fashion creative, simple appropriation and collage of design styles is no longer the fundamental way out for ethnic design. It is not helpful to directly borrow and transplant traditional things without reformation, while fragmentation deconstructs the integrity and lays the foundation for collage-type reconstruction.

In the expression of ethnic fashion, appropriation and collage with their mutual generation involve the deconstruction of tradition and the reconstruction of the sense of current fashion in the dialogue with existing styles. This kind of dialogue takes place between elements and texts, and between texts and contexts. Derrida advocated first of all establishing a non-inevitable connection between the signifier and the signified in the text, with the purpose to highlight the arbitrariness of collocation between the signifier and the signified, as well as the difference and non-simple correspondence between them, so that the signified can get rid of its attachment to the given signifier, and solidified structuralist ideas can be disturbed and deconstructed. The broad sense of collage is actually the core idea of the word, that is, a wide reference to diversity, coexistence, randomness, borrowing, etc..

The automatic conceiving principle of collage is in an irrational juxtaposition with its theme, which may cause transformation and novelty. Appropriation and collage did not completely abandon the meaning of traditional elements, only the relationship between meaning and context changes. In essence, all modern fashion ideas are closely related to deconstruction and postmodernism. Of course, "in the history of fashion there is no obvious, well-proven stage of modernism."[2] Collage also generates strangeness and alienation rarely seen in the original framework and context. The technique is widely used in fashion creative and design, especially in the generation of current fashion sense. No doubt collage can also be applied to fields such as photography, architecture, literature, and music.

The collage in a narrow sense is a painting technique, referring to pasting clippings of paper, cloth, or other materials on canvas or other surfaces to form a specific composition or layout of picture. From the perspectives of theory and method, collage is a method of discourse construction with postmodern meanings and traits, generating a fashion sense different from impressions given by previous elements and traditional combinations. For example, the radical expression of punk-

---

[1] McRobbie A. Postmodernism and Popular Culture [M]. Tian Xiaofei (tr). Beijing: Central Compilation & Translation Press, 2001:18.

[2] Connor S. Postmodernist Culture: An Introduction to Theories of the Contemporary [M]. Yan Zhongzhi (tr). Beijing: Commercial Press, 2002:293.

style collage aesthetics usually reuses dirty clothing fragments and debris of urban life like pins. Although collages are often accidental and casual, there is still a question of how to create a sense of fashion.

It can also be said that collage is to mix different works, paragraphs, sentences, and words together, thus producing a new, strange and non-daily feeling and aesthetic experience. In this age of pluralism, it has been very difficult to talk about art and aesthetic stipulation with absolute certainty. All existing elements and their compositions face challenges from fashionization. Modern art not only loses the basis on which traditional art is built, but also derives unintelligible interpretation about itself in its process of evolution and generation. In fact, collage has been used in apparel design for a long time. For example, patch patterns in clothing fabrics are typical patterns of traditional collage. Contemporary art has also developed large quantities of collage methods, providing much possibility for the expression of fashion and texture.

Whether to understand the meaning associated with art in its existence, or to open up the existence and the cover of art in discourse, are questions that need to be answered in postmodern ideological context. In fashion creative and design, we must fully consider the coordination between reconstructed artistic expression and various conflicting factors, and the ways of reconstructing novelty of art and fashion expression in deconstruction. But even in the context of contemporary art and fashion creative, there is still a question of how to achieve a chic beauty in collage. Compared with traditional collage such as that used in the official uniform of the Qing Dynasty, collage as a contemporary fashionizing technique emphasizes more the change and reconstruction of existing rules and traditions, rather than maintaining strictly certain grade or class as a social label and cultural symbol.

In fact, the basic method of collage is nothing particularly innovative, as it merely connects things and images seemingly unrelated to each other, aiming to change the relationship and composition of artistic elements in traditional expressions. It should be admitted that, "Coordination is an indispensable rule for the formal beauty in clothing. Since clothing is made up of multiple elements, the choice of styles, the use of colors, the combination of fabrics, the addition of adornments, the matching of accessories, etc., should all comply with overall designing requirements." ❶ However, the coordination and unification of various elements of clothing is a response, rather than a complete elimination, to change and difference. Collage has completely subverted the continuity and consistency of traditional art, making the continuous vein and coherent changes of art text disappear. Of course, all avant-garde fashion concepts and techniques

---

❶ Ma Rong (ed). The Application of Ethnic Costume Language to Fashion [M]. Chongqing: Chongqing University Press, 2009:54.

are still inseparable from the ideological dialogue with traditional culture.

The problem here is, due to the diminishing or even disappearance of basis and foundation, artistic expressions such as fashion can often be understood only in its own discipline. The relevant consequence seems to be that, on one hand, the boundary between art and nature or life is rapidly disappearing; on the other hand, the distinction between art and popular culture is also blurring. Because of these changes and trends, clothing and fashion urgently need to seek aesthetic and cultural tension between getting close to and away from the mass lives. In contemporary times, the fashion industry is trying to push the most cutting-edge works into daily life, which means when the original boundary between art and life or popular culture is inevitably broken, their connection and fusion in a new perspective should also be promoted.

Collage provides a unique perspective for people to understand anew traditional elements and their generative traits, as well as construction and deconstruction of related texts. After the birth of modern art, collage has become a way of fashion expression with special significance. After dissolving traditional theories and ideas, postmodernism has not really led to the termination of art and aesthetics, but greatly changed people's understanding of art, fashion, and deconstruction of related texts. Moreover, postmodernism provides a broader horizon and unexpected possibilities for the expression and aesthetics of fashion creative. Therefore, art and beauty will be re-thought, deconstructed, fashionized and reconstructed aesthetically from multiple perspectives. In contemporary art expression and fashion design, applications of appropriation and collage often bring forth unique and exotic effects.

Deconstruction and reconstruction are always mutually generated. There has never been a simple or absolute deconstruction, which is the process of generating new ideas in itself, and any new construction or reconstruction will lead to new deconstruction in turn. The reconstruction and deconstruction of fashion not only distinguish themselves from each other, but also interact and interweave with each other. The reconstruction in a postmodern context is neither a second systematization of ideas and thoughts, nor a new metaphysical mode of thought. In the eternal changing and generating, new art and ideas respond to existing traditions by ways of appropriation and collage, which obviously constitute the generative trait of fashion.

As techniques of creative and design, appropriation and collage are not unrelated to original materials and elements, which would be reconstructed in new aesthetic, cultural and theoretical horizons to achieve innovative expressions. Actually, the style, the nature and the characteristics of art are all historical and generative, free from fixed rules and regulations. Previous elements and issues will also make new appearances in the creative and design expressed through appropriation and collage. In appropriation and collage, the clear classification of elements and their combinations obviously no longer has original fundamental meanings and values, but this deconstruction is also a contemporary reconstruction of ethnic elements and culture. It is in the historical generation of rules and methods that it is possible to reconstruct the sense of current fashion and its cultural significance.

In fact, appropriation and collage are not newly-emerging artistic expressing techniques. Among popular folk arts such as paper-cutting, embroidery, wall painting, and cloth paste painting, appropriation and collage can be found in various aspects like designing, modeling and composition. Therefore, appropriation and collage can be used both in traditional folk crafts, and in contemporary expressions of fashion creative and design with deconstructive characteristics. Of course, in their applications appropriation and collage also involves artistic expression styles and related aesthetic and cultural contexts, so as to reconstruct the contemporary meaning of ethnic elements with their unique deconstructive means. In other words, appropriation and collage can transcend the traditional boundaries of artistic materials and techniques, and generate alternative artistic effects and aesthetic experiences full of fashion senses.

The ethnic fashion sense generated on this basis can be traditional and historical, yet at the same time uniquely novel and alienated. "Thus, on the one hand, fashion means the unity of the same class, or the commonality of a social circle characterized by it; on the other hand, it breaks through the boundaries between different classes and groups constantly." ❶ When it comes to dissolving the inherent stratum of fashion, methods like appropriation and collage often produce unexpected bridging effects. And those methods applied to fashion creative and design usually attach great importance to elements and culture of a certain ethnic group.

Of course, any interpretation of ethnic elements and culture through creative design and artistic expression is inseparable from the issue of fashionization. In the application of appropriation and collage, those seemingly irrelevant fragments are uniquely connected, breaking down the narrative and expressing modes of traditional art as well as their understanding. The dissolution of appropriation and collage can generate the artistic and aesthetic effects of strangeness and novelty, which would give people deep impression or strong mental impact. All generative relations between elements and culture are inseparable from the ways people make aesthetics and cultural construction. It can also be said that appropriation and collage are techniques or strategies used by artists and designers in the creation and generation of texts, and the techniques are characterized by a reexamination and reconstruction from an overall perspective.

To be specific, the fashionization of ethnic costumes involves both the utilization of myths,

---

❶ Simmel G. The Philosophy of Fashion [M]. Fei Yong, Wu Yan (tr). Beijing: Culture and Art Publishing House, 2001:73.

legends, and totem beliefs, and the modern reconstruction by means of appropriation and collage. Although each part of the fashion creative and expression is original, design skillfully integrates these different parts together, which, of course, does not mean a simple stacking of original parts, otherwise the text would appear too rough. The diversified applications of appropriation and collage not only produce changes in the color, texture and quality of the creation, but also present post-modern effects such as game style and irony.

In Baudrillard's opinion, fashion is a simple game of signifiers, producing nothing but codes, with no concerns about value or morality. "Different art forms, from the cubist art to Dadaism, Futurism, Surrealism, etc., have fully borrowed and advanced the techniques of appropriation and collage. Given all these characteristics, it is clear that fashion is a part of the postmodern world." [1] At the same time, unreal and surreal concepts and techniques have become important means of fashion creative and artistic expression. Art forms of appropriation and collage continue till today, keeping emitting unique and chic fashion charm, and getting constant improvement and innovation by artists and designers. For surrealist artists, appropriation and collage are means to express the true self and subconsciousness.

In the aesthetic and cultural reconstruction of ethnic elements and art, appropriation and collage will also produce an effect both traditional and exotic. The composition of patterns in punk fashion involves a combination of grotesque style, black humor, and various conflicting elements. More than being creative techniques, appropriation and collage are also ways of responding to and interacting with contemporary art, aesthetics and culture, because they concern ideological factors embedded in artwork creating manners. In this era of globalization, the homogeneity in fashion creative and design not only eliminates unique cultural purports of fashion arts, but also ignores cultural differences between ethnic groups and places.

As anti-tradition fashion discourses, appropriation and collage could also constitute new fashion texts. In the reference to appropriation and collage, we should pay attention to the exploration and the contemporary reconstruction of ethnic elements and culture, and cope with the homogeneity caused by vulgar, mediocre and simple borrowing. "Collage can combine materials of different styles and ages to present a seemingly random but actually unique new realm." [2] The fashionization as a deconstruction involves overturning and reconstructing the traditional and existing styles. If fashion design simply evacuates, transplants, or even eliminates the original ethnic character, it will undoubtedly lead to fragmentation, and the ethnic elements in

---

[1] Ritze G. Postmodern Social Theory [M]. New York: The McGraw-Hill Companies, Inc, 1997:94.
[2] Su Yonggang (ed). The Refinement and Application of Fashion Elements [M]. Chongqing: Chongqing University Press, 2007:75.

contemporary fashion design will lose their context for cultural reconstruction.

In addition to Marcel Duchamp's Dadaism, Robert Rauschenberg stuffed everything he could find, including even fed goats, chopped newspapers, cloth pieces, clocks, photographs, paintings, etc., into his work, and put them together through colors. Rauschenberg broke the boundaries of traditional painting, sculpture and craftsmanship, thus forming his own unique artistic expression and aesthetic experience. In fact, appropriation and collage are both interrelated to and generated from each other, constituting together a way of responding to the original text, that is, they both utilize and deconstruct original elements and texts. In fashion creative, appropriation provides a possible basis of text for collage, which in turn reconstructs elements and texts that have been appropriated. As tradition and modernity become increasingly intertwined, how to break established frameworks and systems to achieve current innovation is undoubtedly an artistic, aesthetic and cultural issue in urgent need of exploration.

3. Fashion Meaning Based on Disassembly and Reassembly

If modernism focuses on the self-discipline of form and the appeal for consistency, then postmodernist fashion design intends to break down previous unity, balance and harmony, and emphasizes such design principles as the sense of integrity, so as to highlight the diversity and flexibility of design method. For example, "the use of buttons, zippers, snap-fasteners, hooks, or nylon hasps can reassemble clothes by increasing or decreasing elements on them."❶ It is through such deconstructive techniques as disassembly and reassembly that a fashion meaning could be generated and aesthetically constructed. In structuralism, relationship is fully recognized and regarded as a substitution for entity, because structuralism aims to overcome the dilemmas of epistemology and ontology.

But this emphasis on relationship and structure was later opposed by post-structuralism and deconstructionism. According to Derrida, "disassembly is directed against the principle of absolute obedience to structure as the center", as well as the identity, centrality, and integrality of modernism. Like Vivienne Westwood, Flsa Schiaparelli disassembled the so-called mainstream design with joking manners, making designers and the fashion industry to rethink about beauty. All existing modern fashion texts and their meanings are inevitably based on established relationships or structures. Therefore, the continuous generation and construction of fashion creative has to involve the disassembly of existing fashion elements and their structures. Here, disassembly has brought about the emphasis on the distinctive characteristics of each text, and then the dissolution

---

❶ Calderin J. 100 Keywords of Creative in Fashion Design [M]. Cao Shuai (tr). Beijing: China Youth Publishing House, 2012:118.

and deconstruction of the structure center of original text with the introduction and reference to external differences.

Because structure is generally characteristic of fixity and definiteness, opposite structure would often produce similar meanings, which shows that construction and deconstruction need to be alternated with each other constantly. Modern art has a preference for depth perception or single root, and shows dependence on interpretation. In particular, modernism emphasizes those conceptual systems and knowledge systems that play a stipulative role in the interpretation of texts. In contrast, postmodernism emphasizes planarity and superficiality, that is, characteristics of fibrous roots, as well as the importance of misreading in the interpretation of art. If modernism still values the signified, emphasizing the one-to-one correspondence between the signifier and the signified, and therefore showing metaphysical influences in the interpretation of art and beauty, then postmodernism is ironic, and represented as a game of signifiers.

It is noteworthy that Derrida's deconstructionism is directed at a series of binary separations in the Western philosophy and thought, such as speech and writing, truth and fallacy, nature and culture, etc.. In the contemporary era, the disassembling and deconstruction of traditional clothing is manifested in the subversion of dichotomy between internal and external, thin and thick, etc.. For example, jackets can be worn with outside turned in, and exquisite workmanship can be replaced by rough edges and unfinished seams, but clothes are actually designed in these unique ways on purpose. In fact, it is the original dichotomy that constitutes the hierarchical order identified by people and leads to many cognitive problems and ideological dilemmas. In the designing process of ethnic fashion, this traditional dichotomy is also represented by the separation of men and women, elegance and vulgarity, but these hierarchical systems have been challenged by dissolution.

In the postmodern context, the signifier does not actually point to any signified, and the correlation between the signifier and the signified no longer has any substantial meaning. In this era of globalization, modernity regulates high esteem and strong appeal for consistency, which will inevitably lead to the homogeneity of art, aesthetics and culture. In fact, "contemporary postmodernism has gradually turned to popular cultural practices in this way, so as to seek cultural diversity and resisting models."❶ As far as creative and design are concerned, many fashionable clothes are not only homogeneous and uncharacteristic, but also vulgar and shallow, without inherent spiritual content or aesthetic cultural characteristics at all. However, those overly moralized evaluation and treatment should also be opposed.

If modernism still emphasizes creation, narrative, and grand history based on subject and

---

❶ Connor S. Postmodernist Culture: An Introduction to Theories of the Contemporary [M]. Yan Zhongzhi (tr). Beijing: Commercial Press, 2002:296.

rationality, then postmodernism, especially deconstructionism, highlights aesthetic acceptance, and rebellion against grand narrative. According to Jean-Franco is Liotta, it was the Enlightenment that contributed to the generation of grand narrative. Postmodernism pays attention to the dissolution and deconstruction of creation subject, and stresses the personal language pattern which is anti-narrative and concerned with personal surviving experience. But there is no strict distinction between modernity and postmodernity, which are intertwined and mutually generated. In fact, breaking the wholeness and identity of structuralism helps to cultivate the skepticism and pluralistic cultural mentality of the audience.

Since the appearance of Pop Art, disassembly and reassembly, which deal with old elements, texts (including images), etc., are still most common techniques for post-modern artists and designers, while whether there is originality or authenticity is completely unimportant. The disassembly of traditional elements and structures not only provides possibility for the reassembly of ethnic signs and culture in the contemporary context, but also lays aesthetics and cultural foundation for the generative association between ethnicity and globality, tradition and contemporariness. Disassembling is the process of constantly breaking the old structure and forming a new structure, that is, it has subverted general concepts and conventional meanings of traditional fashion, and keeps seeking expressing ways of art and fashion creative in continuous deconstruction.

In deconstructionism, existence is constantly denied, and center is constantly shifted, whose vacancy is to be supplemented by the coexistence of absence. According to Derrida, works are always open to readers, whose reading is also a creative process. We can even say that the interpretation on the text of dress by the wearer is never finished and determinate, as any interpretative perspective would open the text and close over it at the same time. "In the film *A Zed & Two Noughts*, the British filmmaker Peter Greenaway disassembled a taxonomic tradition that grew out of the Enlightenment."[1] In fact, disassembly points not only to different issues, but also to various art styles. In this era of globalization, fashion exchanges between countries, places and ethnic groups are becoming increasingly frequent, and the local character of clothing has also received worldwide artistic and cultural response and reconstruction.

At the same time, deconstruction and restructuring involves making the symmetrical, the regular, and the formatted asymmetric, irregular, and unformatted by ways of intersecting, twisting, displacing, and reversing, so as to generate and construct unexpected beauty of changes and dynamics. In the contemporary world, the speed, rhythm and diffusion of fashion are getting faster

---

[1] Richards K M. Derrida Reframed [M]. Chen Si (tr). Chongqing: Chongqing University Press, 2016:174.

and faster. For example, the fashion just released at major Paris fashion shows will appear the next day in fashion boutiques at every corner of the world. In this contemporary fashion trend of rapid dissemination and consumption, people's pursuit of individuality has gradually become the purport of fashion designers, but this kind of effort often loses its uniqueness quickly because of immediate imitation.

Starting from the elements and structures of ethnic costumes, designers use the artistic expressions and techniques of disassembling to break the inherent relationship and pattern of original elements, so as to present different sensory experiences to wearers and viewers. Various ethnic elements undoubtedly provide cultural diversity for fashion creative. In Derrida's view, "deconstructionism doesn't mean demolishing or destroying, and if it is anything, ... then it is a thinking about being and metaphysics, and thus manifesting itself in the discussion about the authority of being or essence, while such a discussion or explanation cannot simply be a negative destruction." ❶ But artistic characteristics and clothing cultures of different ethnic groups cannot be automatically integrated to fashion works, for which constant dissolution and reconstruction are indispensable.

The fashion meaning generated by disassembly and reassembly is obviously inseparable from the living world of a certain race or ethnic group. Fashion sense is always achieved by reassembling the previous elements with their relationship disassembled. For example, the 1960s brought the popularity of beggar clothing with decadent style and street characteristics, which was later pushed onto the catwalk by Yohji Yamamoto and Comme des Garcons, and today it is still the fashionable dress among college students and youths. The living world of an ethnic group (including clothing life) is inseparable from popular culture. Popular culture often has a specific ideological function, and it deconstructs some original meanings of traditional culture. Moreover, disassembly and reassembly can also be targeted at established fashion.

As the representatives of anti-fashion behavior and culture, people like the Beatles, Rolling Stones, and Bob Dylan often express their unconventional appeals with their unique costumes. Of course, popular culture also provides artistic and ideological possibilities for the reconstruction of fashion. In fact, the disassembly and reassembly of ethnic fashion have always been complementary to each other, and on the basis of which, design could generate its own purport. Here, disassembly and reassembly mean actually to analyze and organize anew codes or symbols, so that all the deconstructed clothing codes are encoded afresh. Clothing styles and aesthetic cultures of different ethnic groups have laid the cultural foundation for ethnic culture, but how

---

❶ Derrida J A. Madness Guards Thought – A Collection of Interviews with Derrida [M]. He Peiqun (tr). Shanghai: Shanghai People's Publishing House, 1997:18.

to disassembly and reassemble remains an important issue in contemporary fashion creative and design.

Based on continuous decoding and encoding, fashion generates the purport and the meaning intended by the creative. All ethnic elements have characteristics of art, aesthetics, and in the contemporary disassembly and reassembly of which, rough misreading and destruction can only be avoided through continuous exploration. Here is the problem: disassembly and reassembly can never completely get rid of misreading or distortion. The question that, in which sense the interpretation achieved through disassembly and reassembly is a misreading, depends on people's aesthetic and cultural understanding of the design. Since current concepts are always in the process of transformation and renewal, disassembly and reassembly of ethnic elements should be a historical process, rather than a conceptual view and a visual mode that can be simply copied and transplanted. In other words, ethnic elements are always in the generation of ideas and visions.

Also, disassembly and reassembly are important means for these elements to emerge through construction in fashion art. Therefore, in the designing process, we should to pay attention to the openness and variability of ethnic elements, as well as the generative text style full of ambiguity. This variability provides the possibility for disassembly and reassembly, which in turn bring on the disclosure and interpretation of multiple meanings of text. The generative relationship between elements of different ethnic groups and cultures is not simply juxtaposed on the visual appearance of a text; rather, it generates a new meaning of fashion in a deep dialogue. In addition, ethnic elements and texts leave plenty blanks among their signs, allowing designers to have ideological dialogues and cultural communications with them, so that different ethnic groups and cultures could achieve reconstruction in the field of contemporary clothing.

Fashion has constructed a broader social and cultural context for people, making fashion creative occur with concern for ethnicity and globality. In fashion creative and design, we must break inherent aesthetic tendencies and cultural stereotypes brought by history, because "the alienation theory is always rooted in the numbness and blindness of everyday life, and bound to alienate us from everyday life; ..." ❶ In other words, we can endow ethnic elements and culture with new meanings and purports through disassembly and reassembly, and make dialogues and collisions of ethnic cultural vocabulary in different periods possible, thus generating creative interweaving and intertextuality based on aesthetic and cultural distinctions.

In creative and design, ethnic elements are often generated and constructed in open aesthetic and cultural contexts, and integrated into the construction and continuous reconstruction of

---

❶ Jameson F. Brecht and Method [M]. Chen Yongguo (tr). Beijing: China Social Sciences Press, 1998:97.

multiple arts and cultures. In fact, sense of strangeness and alienation is an issue to be considered in ethnic fashion design, which involves not only unique traits of ethnic arts and cultures, but also expressions achieved through various techniques of disassembly and reassembly. When disassembly and reassembly is target to the established system and structure, it is actually a regenerating process of art, aesthetics and culture. In order to generate novelty and strangeness in fashion design, it is necessary to deconstruct existing relationships and patterns, which will inevitably lead to certain ambiguity and polysemy. To disassemble and reassemble the original elements of an ethnic group and its inherent structure aims to produce a sense of novelty out of daily life.

However, the effect of strangeness and alienation is not necessarily curious things, nor artificial fabrication or imagination; instead, they may be the disclosure and rediscovery of the fashion sense that has been masked. The rebellion against meta-interpretation, grand narrative and metaphysics by postmodernism provides the possibility for the reconstruction of ethnic elements in fashion creative. This rebellion emphasizes the role of irrational factors in achieving ease and tolerance in design. Postmodernism has never been a specific, onefold style, and postmodern style can never be defined just according to the age of the work. In fact, there is no inherent concept or rigid system of postmodernism, because all forms of metaphysics are to be disassembled and overcome by postmodernism.

Disassembly breaks the original relationship and structure between the elements, into many constituents for reassembly, to generate a unique and novel sense of currency and fashion, which often bears ethnic artistic characteristics and cultural tastes. From the perspective of art anthropology, all ethnic groups have their irreplaceable uniqueness, but the ethnic characteristics that distinguish them from each other are not completely different. In structuralism, the priority of the whole over the parts is emphasized, and everything belongs to a complex and indivisible generative whole. The nature of any one component can be understood not in isolation but together with other components in an integral relationship and context, that is, by being related to various other components. From the perspective of structuralism, the relationship between parts is related to that between the whole and the parts.

However, the deconstruction and continuous reconstruction of the existing structure have become an important way to reveal fashion traits from daily life. The essence and primary principle of structuralism is to reveal the complex relationship that links and combines elements, rather than to analyze individual elements in a disconnected way. The occurrence and current construction of ethnic fashion creative involves the disassembly of the existing structure of ethnic elements, which, however, is not simply negating and destroying previous traditions and thoughts, but aimed at activating traditional elements and cultures and the relevance among them, so as to reassemble and construct the special fashion meaning of the moment. For example, suits originating from Europe and the West have developed into a variety of etiquette clothing in modern times, and have spread across the world as a contemporary interethnic costume.

In different regions and historical periods, the designs and styles of suits have obviously changed. Essentially, the fundamental strategy of deconstruction is to dissolve the original structure and order of elements. For clothing and fashion design, it is existing relationships and structures, as well as consequent visual and aesthetic expressions and habits, that are mainly disassembled. For example, "The colors used in fashion vary from culture to culture, for example, they can be red, green, and gold in Africa, and red, green, and black in America." ❶ Of course, original structures and orders are related not only to art and culture, but also to all aspects of society and human lifestyles. Disassembly also involves design ideas that break conventional impressions to bring unique and novel creative and artistic effects. It should be realized that different ethnic groups have different understandings of and preferences for elements.

The recurrence of ethnic fashion is not simply a return and restoration, but a reconstruction of the original meaning and purport in retrospect. Disassembly and reassembly exist widely in the field of fashion design, bringing special effects unique for fashion art. It is this disassembly that breaks the existing order and structure of ethnic elements and creates a novel and chic fashion sense related to ethnic culture. In the era with increasing attention to personality, the reappearance and contemporary popularity of retro style have made people focus more on the disassembly and reassembly of traditional elements. In the disassembly and reassembly, the characteristics of different regions and times are embedded in the new fashion text, and any either-or approach will be dispelled in the generation of fashion sense. Disassembly and reassembly are neither abandoning of the tradition nor simply returning to it.

Through the analysis on various retro styles and elements, we are here to explore how to disassemble and extract classic clothing elements for reassembly. For example, a fashion style called Afrocentrism is obviously related to the local character and traditional culture of Africa, but it is also closely linked with the fashion sense of contemporary world. In disassembly and reassembly, prejudice and misreading are unavoidable hermeneutic events, but they can be overcome through constant dialogues and discussions. If modernism is often concerned with semantics in art and fashion design, then postmodernism pays more attention to rhetoric and discourse generation, aiming at the contemporary rhetoric reconstruction of clothing elements.

---

❶ Calderin J. Form, Fit, Fashion [M]. Zhou Mingrui (tr). Jinan: Shandong Pictorial Publishing House, 2011:83.

Again, if modernism mainly emphasizes paradigms, principal-subordinate structures and metaphors, then postmodernism stresses the reference to syntax, coordinate structures and metonymy.

Modernism emphasizes origin and determinacy, while postmodernism emphasizes difference and non-determinacy. In the process of disassembly and reassembly, all things of fashion and non-fashion are incorporated into an intertext. The extreme situation is that fashion even becomes non-fashion or anti-fashion, that is, the latter two intervene in the field of fashion and become a new fashion and aesthetic style. In the opinion of Appiah, "postmodernism rejects all claims of exclusivism and universalism." ❶ In the process of fashion designing based on disassembly and reassembly, people must pay attention to the revelation of cultural connotations of certain ethnic elements, as well as achieve the contemporary reconstruction of fashion aesthetics and culture. In fact, making use of disassembly and reassembly is undoubtedly a new access to the creative and design of ethnic fashion.

Section 3   Generation of Fashion Creative on Ethnic Elements

It is the intention of design to develop, from the system of concepts and thoughts, the conception and current construction of creative ideas, and to express them in visualized ways. For fashion design, in addition to advocating novelty and chic, creative ideas and concepts should also take intrinsic spiritual and cultural characteristics as the fundamentals. In fact, design can be understood in its nature as the visualization and production of creative ideas, and the response to changes of fashion concepts through continuous deconstruction of visualization. Although creative ideas are of irreplaceable and important significance and value, it does not mean that the more abstract and esoteric they are, the better it is. After all, the possibility of realizing visualized expression is to be considered, so is the question how creative ideas could be accepted in everyday life and popular culture. Although the visual expression and transmission of ideas are under certain limitation, they are expected to be incisive and vivid, in perfectly close connection with creative, which is the fundamental appeal of culture and aesthetic expressions of fashion creative. Besides, no creative idea can be rigid and fixed, as it is in the continuous process of generation, construction and reconstruction.

---

❶ Wartenberg T E. (ed). The Nature of Art [M]. Li Fengqi, Zhang Yun, Xu Quan, et al (tr). Chongqing: Chongqing University Press, 2011:323.

1. Cultural and Ethnic Characters of Fashion Meaning

The inseparability from the inner spirit of culture is undoubtedly the fundamental characteristic of all arts and designs, including fashion artistic expression and creative design. Fashion has entered people's living world and public domain as a popular trend. The word fashion is widely used and familiar to everybody, frequently appearing in newspapers, media and communication among people. "The essence of fashion exists in the fact that it is only used by a specific group of people, and most others are just on the way to its acceptance." [1] In the context of popular culture, the pursuit of fashion has become the order of the day, and hence an important way of life. In the emphasis on the visualization of concepts, the ethnicity and aesthetic expression of fashion creative and design present unique images and artistic charm.

Therefore, those creative and design concepts with individuality, as well as unique and novel techniques of expression and production, are essential prerequisites of fashion art and culture. In fashion creative, all the returns and rebellions that people try to achieve cannot completely get rid of ethnic characteristics, which may be involved in a deformed or abstract way though. In other words, as a form of subculture that cannot be ignored, fashion is always inseparable from a certain race or ethnic group. At the same time, fashion often tries to go beyond the limits of ethnic characteristics. However, in the classification of culture, fashion is constantly breaking through the restrictions on subcultures. Fashion can be understood as the clothing life style that is initiated and tried by a few people in a certain period of time, and later imitated or even admired by the general public.

An indispensable trait of fashion is the sense of uniqueness and novelty, which also forms an open perspective to ethnic costumes and traditional culture. But this openness and disclosure will inevitably obscure existing perspectives in turn. In terms of clothing, fashion is often expressed through clothing designs and styles. It is worth noting that the origin of fashion does not have a strict time limit, therefore, although fashion emphasizes the current sense and immediacy, it is also a historically generated cultural style. In the Middle Ages, fashion was closely connected with the aristocratic class, namely, inseparable from the people and cultural characteristics of this class. Nobles often hire famous fashion designers to customize their distinctive dress out of their appeals for life tastes and styles.

It is because of this stratifying feature of fashion that defines the hierarchical nature of fashion lifestyle. Today, although fashion still possesses hierarchical sense and symbols, the hierarchy is not as stable as that in the Middle Ages and modern times. At the same time, fashion is still

---

[1] Simmel G. The Philosophy of Fashion [M]. Fei Yong (tr). Beijing: Culture and Art Publishing House, 2001:76-77.

playing differentiating role among social communities, groups and individuals. It should also be noted that "to this day, it is still difficult for us to judge a person's social class, economic status, occupation, or ethnicity purely from his appearance," [1] which, however, does not mean that ethnic elements and clothing culture are not important. All established cultural traditions are inseparable from historical heritage, as well as from people's lifestyle and cultural consciousness. In traditional social and cultural context, if people want to live a fashionable and popular lifestyle, they must understand the characteristics and cultural tastes of the class that they belong to.

Generally speaking, the cognition and understanding on the life and cultural context of one's class can prevent one's fashion style from being nondescript, but this connection or even correspondence between fashion and class has been challenged in contemporary times. For fashion, its meaning and connection are not only structural, but also open and generative. In the generation of fashion meaning, the generative connection between ethnic group and culture are indispensable. In fact, fashion has long been involved and immersed in many aspects of human lifestyles, such as clothing, dressing, diet, behavior, dwelling, consumption, emotional expression and thinking. At the same time, fashion is often understood in the same sense as popularity is. No doubt the two are closely related, but they are not equal to each other.

To put it simply, fashion obviously could be, and it is often, popular, but if it is widely popular and made far too so, it will inevitably be ended. "The purpose of art is to make you feel things as you see, not as you perceive; one technique of art is the defamiliarization of things ..." [2] This technique is often fully used and reflected in fashion, though returning to historical traditions would actually produce the sense of strangeness as well. Popularity and trends in a certain degree and period are undoubtedly indispensable symbols of the generation of fashion.

Fashion appeal is also related to the art and aesthetics of life, and lifestyle focus is more on the sense of current fashion than on the long history of clothing. However, no fashion can exist without the sense of history, and the historical and cultural characteristics of an ethnic group are embedded in fashion styles. As a clothing lifestyle, fashion is undoubtedly inseparable from culture, being an important art and cultural style in itself. Of course, fashion culture is often a temporal subculture, expressing itself through the alienation from and supplementation to the so-called mainstream culture, but it is never an insignificant cultural style. For fashion clothes, imitation and conformity actually mean the primary stage of fashion life. At the same time, from the process of fashion

---

[1] Perna R. Fashion Forecasting [M]. Li Hongwei, Wang Qianmei, Hong Ruilin (tr). Beijing: China Textile & Apparel Press, 2000:91.

[2] Shklovsky V, et al. Selected Literary Theories of Russian Formalism [M]. Fang Shan, et al (tr). Beijing: SDX Joint Publishing Company, 1989:6.

recurrence, new sense and taste should be revealed on the changes of fashion.

In the clothing lifestyle, fashion style and cultural taste are a matter of general concern. However, the pursuit of fashion does not lie in passive following and imitating, but in constructing a unique and suitable sense of fashion, as well as a special understanding of fashion lifestyle. And this aesthetic understanding and cultural interpretation of fashion is always related to a certain ethnic group and its spiritual characteristics. In fact, fashion tentacles have reached into all aspects of human life, being inseparable from the lifestyle of certain ethnic groups. Generally speaking, fashion brings people a sense of joy and elegance, in particular, a unique experience and insight for their routine daily lives.

Fashion may also give people a different temperament and taste, as well as a unique lifestyle and personality. Human preference for fashion and appeal for popular culture have contributed to the mutual orientation between life and aesthetics, and all things related of fashion can't be void of ethnic heritage and cultural characteristics. There is no doubt that fashion is a cyclical yet forever updated art and cultural style. Nowadays, people still like to pursue embellished details to achieve a fashion style, especially when a variety of fashionable jewelry and trendy clothes, refreshing and dazzling, turn up with the continuous replacement and acceleration of fashions. The generative relationship between fashion, ethnicity and culture cannot be ignored, and it depends on people overcoming and breaking through traditional epistemology in their understanding and interpretation of fashion.

Some people may hold that fashion is simplicity, and simplicity is superior to luxury, though in daily life the latter is often considered synonymous with fashion. In the contemporary lifestyle, people vary in their understanding of fashion, but in terms of the aestheticization of daily life, "if being in an environment with plenty artistic and cultural traces, then the fashion consumer who shows a preference for art can better understand and appreciate the designer's work."[1] It is noteworthy that sometimes fashion only tries to curry favor with eccentricity, gimmicks, or even claptrap, lacking substantial aesthetic value and cultural connotation at all. Such a fashion is at best a visual imagery.

In daily life, those people or things out of sync with fashion trend are often regarded as obsolete and outdated, but the dress that is inconsistent with the trend are unnecessarily wanting in fashion meaning. Some fashion objectors believe that fashion is a vulgar and popular style of mass culture, constructing illusions and simulacra about pop and fashionable life through nothing but novelty, vulgarity, and irrational stunts, thus fashion is seen as a lifestyle of conformity lacking

---

[1] Calderin J. Form, Fit, Fashion [M]. Zhou Mingrui (tr). Jinan: Shandong Pictorial Publishing House, 2011:224.

independent value judgment. Different views on fashion, related to the differences of certain groups and classes, constitute the theoretical and ideological diversity of fashion evaluation. In fact, although fashion often means a current fashionable lifestyle, it is ultimately inseparable from the ethnic and cultural context in which people live.

At the same time, the masking over the sense of history is an expedient measure of the current fashion. In this seemingly superficial obscuration, fashion suspends the sense of history based on temporality, and this suspension brings fashion into the coming past. Although fashion stands on the present and looks into the future, it has never been and cannot be completely separated from the past lifestyle. Here, different fashion creative can often be regarded as different historical responses to bygone arts. As a symbol of art, beauty, and culture, traditional clothing, together with its contemporary aesthetization and fashionization, is actually an important component in the construction of the ethnic and cultural significance of fashion.

Since ancient times, across the world, clothing lifestyle has always been closely related to certain ethnic group and culture. In fact, leaving deep impressions and meaningful symbols to the contemporary and next generation is an inherent appeal of artistic, aesthetic and cultural generation. No doubt, clothing and fashions of all ethnic groups are constructed by aesthetics and culture, which in turn, get constructed by clothing and fashions. Fashion art and culture fuse with the values and tastes of life in the corresponding times. With the ever rising of the threshold to receive visual impact, people await increasingly strong aesthetic shocks more eagerly.

Although fashion is typically reflected in people's clothing styles, it is not limited to this field. Extending to the fields of contemporary art, architectural design, folk crafts, etc., fashion is actually the cultural event that occurs widely in people's daily lives and spiritual world. At the same time, fashion is a rediscovery on the meaning of everyday life, though lacking a certain depth due to the rapid change of trend. Fashion has always been injected with and immersed in ethnic and cultural characteristics, but often in a deformed and rhetoric manner. In the process of fashion expression and design, ethnic and cultural characteristics are sheltered in the visual images, and through them respond to the inner mental schema of the ethnic group.

Moreover, avant-garde fashion is often a form of subculture, intervening and penetrating into various artistic and cultural styles. Subculture injects into the constitution of culture the heterogeneity related to specific ethnic group and class. In fact, a subculture not only contains the values and concepts related to the main culture, but also has its own unique values, concepts and lifestyles. Ethnic fashion explores, organizes, and reconstructs the historical memory of an ethnic group, aim to generate a fashion style that possesses both the ethnic cultural characteristics and the sense of currency. In the context of generative theory, culture means a process of becoming the culture itself, that is, culturalization, just as ethnicization means becoming the ethnic group itself. However, ethnicization does not imply a simple conversion among ethnic groups.

If ethnic fashion prevails in contemporary daily life, it becomes an important component of the aestheticization of daily life, which is related to mass art and pop culture. For example, young African Americans and Mexican Americans used to wear Zoot suits. "In order to avoid being mistaken for general suit, Zoot suit has to make greater changes to general suit." ❶ In the mutual promotion between aestheticization of daily life and ethnic fashion, there are not only changes in the original expressions and meanings, but also the intertwined and fusion between the old and the new. Ethnicity has always been the basis of fashion and its local culture, and in turn this local character has provided a kind of ground for the presence of ethnicity.

Generally speaking, ethnic culture is characteristic of regionality, diversity, and original ecology. Those ethnic clothes and fashions present not only exotic fashion styles and unique experiences, but also local and diversified cultural characteristics. Although any ethnic group does not form its own culture by depending on other cultures, the connections among different ethnic groups and cultures cannot be denied. There is no label of being superior or inferior, advanced or backward, on various ethnic cultures. In the existence and clothing lifestyle of human beings, any ethnic group cannot avoid associations with other ones, thus certain hybridity has been infused into the coexistence of ethnic groups. For clothing art and aesthetics, among the essentials are the ethnic and cultural characteristics of creative and design.

What Taylor put forward was an early classic doctrine of culture in a narrow sense. Later, the Diffusionist School pushed the phenomenon of cultural communication to the extreme, opposing the revelation and interpretation made by evolutionism on cultural communication. The generation of various ethnic arts and cultural creative, as well as the artistic, aesthetic, and cultural exchanges among ethnic groups, produces significance that cannot be ignored in the aestheticization of daily life. Moreover, this cross-cultural communication of art and fashion is based on the local character of an ethnic group and its culture, but at the same time it is constantly breaking through the restrictions and limitations of certain regional characteristics. The relationship between ethnic fashion characteristics and traditional culture is undoubtedly an unavoidable issue for ethnic self-identification and its contemporary construction.

With the rapid development of social economy and the gradual decline of ethnic customs and unique lifestyles, the diversity of ethnic culture is often regulated in some kind of consistency. "After ages of accumulation, fusion, transformation and innovation, Chinese clothing culture has become

---

❶ Barnard M. Art, Design and Visual Culture [M]. Wang Shengcai, Zhang Aidong, Qin Shangli (tr). Nanjing: Jiangsu Fine Arts Publishing House, 2006:149.

increasingly delicate and lush with unique ethnic characteristics and cultural traditions, fully manifesting Chinese spiritual and cultural features." ❶ In the era of globalization, ethnic and local cultures are confronted with severe challenges. Therefore, it is urgent to construct the aesthetic and cultural tension between uniqueness and consistency from the dialogues among creative ideas and designs. Each ethnic group has formed a unique set of lifestyle, belief, ideology, etiquette, custom, local circumstance, etc., which have constructed distinct aesthetic styles and cultural characteristics of each ethnic group.

Various ethnic groups have formed their unique and distinctive clothing cultures, but with the economic and social development, ethnic costume and traditional culture are faced with the danger of diminishing or even disappearing, so the issue of respecting and protecting ethnic traditional cultures come to the surface. Rather than being a simple return to the original clothing lifestyle, exploring ethnic elements emphasizes the reconstruction of ethnic elements and traditions in the contemporary cultural context. In order to protect and inherit the costumes and traditional cultures of ethnic minorities, it is urgent to systematically collect and sort out ethnic cultural heritages for their preservation.

Of course, ethnic costume art and culture will be protected and inherited with inevitable connections with other ethnic cultures, and be recreated and interpreted in the contemporary social and cultural context. The generation of ethnic characteristics is inseparable from a community, a specific historical process and a common cultural context. For example, on the raglan sleeved linear tunic worn by ancient Greeks and Romans, conspicuous changes were made later in its sleeve shape, length and decorative details, which exerted great influence on fashion creative and designs of subsequent generations. Fashion art and design expression are always related to the lifestyle of certain ethnic group, but they cannot be simply attributed to the ethnic and traditional category.

Culture is a revelation of the basic existing way of an ethnic group, while the existence of an ethnic group is the ontological basis for its culture. Of course, the reconstruction of fashion based on traditional cultural foundations is essential. Take Lacroix for example. His creative inspiration is closely related to his ethnic culture, because "his design is deeply influenced by his hometown Arles – a place with primitive and innocent paintings, gypsies, bullfights and ethnic costumes." ❷ But if there is no reconstruction in the current context, neither ethnic element nor tradition can automatically undergo a fashionized transformation, which is essentially a visual, aesthetic and

---

❶ Lou Huizhen, Wu Yong, Zheng Tong. Chinese Traditional Costume Culture [M]. Shanghai: Donghua University Press, 2004:3.
❷ English B. Fashion Design [M]. Huang Hui (tr). Hangzhou: Zhejiang Photography Publishing House, 2012:42.

cultural construction and generation.

Fashion art and culture is an extension, expansion and enrichment of traditional culture, rather than a pure fiction and conjecture separated from ethnic and traditional culture. Through historical associations with various lifestyles, the protection of ethnic costume art and the inheritance of cultural tradition have become a discovery on the meaning of ethnic life. This discovery is inseparable from various artistic expressions, and it is necessary to dissolve and deconstruct the anthropological presence of each ethnic group and the possible traces of subject theory through the disclosure of this anthropological presence, so as to highlight the intertextuality and mutual generation between ethnicity and culture. In the process of design, to reveal the generation of the fashion meaning of ethnic elements is undoubtedly an important research subject on fashion art, aesthetics and culture.

2. Generation of Fashion Meaning on Ethnic Elements

Fashion not only has the characteristics of general art and design, but also possesses unique and irreplaceable aesthetic and cultural traits, because fashion is more closely related to people's lives, bodies and history. When reconstructing various ethnic elements and cultures to produce special meanings and purports of fashion, we should figure out what on earth fashion meaning refers to. In addition to having a strong sense of the moment, fashion is often associated with ethnic elements and traditional culture. Revealing the potential implication of ethnic elements through defamiliarization is fundamental to the generation of novel and unique fashion meaning.

Defamiliarization consists in the deviation from daily life and routine, which leads to a strangeness in language understanding and feeling. In terms of referent, defamiliarization makes things that are commonplace in real life novel in meaning and purport. For instance, in designing the 1995 autumn and winter series, Westwood used Scottish tartan to reconstruct the clothing silhouette of the 19th century, the fabric, lines and accessories rendering a strong British style. And in terms of language structure, common grammatical rules would be transformed into language art with new forms and aesthetic values. Anyway, the basic constitutive principle of defamiliarization is the confrontation and conflict between factors irrelevant on the surface yet connected inherently, thus forming an unusual feeling and a novel impression.

Of course, defamiliarized expressions of fashion sense are not just deconstructive, and all artistic techniques could actually be adopted by fashion expressions. It is the opposition and conflict that result in defamiliarized presentation or presentative defamiliarization, which gives people sensory stimulation or emotional shock. No doubt defamiliarization is often relative to everydayness. For example, "traditional art is committed to producing beautiful, rather than novel, things, while today's art does exactly the opposite." ❶ Generally speaking, people often give attentive and curious psychological responses to outside stimulations, and those familiar and routine things or situations can hardly arouse or maintain people's interest and concern. Only new and unique creative designs can evoke people's peculiar artistic experience and aesthetic taste, thereby generating a fashion sense that people expect or favor.

On the basis of alienation, people have developed a new consciousness and identification of their selves, and defamiliarization is an important way to turn familiarity into novelty. The concept "defamiliarization" can actually be traced back to Aristotle. Of course, Aristotle did not formally propose the concept of "defamiliarization", but used such terms as "surprise" "strangeness" and "unusualness". People tend to be accustomed, or even turn a blind eye, to things around them. It can be said that the wide spread of fashion means the end of it, and lays a historical foundation for future fashion and vogue. In this cycling of fashion, the shading and revealing of meaning are both distinguished from and intertwined with each other. Defamiliarization makes bland things unusual, thereby increasing the novelty and freshness of art and design.

At the same time, defamiliarization is to ensure the need for aesthetic distance and to answer people's psychological appeals for novelty. Edward Bullough's theory of aesthetic distance holds that in the process involving art, design or aesthetics, people should maintain a certain aesthetic "distance" psychologically. The construction of ethnic elements and cultural characteristics not only provides cultural possibilities for the generation of unique fashion meaning, but also lay the foundation for overcoming homogenization and relevant problems. The way to see things through distance is a special perspective of observation. Because people generally lack the ability to maintain distance, apt to reach the limit of distance and experience distance loss, so they cannot think and operate like artists to appreciate things with innocent artistic and aesthetic eye.

For the generation of fashion sense, the irreplaceable uniqueness of ethnic elements and culture provides a practical possibility for setting aesthetic distance. Once art and aesthetics enter society and reality, life tends to become trivial, extravagant and vulgar. The lack of proper aesthetic distance will lead to people's aesthetic fatigue and weariness, making them fall into a kind of average and dull everydayness. Because of concerns on utility and practicality, people often lose their excitement on art and aesthetics, experiencing hardly aesthetic novelty or pleasure, or even worse, undergoing tiredness and disgust. If there is no aesthetic distance between people and things, people will inevitably lose interest in any person or thing. For fashion creative and design, the lack of aesthetic distance leads to aesthetic fatigue and an obvious declining of the sense of

---

❶ Tatarkiewicz W. A History of Six Ideas [M]. Liu Wentan (tr). Shanghai: Shanghai Translation Publishing House, 2006:46.

beauty.

The fashion sense and cultural meaning of ethnic elements can be expressed through specific styles, modelling, and colors. The alienation and the fashion sense of ethnic elements and culture are revealed and manifested through unique ethnic traits. The Chinese fashion designer Wu Haiyan has a special fondness for ethnic elements and traditional culture, but what she advocates is not just Chinese red, but a kind of eastern beauty with more inclusiveness. Without ethnic characteristics, fashion may be lost to homogenization, nevertheless, it is not advisable to attribute fashion simply to ethnic character. An inherent characteristic of ethnic culture is its conservatism, the ways and degrees of which vary in different ethnic groups. And the reason why the culture of an ethnic group can last for long is inseparable from this conservative nature of culture.

The ethnic characteristics of each culture are passed down through dynasty changes, historical sediment of culture, and deconstruction and reconstruction of subsequent eras. The characteristics of ethnic art and culture are relatively stable, solidified and complete, such as ethics, values, living habits, social etiquettes, languages, etc., which will all be directly expressed and conveyed in fashion through vision. "Some of the philosophical ideas that the artists are working on or looking forward to will help produce certain visual effects. And no matter how limited these views may be, the artistic effects can go beyond the specific historical environment of the work."[1] Therefore, the visual effect of fashion is always associated with specific historical character. Of course, ethnic groups and traditional cultures are changing in themselves, presenting different historical traces and cultural characteristics.

As a way of generating fashion sense, defamiliarization can be divided into different levels or dimensions, which are related to each other in generating fashion meanings. At the first level, it emphasizes the separation of fashion from daily clothing; then, it brings novelty to fashion through avant-garde artistic expression; and finally, it rediscovers meanings and purports of fashion elements and expressions by returning to daily life and conventional art. Here, daily life is actually the life that people have to live every day, which changes of course in different societies and times. In the modern lifestyle, the fashion senses out of different materials are also different, and these differences are to be understood and explained correspondingly in specific ethnic groups or strata.

In the construction of the fashion sense of ethnic elements, people often choose specific materials for expression according to different purposes, so as to generate interesting meaning and novel sense. However, due to differences in environment, climate, custom, and culture, various ethnic groups have formed distinctive and colorful ethnic styles in a long period of existence.

---

[1] Crowther P. The Language of Twentieth-Century Art: A Conceptual History [M]. Liu Yiping, et al (tr). Changchun: Jilin People's Publishing House, 2007:168.

But even in the ethnic lifestyle, it is still difficult to get rid of equalized and routine patterns and customs, so the appeal for novelty is helpful to the aestheticization of life. Regardless of ethnic lifestyles, the generation of fashion sense means its distinction from the daily life.

It is in the distinction from daily life that fashion has become a novel way of life. As an important part of the ethnic daily life, the fashion art and clothing lifestyle of an ethnic group also constitute a challenge to its daily life. In the ethnic fashion art, the ethnicity and culture have been uniquely reflected, bringing novelty to the ethnic daily life. Ethnicity is related to the psychological state manifested in ethnic culture, and inseparable from the psychological and cultural characteristics identified commonly by an ethnic group. In fact, the forming of ethnicity is a long-term process of accumulation and construction. At the same time, it has to be affected and restricted by many factors, the most important one being the spirit and culture of the ethnic group. Fashion should not be understood just as different from regular clothes, for its fashionability sometimes is not clearly distinguished from everydayness.

How to dialogue with heterogeneous cultures is obviously an issue that all fashions should respond to in creative. Noting and respecting the inherent regularity of ethnic elements and culture is indispensable for the construction of ethnic art and fashion culture. In his research articles, Raymond speaks highly of the French fashion industry. For example, "Raymond associates the superiority of fashionable Parisian girls with French fashion and French ethnicity, which confirms how the discourse of fashionable Parisian girls promotes the French fashion industry in the interethnic environment."❶ Moreover, ethnic culture sometimes shows strong exclusivity, especially when it may shut out heterogeneous cultures. Therefore, the communication and exchange between heterogeneous cultures is indispensable for the generation of ethnic fashions.

Because of the cohesion inherent in cultures, it is easier for individuals within a homogeneous culture to understand each other. As a sign, fashion meaning is related not only to artistic texts, but further to society, history, and culture. The contemporary interpretation of the fashion meaning of ethnic elements will definitely involve inspiring perspectives of many disciplines and cultures. Ethnicity reflects the innate and irreplaceable uniqueness of an ethnic group, represents the inheritance of specific ethnic culture and the characteristics of particular regional civilization, and has much bearing on the particular spiritual and cultural characteristics of an ethnic group. Therefore, ethnic fashion should not only maintain the individuality and traits of ethnic culture internally, but also relate itself to some generality of global culture externally. In the communication between clothing lifestyles of different ethnic groups, cultural adaptability is also

---

❶ Iskin R E. Modern Women and Parisian Consumer Culture in Impressionist Painting [M]. Meng Chunyan (tr). Nanjing: Jiangsu Fine Arts Publishing House, 2009:229.

an issue connected with fashion meaning.

In fact, the unique sense of novelty can also be brought to ethnic fashion art and aesthetic culture through avant-garde artistic expressions. As one of modern art genres, avant-garde art generally refers to new artistic expressions and styles, often with rebellion and subversion against tradition. As a reaction to the existing art system, the avant-garde art always shows its vanguard nature in a historical context, and inevitably experiences continuous deconstruction and dissolution. However, postmodernism does not simply rebel against artistic tradition; instead, it also reconstructs traditional elements through art and design, generating a current sense of fashion and clothing lifestyle. We can neither classify fashion into a kind of avant-garde art simply, nor deny the fashion traits possessed by many avant-garde arts.

Avant-garde art appears in the intent of Western modernity. It is a concept proposed by Western modernity and related to postmodernism. Avant-garde fashion consists in the application of avant-garde artistic techniques to the creative and designs of fashion (including ethnic fashion), so as to form the contemporary ethnic fashion with avant-garde awareness and feeling. The generative association between avant-garde style and ethnic elements actually results in the ethnic avant-garde fashion. Arts and cultures of various ethnic groups are intertwined and intertextual with each other, for example, the Central Plains culture in ancient China coexisted well with surrounding regional cultures ethnic minority cultures. Therefore, the mental schemas and visual habits of different ethnic groups are often interwoven together historically, difficult to be separated from each other.

Compared with ethnicities of other regions, ethnic minorities are more peculiar with regional characteristics and more inseparable from their spiritual schemes. In today's globalization, the ethnic culture of China, like that of any other place in the world, is facing new challenges and dilemmas of cultural choice. Whether the ethnicism adhering to ethnic conventions or the ethnic nihilism moving towards Westernization, cannot position ethnic culture properly in the forest of world culture. In fact, the fashion meaning of specific ethnic elements is generated in dialogues with and cultural responses to other ethnic groups. The defamiliarization of ethnic fashion based on uniqueness is a vital characteristic of ethnic art and fashion creative, forming the sensation basis to generate the fashion meaning.

In the prediction of fashion trends, though it is not necessary to trace each specific ethnic origin of fashion, this ethnic origin is an inseparable historical context for the meaning generating of ethnic elements. Cultural heterogeneity exists among different ethnic cultures, which may serve as the generative prerequisite of constructing fashion sense in a specific ethnic group or culture. "However, all those engaging in fashion prediction should understand that the taste of certain ethnic group will be the main driving force guiding the requirement of the entire clothing market." [1] Parallel to heterogeneous culture is homogeneous culture, which refers to the common or similar cultural characteristics shared by people of different ethnic groups and cultures. It can also be said that modern art and culture are the combination and blending of multiple heterogeneous cultures.

Therefore, the coexistence of various arts and cultures has become the indispensable living, historical and cultural context for fashion creative. At the same time, heterogeneous arts and cultures existing in various regions are inevitably melted into the heterogeneous connections of art and aesthetics, and respectively show a sense of strangeness in their coexistence. Homogeneous art and culture are a more stable part of the world's culture, making possible world-wide dialogues between arts and cultures. However, due to differences in human living environment, folk ritual, and life taste, ethnic elements and cultures present their unique characteristics in their expressions. It may be said that, the interpretation of any ethnic element on its meaning and purport is inseparable from the cultural context related to specific place and history.

Human beings vary with regions and races in the means by which they are connected with nature to obtain surviving opportunities, and also in their ethnic psychology accumulated through a long time. This local character is not only related to the entity and its space, but also fundamental for the construction of the living world of a specific ethnic group, providing the place where the memory and collective unconsciousness of that ethnic group occur. So, people's fashion lifestyle shows local character and heterogeneity, resulting in the forming of a peculiar cultural system, which is, of course, an important part to the integral culture. But different regions and ethnic cultures can become each other's heterogeneous culture in a relative sense. Creative designs of fashion distinguish themselves from each other and generate unique fashion senses with their respective characteristics.

Obviously, fashion creative aims to reveal the free nature of designing. The differences between all ethnic cultures can only be relative, as the differences of codes existing in art styles and costume cultures are not simple black-and-white opposition or consistency. For the evaluation of art, aesthetics and culture, creative is always completed in the value system of certain culture. And because each person has his own experiences, he develops an individual understanding on the cultural differences of design. These various cultural characteristics are intertwined and generate fashion meanings historically in cross-cultural fashion communication. The relative and historical characters in the generation of fashion meaning appear prominent in heterogeneous fashions and cultures.

---

[1] Perna R. Fashion Forecasting [M]. Li Hongwei, et al (tr). Beijing: China Textile &Apparel Press, 2000:118.

Here, the heterogeneity and homogeneity often exist in comparison, and together they constitute the cultural characteristics of art and design; while open creative ideas and designing texts provide the possibility for the mutual generation of heterogeneity and homogeneity. It should be pointed out that "ethnic groups or individuals are actually different in their aesthetic conception, which, though forms the basis of all artistic creations, is not the only reason for ornamental creation."❶ Moreover, no design can resort only to heterogeneity or homogeneity. In a certain process of becoming heterogeneous or homogeneous, seeking unique ethnic creative is a vital aesthetic and cultural appeal. The generation and interpretation of any fashion creative and meaning are inseparable from the exchange and intertextuality between various ethnic cultures.

However, ethnic elements with different cultural connotations and characteristics do not appear in fashion creative design in a single and pure form, but generate and achieve their unique fashion significance of the moment in the blending of various ethnic cultures. In the process of globalization, the generation and historical occurrence of ethnic fashion culture always present two seemingly conflicting situations, namely, the paradox of heterogeneity and homogeneity, which is hard to dissociate in all fashion creative and designs. In fashion creative and design, people are paying increasing attention to the absorption of different ethnic elements and cultures, and trying to construct unique fashion in the artistic and cultural dialogues between ethnic groups.

The relationship between heterogeneous cultures, through mutual adaptation, complementation and fusion, generates a new sense of heterogeneous culture. Here, the clothing lives of various ethnicities and ethnic groups are all faced with aesthetic and cultural conflicts between heterogeneity and homogeneity. In particular, when the foundations of fashion cultures in different ethnicities often have their own continuity, stability and otherness, the cultural consciousness of non-Western countries has got exceptional attention and reinforcement, which is actually a reaction to the appeals of modernity and uniformity in the era of globalization. However, both various forms of colonialism and extreme forms of ethnicism should be avoided and criticized in contemporary ethnic fashion designing, and cultural exchanges and mutual recognition among ethnic groups are indispensable anthropological foundations of ethnic fashion creative.

3. Generating Methods of Ethnic Fashion Creative

All fashionization processes and expressions of ethnic elements in fashion designing need to be revealed and explored by specific method of artistic manifestation. The generation methods of ethnic fashion creative are related not only to various artistic expressions and technological

---

❶ Hadden A C. Evolution in Art: As Illustrated by the Life-Histories of Designs [M]. Agazuoshi (tr). Guilin: Guangxi Normal University Press, 2010:171.

processes, but also to ethnic psychological, social and cultural issues. It should be emphasized that "art and design are open disciplines: there is no so-called right answer to a given question or situation, which is the very reason why this discipline is extremely charming for designers."[1] It can be said that the designing creative involving the relationship between form and material is fundamental to the creative and designing of fashion, which helps to break through constantly the traditional restrictions on the conceptual frameworks of form and material.

Of course, fashion creative designing is quite different from general designing, just because fashion has to respond to its unique relevance to body, as well as to the ways that art and aesthetics construct current fashion sense. In art and designing, the generative relevance between form and material keeps an issue to be meticulously considered and revealed. In Aristotle's view, form, material and other concrete things are all substantive in nature. Although being different from non-utilitarian free (pure) art, design is undoubtedly inseparable from artistic expression and aesthetic experience. Sometimes, the production of utensils may be properly separated from creative designing, but design should also provide an aesthetic consideration for production.

It should be noted that non-utilitarianism and aesthetic generation are also involved in designing, so that designed product can acquire a transcendental beauty. Kant's distinction between dependent beauty (adjunct beauty) and free beauty (pure beauty) lays the foundation for the division between design art and free art, but the boundaries between these opposites are inevitably subject to continuous dissolution and reconstruction. In particular, when aestheticism keeps encountering problems and dilemmas, the traditional distinction between design art and free art has become increasingly blurred. For example, in the fashion history across the world, different ethnic groups have different styles of dresses, such as Scottish short skirts, Russian long skirts, etc., which show different designs, lengths and characteristics in different historical periods. As a modeling activity based on purpose and creative, art design is obviously not only a process of technology and implementation, but also a cultural construction related to vision and aesthetics.

As far as fashion clothes are concerned, creative is the most important and fundamental part of any design, as well as the conceptual and ideological basis on which fashion sense can be generated and constructed. All creative and designing are inseparable from the visualization process, in which a unique sense of fashion and aesthetic taste can be built. Here, visualization aims to activate the imagery thinking of designers and audiences, and present visually acceptable images in their minds, thereby artistic expression and aesthetic experience could be generated and disseminated. Although the beauty of design is generally divided into functional beauty, form

---

[1] Clay R. Beautiful Thing: An Introduction to Design [M]. Yin Tao (tr). Jinan: Shandong Pictorial Publishing House, 2010:17.

beauty and material beauty, such simplified divisions on beauty and aesthetic experience are no better than ideas of expediency.

In traditional costume design, various artistic expressions and aesthetic perspectives are the manifestation of the spiritual pattern of specific ethnic group. In the aesthetic expressions of design, functional beauty is related to the perception, emotion and aesthetic experience generated in a person after his physiological need is satisfied; while formal beauty generally involves the relationship between shape, sound and color of a product. As Clive Bell holds, "I call these combinations and relationships of lines and colors, and these aesthetically appealing forms as 'forms of intention', which is the commonality of all visual art works."[1] In general, the constituent factors of formal beauty involve the combination or composition of perceptual materials, as well as the fashion styles and aesthetic emotions of different races or ethnic groups. Here, the relationship or the composition of the perceptual materials that makes up the form beauty can actually be regarded as the rule related to the form beauty of design product.

In creative designing, the main rules related to formal beauty are: uniformity and variance, symmetry and balance, proportion and scale, golden section, transition and echo, calmness and lightness, rhythm and cadence, penetration and hierarchy, quality and texture, harmony and contrast, diversity and unity. However, the simple application or direct borrowing of any rules can hardly produce a true and unique sense of fashion. In fact, the occurrence of any ethnic creative design is a unique response to or even a breakthrough of existing rules. In other words, these formal rules, revealed by human beings from creating and aesthetic experiences, are ideal standards and appeals stipulative for creative designing. According to Kant, formal beauty, being pure, is independent of material and function, but in the modern and contemporary period they are closely related to each other.

Therefore, fashion creative is inseparable both from visual and aesthetic expressions, and from human world of daily lives. In aestheticism and formalism, the purity of the art form is fully emphasized, namely, the independence of art and aesthetics and the absolutization of form are extremely important. Formalism also highlights independent aesthetic meanings of art forms. In the context of generative theory and phenomenology, the ethnic fashion meaning is always achieved in the distinction between ethnicities. Aestheticism has exerted great influence on abstract and non-reproducible modern art movement, and further promoted the appearing and developing of structuralism and semiotics. Besides, the tendency of modern architecture to pursue blank and neutral formal structures actually comes from the deep influence of aestheticism and formalism.

---

[1] Bell C. Art [M]. Xue Hua (tr). Nanjing: Jiangsu Education Publishing House, 2005: 4.

Aestheticism and formalism are also important to ethnic fashion, because for various races or ethnic groups, in addition to emphasizing the functional relevance between designing and life, ethnic fashion should also express distinctive aesthetic effects. "As far as the nature of beauty is concerned, the diversity of beauty is better described as the varieties rather than types of beauty."[1] Therefore, aesthetic fashion texts respond with its openness to the issues involved in the social, historical and cultural context. In fact, ethnic elements and sense of fashion are generated in the construction of unique beauty. Moreover, the construction of fashion beauty is not limited to the traditional classification of beauty.

From Plato to Hegel, Western philosophers regard material as dark, murky and inert, often discussing the issues of artistic expression and aesthetic experience from the perspective of form. Although pure form seems to be between material and idea, it actually accepts the fundamental stipulation of the latter one. In ancient Greece, the idea itself was often embedded with visual and formal meaning. In ethnic costume culture, various colors have their own meanings and emotional connections, experiencing historical changes and continuous reconstruction of meaning. In terms of material, fashion creativity and performance are generally achieved through clothing fabrics, and it is an important issue in fashion design to express ethnic elements on the basis of material characteristics and texture. According to Aristotle, the world is made of things harmonious in forms and materials.

Aristotle explores the generation and change of things in light of combination. The paired category material and form was originally used in the description of appliance and design, but later was extended to the expression and evaluation of free art. In Aristotle's opinion, there are four basic types of cause. The first one is material cause, which is the main substance that forms an object, also involving various materials used in fashion clothes. If fabrics provide the material cause for apparel and fashion, then styles are the form cause, hands and production tools the motivation cause, while functions objective cause. Aristotle holds that there is neither a form without material nor material without a form, hence a close connection exists between the two.

However, material and form still face the inevitable dilemma of binary separation. Although aesthetics was once defined as a perceptual learning, originally focusing on the study of free art and aesthetic experience, it still has to respond to designing and functional issues, unable to get rid of its connection with technology. That means, "beauty is shown to us in a contact with the object, now more intellectual, and then more physical. And it is in this experience that the object

---

[1] Tatarkiewicz W. Dzieje Szesciu Pojec (A History of Six Ideas) [M]. Liu Wentan (tr). Shanghai: Shanghai Translation Publishing House, 2006:159.

of technology could be aestheticized by us."❶ Here, the beauty of material refers to the beauty manifested in the texture of the material involved in designing and artistic expressions. For example: simple and mysterious clothing is associated with dusty history; bright and magnificent metal decoration reminds us of future technology; while soft and subtle fabrics undoubtedly put a cozy family atmosphere in our mind.

Generally speaking, flowing elegant curves and accessories remind people of bustling city and romantic emotion; and tough fabrics peaceful countryside. The generation of fashion meaning is inseparable from the process of aestheticization, which reveals and reconstructs ethnic elements. Fabric can not only reveal and interpret the style and characteristics of clothing, but also affect directly the color, shape and effect of clothing. In ethnic fashion designing, fabrics could be of various color and style, injecting a unique aesthetic taste into the generation of creativity and fashion sense.

Generally speaking, high-quality fabrics have such advantages as being comfortable, absorbent, breathable, straight, smooth, noble-looking, etc. Therefore, the design and production of clothing worn on formal social occasions usually choose fabrics like pure cotton, pure wool, pure silk, and pure linen. Different from general forms of free art, fashion design must also fully consider the functional appeals of the wearer, which could not be separable from his aesthetic expectations to clothing. Kant paid attention to the difference of feelings and experiences as well as their inner relations. The generation of fashion sense and meaning is closely related to this kind of aesthetic synesthesia, but not limited to the text of aestheticism. Free beauty is not premised on the concept of an object (i.e., objective purposiveness), while dependent beauty is premised on such a concept and on the completeness of the object according to that concept.

In Kant's view, when an object stimulates us, it results in our sensation in the aspect of imagery ability. Therefore, the intuition that is related to the object through sensation is called empirical intuition, and an unspecified object of empirical intuition is called phenomenon. It should be noted that although fashion beauty has a certain dependence on function and reality, it is also affected by free art and its aesthetic style. Among phenomena, what corresponds to the sensation is called the material of phenomenon. According to Kant, the materials for all phenomena are only acquired later on, but their forms must be innately prepared for these phenomena inwardly.

The ideas of aestheticism, "art for art's sake", and formalist aesthetics actually come from the free beauty proposed by Kant, which is, in other words, pure and non-utilitarian formal beauty. In this sense, "Kant may be the first and truly prestigious fashion theorist who emphasizes that

---

❶ Dufrenne M. Esthetique et Philosophie [M]. Sun Fei (tr). Beijing: China Social Sciences Press, 1985:214.

newness is the essential quality of fashion ..." ❶ Kant also denied the simplified relationship between fashion and beauty. Fashion design, regarded as an artistic activity and an important form of art production, cannot separate the creative from certain material to express beauty. As far as ethnic fashion is concerned, the generation of creative is separable neither from the newness of ideas, nor from the specific spirit and cultural characteristics, which would bring forth unique meanings and charms related to specific group of people.

In fact, unique creative is toward a return to ethnic spirit and cultural charm, or, a return to the specific spiritual realm and context related to ethnic existence and culture. Moreover, only starting from ethnic spirit and the reconstruction of its schema, can we fully express and elucidate the current fashion creative and taste, as well as the unique artistic and aesthetic experience. For example, because of its peculiar and novel connotation, asymmetry has been widely adopted and used in many designs. Actually, this reenchantment is a reconstruction of the ethnic charm, showing differences in creative style between different ethnicities. In the creative of ethnic fashion, certain costumes are inseparable from their designing purpose or function, manifesting some kind of continuity between them that is difficult to break.

Undoubtedly the generation and existence of creative and design are related to form and material, thus overcoming the problems of traditional model in the relationship between form and material. For example, the crown that once symbolized status, power and honor is still used in the coronation ceremonies of some monarchy countries. As to the freedom of revealing symbols with new primitive style, Blanche, Jacques Emile believes that "designers seek the creative points of their own recognition, and the construction of their own language codes makes them look like tribal leaders." ❷ The aesthetic psychology to material also involves the connection and fusion between different feelings. That is to say, fashion creativity and aesthetics require the co-intervention of multiple senses, and aesthetic synesthesia plays an irreplaceable role in the aesthetic observation of material.

In Aristotle's view, Plato's theory of ideas cannot explain the existence of things, because Plato's ideas are separated from individual things. The so-called "material" cause is "the initial substrate" of things, that is, the original material that constitutes everything. At the same time, "form" cause refers to "the essential stipulation" on things. No design or creation can get rid of the conceptual schema of material and form, but all involve unique response to and reconstruction of this schema. According to Aristotle, the relationship between material and form is that of between

---

❶ Svendsen L. Fashion: A Philosophy [M]. Li Man (tr). Beijing: Peking University Press, 2010:21.
❷ Marglin V. (ed). Design Discourse: History, Theory, Criticism [M]. Liu Sha, et al (tr). Beijing: China Architecture & Building Press, 2010:35.

potential and reality. Form, being the active and positive cause during the formalization of material, stipulates material and makes it an individual of reality.

Material needs to be shaped by form, and form is always related to spirit in creative and expressions. Form, as the essence, definition, existence and reality of things, is distinguished from the material that serves as the potential of things, but the two cannot exist without each other. In Aristotle's view, teleology presupposes a certain purpose, and then analyzes the ways to achieve the purpose. So how to make material and form related and responsive to each other in creative and designs has become an unavoidable issue in the generation of fashion meaning. In the texture beauty of visual arts, form and material share a close generative relationship. In fact, the simple dichotomy between form and material limits the full disclosure and expression on them.

Although Mikel Dufrelnne believes that in logic, form is not the form of an object and is not closely related to material. However, aesthetic form should make material possess a form. In modern times, form is no longer simply determined by content, and the traditional association between content and form is inevitably deconstructed. For creative, the essence of fashion is that, "it feels a kind of 'spirit' going beyond words, and it is a supreme abstract process that comprehensively summarizes scattered elements."[1] Thus, the expression and construction of form in contemporary fashion creative are no longer constrained by the traditional relationship and dilemma between material and form.

Only by overcoming the traditional relationship and problems between material and form can designing reveal the generative meaning and purport embedded in form. Besides special ethnic cultural meaning, sense of form is also an important appeal of expression in fashion creative. From modern to post-modern period, the stipulation of Western thought has changed from existence to language or discourse. Fashion creative and designing are actually from diversified perspectives, being both a response to the tradition and a current reconstruction. Postmodern arts eradicate modern artistic and aesthetic concepts, being fundamentally deconstructive in their thoughts, and uncertain, scattered, random and plain in their expressions. If modern aesthetics still pay attention to form in the realm of existence, then postmodernism insists on a strong anti-form tendency, which could provide an important opportunity for the contemporary generation and expression of ethnic fashion creative.

---

[1] Barthes R. Système de la Mode [M]. Ao Jun (tr). Shanghai: Shanghai People's Publishing House, 2000:123.

第二章

民族时尚创意的生成与视觉表现

一般来说，时尚艺术与表现无不具有视觉性及其相关特征，且在视觉表现里彰显自身的创意诉求与设计表达。实际上，民族的时尚创意本身就是与视觉及其表现相关的，并由此构成了一种重要的审美经验与视觉文化样式。时尚创意与设计的艺术表现，无疑也是一种视觉性的艺术存在。与此同时，民族时尚创意还涉及民族风尚与传统文化的视觉性关联问题。创意的视觉化转换就是将新的观念、想法，经过艺术化的可视性处理来加以表现与传达。在西方艺术史上，视觉一直具有特别重要的规定性意义与价值关涉，甚至可以说在很大程度上，西方艺术史往往就是一部西方视觉艺术史。但这并不表明，一切民族的元素与文化都是简单可视的，因此不能说，非视觉性因素之于艺术表现忽略不计或无足轻重。

其实，许多观念并非都是直接通过视觉来传递与感受的，但它们大都可以经由视觉化转换而被感性重构。民族时尚创意的生成离不开视觉性表现问题，必定还涉及观念表达与视觉思维的关系。对时尚创意来说，这种视觉表现总是重构性的与不断生成的。但视觉重构的发生不只是一个艺术与表现的问题，同时也是一个极其重要的社会与文化问题。在创意的视觉化过程中，抽象的或不可见的观念在视觉里得到了表现与重构，而这种视觉表现本身就是一种审美与文化建构。在民族时尚的创意过程中，审美建构还关切到民族的生活方式与人类学存在。还要看到，创意的视觉表现所关联的是一种动态的、开放性的文本，这种文本当然也是创意与接受的对话及其发生的生成论基础。

第一节　创意的视觉转换与图式化

在时尚设计过程中，创意就是一个从观念、想法到视觉传达，以及将这种视觉化得以实物化或成品化的过程。时尚表现的视觉传达之所以成为可能，是以创意观念与想法的视觉化为前提的。在视觉表现与文化语境中，设计就是把创意的观念与想法加以转换，变成可经由视觉来感受的要素及其关系图像。这种视觉化转换及其实现方式，也是创意的视觉化所要考虑的审美与文化问题。而且，创意经过视觉化的转换与艺术表现，还要成为在视觉中加以识别与接受的图式。这里的视觉转换并不是将创意的观念与想法直接与简单地加以比附，甚至是穿凿附会的图解，而是创造性的视觉转换与审美和文化重构的过程。在此基础上，再将所要表达的图像意味与含义加以编码，并在设计与制作过程中解码与传递出来，从而被人们，尤其是时装的使用者所认同与接受。

一、创意：从观念到视觉

应当说，创意之于时尚设计的重要性，不仅是因为设计做得与创意密切相关，还由于观念与思想都从创意进入设计之中。创意其实就是从观念的发生与视觉化的转换，最后实现视觉表现与形式的表达这一完整过程。当然，创意过程也为制作的可能性提供切实可靠的基础，实际上，在创意本身就蕴含着制作得以实现的可能性。还可以说，观念在创意活动中具有首要性的作用，它在很大程度上规定着设计的品质与优劣。自从古希腊以来，理念或观念就受到过充分的重视与研究。任何艺术表现与设计，都无不涉及理念或观念的问题。

柏拉图把"理念"这个词用到哲学中，还赋予观念以实体化特征，即可以脱离可感事物独立存在的特性。"理念"一词来自古希腊语的两个词，即"idea"和"eidos"，前者源自动词"看"，逐渐引申为心中的观念。而且，"这样独立的模式或理念是无数的，没有任何东西因为太卑下或不重要而没有它的理念"。❶ 对理念的模仿其实就是艺术与美接受这种理念的规定。在模仿说看来，艺术模仿针对现实进而指向了理念。视觉化表现就是从上到下的过程，它与从下到上的模仿相互呼应，从而构成了设计与艺术的密切相关性。

在柏拉图那里，理念是实在界的原型，感官所及的世界均是以它为依据而成形的。柏拉图的思想奠基于理念之上，他认为文艺与美的事物在本质上是对理念的模仿。虽然柏拉图理念论与模仿说都难免存在自身的问题与困境，但这些理论与思想却深刻地影响着后世的艺术、设计与审美。尽管柏拉图继承了苏格拉底模仿说的基本精神，但他又从理念论的视角对苏格拉底的模仿说加以重构。柏拉图认为，理念甚至是一种无所不在的思想性存在，同时也是形而上学所指向的根本性旨归与诉求。

在创意与设计过程中，各个民族的精神图式与理念、观念无疑是密切相关的。也正因如此，艺术就像模仿的模仿、影子的影子，因此与理念的真实似乎隔着两层。柏拉图之所以排斥文艺，是因为文艺是对自然世界的模仿，因此比自然实体还要等而下之的东西，由此导致的二元分立与对艺术的轻视受到了后世的批判。柏拉图认为，理念是独立于事物而存在的根本规定。柏拉图对创意的重要启发是，理念或观念是一切创意与设计表现的根本来源。对理念加以视觉化转换，可以说是所有设计发生的根本性方式。当然，设计与制作只有理念是远远不够的，显然还要经过这种视觉化转换的过程。

理念成为设计所关涉的模型、样稿与雏形，也就成为设计出的产品原初所依凭的思想原型。但还应看到，"柏拉图关于艺术的理论，即艺术是对模仿品的模仿，与他所提出的'形式'论密不可分"。❷ 到了黑格尔那里，美被界定为理念的感性显现，因此，艺术与美的显现仍然不得不接受理念的规定。与之相关，艺术在于用感性形象来表现理念，以供直接观照与提供某种生动的感性，而不是用思想和纯粹心灵性的形式来表现。所有的设计虽然都涉及观念的问题，但对观念的强调在概念设计达到了极致。

因此，黑格尔的美学与哲学思想，对于理念的视觉化与设计具有重要意义。在黑格尔

---

❶ 梯利.西方哲学史[M].葛力，译.北京：商务印书馆，1995：66.
❷ 沃特伯格.什么是艺术[M].李奉栖，张云，胥全文，等译.重庆：重庆大学出版社，2011：15.

那里，艺术以其直观与可感性特质区分于宗教与哲学。根据黑格尔所言，最初的艺术是象征型艺术，在这个阶段，人类想把认识到的理念表现出来，但还找不到合适的感性形象，于是就用对形式的强调来象征所要表达的观念。但在黑格尔那里，仍然面临着理性形而上学的问题与困境。当然，这种象征意味并不局限在黑格尔的象征型艺术中，因为在现当代艺术表现与设计中，符号仍然具有重要的艺术意义与审美价值。到了黑格尔所说的古典型艺术时期，艺术的内容和形式达到完美的关切与契合。

而且理念和感性统一的古典型艺术成为最完美的艺术。最后，才是浪漫型艺术。在浪漫型艺术中，无限的心灵发现有限的物质不能满足表现的需要，于是又从物质世界退回心灵与精神世界。在当代设计中，观念及其视觉化虽然也涉及诸多成对概念，但这种视觉化又总是与二元分立的解构分不开的。其实早在古希腊，理论理念本身就已经表现出这种视觉性的特质，而视觉作为最基本的感觉，规定与支配着其他的感觉。正因如此，古希腊的视觉艺术有着比诗歌与音乐更优越的地位。

甚至可以说，艺术、美总是与视觉表现密切相关。在古希腊，神话对艺术产生了广泛而深刻的影响，同时也为创意的生成与文化建构提供了语境。特别是随着荷马史诗的出现，以及以宙斯为核心的奥林匹亚山的诸神系统，为以希腊神话为主要题材的希腊美术的产生作出了准备。其实，视觉最初的含义也是与逻各斯相关联的。逻各斯把某种东西展示出来让人看，也就是朴素地让人看某种东西，从而让人觉知存在者，但它后来被遮蔽在逻辑与理性哲学中。然而，相关于民族精神图式的创意观念，在此并不局限在任何既有的概念与体系中。还要看到，最早的理性是出于逻各斯并与视觉相关的理性。

应注意到，作为光明之神、造型之神，日神阿波罗把光辉洒向万物与存在者，从而使万物显现出美的外观与形式。自古希腊到近代，模仿说在西方艺术与美学界一直占据着支配地位，从而影响了西方现实主义艺术风格与审美经验。对视觉艺术与表现而言，模仿主要指赋形与外观上的相似、逼真。虽然在古希腊，艺术只能模仿外形，而无法模仿实质，但却不能说这种模仿与形而上学本质无关。一般来说，柏拉图推崇理念和哲学，贬低艺术，主张把迷狂的诗人逐出理想国。在亚里士多德那里，所有的艺术都被把握为一种再现。

在艺术与美的问题上，亚里士多德虽然也坚持模仿说的基本观点与思想，但他的模仿说与柏拉图的模仿说又有了很大的不同。根据亚里士多德，只有一重现实的世界，艺术模仿现实，艺术与现实都是真实的，诗（艺术）甚至比历史更真实。其实，理念与视觉的关联从来都是不可回避的问题。"我认为理念与有形的形式之间的相互作用，在比拜克认为莱加艺术家从其雕刻品中意识到'文化类型'的观点中也得到了说明。"❶ 但艺术仍然涉及形式与质料及其关系，这当然也是艺术创意与设计所要面对与回应的问题。而且，如何克服形式与质料及其二元分立，无疑也是艺术、设计与审美研究的问题。

---

❶ 罗伯特·莱顿.艺术人类学[M].李东晔，王红，译.桂林：广西师范大学出版社，2009：37.

亚里士多德认为，理性分为理论理性、实践理性与诗意（创造）理性。同时，他还把美的形式归结为与视觉相关的秩序、匀称与明确等。逻各斯规定了，理性原初表征为理论理性，而理论理性与洞见、视觉相关。作为一种反思，理性相关于光的反射，并规定了看与思的一致性。看离不开光，光决定了是否能够看见。从一开始，视觉艺术就涉及对光的把握与处理。在希腊化与古罗马时期，视觉艺术与享乐、功利、世俗生活发生了密切的关联。在现当代，设计的视觉化与人的感官，经由表现及其理解与阐释，而又涉及民族精神与文化特质。

显然，观念的视觉化是创意得以生成与实现的根本前提，它也是设计的社会与文化建构不可缺少的过程。还应意识到，新的视觉文化把本身非视觉性的东西视像化，并将之纳入视觉化语境加以解读与阐释。在亚历山大·麦昆那里，时尚、艺术与概念及其密切关联融入了设计，他始终注重野兽与文明、男人与女人、科技与自然等之间的平衡的维系。在观念的发生与创意过程中，视觉化如何涉及不同表述间的关系，也与各族群对这种关系的理解分不开。但如此强调视觉形式之于艺术表现的重要性，并非仅仅局限于视觉而排除一切其他感觉。创意关切于视觉经验与其他经验，旨在将观念加以视觉表现，并经由通感把经验建构与整合起来。

毫无疑问，各种民族的服饰艺术与时尚设计，都是与传统视觉艺术密切相关的艺术样式。而且，时尚创意还关涉各种不同观念与经验的生成性关联。就时尚创意而言，"时装设计师经常需要快速描画，匆匆记下飞逝的构想，捕获短暂的瞬间，迅速地构思出足够多的想法以编辑出连续一致的整体"。❶ 在视觉人类学中，通过可视符号来建构设计产品所关涉与呈现的文化得到了强调。在创意中，草图表现也是概念与想法的视觉化过程。视觉化主要是以文字、图形、色彩为基本要素的表现过程，在精神与文化领域以其独特的表现影响着人们的感情，并对人们的生存与日常衣生活加以审美与文化建构。

视觉传达是人们利用"看"所进行的交流，也是通过视觉语言进行表达与传播的方式。不同地域、肤色与使用各种语言的人们，通过创意符码与视觉进行观念的传达、情感的沟通与文化的传播。显然，这种跨文化的交流与传播，还涉及诸多族群及其文化差异的问题。在一定程度上，视觉的观察与体验可以克服彼此语言间的障碍，还能消除文字不同及其所关涉的文化阻隔，凭借对图案与纹样的视觉共识实现相互沟通。但就如何揭示与理解服饰的视觉性特质，仍然涉及对这些可视符码的社会与文化阐释。

其实，视觉传播从来都是人与人之间交流与对话的直观方式，并对人类历史文化的传承和人们精神生活的建构都有着深远的影响。视觉表现借助特定的媒材与技法，构成了民族服饰艺术及其款式与纹样等，彰显与建构着与民族性特质相关的创意文化。还要注意到，"在思维与视觉之间的许多相互依赖的联系不能被简单地分割为一组零部件"。❷ 因为，一切

---

❶ 苏·詹金·琼斯.时装设计[M].张翎，译.北京：中国纺织出版社，2009：82.
❷ 朗·伯内特.视觉文化——图像、媒介与想象力[M].赵毅，等译.济南：山东文艺出版社，2008：17.

时尚风格都有其不可还原的整体性特质。从意大利时装的柔软与优雅、德国时装的蓬松与华丽，以及西班牙时装由优雅变成僵直等应意识到，这些不同民族或国家的创意，都有其不可分割的社会与文化语境，而这种语境性关联也会进入创意与设计文本中。

作为一种传达或传播方式，视觉化当然有其自身的表现方式与技巧，对视觉化的理解与阐释关涉不同的学科与视角。人们力图通过自己的眼睛去看，往往离不开对图像及其文化意趣的自我理解。因此，将各种规定与想法通过视觉化表现出来，无疑是一个重要的艺术、设计与文化问题。既然说视觉化是文化对话与理解的一种直观方式，那么，对话的双方应对同样的形象符号具有可沟通性。对在识别与理解上有差异的创意图形，可通过文化上的沟通甚至包容来对待差异。视觉语言可看成是基于基本元素和原则，而构成的一套传达意义的规范或符号系统。

实际上，各个民族都有其独特的思考方式与视觉习惯，这其实也是民族元素与文化的时尚表现所应考虑的。在视觉艺术的表现中，设计师总是赋予那些经典图案以传统的意义，这是理解创意与达成沟通的思想基础与文化前提。"在设计中，人们有时能够发现设计师们一次又一次地在做着形象化的陈述……"❶ 值得注意的是，创意设计总在考虑如何突破传统的解读，从而获得一种新的时尚效果与解读方式。具体而言，时尚设计原则包括布局、对比、节奏、平衡、统一等，这些都是设计师用来传达意义的准则和方法，但各种不同的视觉化设计又会对这些原则加以独特的应用与强调。

根据特定生活方式与审美的需要，选择相应的材料与表现形式，以及建构元素之间的独特关系，从而形成能够传达特有意义的图像。但视觉思维并不局限于直接的知觉内，其还被广泛地拓展到民族审美经验与文化的建构中。但不应把图像仅看成一种再现方式，它其实也是一种关于物象甚至自我的重构。创意的视觉化总是与观念发生着密切的相关与对话，这也是对观念与图式及其生成性关联的揭示。这里可以说，视觉化的表象只是力图揭示的东西的一种呈现。而且，视觉化还要关注与探究图像及其所涉及的社会与文化意义如何解读与理解的问题，同时也关联到不同民族或族群在创意上的勾连与对话。

而且，观念的这种视觉化还涉及表象与内在精神复杂的生成性关联。在观念的视觉化过程中，还涉及可感元素与非可感元素的生成性关联与转换问题。在文艺复兴时期，"当时的贸易和旅游都在增长，而人们对于时尚的观念也随之得以交流，但服装仍呈现出很大的民族特性"。❷ 这种跨文化的时尚传播也是各民族对自身传统再认识的重要契机，它相关于如何在观念与创意里对民族特质加以视觉化表达的问题。一种跨文化的服饰与时尚传播，既关涉到从观念到视觉的转换问题，又与不同民族元素和文化的交流与认同分不开。文化的适应性问题在时尚创意的视觉化，以及与之相关的跨文化时尚传播里得到了突显。

---

❶ 彼得·多默.1945年以来的设计[M].梁梅,译.成都：四川人民出版社，1998：169.
❷ 琼·娜.服饰时尚800年：1200—2000 [M].贺彤,译.桂林：广西师范大学出版社，2004：24.

二、创意的视觉转换及其可能性

在很大程度上,古希腊的理念及其视觉性特质规定了西方的艺术与审美。西方文艺复兴的基本风格与表现技法,构成了近代视觉艺术与文化的主要传统。在造型艺术方面,文艺复兴以写实作为出发点与基本传统。在达·芬奇看来,透视是一种理性的表现,物体的轮廓线汇聚于人眼。同时,线条也基于人的理性的控制之中。人体解剖的研究和透视学的完善,在视觉艺术的创作中得到了广泛应用。文艺复兴以后,视觉艺术及其新的意味与旨趣,对时尚创意的视觉化产生了深刻的影响。

其实,近代的透视与视觉化在艺术与设计里的密切相关,也是与当时的理性与古典主义分不开的。就广告与视觉传达而言,古典主义往往意味着理性、秩序与控制。"也许这一广告的古典主义风格表现得异乎寻常的强烈,但它所代表的普遍的风格发展趋势却在大部分高档时装形象中具有典型意义。"❶但17世纪以来,西方艺术从宗教走向了世俗生活,从而让理性之光关注与照亮人性的存在。在近代,勒内·笛卡尔为艺术和思想奠定了一个理性的基础,进而敞开了一个由理性所规定的艺术与美。在现代,由于对人的视知觉的研究不断深入,透视学的范畴、内容得到了极大的拓展与延用。

实际上,人们总是经由对民族服饰与时装的感知与审美经验,去理解、阐释与把握设计所传递出的创意与文化的。在创意的视觉转换过程中,中国传统的艺术表现与西方透视学的差异应引起关注,因为这涉及对不同民族或国家时尚的理解与阐释问题。鲍姆嘉通认为,审美是感性认识的能力,这种感性理解与创造美,并在艺术中达到完美。但仅仅靠西方近代的这种理性与理解,难以深入领会不同民族内在精神的可视化问题。黑格尔认为,在绘画艺术之中,人的理性之光的重要性远远超过了自然的太阳光。

不同于古希腊的理论理性、中世纪的实践理性,近代的理性往往相关于诗意与创造。应当注意到,黑格尔把艺术与美阐释为理念的感性显现,显然也关涉观念的这种视觉化问题。在黑格尔那里,艺术中一切感性显现的东西最终都要受理念的规定。但这并不是说,视觉艺术不再相关于感性与审美经验,而是表明理性在艺术经验中的规定性影响。一般来说,形式美指事物的色彩、形状、线条、声音等及其关系所生成的美感,它无疑是视觉艺术与审美经验的根本性之所在,同时也是创意的视觉转换所应考究的重要问题。在古希腊,毕达哥拉斯学派提出的黄金分割律认为,凡符合黄金分割比例的形式总是美的。

作为形式美的重要构成规则,黄金分割在现代被广泛地借鉴与应用到绘画、工艺、建筑与设计等领域。但在近代,就艺术与美的探究而言,形式总是与内容密切相关的,它们是一对不可分割的范畴。而且,形式与内容等范畴,成为把握视觉艺术的概念框架。应当看到,几何学与科学给视觉与艺术表现带来了深刻的影响。基于科学与几何原理的透视,被广泛地运用于视觉艺术与设计之中。近代视觉艺术中的透视,主要有焦点透视与散点透

---

❶ 保罗·梅萨里.视觉说服:形象在广告中的作用[M].王波,译.北京:新华出版社,2004:86.

视。但不同于一般的比拟之处在于，创意及其视觉化所凭借的比拟与精神图式密切相关。与此同时，将观念视觉化进而在质料与形式的关联里实现造物。

在这里，创意的视觉转换及其可能性，是以观念或想法的可视性为基础的。应当说，质料与形式及其关联的原始含义就是适切于造物与器具的，后来才被移用到自由艺术的实践中。应当说，透视原理与方法的借鉴与应用，拓展了视觉艺术表现的崭新空间。但要看到，"视觉能指和神灵力量理念之间的关系要比杜尔干或者列维-斯特劳斯的图腾模式复杂得多"。❶ 其实，对视觉的理解本身也离不开理论与文化的建构。近代以来的造型艺术用一定的材料，通过构图、透视与用光等艺术手段，塑造直观的平面或立体的艺术形象。毫无疑问，这些都是创意及其视觉转化不可或缺的表现方式。

而且，一个观念或想法的可视性究竟何在，则与族群的想象力与文化理解相关，这种理解又是与族群的内在精神图式分不开的。这里的可视性并不是说观念可以被直接看到，而是旨在强调观念能够转化为一种视觉图像的可能，人们再经由图像的意味领会观念所蕴含的思想。还可以说，传统意义上的可视是强调视觉上的通达性。其实，艺术人类学为不同族群的观念的视觉转换及其理解提供了文化的可能性。但与创意相关的不仅是视线的可通达，实际上还包括非视线的可通达，如沟通与可理解的达致与实现，以及发生在视觉与非视觉间的沟通与对话。视觉转换不仅是一种生理与知觉上的可感性的体现，它也是一种相关于民族的审美与文化实践。

这里的根本问题无疑在于，观念究竟如何才能具有可视性特质。这里所说的可视性，往往指观念何以能表征为一种视觉印象，并被人们加以理解与阐释。在当今时尚设计界，"真仿古、伪前卫的时装设计师们很少躬身探究时尚的真正意义，他们更多地热衷于昙花一现、顾影自怜、毫无意义的形象展示"。❷ 这里还涉及一种民族时尚创意与设计，如何才能通过视觉图式将文化的历史性揭示出来，并在这种时尚化了的视觉图式里理解民族生活方式。实际上，古希腊的理论理性就具有某种视觉性的特质，而这就在根本意义上规定了理论的可视性基础。

在对时尚创意表现加以接受的过程中，人们就开始用视觉观察去感受设计企图表达的想法，并在一定思想与文化语境里去重构所获得的视觉印象。理论与观念的建构本身就不可能没有想象力，而这种想象力为可视性的拓展又作出了某种奠基。虽然想象力离不开直观、形象与生动的意象，但它也是与认知、理论与思想分不开的。对创意观念加以视觉性的生成转换，这既相关于人们的想象力对图式的建构，还与如何对抽象与观念的东西加以分析分不开，进而凭借特定的视觉化表现方式，将创意转化为具象的可感性及其视觉经验。

但是，并不存在所谓绝对纯粹的感性可以让我们依靠，因为，对任何抽象观念的理解也需要想象力的介入。在认知过程中，知性用概念统一表象以形成知识。当想象力把感性

---

❶ 罗伯特·莱顿.艺术人类学[M].李东晔，王红，译.桂林：广西师范大学出版社，2009：114.
❷ 多米尼克·古维烈.时尚不死？关于时尚的终极诘问[M].治棋，译.北京：中国纺织出版社，2009：128.

杂多集合起来后，不是像认知那样去统一表象，而是让想象力与知性去自由游戏。可以说，"在中国画家看来，任何有特征的自然风景画面都与人类的某些精神方面相对应"。❶ 在审美的自由游戏之中，知性与想象力虽然有所冲突，但它们必须相互共处与协调起来。与此同时，知性与想象力既都不能缺席，也不能一方胜过另一方，而是在它们之间保持一种恰当的张力。在民族时尚创意的视觉化转化过程中，不同民族的心理与文化也具有其自身的特质。

在本性上，抽象是观念抽离原本客体的思想生成过程，但观念创意与视觉化的关系并不能理解为抽象与具象等概念模式。因此，对抽象事物的理解与有效沟通，往往需要基于沟通的知觉或共同的经验。被抽象化了的经验与感官印象，在时尚创意观念及其向视觉转换时，有待于在艺术表现与产品诉求的语境里得到重构，同时还要在对这些时装的解读里来领会内在的精神意象。不同于抽象，具象更多地相关于形象思维，以及人的直觉与情感，而具象的表现也必须对抽象观念的可视性要素加以分析。

但人们的视觉观察并不是空洞的、没有理论支撑的，其离不开理论及其所建构的视觉图式。在时尚创意观念的视觉化转化中，具象与抽象本身其实都不是分离的，而是密切相关与相互交织的。而且理论与观念在人们观察活动中的意义是不可或缺的，因为没有任何观察可以绝对地与观念无关而得以展开的。在民族时尚创意过程中，往往借助各种理论视角对民族元素加以分析，并在此基础上对观念视觉化的可能性加以探究。在这里，观念视觉化的诸多可能性，其实还涉及深层与表象及其复杂的生成性关联，以及如何对两者间的审美与文化张力加以建构的问题。

在创意观念视觉化的研究中，一切所凭借的理论、思想与观点都应与设计目的相关联。还要看到，不同的设计师甚至同一设计师在不同条件下，所想象到的东西与做出的创意其实也有所差异。虽然说，"理性知识有时有助于形成一个视觉概念，但只有在这些知识可以转换成视觉的属性的时候才能起到作用"。❷ 因此，设计将不可见的创意进行转换，使之具有可见性基础。但在不可见与可见之间，实际上并没有一条绝对的与不可逾越的界限。应当注意到，由于观念自身的抽象性与复杂性，比较难以通过直接的视觉去理解与把握。早在亚里士多德时期，形式、质料和具体事物都是实体性的。

在笛卡尔那里，观念被分为天赋的、外来的和虚构的等三类。戈特弗里德·威廉·莱布尼茨认为，观念是作为倾向、禀赋、习性或自然的潜在能力。莱布尼茨反对经验论，尤其是洛克的经验论。乔治·贝克莱认为，心中的观念是构成现实事物的本原，事物就是"观念的集合"。还要看到，这里的观念往往都是抽象的，因此难以被人的眼、耳等感觉器官感知。在观念的视觉化过程中，其实也涉及对某种可见之物形制的建构。在海德格尔那里，艺术乃是一种存在论意义上的存在，它与作为存在者的艺术家、作品，构成了一种共同存

---

❶ C.A.S.威廉斯.中国艺术象征词典[M].李宏，徐燕霞，译.长沙：湖南科学技术出版社，2006：178.
❷ 鲁道夫·阿恩海姆.艺术与视知觉[M].腾守尧，朱疆源，译.成都：四川人民出版社，1998：128.

在与相互生成的关系。

对艺术与设计创意来说,史论、批评与跨文化传播都是不可忽视的。但观念与形式的生成性关联,可以说就是创意的视觉表现所要实现的。在创意的视觉转换之中,现象学所说的视觉直观无疑具有重要的意义与价值。"因此,构成形式的综合是一种思维活动,而统一感属于自发意识,是对那些可以分别感知的可感要素之间关系的洞察。"❶ 在直观的诸多形式之中,视觉感知的感性直观是基本的样式。埃德蒙德·胡塞尔认为,审美对象是一种意向性对象,现象学直观与纯粹艺术中的审美直观是相近的。在民族元素的创意与重构之中,也会关联到民族集体无意识所支配的意向性指涉。

在艺术与时尚本文所处的语境中,后现代是对现代性面临的问题与困境所作出的回应。当然,现代性与后现代性之间的复杂关系,无疑是全球化时代民族时尚创意所不可回避的。视觉在创意表现中不仅具有一般的规定性,它更是传递思想与建构可理解性的基础。梅洛-庞蒂从知觉的角度赋予直观以重要意义,他把知觉而非情绪体验当作人的存在的先验结构。而且,视觉转换所呈现的艺术构图与印象,也成为通达审美、文化与精神的直观性路径。在当代,人们对生活世界审美化的诉求与期盼,往往相关于时尚创意及其视觉化表现。随着人们视觉在审美过程中的不断延伸,可视性彰显出不同层面上的精神与文化关涉。

对创意可视性特质的理解与阐释,无不相关于特定族群的内在精神图式,而不同图式间的对话仍然是时尚不可忽视的跨文化问题。实际上,审美通感借助联想引起感觉之间的转移与彼此交织。应当说,"视觉设计涉及图像,而图像的功能就是传播与形象地传达符号、象征、形式与色彩的意义,以及它们之间的关系"。❷ 感觉与审美经验难以摆脱独特的民族性,以及不同民族之间可能发生的相互沟通与认同。除了诉诸视觉外,时尚也是一种别致与陌生的审美通感。在这种陌生感里,就不乏民族精神与文化的贯注,以及不同族群之间的文化异质感。在观念视觉化的可能性的探究中,不同民族艺术与文化之间的对话依然是必要的。

三、创意的图式化与视觉表现

在艺术与设计之中,视觉表现所呈现出的印象与经验,其实并非与民族性特质毫无关联。甚至可以说,时尚表现还相关于某种特定族群的精神图式。人类的精神图式对于视觉表现所具有的规定性,表征在艺术与时尚所蕴含的独特意义与特质里。康德认为,图式作为一种先验范畴,被看作潜藏在人类心灵深处的一种技术与技巧。根据康德的观点,理念是指在日常生活里无法完全体验的概念。如在日常生活之中,就找不到可完全体现"美"这一概念的例子。而且艺术所具备的可超越日常生活的特质为理念的表达提供了可能。

在民族创意的视觉化表现之中,精神图式在根本意义上规定着意义与旨趣。通过实验

---

❶ 乔治·桑塔耶纳.美感[M].杨向荣,译.北京:人民出版社,2013:72.
❷ Bruno Munari. Design as Art [M].London: Penguin Books Ltd., 2008:33.

研究，让·皮亚杰赋予了图式概念新的含义。在皮亚杰看来，图式是包括动作结构和运算结构在内的从经验到概念的中介，也是主体内部的一种动态与可变的认知结构。这种图式在认识过程中发挥着不可替代的作用，即能过滤、筛选、整理外界的刺激，使之成为有条理的整体性认识。皮亚杰认为，在适应外界与环境的过程中，图式就会不断变化、建构与丰富起来，但他的认识论及其二元分立的根本困境并没有得到彻底的克服。在这里，不同民族的艺术图案与造型及其特质，无疑也涉及民族内在精神图式的差别。

但不同图案间的层级性差异，并不表明各个民族间的不平等。与此同时，流行其实也涉及符号的修辞问题，比如说，"它竭力要在直接意指的地方炫示含蓄意指，采取纯修辞的形式勾画直接意指低下的形象"。❶ 对于艺术设计与审美表现来说，认知本身也涉及如何被突破以达到善的问题。但所有图式都不是各个部分的简单加和，而是一个难以分离与不可还原的整体，这在时尚品牌及其风格的整体性特质里得到了表征。在视觉文化里，民族衣生活方式存在着不可忽视的习俗差异。

实际上，图式本质上与特定民族的精神结构相呼应。应提到的是，英加登从作品本身出发，强调艺术作品的本体论地位，进而分析了不同种类艺术作品的内部结构。在英加登看来，音乐作品只有一个层次，即音乐中的声音组合。绘画通常包含两个层次，即再现的对象中被描绘的图式化观相所构成的层次和再现对象本身所构成的层次。但是，人们能体验到的往往只是事物的具体观相。根据英伽登的观点，具体观相是变化的，而在诸多变化的观相中，能够保持自身同一与不变的东西，就是图式化观相。在创意图式化的问题上，艺术与设计既与内在精神结构相关，同时也通过结构本身的开放性，而与社会、历史和文化语境发生联系。

也就是说，图式既可描述事物的必要特征，同时又包括其非必要特征。图式的视觉表现之所以可能，其实也是因为视觉本身就是可以思维的。在这里，语言、言语与思维之间的密切联系，以及语言与图式之间的相互转化并表现为符码，是与语言的修辞表达和话语建构分不开的。尤其是到了现代，对人类精神图式与文化传统的简单图解也是设计所应克服的。当然，设计离不开理念的元素及其关联向视觉化了的形象创造性地转换。作为一种生成性的语境，理念的视觉化为拟象的产生提供了观念与思想性的基础与前提。

其实早在中世纪，可感知与可理解的关系就是艺术与审美的问题。但到了近代，这种关系则主要表现为感性与理性的问题。在新古典主义艺术与图像美学之中，"'思想'的观念与图像或刻印的记号是不可分离的，这是经验在想象中留下的'理想'印象，特别是典型的视觉经验留下的印象"。❷ 创意的视觉化表现化为了具体而直观的形象，但每种视觉形象又内在地相关于人的精神结构。但这种严谨与理想的关联及其预设，在现代的艺术与时尚的表现里遇到了困境。还要注意到，符号与人类各种活动的发生密不可分，人类社会和

---

❶ 罗兰·巴特. 流行体系：符号学与服饰符码[M]. 敖军，译. 上海：上海人民出版社，2000：303.
❷ W.J.T.米歇尔. 图像学：形象，文本，意识形态[M]. 陈永国，译. 北京：北京大学出版社，2012：154.

文化的生成与相互关联离不开符号。

在时尚创意的视觉表现中，经常可以发现各种不同的符码象征，而这些象征的当代发生、变形与重构，又都与特定族群的精神和文化分不开。实际上，创意的观念及其图式化表现就是基于人类精神与文化的，特别是，各个民族或族群文化生成了创意表现的特质，并成为创意的视觉与图式化得以实现的文化基础。与此同时，这种图式化表现又往往是经由视觉方式来实现的。在英伽登那里，崇高、神圣与平和等审美中的形而上学得到了强调。实际上，时尚创意的图式化也是与这些形而上学相关的。

弗迪南·德·索绪尔认为，一个符号包括了两个不可分割的组成部分即能指和所指。在符号的表达之中，基本问题就是能指与所指的关联问题。因此，可视化的能指总在意指着某种所指及其意义。譬如，在波尔西默斯看来，"地域性品牌是通过民族服饰（像是印度的纱丽、巴西的比基尼）将品牌象征意义可视化的，时尚则是定期将区域性或民族性品牌的叙事织入其乌托邦愿景的符号结构中"。❶ 索绪尔指出，语言符号的特性就是符号的任意性与符号构成的线性序列。索绪尔看到，语言虽然作为符号系统文化中极其重要的例子，但除此之外，文字信号、礼节仪式、风俗习惯等也具有同样的性质。

但是，能指与所指的关联又会因为所指被消解而失去确定性，因此许多视觉表现在后现代难免成为能指的游戏。当然，能指的游戏也是与所指的多元性分不开。应当说，感觉与观念的二元论总是与观念至上论联系在一起。观念至上论认为，在认识活动中，占主导地位的不是感觉，而是观念。但在创意及其视觉化表现过程中，观念至上论摆脱不了认识论与形而上学的限制与困境。符号的任意性其实就是说，所指与能指的相互联系是任意的，两者之间没有任何内在的、自然的联系。

当然，所指与能指的这种联系一旦建构出来，就具有了一定的传承性与历史性特质，这也是创意表现的编码与解码得以存在的基础。鲁道夫·阿恩海姆认为，象征的意义应当通过构图形式特征直接传达于视觉。如在西班牙的斗牛节中，"服装上的金饰和公牛的鲜血，不正是西班牙国旗的颜色吗？"❷ 在阿恩海姆那里，视觉具有可思维的特质，它本身就是一种思维样式。还要注意到，各种民族元素与传统文化特质，无不渗透在民族日常生活与节日活动中。阿恩海姆吸收了格式塔心理学的思想，即视觉形象并不是对感性材料的机械把握，而是对现实的一种创造性把握。与语言符号不同之处在于，象征永远不会是完全任意性的。

而且，能指与所指关联的这种约定俗成，对民族观念及其视觉化的理解是不可缺少的。在某种意义上，能指与所指的关系就是感觉与观念的关系。在时尚创意的表现之中，视觉叙事其实也是视觉表现的一种重要方式。因此可以说，视觉叙事也涉及历史、社会与文化的问题。罗兰·巴特认为，任何材料都适宜于叙事，除了文学作品外，还包括绘画、电影、

---

❶ 伯格，等.时尚的力量[M].韦晓强，等译.北京：科学出版社，2014：272.
❷ 本内迪克特·拉佩尔.欧洲脸谱[M].刘玉俐，译.北京：中国人民大学出版社，2015：86.

连环画、社会杂闻、会话。当然，民族服饰本身也是一种衣生活与文化叙事方式，与此同时还有关于某种服饰的传说与故事等。举例来说，关于西兰卡普（土家织锦）的民间叙事，可通过视觉与图式化表征在服饰上。

而且，叙事承载物是口头或书面的有声语言、固定或活动的画面、手势，以及所有这些材料的各种混合。符号学就是意指系统的一种等级分析学说，一个意指整体可以分为深层结构、表层结构与表现结构。在面料的选择及其阐释上，其实也涉及不同的层次与结构，例如，"迪奥会选用奢华精细的布料，如素库缎、塔夫绸、土耳其绸、羊毛绉绸和天鹅绒，这些布料的视觉效果甚佳，颇受大众喜爱……"❶通过视觉化所表达的这种意指，在创意设计里也涉及不同的层次与结构。符号学以语言学的语义研究为基础，但又增加了与社会和文化相联系的内容和分析方法。

作为中国的一种传统纹样，龙凤呈祥以祥瑞神异动物为装饰纹能指，象征着婚恋美满、吉祥福瑞与阴阳和谐等所指。当然，民族服饰与时尚不仅是一种艺术样式，还是一种不乏符码与象征意味的文化。而且，时尚的流行可以说是一种艺术与文化的传播，它往往还发生在不同民族的文化之间。虽然，民族服饰涉及众多的艺术与文化关联，但通过视觉化来实现这种创意与思路，却是让设计被公众理解的重要方式。对于民族时尚来说，跨文化传播无疑会涉及文化认同的问题，而且关联到各个社会、历史与文化语境，但这些都是以创意的视觉化为生成论基础的。

叙事学还由"故事"层深层结构的探索，发展为对"话语"层叙事结构的分析与阐释。而民族创意与观念的视觉表现，其实也是符码象征与叙事话语生成的过程，并由此关涉精神与文化的诸多层面。实际上，"在假面表演中，面具和服饰改变了面具佩戴者的形象，但是改变只是暂时的"。❷ 因为，一旦面具表演结束后，佩戴者就会回到本身的模样与日常生活状态。在服饰与时尚的跨文化传播之中，必定还涉及对创意图式的理解与阐发的问题。其实还可以通过视错觉的表现手法，在时尚感的生成上将创意与民族叙事相结合。

但传统叙事学往往局限于神话、民间故事，尤其是小说等以书面语言为载体的叙事作品中，因此有待于向各种视觉符码与图形叙事介入与不断拓展。在创意及其视觉表现过程中，视觉艺术思维导图是通过图形化手段进行的明了与有效的传达。但是，这种导图并不是为了传达而设计成无意义的可视性图形，同时也不意味着只是为了追求美而设计成某种唯美图式。在这里，民族时尚创意的图示化是与民族生活及其叙事相关联的，但应看到，这种创意即使进入非语言材料构成的视觉叙事领域之中，也是以用语言作载体的叙事作品的研究为参照的。为了有效地传达创意所旨在表达的意图，视觉化和审美对原来观念与想法进行分析整合，并以非常直观的视觉化手段加以陌生化表达。

应当说，图像学对艺术作品在其历史与文化语境里的意义加以研究，这种研究与阐发

---

❶ 琼·马什.时尚设计史：从"新风貌"到当代[M].邵立荣，徐倩倩，译.济南：山东画报出版社，2014：14.
❷ 约翰·马克.面具：人类的自我伪装与救赎[M].杨洋，译.广州：南方日报出版社，2011：20.

又是基于对图像本身及其含义进行解读的。在这里，图像学旨在发现和解释艺术图像的内在含义与象征意义，以及图像的形成、变化及其所表现或暗示出来的思想观念。在这个图像时代，"我们需要一个可视的过去，一个可视的连续统一体，一个可视的起源神话，它消除了我们关于目的的疑虑"。❶ 但视觉与图式化及其表象主义问题与困境，却是艺术与设计亟待加以回应与克服的。还要注意到，与图像志对艺术作品内容的描述和阐释有所不同，图像学着重发现和揭示作品在纯形式、形象、母题、情节之后更为本质的东西。

第二节　民族时尚创意及其视觉文化

在民族时尚创意与设计研究之中，不仅要提出富有新意的各种想法、思想与可行方案，还要对观念、文化及其与视觉的可表现性的关联加以探究。与此同时，把这种关联性置入民族的生活史与视觉文化语境里加以阐发也是不可或缺的。实际上，不少设计的创意与想法虽然都是不乏新意的，但它们尚未在视觉的可表现性上得到较好实现。在日常生活与大众文化的语境里，如何关注各个民族自己的与特有的艺术与文化样式，对于民族时尚创意的审美表现无疑具有重要意义。而且，视觉文化还将民族时尚的创意与观念，纳入当代时尚艺术与审美的文本与话语里，并对之加以创造性的解读、阐释与生成性建构。在全球化的艺术与文化语境里，视觉文化建构关涉日常衣生活与时尚文化的民族性特质，以及这些民族时尚文本与话语在当代的审美与文化重构。

一、民族的生存、创意与文化

应当说，民族的生存与日常生活方式，总是与特定的自然环境与文化语境分不开的。在生存的问题上，海德格尔强调了在世界之中存在的不可避免性。海德格尔力图经由对此在的生存状态的分析，揭示此在的存在本性与存在自身的意义。对于特定民族来说，民族性此在在本性上也就是在世界之中存在，这种世界既是世界本身，同时也关涉民族的生活世界。其实，海德格尔对存在的追问是离不开世界，以及此在与世界的生成性关联的。实际上，此在即在世界之中存在，这表明此在存在于一个不可分之整体中。

当然，地理环境、文化传统与社会心理等多种因素，也从不同层面影响生活方式的生成，以及在时尚创意里所表现出来的视觉文化特质。"从纯粹意义上讲，在人类出现的最初时期，所谓服装只不过是一件凋敝寒衣，而且很可能是由磨损严重的兽皮拼成的，勉强起到服装的作用。"❷ 但随着人类生存与生活的变化，以及服饰各种功能的不断实现与满足，对创意与文化的诉求推动着后来服饰的美化。如果说，只是简单地把人作为动物的人和文化人来区分的话，那就不可能全面地理解人的本性及其复杂性。其实，把人的动物性与文

---

❶ Jean Baudrillard. Simulacra and Simulation [M]. Ann Arbor: The University of Michigan Press, 1995: 7.
❷ 弗朗索瓦-玛丽·格罗. 回眸时尚：西方服装简史[M]. 治棋, 译. 北京：中国纺织出版社，2009：13.

化性绝对区别开来是根本不可能的。

可以这样说，动物性与文化总是交织在身体存在与生活方式中，但文明又尽可能将这种动物性规限在最低的限度内。人类学趋向于考察人类种族，以及这些族群在身体、社会与文化上的差异与多样性，以阐明人体和文化的关联为目的。在旧石器时代，随着生产力的提高，人类的穿着可以按其所需而自由制作，这时的服饰已经脱离了原始的萌芽状态。但进入新石器时代后，尤其是随着初级纺织技术的发明，服装材料就有了人工织造的布帛，服装形式也随之发生了相应的变化，功能性得到较大的实现与改善。

在新石器时代，除了笼统式服装外，还从一些陶塑遗物发现了冠、靴、头饰、佩饰。到了渔猎、畜牧与农业时期，人们对着装上的美化和审美有了自觉。人们不仅寻求与探究服饰自身式样的合度，还对服饰外的各类附属饰件加以美化。在纺织品出现之后，作为中国原始社会的一种袍衫类服装，贯头衣已成为一种定型服式，并在相当长的时期、极广阔的地域，以及较多的民族中得到了使用，基本上替代了旧石器时代的部件衣着。实际上，贯头衣和披单服等披风式服装已成为典型的衣着样式。在不同的地域与历史阶段，服饰与人的生存、创意的生成性关联，显然也彰显出了不可替代的艺术与文化特质。

由于服饰极难保存，原始陶器彩绘与雕塑的人物形象，以及玉器人形刻纹，成了考察当时服装款式的珍贵资料。服装既是人类衣、食、住、行不可或缺的构成，同时也是人们身份的审美、社会与文化象征。正因如此，"虽然越来越多的人接受裸露上身做日光浴的想法，但是看来比基尼仍然会存在下去"。❶ 应当说，在着装及其审美过程中，还关联到各民族的视觉习惯与文化心理。其实，服饰的产生、样式的变化与创意的发生，无不与人类的生存状况、审美观念与文化相关联。为了在寒冷时保持身体的温度，就要穿较厚的衣服以防被冻伤。在原始人类的生活方式里，服饰的功能性无疑是至关重要的。

但各个不同民族的原初服饰，依然在不断影响着后来时尚创意与服饰文化的建构。在这里，护体与保温是从生理、体质与生存角度来解释服装起源的。但在不同的地域，如何着装又有所差异，这种差异还影响对创意与文化的理解，如居住在热带地区的民族，也几乎没有全身裸体的。随着社会发展与文明时代的到来，人们将服饰作为一种装饰文化来看待。一切古老与传统的艺术与服饰，显然又将在现代的语境里得以重构。例如，现代的原始主义装束风格显得古朴，它的创意灵感来自非洲、因纽特与太平洋岛屿等原始图腾文化。

在人类衣生活中，既有为了逢凶化吉而把护身符带在身上，也有把作为特定社会阶层标志的东西佩戴在身。其实，创意表现与质料（面料）也是密切相关的，不同材料的表现手法与体验也有所差异。举例来说，"在古代，虽然灯芯草、棕榈和纸莎草也被用作织物纤维，但最为普遍的还是亚麻"。❷ 作为一种纯天然纤维，亚麻由于其吸汗与透气性能良好，以及对人体无害等显著特点，越来越被当代时装设计广泛使用。还要注意到，任何单一的

---

❶ 安德鲁·塔克，塔米辛·金斯伟尔.时装[M].童未央，戴联斌，译.北京：生活·读书·新知三联书店，2014：67.
❷ 詹妮弗·哈里斯.纺织史[M].李国庆，等译.汕头：汕头大学出版社，2011：16.

服装起源说，都不足以阐发衣服发生的全部缘由，当然也只是一种看问题的视角而已。在服装起源的问题上，不同的起源说都在建构着特定的理解与阐释。

毋庸置疑，服装的创意与设计还与特定族群的生活方式和环境有关。譬如，居住在热带雨林地区的未开化民族，所穿的往往是最小限度的衣服，几乎仅仅是遮盖了生殖器而已。即使如此，这也可以在相当程度上防止外部的伤害。羞耻感的产生与服饰的出现是密切相关的，但仍然难以对谁先谁后加以简单的区分。对裸露的身体加以遮蔽，特别是首先遮蔽何处，在各个民族里又是有所不同的。

一般来说，汉民族服装上下连属的形制，是与所在地域的农耕生产方式分不开的。对北方的少数民族来说，因为生活在草原、平原或沙漠等地区，为了满足狩猎与放牧的生存性需要，所穿着的服饰（如胡服等）就是上衣下裤，这样就便于适应马上的生活与征战。由此可见，穿衣得体与否的问题受到了习惯与风俗的影响。衣服对于古埃及人并非仅为了遮体，而是强调衣服的象征意义和价值，其实这才是着装的主要目的之所在。

与此同时，人类的衣服与男女间的相互吸引不无关联。在原始人类的生活方式里，服饰也是一种象征着装者社会地位的符码。实际上，想要别人看到自己的服饰美是人的一种诉求，并经由服饰艺术建构出民族的衣生活与文化。譬如，那些尚未开化的民族的人们，在以野兽皮制作的防寒衣上所加的刺绣与配饰，其实就是关于身体之美的一种独特表现。先民们还从身体的涂色与装饰开始，尤其是像耳环、头饰、腰饰、脚环等的佩戴，这种想方设法装饰身体的心理与审美欲求，甚至可以说与人类生存的本能同样强烈。虽然人类今天的生存环境已不同于以前时代，但生存与身体的关系却一直影响着时尚设计。

毫无疑问，服饰难免受到不同历史时期人类精神与文化的影响与制约，这种历史性特质早已沉淀在各个时代的服装款式与风格中。从历史性的视角来看，民族服饰文化是一个变化着的，并有着分明的时代性、地域性与风俗性特质，以及艺术表现与设计的民族性关联的文化样式。"有迹象表明，'剪裁'这一概念正是起源于远古的克里特，这是因为，当其他早期文明的人们还只是简单地以布裹身时，米诺人的穿着就已经很得体了。"❶ 在一定历史时期与社会语境里，民族的创意与设计是该民族精神与文化建构的重要方式。

在远古时代，人们把身边能找到的各种材料做成粗陋的衣服，用于护身或对身体进行的修饰与美化。人类最初的衣服往往是用兽皮制成的，包裹身体的最早织物由麻类纤维和草制成。处于不同生存环境与文明形态的民族，对着装的理解与服饰文化的建构并不一致。在人类社会早期，服装就出现了，并与人类的生活方式密不可分，成为人类文化与精神的一种符码与象征。在原始社会阶段，人类采集野生的纺织纤维等材料以供服饰制作之用。但随着农牧业的发展，人工培育的纺织原料渐渐增多，制作服装的工具由简单到复杂，服装用料品种也日益增加。实际上，服装的变化趋势更注重服装的美观性，满足人们精神与

---

❶ 普兰温·科斯格拉芙.时装生活史[M].龙靖遥，张莹，郑晓利，译.上海：东方出版中心，2006：34.

文化上的享受诉求。

因此，创意与设计在服饰与时尚表现中更凸显出重要性，而人类早先生存与生活方式从来都会在当代设计里得到回应与重构。实际上，影响时尚艺术表现与审美经验的因素是各种各样的，如纺织品的质地、色彩、花纹图案、坯布组织、形态保持性、悬垂性、弹性、防皱性、服装款式等。同时，织物的原料、组织结构和生产方法也相关于服装形式。一般来说，用粗糙、坚硬的织物只能制作出结构简单的服装，只有具备了更柔软的细薄织物的时候，才有可能制作出复杂而有轮廓的服装样式。兴起于20世纪60年代美国的印第安式着装，其实也是对印第安服饰特质的一种借用与重构。

作为一种最古老的服饰，腰带往往被用以挂上武器等必需物件。甚至可以说，装在腰带上的兽皮、树叶以及编织物其实就是早期的裙子。居住在不同气候、山川、地貌等地理环境中的居民，其生活方式也因此具有独特的风格与习性。在长期的生存与生活之中，各个民族所形成的独特精神特质与文化语境，又使其衣生活方式呈现出丰富多彩的民族特色。在东方的一些国家，人们还通过含蓄的方式来表达自身的着装与他者的区分。几乎是从服饰起源的时候起，人们就已将其生活习俗、审美情趣、色彩爱好，以及种种文化心态与信仰旨趣，都积淀在服饰的艺术表现与设计之中。

尤其是在服饰功能性得到满足后，审美、社会与文化的诉求也会在创意设计之中实现。毋庸置疑，追求艺术与美是人的天性，衣冠之于人的生存与生活方式，作用不仅在遮蔽与保护人的身体方面，实际上更在于是否具有美化的价值，以及它在社会生活里所具有的象征意味。当然，"美或功能，无论哪个更重要，美都会存在于设计的方方面面"。❶人类祖先在与猿猴相揖别以后，终于艰难地跨进了文明时代的门槛。与此同时，人类创造出又一个承载文明的衣生活方式。

而且，人类知道服饰符码有助于辨认出其传递的信息，这与人们的生存、生活方式密切相关，民族心理与文化积淀构成了创意解读的重要语境。如果说从各个族群或民族对于同一种衣物、装饰的态度，可以解读出不同的审美旨趣与社会、文化意蕴，那么，穿衣者可能会激发出一些自己所没有预料到的情感反应。实际上，世界各民族与国家都有与其文化相关的时尚创意，并呈现出特有的艺术表现方式与审美风格。而且民族或本土时尚并不能仅仅局限在某一特定民族的生活世界里，还涉及由一个民族向另一个民族的跨文化传播事件，以及各个不同民族的服装与文化之间的理解与相互阐释的问题。

各个民族在自己的衣生活方式里，所关注与强调的审美与文化也有所差异，这既相关于生存与生活史的内在精神特质，同时又是不同文明自身相区分的重要标识。"……譬如法国的豪华高级时装、意大利的孤冷高雅、英国的荒诞流行、日本的功能主义、中国的古典美、非洲的原始美以及澳洲的实用主义。"❷实际上，生存不仅需要自然与物质性空间，更

---

❶ 罗伯特·克雷.设计之美[M].尹弢，译.济南：山东画报出版社，2010：7.
❷ 丽塔·裴娜.流行预测[M].李宏伟，等译.北京：中国纺织出版社，2000：144.

需要与之相关的社会与文化性空间。当然，对时尚文化的建构也不是一味地继承与沿袭，更不能放弃对本土文化的分析、反思与文化批评。当然，这些各具特色的创意与风格的区分是相对的、历史性的。

也可以说，各个不同民族在创意与设计上的差别，也是这些民族之间在艺术与文化人类学上的区分。其实，艺术与时尚的创意与表现起源于人类的创造力、技能和才华，以至于可以说人类文化本身就是创意、创新的生成之物。但如果只是一味地坚持自民族文化而拒斥他民族文化，自民族与本土文化就会陷入封闭与僵化之中，艺术与服饰文化的传承与发展就要受到极大的限制。将一个民族的创意与设计特质，历史性地还原到该民族原初的生活方式里，无疑是后来关于创意理解的人类学建构所需要的。在这里，民族文化的坚守还涉及多民族文化及其关系与文化相互认同的问题。

二、创意视觉化的文化语境

时尚创意与设计，离不开视觉化的表现与传达，虽然说，视觉并非服饰艺术唯一的相关感知觉，但视知觉往往具有某种不可或缺的规定性。因此，研究艺术首先要研究人的知觉结构及其特质。鲁道夫·阿恩海姆认为，在人类认识与审美活动之中，视觉思维可以说是最有效的知觉方式，这种知觉方式同样具备思维的理性功能。民族服饰创意的视觉化，既是一种建构社会意义的活动，同时这种视觉建构又离不开文化语境。应当注意到，对于民族元素及其创意与重构而言，视觉化的文化语境无疑是难以回避与缺失的基础。

在民族服饰与时尚的创意过程中，文化语境不仅是极其重要的历史性基础，同时还涉及不同族群的文化及其特质与关系。值得注意的是，"我们的过去经验、我们的教育和训练，以及我们的观点和其他种类的知识没有触及的感官意义上的纯粹知觉也不存在"。❶ 考虑到与思维活动的联系，艺术与审美有待于从完形出发，从视知觉及其同艺术、审美的关系分析上入手。应当说，视觉在艺术与审美中并不是孤立的活动，但如何从中读出某种特定意义却与文化的介入分不开。当然，视觉思维并不限于直接的知觉范围，广义的知觉还包括心理意象，以及这些意象与直接的感性之间的联系。

服饰艺术、民族时尚与文化创意，都离不开经由视觉表现及其所通达的文化旨趣。尽管说，视觉文化并非只是不依赖或局限于图像，但图像化却是视觉文化不可缺少的关涉，当然这种关涉并不能简单归结为某种既有的模式。因为，人们的读图既是开放性的、多元的，同时也是历史性的与语境性的。更重要的是，不能只是把图像看作一种再现的东西，亦即模仿物体的某种视觉化的人造物，而应把图像看作与那个物体密切相关的东西，甚至是和那个物体同一或等同的视觉替代物。

而且开放性既可吸收语言并使之文本化，又能将一个文本转化为另一文本的语境。在

---

❶ 阿诺德·贝林特.艺术与介入[M].李媛媛，译.北京：商务印书馆，2013：125.

民族时尚文本与文化语境之间，无疑是一种相互生成的生成论关系。艺术及其结构是在民族生存的文化语境下形成的，它自身就是人类活动的结构化及其在艺术上的表现，并由此显出民族文化的独特意味及其相关语境。应注意到，"文本的形式元素并不是独立存在的，它们需要一个语境使其有意义"。❶ 所谓的服饰元素及其文化创意，就是要将抽象的民族元素与文化底蕴，转化为可以通过视觉化来表现的东西，并使之在一定的社会、历史与文化语境里得到解读。

换言之，创意就是力图将原创性、变化性与陌生感，融入具有精神特质的民族元素与文化之中。艺术文本的生成不只是抽象元素的关联与聚集，而是对文化要素有意味的、象征的特定关切的表征。而且服饰与艺术创意生成的游戏，还彰显了其特有的文化及其生成本性。尤其是在不同社会与历史时期，人们的尚新心理与族群的集体无意识，生成了时尚艺术与文化的相关语境，并使时尚成为现代社会不可或缺的文化消费。在这里，时尚艺术与文化既可以映射一定的政治与经济形态，同时又能够将这种回应内化为文本性因素。

在一定程度上，新的视觉创意体现着文化生成与建构的趋势，它往往具有崭新性、前沿性与活跃性等特质。时尚艺术与文化总与大众传媒紧密地关联在一起，而大众传媒又是时尚生成与传播的重要发生地。实际上，创意的视觉化还与时代、文化密切相关。譬如，"在20世纪60年代前，帽子曾经是传统着装方式的一部分"。❷ 对于大众的日常生活来说，时装能够充分满足人们对时髦的消费欲求。但这种时尚消费及其生成与实现，与特定族群的习惯和文化语境分不开。与此同时，时尚对传统文化难免会起着某种解构与重构的作用。

在日常衣生活方式里，各个民族既把服饰作为自己的实用必需品，还通过着装来建构生活自身的社会与文化意义，这种建构活动的发生有时并未被人们充分意识到。譬如说，以嘻哈文化为代表的新一代时尚文化重在张扬个性与展现自我，这一精神必须通过各种创意与技能的展示来加以表现。而且时尚亚文化往往是偶发性的、变化性的与参与性的，似乎根本无须进行什么过于专业与特别的技术训练，在街头巷尾就可以直接从事与传播这种生活方式。除此之外，时尚与所有亚文化样式一般都具有天生的竞争性特质。

考虑到创意与设计通过交流与对话来表现意义，因此，这种文化语境也是时尚研究不可回避的问题。在当代，大众时尚文化大都主张自由自在与自我表达，一切创意往往从个人的感受与情绪出发，旨在生成与建构所谓自由的生活方式。在加利亚诺那里，时尚创意灵感来源包含各个时期与不同地方的多元文化。但在技术所规定的大众文化里，一致性正是民族创意与设计所应回应与消解的。创意视觉化涉及对观念与想法的视觉化转换，究竟如何生成与实现这种视觉化转换，就涉及一定族群的生活方式与文化及其关联。在视觉化转换过程中，还要关联到如何与特定文化相呼应的问题。

但还要注意到，不同族群的着装往往是一种日常生活事件，因此创意与设计有时也不

---

❶ 维多利亚·D.亚历山大.艺术社会学[M].章浩,沈杨,译.南京:江苏美术出版社,2009：329.

❷ Ffoulkes F. How to Read Fashion [M].New York: Rizzoli International Publications, Inc, 2013:176.

必过度考虑文化问题，至少不应对相关文化要素作太过直白的图像。消费时代是一个关注视觉奇观化的读图时代，但文字与语境的重要性却是不可忽视的。实际上，"在我们用引申含义谈论之处，无文字的民族都用本意来表达"。❶ 但无论是图像，还是文字，其实都是文本表现的重要样式。如何从无文字的民族生存与文化里解读创意，也是民族时尚设计所应思考的问题。传统的视觉中心主义所建构的中心化主体，难免在当代的视线编织中坍陷与解构。

在民族的读图、创意与表达过程中，文字产生了不可忽视的、深刻的社会与文化影响。如果说，雅克·拉康主要是在精神分析的欲望运作之中，把主体的建构（被建构）回置到其文化与语言环境。那么，米歇尔·福柯则在这种文化和语言环境里，揭示了主体被建构的权力运作机制。其实，现代视觉经验大都是一种技术化的视觉经验，世界其实正是通过这种视觉机器被编码成图像的。在创意过程中，如何将理念、观念，转换成与特定族群文化相关的视觉拟象是至关重要的。在这种拟象里，创意的视觉化所建构出的图像的仿真也有待于在文化上回应。视觉化为拟象生成提供了根本性语境，但拟象的生成还必须借助生成论及其经验。

不同于一般的现象学，生成论将经验的生成作为现象学的事情本身，并为走向经验的生成本身提供了可能。在这里，视觉化的观念还必须转化为一种视觉经验，这种视觉经验既是对理念的激活，也是观念视觉化的意义生成物。创意视觉风格的写实与写意既相互区分，又构成了在审美与文化上的交织与互文。当然，这种意义生成物正是创意拟象的根本性来源，同时它又把创意拟象重新置回到相关的文化语境里并加以建构。与此同时，一切相关的文化语境本身也可以被重构为民族时尚文本。

因此，文化语境在创意视觉化过程中具有极其重要的意义，它甚至是一切民族时尚创意与设计不可或缺的底蕴。其实，观念的视觉化从来都是语境性的，它将诸多因素作为理解的相关之物，而视觉化的观念则为创意提供了艺术与思想的经验。因为，"尽管艺术有表征的特质。这些例子在建立视觉交流体系中的意义勾勒了文化传统的重要性，说明了视觉与语言表达之间存在的真实的相似性"。❷ 人们还要借助特定的机器与技术，并通过图像来获得有关世界的视觉经验。在人们观看的行为、图像与机器之间，无疑还存在着复杂的生成性关联。对于民族创意的视觉化表现来说，可视性的理解与阐释也相关于各种非视觉的语境因素。

而且设计者想要表达的东西通过视觉经验，传递给每一个接收到这个经验的接收者，而视觉经验就起到了传达与文化传播的作用。视觉传达设计所涉及的领域确实不少，许多创意设计都属于视觉传达及其相关的领域。一般来说，视觉文化的视觉性关涉因其形象性、可感性，从而吸引了人们的眼球与各种相关的心理诉求。当然，不同族群对视觉经验的心

---

❶ 克洛德·列维-斯特劳斯. 看·听·读[M]. 顾嘉琛, 译. 北京：中国人民大学出版社, 2006：174.
❷ 罗伯特·莱顿. 艺术人类学[M]. 李东晔, 王红, 译. 桂林：广西师范大学出版社, 2009：129.

理与文化理解又有所区别。作为民族创意视觉化的语境，民族文化的构成及其开放性与生成性也是极其复杂的。与此同时，视觉世界与现实社会之间的冲突与和解，也是时尚创意与设计所应关注与回应的问题。

虽然不能简单地将西方文化归结为个体性的，也不能把东方文化仅仅看成是集体性的，但这两种文化的侧重与互补却是不可忽视的。而且不同的政治、经济与社会语境，造就与改变着艺术与文化的观念及其特质。正因为文化作为语境的介入，民族创意的视觉化才不至于陷入空洞，同时有助于克服视觉表象与内在精神的分离。在这个全球化时代，亟待促进东西方艺术与文化的互补和融合。正是由于东西方艺术与文化的相互生成，差异性与多元性的和谐共存才能得以真正实现。

还要看到，后现代主义的大众文化的无深度诉求，呼唤与推崇大叙事的艺术与话语风格，以及与之相关的、直观浅白的视觉文化样式。但只有在一定的文化语境及其特质里，民族的创意与设计才能避免陷入同质化的误区。创意与设计所涉及的元素无疑是多元的，并在各种文化语境里相互关切与彼此生成。而且创意视觉化与文化语境的关联是历史性的，同时还与族群或民族的存在和生活方式分不开。在"人类学之父"爱德华·伯内特·泰勒看来，在广义民族志意义上，文化或文明是作为社会成员的人们习得的复杂整体。因此，文化是人们长期沉淀与习得的精神生成之物。

其实，文化的历史性特质表明了它的连续与传承，这种传统有助于对粗暴干预与人为伪造的拒斥。而且文化的历史性与族群的生活方式、精神诉求密不可分。当然，"今天的生活风格不再止步于民族文化的边界，而是超越了边界，以同样的方式见之于其他文化之中"。❶ 在不同民族的创意视觉化过程中，简单的非此即彼的区分已不再具有实质性的意义，而应以民族之间的艺术交流与文化对话为生成论基础。应当说，每一个民族都有自身独特的文化符号，以及这些文化符码之中的民族精神图式。

当然，一切民族的独特文化符号，都可以通过民族符码与艺术表现来呈现。而且，社会群体中不同的成员都是具体与独特的衣生活者，这些个体基于自己的需要，根据对情景的判断和理解采取着装行为。在当今世界，还应认识到民族与传统的艺术样式，以及文化遗存多样性的意义与人文价值，这些都是民族服饰与时尚创意设计不可或缺的语境。但如果过于强调某一民族的优越感，而忽视了其他民族的差异性与文化特质，显然也是时尚艺术与文化建构不可取的。所有观念与创意都应以一定的视觉方式表现出来，但这种视觉表现是否在何种程度上切合观念则是设计极其重要的问题。

在这里，应以多种方式注重民族服饰与文化传统的保护，以免这些传统在全球化趋势下式微甚至消失。如果不同族群的人们能够共享多民族文化，充分尊重各民族的信仰与文化差异，那么就能够有效地沟通并消除民族隔阂，促成各民族在生存与文化上的相互理解

---

❶ 沃尔夫冈·韦尔施.重构美学[M].陆扬，张岩冰，译.上海：上海译文出版社，2002：197.

与包容。当然，服饰文化可以在不同的族群之间发生传播，既区分又融合着不同民族的生活方式。应当说，文本与语境的相互生成与转化也是值得注意的。作为特定民族时尚的语境的文化，还可以经由文本化成为其他民族的时尚性文本。毋庸置疑，任何创意及其视觉化表现，其实都以一定的社会、历史与文化为根本性语境。

三、民族创意文化的视觉表现

各个民族自身都有其特定的创意文化，这些创意文化既是设计所依凭的前提，同时又有待于经由视觉在服饰里得到生成与表现。可以说，创意文化是关于创意的理解与阐发，以及对创意的意义与价值加以揭示的文化。在创意与设计上，各个民族既有其不可替代的创意文化特质，同时又在不同艺术与文化的交流与对话里，促成对民族服饰艺术与创意设计的理解与阐释。因此，一方面，民族创意的视觉化离不开特定的文化语境；另一方面，民族创意文化本身也是经由视觉化而得到体现的。

毫无疑问，民族创意文化离不开视觉表现来加以实现，而这种表现是创意文化在时尚上的表征。其实，一切艺术与设计无不涉及如何将文化加以视觉表现的问题。在人的诸多感（知）觉中，视觉往往具有某种规定性与支配性。在这里，"视觉语言也像会话语言一样，从一种文化传到另一种文化，从一代传到另一代"。[1] 在民族服饰与时尚设计中，各种艺术流派与风格经由视觉化建构，构成了对创意文化加以揭示的独特维度。从学术规范上来看，一般把美术限定在视觉艺术上，当然，许多设计无不与视觉密切相关。还可以说，一切设计艺术都是以审美与文化为基础的。

不同于古典与近代的艺术，现代艺术强调艺术家的独特感受与个性表达，而各种艺术流派都从某一特定视角对时尚创意加以表现。在现代，对艺术与思想起规定作用的是存在而非理性。与此同时，视觉艺术与人的身体存在发生着密切的相关，身体性甚至成为设计不可或缺的存在论基础。因此可以说，视觉艺术与美在存在的境域里得以生成。也就是说，现代的视觉艺术表现与人们的生存状态是分不开的。在视觉文化时代，图像表征成为艺术创作与时尚传播的重要方式。不同于现代的存在，后现代的身体是在话语建构中生成的。

当然，艺术与设计不仅是视觉与审美的问题，它们还关联到心理与文化的问题。而且视觉的含义、表现及其与文化的关联，以及视觉艺术的内在精神图式与规定性，无不是在一定语境里历史性变化与生成的。有别于设计的同质化，各个民族创意文化的视觉表现，正是文化异质性生成与建构不可或缺的。其实，视觉生成物既可进入与成为文本，还可以作为对创意文化的一种回应而存在。混合、拼贴与全球地方化等多样性，是异质文化建构所不可或缺的方式。作为一种重要的产业样式，文化创意产业是一个迅速崛起、方兴未艾的新兴产业。

---

[1] 卡洛琳·M.布鲁墨.视觉原理[M].张功钤,译.北京：北京大学出版社，1987：55.

还应当注意到，民族创意文化产业既是创意产业向民族艺术与文化的延伸，同时也是创意产业及其民族文化特质的生成与建构之物。当然，创意产业是在欧美发达国家完成了工业化后，开始向服务业、高附加值的制造业转变。也就是说，发达国家很多老的产业与城市出现了衰落，这时就出现了经济转型与文化自身发展的需要。在20世纪60年代，欧美艺术与文化领域出现了大规模的社会运动，各种亚文化、流行文化与社会思潮等风起云涌，对传统的工业社会结构产生了很大的冲击。

与此同时，各种艺术与文化也在很大程度上影响了创意文化的视觉表现。在当代服饰与时尚创意中，设计师们更加重视差异以反对传统主流文化，极力张扬个性的解放与新感性的生成，并对以前普遍认为怪异的另类文化逐渐加以承认。与之相关的，艺术、设计与社会文化呈现出了日趋多元的格局，从而形成了有利于独特视觉创意发生的氛围。在创意文化的视觉表现里，时装所涉及的身体问题其实也是社会与文化的问题。20世纪末以来，尤其是从创意产业的概念面世起，人们就将其视为文化产业的重要构成。实际上，创意与文化产业既不同于传统的艺术与设计，又区分于一般产业的概念、属性与传统分类。

在观念与创意的视觉化过程中，尤其是在时尚图案与纹样的设计上，构思、排列、组合与混搭等手法都被广泛借鉴。就文化创意而言，民族时尚艺术的设计与审美表现，既以一定的技术手段与方式为基础，同时又总是与各种各样的文化相关涉。在如何培养人们创意能力的问题上，"我冒昧地建议，对于创意人来说，最好的训练方式就是研读社会科学领域的著作"。❶ 这是因为，对人文与社会科学著作的广泛研读，既可以对设计师建构理论视角有所助益，同时还能增进人们对特定族群的日常生活与文化的理解。

其实，正是不同的学科与思想，构成了创意视觉化的多元视角。与此同时，技术如何才能更好地揭示文化的根本意义，而不是将文化遮蔽在技术表现的表象之中，显然也是文化创意所要探究与解决的根本问题。在新媒体与大数据时代，民族创意文化的视觉表现是一个亟待关注的课题。如果说，一个创意虽然通过信息技术得到了快速传播，却没有深厚的文化语境作为底蕴与背景，也不可能是一种优良的创意与文化传播，更难以对品牌文化及其精髓加以揭示与彰显。实际上，对民族创意文化的视觉表现的审美评价，是与不同民族的心理与文化分不开的。

在民族创意文化的表现与传播之中，还涉及商品化、消费文化与创意产业的关系问题，同时还关系到对不同的民族及其文化的跨文化传播的理解与阐释。而且，东西方不同的服饰理念与文化，难免构成对时尚创意表现的独特理解，如东方的含蓄与西方的奔放等。还要注意的是，时尚市场的诱导可能破坏创意的自主性原则。正因如此，如何处理市场、商业与创意的复杂关系，对于文化产业的发展也将产生极其深远的影响。如果一味地以商业、市场与消费为导向，往往会削弱创意可能揭示的精神特质，从而导致创意产业丧失所赖以

---

❶ 詹姆斯·韦伯·扬.创意的生成[M].祝士伟，译.北京：中国人民大学出版社，2014：36.

存在的日常生活基础与特定的文化语境。

随着大众艺术修养与审美趣味的提升，那些缺乏精神与文化特质的时尚表象将难以受到人们的青睐。当然，还应对大众艺术、审美经验与时尚文化加以反思与批判。而且，不能简单地将文化创意产业与文化产业作为等同概念来理解，但视觉信息及其传达却是它们不可或缺的构成。可以说，"时尚领域的多样性正是数量庞大的视觉信息的产物，这些视觉信息每天喋喋不休地对我们进行视觉轰炸"。❶ 在这里，视觉所实现的正是对现实的各种图像性重构，从而成为对创意文化的一种直观性表征。基于新的艺术理念、审美视角与文化语境，促成民族文化创意的生成与当代建构是创意设计的内在诉求。

在创意文化及其视觉表现之中，民族的观念与思想的创新无疑是根本之所在。因为，文化创意是依靠创意人的智慧与独特思维，以及当代的理论与思想对传统元素加以揭示，从而产生出既有可行性又不乏文化意味的想法。任何一种时尚创意与设计活动，都离不开特定的族群及其文化语境，以及在此语境里对民族精神图式的视觉表现。在不同的民族或族群之间，创意文化及其与精神图式的生成性关联，显然也不乏在理解与阐释上存在差异。毫无疑问，所有创意从来都不是对传统文化的简单拿来与复制。

应当说，创意往往依靠人们的灵感、想象力与求异思维等，以及各种表现手法在当下语境里来对传统文化元素加以重构。一个民族的时尚除了具有传统的艺术与文化要素外，还必须建构与表现出特定的时代感与当下意识。因此，创意可以从面料、款式、色彩与细节等入手，但这些层面上的表现都与技术、文化密切相关。纵观中国服装史，由于中国幅员辽阔与民族众多，传统服饰艺术与文化呈现出了极大的差异性。实际上，民族的历史性与文化脉络，往往成为民族先民们所恪守的传统谱系。

在服饰创意与设计上，有的民族在质和形上与其他民族看似并无区别，但通过仔细观察还是可以发现某些值得关注的差异。譬如，汉服历史悠久，有礼服和常服之分。虽然主要形制变化不大，但汉服款式众多，且历朝历代皆有其特点。从具体形制上来看，主要有"上衣下裳"制、"深衣"制（把上衣下裳缝连起来）、"襦裙"制等类型。对汉服创意文化的视觉化理解与阐释，离不开特定的形制、仪规与服饰文化。在创意与设计过程中，汉族服饰也因为受到过其他民族的影响而发生变化。

考虑到民族服饰的款式多样、形制各异，应充分关注不同民族的生活方式与文化差异。例如，北方往往严寒多风雪，再加上森林、草原宽阔，北方少数民族多靠狩猎、畜牧为生；南方湿热多雨，山地与盆岭相间分布，生活在其间的少数民族多从事农耕。在传统服饰的设计中，北方与南方的地理与环境差异是不可忽视的问题。甚至可以说，不同的自然环境、生产和生活方式，在一定程度上生成了特定的民族性格、心理与审美文化，当然也就有了各不相同的服饰风格、特点与视觉设计表现。

---

❶ 拉斯·史文德森.时尚的哲学[M].北京：北京大学出版社，2010：147.

比如，生活在高原草场并从事畜牧业的蒙古族、藏族、哈萨克族、柯尔克孜族、塔吉克族等少数民族，一般的穿着与日常服饰多取之于牲畜的皮毛，在衣领、袖口、衣襟、下摆镶以色布或细毛皮。哈萨克族的"库普"是用驼毛絮里的大衣，十分轻暖。应当说，哈萨克族的服装风格是宽袍大袖、厚实庄重。不同于北方少数民族，南方少数民族地区宜于植麻种棉，自织麻布和土布是衣裙的主要用料。所用工具虽然简陋，但织物精美，花纹奇丽。因天气湿热，需要袒胸露腿，衣裙多短窄轻薄，其风格生动活泼，式样繁多，各不雷同。在创意文化的视觉表现上，东西南北都有其相关于特定地域的时尚样式。

对于日常衣生活的理解与阐释，显然是各民族创意文化的视觉化表现不可或缺的。其实，诸多各不相同的民族性特质，正是民族视觉表现的文化人类学基础。对于不同地域与民族来说，服饰与着装风格的多种多样与彼此区分，无疑构成了少数民族服饰艺术与文化。在不同民族的创意文化及其视觉表现上，各种形制与风格建构着各自的审美习惯。在现当代，作为西方主流文化的所谓他者，富有东方意味的视觉图像正在成为时尚界的一种异国情调，这种异国情调的图式与风格又反过来影响着东方创意文化与时尚设计。

一般来说，少数民族服装用料多，装饰烦琐，工艺复杂，制作困难，穿着不便，难于洗涤。因此，许多少数民族往往改穿汉族服装，个别地区甚至已经见不到民族服装。针对这一严峻情况，有待于抓紧抢救与整理少数民族服饰资源，以免导致富有特色的民族服饰文化彻底消失。实际上，"视觉文化在过去常被看作分散了人们对文本和历史之类的正经事儿的注意力，而现在却是文化和历史变化的场所"。❶ 与此同时，视觉文化与文化研究的关联性正在日益受到关注。可以说，民族性特质既是现阶段少数民族服饰文化所要面临的问题，也是现阶段少数民族服饰艺术与文化重构的设计课题。

基于民族服饰及其文化特质，创意与设计应当力求大方与雅致，同时还要美观、简洁与适用，这样便于满足人们生产、生活与审美的需要。将文化与人的关系纳入设计之中，对民族创意文化的视觉化无疑是不可忽视的。这里存在的问题在于，在视觉创意与设计多元化表现中，不少设计师只注重艺术效果表面的华丽，往往忽视了对内在精神图式的理解与阐发。在时尚创意过程中，任何视觉化都应成为对精神图式的独特揭示。为此，理论视角与思想建构仍然有待于深度介入。

实际上，各民族或国家服装文化往往具有鲜明的精神特质，如阿富汗披掩全身的斗篷式女装帕儿锥、日本的和服、印度的女装纱丽、印度尼西亚男女皆穿的围裹裙莎笼、苏格兰的男式短褶裙凯尔特、夏威夷的直统型连衣裙穆穆袍，以及印第安民族的披风式外衣庞乔等。不同民族间的时尚对话与文化交流，无疑是民族创意的视觉表征所不可或缺的。而对各民族时尚的解读与阐释，也必须被纳入民族服饰创意与视觉化过程中。尽管说，视觉化由于界定的暧昧而难以承担起对精神与文化的表述，但视觉化所形成的从不可见到可见

---

❶ 尼古拉斯·米尔佐夫.视觉文化导论[M].倪伟，译.南京：江苏人民出版社，2006：39.

的系列与谱系，则仍然是精神与文化特质的揭示与阐发所不可或缺的。

在视觉化的表现过程中，既可以形成与建构影像化、虚拟性的新质，又将视觉化的生成物渗透到"不可见"之物中，从而重新理解与阐释视觉文化的思想与文化语境。梅洛-庞蒂强调了视觉与所有知觉的身体性关联与基础。但问题在于，除了不同的个人、族群所看见的世界外，向世界本身的切近是一个无止境的现象学还原过程。在后现代主义语境里，在二元对立视域下的图像的模仿、反映等本质观，发生了式微甚至失去了基本的合法性。实际上，笛卡尔式视觉中心主义也难免被颠覆与解构。

应当说，近代的理性与感性及其二元分立，在现代的存在论里已丧失了根本性的意义与旨趣。对于创意的视觉表现及其民族性来说，各个民族的精神图式与独特形式感无疑是有差异的。在东方主义的问题上，"批评东方主义的西方批评家常常用对抗性的术语来描述东方主义，因此，这种长存不灭的吉卜林式论调就将东西方理解为永远相互敌对的两极"。❶ 如果只是借用语言哲学的观点与思想，从而把图像理解与把握为一种语言符号，这也依然不可忽视民族间的习俗与文化差异。即使到了后现代，关于精神、创意及其视觉化的表现与传达，仍然会不断地陷入二元分立的问题与困境之中。

因此，对不同的视觉与图像的差异性的无视，难免会遮蔽视觉表征及其独特性本身，特别是这种独特性的人类学牵涉及其意义。在后现代艺术与文化语境里，仿佛为大众制造了一个虚拟的、拟真的幻象，而世界的视觉再现的真实性往往被质疑。在一定程度上，视觉实现的是对理性与秩序等观念的解构，从而导致视觉的异化、虚拟与茫然狂欢。其实，后现代思潮与消费文化的共谋，促使视觉再现的真实感被瓦解与解构，从而导致了人类陷入前所未有的视觉危机之中。正因如此，对民族创意文化及其视觉化表征的研究，需要我们对视觉表象问题进行分析与克服。

第三节 民族性的生成与时尚的视觉表现

在时尚创意及其表现方面，民族性的东西并非什么实体性的存在者，同时也不是所谓固定不变的现成品，而是处于不断变化与生成中的建构之物。对创意的视觉表现的理解与阐发，无疑是时尚设计得以表达的文化基础，也是时尚文化及其传播与接受的前提。实际上，并没有一个为所有人所接受的民族性，民族性从来都是在不断建构与重构中来显现自身的。时尚的创意设计与视觉性表现，不仅要对一般的设计问题加以分析与探究，还要针对民族的存在及其生成性特征给予阐释。时尚创意不仅关涉特定的民族存在，还涉及众多民族之间的文化沟通与跨文化理解的问题。应当说，揭示民族性元素的精神意义与文化价值，以及它们究竟是如何在历史性的语境里生成自身的，对于民族服饰与创意设计来说无

---

❶ J.J.克拉克.东方启蒙：东西方思想的遭遇[M].于闽梅，曾祥波，译.上海：上海人民出版社，2011：299.

疑是不可或缺的。

一、创意的民族性及其生成

无论是一般的自由艺术，还是服饰设计与时尚艺术，它们无不是人类文化及其在特定领域里得以展现的重要样式。在西方的文明与文化语境里，视觉艺术一直占有支配与主导的地位，并对现代时尚创意与设计产生着重要的规定性影响。因此，对服饰与时尚创意的视觉性表现，就成了创意文化与产业所不可忽视的问题。在这种视觉性表达与传递之中，特定民族或人群是应当加以考虑的人类学的存在。创造性的民族性特质并非固定不变的实体，而是处于不断建构与重构的生成之物。在这里，民族性被表征和阐明为民族自身存在的独特性。同时，既然说民族性是一种生成性的特质，那么对这种民族性的揭示也是不断生成的。

在民族时尚创意之中，民族性特质之于创意的规定虽然极其重要，但也不能将这种规定性看成是一成不变的决定论。而且时尚创意总是与一定民族、群体的存在及其文化语境分不开的。还要看到，"对人类外表的审美关注，还包括美发、服装，或文身、身体绘画与饰物等修饰形式。"❶ 但这种审美关注及其理解与阐释，又离不开各个民族的精神与文化特质。因此可以说，民族性及其与精神的生成性关联，甚至成了时尚文化创意的重要来源。在民族时尚创意及其表现方面，涉及众多的因素与各种复杂的关联，以及与之相关又无所不在的多元文化语境。

毫无疑问，时尚的文化创意如何与民族元素发生关联，应给予认真关注与深入探究。时尚创意的发生与艺术表现，关切于一切观念、想法的视觉化问题。因为时尚艺术主要是经由视觉化来表现的，这里也就涉及民族元素及其视觉性重构。民族的生存及其民族性特质，既是民族文化及其建构的根本性基础，也是民族时尚创意的思想与观念之源。但这并不是说，存在着一个单一的民族性特质，而这种民族性又以一种简单的方式规范着时尚创意的发生与表现。

倒不如说，民族性渗透在一切民族时尚创意的根基里，以及所有与时尚相关的各种元素及其构成之中。与此同时，任何民族的民族性其实都是非实体性的。民族性在时尚中之所以重要，这是因为，"在当今这个充满异质标准和混乱的机械喧闹的时代里，这个或那个民族的文化都以许多方式强烈地吸引着我们。"❷ 还可以说，民族性是一个民族时尚创意的人类学基础，同时也是时尚表现试图揭示的精神与文化特质。而且，不同民族的服饰与文化不仅相互区分，且又在共同生活与跨文化的交往里彼此关联。例如，在隋唐时代，不同民族的服饰与文化已经有了显著的借鉴与融合。

作为民族艺术与文化的根本性规定，民族性以自身的生成、建构与艺术、文化相呼应。更为重要的是，民族元素及其向时尚艺术的介入与渗透，还应考虑究竟如何实现其时尚化

---

❶ 范丹姆.审美人类学：视野与方法[M].李修建，向丽，译.北京：中国文联出版社，2015：37.
❷ 露丝·本尼迪克.文化模式[M].何锡章，黄欢，译.北京：华夏出版社，1987：15.

的问题,以及怎样才能通过特定艺术表现来获得这种时尚感。例如,在高田贤三的时装设计里,和服与东方民族服饰的形制成为人类学基础,他也广泛地借鉴了世界各地的服饰风格。在民族的时尚创意与文化建构之中,要充分注重民族元素及其特征的揭示与阐释。与此同时,在对民族独特性加以强调的基础上,时尚创意才能建立民族性基础与民族文化底蕴,而这种民族精神特质与文化又应由时尚化的方式来表达。

但不同民族的衣着与文化间的界限,从来都不是分离与固定不变的,而是处于彼此借鉴与历史性变化之中。在一定地域范围内,共同生活的人们往往不乏类似的生活方式,同时还离不开一些相似的风俗与文化。而且,处于一定生态与文化语境里共同生活的人们,在思维方式、生活方式、行为习惯,以及风俗习惯上可能与其他族群区别开来。即使在现当代的时尚艺术里,不同民族密切相关的文化构成也得到了表现与回应。在人之所以成为人的历程里,这种民族性区别和文化差异的存在,往往可以通过共同生活的整个族群体现出来。族群与族群之间存在的区别与差异,其实就是各个民族不可或缺的民族性特质。

随着社会与文化的历史生成,各个族群内部都建构出了特有的习惯与传统,族群的成员大都会受到这种习惯与传统的影响,但不同族群的习惯与传统的差异并不是绝对的。因此,"可见民族融合、服饰互渗等方面的跨文化传播,对于隋唐王室来说,不只是统御天下的政治谋略,而且从某种角度来说是与生俱来的生活渗透与文化承传"。❶ 各个民族生活方式与着装行为的发生,总是以自身的民族特质为基础,同时又与其他民族在衣生活领域区分开来。在原始社会,促使成员共同生活的原动力或许就是迫于生存的需要。

也就是说,离群索居的个人很难独立地生存与生活下来,一定地域内的人们会自然地汇集在一起过共同生活。在精神寄托与文化习得上,族群成员往往倾向于认同本民族的传统,在衣生活上大多会沿袭已有的着装范式。因此,民族意识和民族文化构成了民族内部连接与整合的精神性基础。这里的历史性并非编年史,而是历史的基础与根本,艺术与服饰可以说正是在历史性方面与民族的存在相关切的。例如,景颇族男子穿着白色短上衣、缠白头巾,头巾两端饰有绒球,女子一般穿着黑平绒紧身短衣和红色毛织花筒裙。对于艺术与服饰设计来说,一种民族性如果要生成与成为自身的话,无疑就应基于特定的社会、历史与文化语境。

在不同民族的生存与相互交往之中,它们之间的相互影响是一个不得不面对与回应的艺术与文化传播问题。但绝对不能以某一民族的艺术与文化,来压制与取代其他民族的艺术与文化。比如说,"北魏的拓跋氏全面采纳汉人姓氏、朝政礼仪和服饰,这被视为高度的汉化"。❷ 各民族的彼此尊重与平等交流,显然是设计及其文化传播得以发生的理性基础。作为文化的一种原始样式,原始文化是艺术发生的本源与原始规定,也就是说,艺术本身就是原始文化的生成与建构之物。如早期的面具,它就多用于宗教与巫术活动之中,后来

---

❶ 张志春.中国服饰文化[M].北京:中国纺织出版社,2009:228.
❷ 杜朴,文以诚.中国艺术与文化[M].北京:北京联合出版公司,2014:131.

逐渐变成一种戏曲、舞蹈的道具。在这里，神话往往以想象性、寓言式的方式对自然规律加以解释。

对象征性地存在于特定文化里的故事，以及这些故事与其他文化里类似故事的关系，所进行的研究与阐释构成了神话学的基本话题，这为创意的民族性及其建构提供了话语基础。作为一种文化样式，服饰揭示与彰显了人们对非功利审美的诉求，它与民族文化处于相互的生成与建构之中，而不是任何简单的部分与整体之间的关系。因为，整体与部分的逻辑关系如包含与被包含等，难免遮蔽服饰与文化之间相互生成的本性。当然，民族艺术的表现及其审美经验，并不一定是纯粹非功利的与自由的，它往往与实用、生活发生着密切的关联，民间工艺就是如此。

但在服饰的设计过程中，既要关注功能性诉求，又应超越这种实用性特质，而注重审美与民族文化的建构。在创意及其与民族性的生成性关联里，共时性与历时性之间也可以相互生成。而且民族性的历史性存在及其在创意里的揭示，其实也可以看作民族艺术与文化的重构过程。譬如，作为一种民族文化样式，土家族义化是土家人的生存状况、群体心理与民族此在等独特的产物。毫无疑问，民族文化意味离不开民族的历史、文化的遗存，甚至可以说，这种文化就存在于民族的历史性发生过程中，虽然它经常被隐藏与遮蔽在民族的日常生活方式里。

在一定意义上，正是各民族风俗与习惯的差异，构成了民族文化的独特存在与精神特质。各民族的风俗与习惯本身，都是以歌曲、舞蹈与服饰等样式来表现的。各民族往往通过自己的风俗与习惯，来保护和传承自己民族的文化艺术。有的民族服饰相对稳定，变化不大，比如，"罗马尼亚的民族服饰，在经历了多少个世纪的发展后基本上没有发生变化，基本的风格和款式一直沿袭到了现在"。❶ 但许多服饰艺术表现方式与着装传统，都难免在与其他民族的共同生活中有所改变。在民族艺术与文化之中，不仅体现了民族性与集体无意识，又不乏世界性艺术与文化的民族性基础。因此，从艺术的文本、语境回到民族艺术生成自身，就是从民族性的视角去揭示与阐发艺术及其生成。

在民族服饰与时装的设计上，应充分考虑不同族群的生活方式与接受习惯，以及民族文化积淀所形成的无意识的民族性。任何民族及其民族性的生成，都与该民族的集体记忆和集体无意识分不开。各种民族元素的相互关切与互文性关联，显现出艺术与文化的独特风格与精神特质。各民族艺术与时尚的不断生成，在本性上是建构与消解的相互生成，并由此揭示与敞开民族性的历史性发生。当然，特定的文化语境也不是固定不变的，而是随着族群的生存与文化的历史性而流变。在时尚文本及其文化语境的生成之中，民族性对设计及其审美风格的形成具有独特的规定性与文化影响。

艺术与服饰的生成性创意游戏，彰显了特有的民族文化及其生成性。虽然完全脱离民

---

❶ 吴妍妍.欧洲民族服饰概论[M].北京：中国纺织出版社，2016：28.

族及其历史性的设计是不可能的，但又不能把时尚归结为对民族性的简单图解。在这里，民族性特质的历史生成及其揭示，不仅使民族艺术与文化成为重要的艺术与文化样式，同时也彰显了不同民族的艺术与文化间的区别。欧美乃至世界各国或各地区的时装，其实无不以其特定的民族性特质相互区分，但这些民族性特质又在不断的时尚化中得到独特表现，而且不同的民族性之间的边界往往还因交织而变得模糊与游移。

作为一种具象性的创作活动，服饰设计还不可避免地涉及民族性与时代性的关系问题。应当说，艺术文本的民族性及其文化特质，其实并不只是诸多抽象元素的集合与关联，而是具有各种要素及其独特关系的有意味的象征，以及时尚创意的特定关切的一种审美与文化表征。实际上，"世人皆知，意大利时装细腻的色彩搭配和面料运用甚至超过了法国时装，他们出产的毛织物更厚，也更加柔软"。❶ 但对于民族性特质的这种符码象征，又应不断还原与回归到民族的存在与日常生活中。与此同时，设计活动还必须面对族群身份及其认同问题，以及这些民族文化认同在当代的接受与实现。

在民族时尚创意过程中，设计师要尽可能关注与回应消费者的习俗与文化。因为只有这样，时尚的表现才能对民族性加以揭示与阐发，以及把创意与观念建基在这种民族性之上，并将之转换成一种基于视觉历史性的当代时尚艺术。而且民族的时尚创意及其在文化上的认同，无疑是一个民族性与国民性认同的文化前提，但不同民族间的开放与相互包容，则构成了跨文化传播的基础。针对全球化可能带来的同质化问题，民族时尚的创意与文化认同显然是不可或缺的。

在反对西方文化霸权方面，这种民族艺术与文化认同具有重要的意义与价值。在这里，民族时尚创意所关联的元素众多且关系复杂，各元素又以特定方式与整个民族文化相关联，同时民族性元素及其相互关联也是不可忽视的问题。"通常在时尚研究中，种族的研究会涉及一些明显的体征问题，如肤色、发质、面部特征等。"❷ 而且种族的人类学体征无疑是创意民族性生成不可回避的。应当说，民族元素及其文化彰显了创意的潜在特质，也影响着创意的艺术品质与特定文化意义的生成。作为艺术家的一种自由创造，艺术相关于艺术家的审美经验与精神世界。

但是，艺术并非仅停留在艺术家的精神世界里，因为艺术总是会涉及内在图式的外在表现问题。尤其是当艺术走出了唯美主义的象牙塔之后，它更加广泛与深入地介入了社会生活领域。与此同时，艺术与各种文化发生多维度、多层面的关联，这种内在精神图式的意义就会从与视觉相关的诸多方面呈现出来。如果说，艺术的这种社会、历史与文化关联，存在于一切样式的艺术表现与创意设计之中，那么这种关联又会在时尚艺术里表征得更加显著。在人类学与社会学的语境里，民族时尚创意与族群生活方式及其关联性的研究，对创意的民族性及其揭示与阐发无疑是不可或缺的。

---

❶ 苏·詹金·琼斯.时装设计[M].张翎，译.北京：中国纺织出版社，2009：46.
❷ 苏珊·B.凯瑟.时尚与文化研究[M].郭平建，等译.北京：中国轻工业出版社，2016：62.

二、民族元素的视觉生成与表现

任何民族元素的生成与存在，都涉及民族内在精神与文化特质的构成，并基于构成的开放性与视觉表现生成各种社会与文化意义。人类通过自身创造的视觉形象来传达信息与想法，因此视觉一直是人与人之间相互交流的基本手段。毫无疑问，视觉艺术对传统文化的继承与当代表征，以及对人类精神生活的建构都具有不可忽视的意义。时尚与社会、文化的关联有助于对创意与设计的深入研究。与此同时，对民族元素的发掘、揭示与当代重构，在民族服饰艺术与设计中具有极其重要的意义。

在这里，时尚创意不仅涉及文本自身的表现形式，同时也与符码的社会与文化象征意义相关联。在文字或符码文本里，视觉表象的独特性往往隐藏在抽象性之中。但要意识到，民族元素的视觉化表现无不从文本本身出发。"比如，符号学把每一个图画形象都当作文本，一个编码的、有意图的、习俗的符号，它似乎有意削弱图画形象的独特性，使其成为可阐释对象的天衣无缝的网络的组成部分。"❶ 当然，图像本身就是一种文本样式，但它又与文字文本有所不同，但又与之构成互文。与此同时，视觉艺术表现及其独特的符码与旨趣相关于特定的社会与文化认同。

但在民族元素的视觉生成过程中，既涉及艺术表现与审美经验的问题，同时也关联到不同理解与认同的关系。而且，民族元素与时尚创意的视觉生成与表现，本身就关涉如何将非视觉性的东西可视化的问题，以及这种视觉表现如何从传统中获得重构的问题。如保加利亚中西部的服装所使用的抽象纹样与现代审美观并不冲突。虽然说，民族元素被理解与阐释为揭示与彰显民族精神与文化特质的基本单元，但这种理解与阐释却不能受制于简单与传统的元素论的困境。正如通常所说，视觉文化研究的往往是现代文化和后现代文化，但如此看重视觉及其审美经验的重要性，却并非只是强调视觉而排除与摒弃其他感觉。

在传统的视觉艺术与表现方式里，设计师对经典构图或样式加以揭示与阐发，这既涉及民族元素的创意与表现的一般问题，也关联到构图所采取的手法与独特的重构方式。在民族元素的创作过程中，基于视觉性的表现方式而生成特定形式，进而以这种视觉形式来表达与传递民族的精神与文化。当然，不同的视觉表现方式所表征出来的文化意味也有所差异。视觉语言主要由视觉基本元素和设计原则构成，它们都是具有传递意义的规范或符号系统，以及这些符号所指涉的社会、历史与文化在意义上具有相关性。

毫无疑问，视觉元素是揭示与重构民族元素及其精神与文化所不可或缺的。在这里，设计的原则一般指布局、对比、节奏、平衡与统一，它们是用来组织和运用基本元素传达意义的原则和方法。譬如，"美洲西北岸的人形面具和图腾柱已经成为某种文化遗产的象征，随着旅游观光者的热潮席卷了整个世界"。❷ 当然，各种艺术与设计的方法与原则及其在民

---

❶ W.J.T. 米歇尔. 图像学：形象，文本，意识形态[M]. 陈永国，译. 北京：北京大学出版社，2012：197.
❷ 约翰·马克. 面具：人类的自我伪装与救赎[M]. 杨洋，译. 广州：南方日报出版社，2011：144.

族服饰上的借鉴，无疑应与特定的民族文化、各种相关语境关联起来。因为只有借助文化语境，才能表现与阐释视觉文本所蕴含的精神性特质。

实际上，设计师根据各种各样的需要与独特的文化诉求，选择特定的材料、表现形式与技法风格，在一定的语境里揭示与生成各种元素之间的关系，从而形成能够传达特定生活与文化意义的构图与样式。而且，所有被建构出的构图与样式无疑还会为以后的设计提供借鉴的图式。在现代服饰设计中，民族性视觉元素的构成是多元的、可变的与生成性的，设计师往往依据实际功能、社会符码与文化旨趣的诉求，针对性地运用点、线、面、色或将其加以整合运用。除此之外，还要不断挖掘与阐发视觉表现的各种可能性，包括视觉的吸引、刺激、昭示与情感的表达等，以便更有效地揭示与表达特有的艺术特质和文化旨趣。

在鲁道夫·阿恩海姆看来，人们从艺术形式中所知觉到的张力样式，正是对象的刺激力与生理力的关联。针对各种民族元素及其生成性构成，视觉往往都具有建构与重构及其交织性特质。根据阿恩海姆所说，任何艺术作品的物理样式，都会唤起一种与它的力结构相同的力的样式。甚至可以说，设计就是根据点、线、面等的形态及其审美关联，以及色彩的情感特征进行创作并表达受众诉求的。基于古典艺术的传统标准与审美文化，经由主题明确、色彩匀称、比例和谐等一系列的范畴与概念而得到规定与表征。

一般来说，古典艺术是一种与优美、典雅相关的艺术样式，此外还涉及崇高、壮美等。在不同的民族衣生活方式里，某种艺术表现与审美可能传递出并不一致的意义与旨趣。有别于古典的艺术样式，现代主义艺术强调的是艺术与审美的自律。"对民族服饰构造方法的借用，可以从两个层面来看，一是服装外轮廓的启发，二是服装内部构造方法的局部借鉴。"❶ 但这两个方面的借鉴与重构又是密切相关的，并共同成为民族时装设计的重要方式与手法。艺术表现进入社会与日常生活，无疑是难以避免与不可逆转的审美趋势，这就相关于艺术文本自身的开放性特质，以及由此所关联到的社会、历史与文化语境。

应当说，古典与近代艺术的表现方式与审美诉求，无疑是与近代认识论及其文化相关的，但这种认识论在现当代不再具有原初的规定性。而且，审美文化既相关于艺术、审美与各种文化及其生成性关联，也是文化对艺术创作、鉴赏与批评及其审美经验的阐释。与此同时，对艺术与设计的解读与阐释，显然离不开各个民族特有的审美文化与生活方式。考虑到现当代艺术表现与审美经验的变化，反艺术、反审美成了一种应对传统艺术与审美的独特方式，它们在本性上其实就是一种新的艺术与审美经验的生成过程。

在某种意义上来说，反艺术、反审美是一种另类的艺术和审美，它们既是对传统艺术、传统审美及其标准的突破，同时也把艺术、审美拓展到与存在、文本的生成性关联上。当代艺术所生成与建构的审美经验，既是一种关切存在及其本性的经验，同时也是一种欲望及其话语表征的文本经验。而且，当代艺术的审美经验影响着视觉文化意味的独特生成，

---

❶ 马蓉.民族服饰语言的时尚运用[M].重庆：重庆大学出版社，2009：52.

以及在当代语境里对民族元素的视觉表现与文化阐释。一般来说，传统艺术主要诉诸人们的静观与直觉，它在实质上并不依赖于欣赏者行为的参与和介入，同时也没有把审美观建立在艺术家与大众的对话与互动上。

在当代艺术表现与时尚设计里，各种民族元素被广泛地引入从建构、解构到重构的过程中。虽然说，关于艺术与审美的规定，一直是西方形而上学致思与探究的根本问题，但究竟何为艺术与审美的本性，无疑仍然是一个极其困难的学术与理论问题。特别是进入当代后，基于对西方形而上学体系与传统的深入批判，艺术与审美及其本质与规定的问题，无疑也受到了严峻的挑战与彻底的解构。作为形而上学在艺术存在中的一种样式，艺术形而上学同样受到了不断的、彻底的怀疑与强烈的批判。

就创意与设计来说，在不同的民族与时代里，裙装都有着彼此相异的长短与艺术风格，这样就构成了时尚视觉表现的多元性与流变性的特质。而且一切时尚的轮回既具有一定节奏与周期，但又在不断地改变与突破以往的各种限制，从而生成与建构出一种意想不到的陌生化审美效果。应当意识到，视觉文化是一种以视觉感知为表现方式的文化样式，它既是视觉印象在文化上的直观表征与阐释，也是文化对视觉事件及其发生的历史性沉淀。但这里的视觉艺术与文化及其观念的密切相关，并不局限于任一或特定民族的生活与文化传统，而是关切所有民族艺术与文化及其跨文化传播的特质。

当然，当代艺术的存在更加强调当下发生的创意观念，而不是传统的、静态的与封闭的理性概念，这其实正是民族元素视觉表现的生成本性之所在。"作为现代消费者，人们通过时装所表现的空间和身体关系建构了他们的民族身份。"❶ 关于民族的服饰艺术与创意表现，显然不能仅停留在视觉艺术的表象层面，还必须进入精神与文化的深层结构加以揭示。这里的困境在于，当代艺术在文化上难免表现为对表象的关注，从而生成了一种基于表象的视觉符码与文化表征系统，这种文化表象又不得不面对艺术的当下发生。

作为一种直观的呈现方式，艺术的视觉表象既是对艺术的显现，同时又是对艺术自身的遮蔽与掩盖。因此，民族元素的视觉表现与时装的生成，就是对那些曾被遮蔽的意义的一种时尚化揭示与阐释。在这里，民族艺术通常包括本土艺术表现样式，以及那些吸收外来因素而后将其化入本族的艺术形式与传统。例如，中华民族的艺术就是由各个民族共同创造的，并具有各自特色的多元一体的艺术及各自的传统。还要看到，民族视觉与文化的这种相互生成性，不仅是与民族的存在、生活相关联的，更建构在艺术文本的社会与文化语境里。值得注意的是，民族服饰的当代创意与设计，也为民族元素及其艺术表现提供了新的可能性。

基于图像与艺术的视觉文化，其实也是艺术观念的一种特定沉淀，往往是经由视觉表象来揭示与实现的，这亟待不断突破表象难以摆脱的二元分立。在民族艺术与表现的过程

---

❶ 珍妮弗·克雷克.时装的面貌——时装的文化研究[M].舒允中，译.北京：中央编译出版社，2000：41.

中，视觉表象方式和文化传统的交织与相互关联，无疑是民族服饰与时尚创意设计的基本构成。以艺术与服饰的民族元素为线索，通过对表层及其所关联的审美意蕴与精神的剖析，还有助于揭示与阐释时尚创意的民族性及其结构性特质。随着艺术与时尚的跨文化传播的兴起与发展，本土文化与外来文化的区分与边界也日趋模糊。

应当说，少数民族艺术指存在于少数民族居住地域内，为少数民族所创造与保存的各种艺术门类与形式，包括传统的与现代的诸多艺术样式及其在当代的重构。但在研究以汉族为人类学存在的民族艺术的时候，显然不能忽视其他民族艺术的存在与相互影响。其实，任何民族都有其不可替代的精神与文化特质，同时又与其他民族处于密切交往与互文之中。与此同时，艺术是观念形态或精神图式得以表现的重要形式，它往往贯穿于各民族的演变与历史过程中。而对民族艺术与文化的理解与生成的阐发，又是与民族元素的视觉表现密不可分，且各民族的元素在视觉与文化上都不是单一与孤立的。

各种元素与民族艺术、文化的关系，显然是相互交织与相互生成的关联。在民族元素的创意与视觉表现过程中，交流、对话与相互的借鉴无疑也是不可或缺的。换言之，每一种元素无不关涉整个的民族性的存在与存在本身。毫无疑问，还可以通过对民族元素的揭示与阐发，来窥探它们之于艺术与文化研究的意义与旨趣。但应意识到，时尚从来都不只隶属于某一特定的民族，各个民族都有属于自己的视觉样式与审美风格，通过特定视觉图像的表现来呈现本民族时尚的精神关联。

对于各个民族来说，服饰的民族间性既可表征与阐发为某种差异，同时还可理解为视觉与文化上的融通感。在墨西哥的早期文明里，神祇在神话与传说中往往被描绘成人形。而且，"数量众多的地方神祇需要通过服饰上的细微差别区分开来，服饰是大部分神祇肖像的主体"。[1] 因此，神话与传说也为服饰艺术与文化的研究提供了视觉的文本与语境。创意所关联的传统艺术与文化上的民族间性，包括少数民族之间、少数民族与汉族之间的民族间性，以及不同民族间艺术与服饰相互的影响与彼此的生成。少数民族服饰与文化包含着大量的独特创意与表现手法，而在表现方式的多样性里隐藏的正是民族精神与文化特质。

在造物与设计过程中，世界各民族古老与独特的传统艺术与服饰风格，建构与保持着难以替代的审美与文化多样性特质。这种多样性既是应加以保护的艺术与文化遗产，也是当代服饰与设计艺术的文化人类学特质。在民族元素及其视觉表现之中，还要注重民族艺术的不断生成与传统文化的重构，而不能把民族传统看作一成不变的古板之物。在跨文化传播之中，民族独特时尚形象是如何得到艺术表现与文化建构的，无疑是揭示与阐发全球化语境里艺术与文化的地方性时亟待回应的问题。在地方性与世界性的张力之中，正是民族元素视觉表现的当代性不可缺少的审美与文化前提。

应当说，后殖民主义、民族主义等意识形态对构建时尚形象的作用，以及通过一定的

---

[1] 布鲁斯·G.崔格尔.理解早期文明：比较研究[M].徐坚，译.北京：北京大学出版社，2014：307.

视觉表现方式加以文化传播，其实都是民族元素的视觉生成与艺术表现所关涉的重要问题。在本性上，民族元素的视觉生成也是民族时尚的发生与建构过程。虽然不能说一切传承与沿袭下来的着装风俗都曾是时尚的，但后来的时尚重构却从来都离不开这些风俗与衣生活的传统。

三、民族创意的时尚表现与视觉艺术

对于设计艺术与视觉表现来说，民族服装、服饰的种类繁多、异彩纷呈、历史悠久，以及其独特的民族性、在地性与多样性等，无疑都是民族创意时尚表现不可或缺的特质，这当然也涉及如何通过艺术来加以表达的问题。其实，从人类造物活动一开始，就有了最早的设计或设计的雏形，尽管它还不是严格意义上的设计。但不同民族的早期艺术与设计传统，往往又通过视觉的历史性保护与传承而得以沿袭。也可以说，只有当设计者（师）有独特想法并付诸实施的时候，才开启了创意设计的生成与时尚的历史性语境。

只有有了设计之后，后来风格的形成与文化传播才有实现的可能，并由此揭示与挖掘创意所内隐的精神图式。在服装设计过程中，视觉艺术的基本元素与形式都可以用于民族创意的生成与建构。同时，由点、线、面所构成的抽象几何形体，在人们的潜意识里会激发出很多相关的联想。在创意与设计过程中，任何点、线、面都必须具有一定的形状、大小、色彩与肌理，这些都是民族创意设计所不可或缺的构成基础。但在不同民族或族群的元素及其视觉化中，涉及的艺术观念与对可视性的理解也并不相同。在民族元素的视觉建构与生成之中，时尚的创意与表现可以获得多种多样的视觉效果。

与此同时，应加以关注的重要问题是民族时尚艺术及其审美风格的当下生成，以及与之相关的时尚文化的建构与传播。还要注意到，"概念的意义与关系可能通过参考其意象而变得易于理解，但概念一旦系统化，它们就成了抽象观念，而不是某种图像语言"。❶ 这里强调的是，概念是根植于隐喻的抽象观念。甚至可以说，民族创意与时装设计及其与视觉的关联性，渗透在从构想、实施、传达到接受等各个层面。毫无疑问，创意在很大程度上规定与影响着设计风格的形成，但这一过程又是经由一系列的视觉表现才能得以实现的。

当然，时尚创意不仅涉及各种想法与见解本身，还关联艺术的表现与设计的实现方式。在创意的时尚表现过程中，身体的存在及其与艺术发生的生成性关联，在一定程度上规定与制约着时装设计活动。虽然说，有的艺术表现并非都是视觉性的，但它们也可以进行视觉性转换，并与视觉艺术及其文化产生相应的关联。时尚表现与人的审美通感的关联，将艺术赋形的美感与经验的形成与建构，从一种感觉样式联通并传递到另一种感觉中。因此，如何经由视觉化而生成与特定人群相关的时尚感，是与不同民族或阶层的精神与文化及其对话相关联的。

---

❶ 艾兰.水之道与德之端——中国早期哲学思想的本喻[M].张海晏，译.北京：商务印书馆，2010：36.

实际上，民族时尚创意生成在基于感觉融合的时尚风格及其传播之中。在时尚的视觉传达与流行趋势中，或许正是人的这种共通感，使人的各种感官的融会成为可能。在不同民族的衣生活方式里，这种审美通感又通过差异化的方式领会与把握。应当说，时尚艺术往往是一种相关于视觉的文化，因此，时尚对通感的关切依然离不开视觉艺术，以及由此所涉及的生活与文化传统。比如说，唐装原指唐代的汉服，今天作为一种时装的新唐装，无疑是一种当代的中式服装，但它仍然保留着汉服的文化意味与旨趣。

与一般的艺术相比，时装艺术与时尚文化更具有生成性的特征，这乃是时尚自身的流行性的审美风格特质，以及这种流行与视觉性及其文化的关联所致。虽然说，一般艺术及其审美也会随着时间而发生流变，但时尚艺术方面的审美经验却显得更加变幻莫测。与此同时，时尚的这种生成性特征经由传播后又得到了强化，当然，时尚随着广泛与极端的流行而衰落，并成为下一流行季的心理预期与生成之物。在民族创意的时尚表现里，其基于视觉艺术而对元素加以当下重构，并形成了与这种视觉性特质相关的审美通感。在这里，民族服饰与时尚创意的文本，无疑是与民族的存在及其文化语境相关。

在艺术与文化建构的过程中，对文本与语境的关联有着不同的理解与阐释。除了强调对视觉文化的真实例子进行实用性分析外，"其次，皮埃尔·布迪厄的文化产生理论主要是用背景来解释文本，而欧文·帕诺夫斯基却相信文本本身的意义可以用来阐明其产生背景"。❶ 其实，文本与语境的这种传统区分本身就是相对的，它们交织与互文在视觉性文化的各种层面上，同时，文本又凭借开放性特征而与语境相互生成。在古代，独龙族并没有严格意义上的衣裳，只是以由麻纤维织制成的独龙毯遮蔽身体，这与当时的生存状况和习惯语境分不开的。

正因如此，风格独特的独龙麻毯就成了一种特殊标志，五色麻布制成的独龙毯自肩斜披至膝，从而显示出粗犷豪放的艺术风格与古朴原始的审美意味。除此之外，还有纳西族的羊皮披肩，以及彝族的"察尔瓦"（披衫）等，这些民族服饰创意都具有将实用与装饰融为一体的效果，但它们在视觉表现方式与审美情趣上无疑又有所差异。应当说，民族时装的创意、设计与生产完成后，就可以进入营销与传播的渠道与领域了，而这也同样与视觉艺术和文化密切相关。民族服饰或时装的流行与文化传播，也是以其特定视觉风格被认同为前提的。在这里，服装风格的社会与文化认同，还促成了民族时尚的不断生成与流行。

正是在艺术与文化传播的语境里，民族创意与设计才能得以流行并被广泛接受与效仿。其实，民族风格与时尚的视觉表现总是相互关联的，并将民族精神与文化特质沉浸到视觉表现里。在少数民族服饰创意与设计中，衣服与饰品彼此关联并构成一种完整与开放的形式美。虽然服装的这种整体美也涉及诸多因素与构成问题，但任何整体美本身一旦形成，就不可能被分解。少数民族独特的配饰与搭配具有重要的意义与作用，它们往往在视觉造

---

❶ 理查德·豪厄尔斯.视觉文化[M].葛红兵，等译.桂林：广西师范大学出版社，2007：77.

型与表现上显示出某种特别甚至夸张的印象。

还要看到，在民族服饰创意与设计的整体搭配之中，色彩起到了不可替代的对比与强调作用。比如，黑彝男子往往身穿黑衣、黑裤与黑披肩，左耳戴缀有红丝线蜜蜡玉大珠，手腕戴银龙大镯，头顶黑布英雄髻。细长锥形的英雄髻，高高地伸出帕外，衬托出黑彝男子格外英武的形象；而倒向右侧的英雄髻与左耳的大型耳饰，形成的则是不对称但却均衡的关系与效果，红黄色的耳饰还起到点缀与强调的作用。在服装创意与设计中，还有一类如披肩、背垫等，因其常与身相随，已成为民族服饰的重要组成部分，无论是从实用，还是审美来看，它们都可以归为配饰。

毫无疑问，各民族的服饰都不乏风格迥异与独特的审美文化特质，之所以如此，是因为民族视觉习惯对时尚的形成与接受产生了不可或缺的影响，业已形成的习惯与风格甚至还成为民族服饰的重要构成。还应注意的是，时尚艺术风格及其变化表征出不同时期时尚的特质。在日本，"平安时代宫廷服饰的奢华风格最终并没有延续下来，其后的镰仓时代贵族服饰就远远没有那么铺张奢靡"。❶ 作为一种表现与传达方式，设计、艺术与文化处于不断的传播过程之中。在不同的时期与各个族群之间，时尚表现风格的关联与区分则是不可忽视的问题。在民族时尚及其审美过程中，习俗与文化具有重要的人类学意义与影响。

比如，纳西族妇女的服装异常朴素，缺乏一般所说的装饰与过度设计，最具特色的饰品便是用作背垫的羊皮披肩，这无疑是与纳西族的习俗和文化分不开的。还可以说，少数民族服饰式样与风格的繁多，往往具有较为强烈的装饰性与视觉性效果。显然，民族创意与设计及其视觉艺术表现，涉及符码与象征及其在社会与文化语境里的生成。在时尚的生成与建构里，服与饰难以分离地关联与交织在一起。应当说，民族性配饰为民族服装添加了不少意趣，无疑成了民族服饰创意与设计的重要构成，服中有饰与饰可成服或许是民族服装的根本性特质。

在这里，民族艺术风格是一个民族在长期的历史性生存中，对本民族的精神图式与文化特质整体性视觉与直观表达。例如，"与明初整齐划一、等级分明的服饰不同，明中期以后的服饰已是花样翻新、众彩纷呈"。❷ 这显然也表明，不同历史时期的民族服饰与时尚的变化，依然有待于在当时的社会与文化语境里加以阐释。但由于不同民族的地理位置与文化语境的差异，其服饰与着装往往也都具有自身的审美经验与风格特质。而且即使那些相隔并不遥远的地域或场所，也存在不同的装扮风格与着装特色。

随着全球化时代的到来，中国与东方各国或主动或被动地加入这股浪潮之中，民族时尚成为民族面对全球化浪潮的裹挟所作出的艺术与文化回应。此外，民族创意在当代的时尚化，还涉及对殖民主义与后殖民主义的回应与批判。从20世纪60年代兴起的嬉皮风格，到近几年再度燃起的民族时尚风格与潮流，民族元素与配饰对个性风格的强化越来越突出。

---

❶ 玛尼·弗格.时尚通史[M].陈磊，译.北京：中信出版社，2016：39.
❷ 杨孝鸿.中国时尚文化史（宋元明卷）[M].济南：山东画报出版社，2011：212-213.

在设计及其创意过程之中，至关重要的就是如何将理念、观念转换成创意的拟象。在柏拉图那里，摹本被看作次于位居其后的观念或形式，而视觉化本身就是对这种观念或形式的模仿。与此同时，视觉化为拟象生成与建构提供了根本性的艺术与文化语境。

在这里，时尚拟象的生成还必须借助生成论及其经验，这样才能避免陷入西方艺术及其所关联的视觉表象之中。还要看到，"对模式的模仿只有在说明了模式的构造规则，在对理念本身进行了描写之后才有意义"。❶当然，这种意义生成物正是创意拟象的根本性来源。不同于一般的现象学，生成论将经验的生成作为事情本身，并为走向经验的生成本身提供根本的可能。当然，视觉化的观念还有待于转化为视觉经验，而这种视觉经验既是对理念的激活与转化，同时也是观念的视觉化及其意义的生成之物。

其实，观念与创意的视觉化从来都是语境性的，而视觉化的观念则为创意与设计提供了思想经验。作为视觉化的观念向创意拟象的过渡，意义生成物既是创意的发生，同时也是一种拟象的建构，更是创意与拟象的相互生成之物。在创意的视觉化中，拟象经由经验的文本及其生成，关切与意指着存在本身。重要的还在于，经验的文本化与文本的经验化是相互生成的，而这种经验文本自身无疑也是艺术与文化的生成之物。观念及其视觉化之所以在创意里显得如此重要，是因为视觉化为拟象与表象奠定了一个生成论基础。通过视觉化的处理与建构，一切理念、观念都向创意设计发生转换。

那些模仿动植物原型的服装设计，虽然也具有艺术情趣与审美意味，但这并不能与摹本对原作的描写相混淆。实际上，设计离不开理念的视觉化转化与文本的生成。作为前提的这种视觉化转化，还需要经过设计对视觉生成物进行仿真。与此同时，一切设计场所与语境都可以解读为某种符码。其实，"只需略施小计，时间和地点的坐标就会被取消，被超越，被转换为符号"。❷但在现象学还原里，符号又可以通过回归到存在而与时空发生历史性关联。创意与设计也可以看作一种拟象的发生，即让理念、观念经由视觉化，转化为创意所必需的拟象或视觉表达。

显然，民族艺术与时尚离不开民族的情调与风俗，而不同民族的创意风格无疑又是有差异的。在很大程度上，不同民族的精神特质规定着服装的时尚情调。但服装要成为一种时尚，还需在艺术表现里强调流行的符号，这种符号在传达时尚与审美经验时，往往具有某种特定的象征性与语境关联。在创意的拟像表现过程中，理念、观念还会以变了形的样式存在，并对设计及其艺术加以特定的视觉性引导。当然，要完成与实现整个设计和创制活动，还必须将创意的拟像转换为某种视觉性传达。

还应看到，视觉传达就是将设计所力图表达的观念，通过艺术的手法加以表现并传递给受众。在设计最终形成的视觉传达中，不仅有理念、观念的历史性沉淀与艺术重构，同时还不乏拟像所蕴含的意味与文化旨趣。可以说，时尚艺术往往经由前卫的或经典的创意，

---

❶ 茨维坦·托多罗夫.象征理论[M].王国卿，译.北京：商务印书馆，2004：158.
❷ 迪克·赫伯迪格.亚文化：风格的意义[M].陆道夫，胡疆锋，译.北京：北京大学出版社，2009：82.

进而通过各种表现手法生成独特个性，而一切经典与前卫的风格及其关联，又将在时尚里发生交织与时尚化重构。其实，民族服饰创意与设计也是时尚风格对艺术与生活加以介入的生成物，这种创意与设计又通过视觉艺术及其表现方式来建构民族时尚感。

应当说，时尚设计的艺术表现与视觉传达，可以理解为理念、观念与拟像的互文性重构。对民族创意来说，时尚的表现总是发生在视觉性文本之中，并经由艺术表现手法加以回应与当代重构。"而且，文本总是处于生成之中，它既不断地存在于一定场所，同时又处在永远的消失之中。"❶ 在生成论语境里，经验经由文本而通达存在本身，进而成了一种永远的游戏活动。在创意与设计过程中，视觉化不仅是理念、观念存在的重要方式，也是艺术与创意拟像可能发生的基础。在这里，拟像与设计的视觉传达和艺术表现，以及它们的关联所彰显与解码的各种诉求，无不与理念、观念的视觉化处于互文的语境之中。

---

❶ 张贤根.艺术现象学导论[M].武汉：湖北人民出版社，2015：116.

CHAPTER 2

Generation and Visual Expression of Ethnic Fashion Creative

Generally speaking, fashion art and expressions are characteristic of visuality, showing creative appeals and design purports through visual expressions. In fact, ethnic fashion creative and visual expression are closely linked to each other, thus constituting an important style of aesthetic experience and visual culture. The artistic expression of fashion creative and designing is also a visual existence of art. At the same time, ethnic fashion creative involves the visual correlation between ethnic custom and traditional culture. Here, the visual transformation of creative means to express and convey new ideas through artistic visual processing. In the history of Western art, vision has always been endowed with particularly important stipulative meaning and value. We may say that, to a large extent, Western art history equals a history of Western visual art. However, it cannot be concluded that all ethnic elements and culture are visible in a simple sense, and non-visual factors are negligible or insignificant for artistic expression.

In fact, not all ideas are directly conveyed and felt through vision, but most of them can be perceptually reconstructed through visual transformation. The generation of ethnic fashion creative is inseparable from issues of visual expression, involving the relationship between idea expression and visual thinking. For fashion creativity, this visual expression is always reconstructive and generative in nature. But the occurrence of visual reconstruction is not only a matter of art and performance, but also an important issue of society and culture. In the visualizing process of creative, abstract or invisible ideas are expressed and reconstructed in vision, which is actually a process of aesthetic and cultural construction. In the designing of ethnic fashion, aesthetic construction will also concern ethnic life-style and anthropological existence. The visual expression of creative is associated with a dynamic and open text, which forms the generative basis for the dialogue between creative and acceptance.

Section 1   Visual Transformation and Schematization of Creative

The process of fashion design is one that involves the change from idea to visual expression, then to product. And the visual conveyance of fashion expression is made possible on the premise of the visualization of creative ideas. In the cultural context of visual expression, design is to transform creative ideas into visually perceivable images of elements and their relationship. This visual transformation and ways of its realization are actually aesthetic and cultural issues to be considered in creative visualization. Moreover, after visual transformation and artistic expression, creative should become a schema to be recognized and accepted in vision. Here, visual transformation is not to make simplified analogies or even give strained interpretations on creative ideas, but to visualize creatively and reconstruct aesthetically and culturally. Then on that basis, the intended meaning of image is coded, decoded and transmitted in designing and producing, so as to be recognized and accepted by people, especially users of fashionable dress.

1. Creative: from Idea to Vision

It should be said that, creative is important to fashion design not only because creative has much to do with the designing effect, but also because ideas and thoughts can go into designing through creative. Creative is actually the complete process involving the generation, the visualization, and the formal expression of idea. Of course, creative provides a practical and reliable basis for production, that is, creative contains in itself the possibility of production. Idea is of primary importance to creative activities, and it determines the quality of design. In fact, since ancient Greece, ideas have been fully valued and studied. It may be said that, all artistic expression and design are related to issues of ideas.

Plato used the word "idea" in his philosophy, giving the word a substantive feature, that is, idea can exist without dependency on perceivable things. The word "idea" comes from ancient Greek, with its meaning originally related to the verb "see", gradually extended to be "the concept in mind". Moreover, "the number of these independent patterns or ideas is countless, and there is nothing too lowly or unimportant to have an idea." [1] The imitation of idea is actually the acceptance of the stipulation of idea by art and beauty. The theory of imitation holds that, art imitation is aimed at reality and then points to idea. Visualization is a top-down process, echoing with the bottom-up imitation, thus forming a close correlation between design and art.

According to Plato, idea is the prototype of reality, and the perceivable world is formed based on ideas. Plato's thoughts are based on ideas, and he believes that beautiful and artistic things are essentially imitations of ideas. Plato's theories of idea and of imitation, although with their inevitable problems and predicaments, have profoundly influenced the art, design and aesthetics of later generations. Plato inherited the basic spirit of Socrates's theory of imitation, but he reconstructed the theory from the perspective of idealism. In Plato's opinion, idea is even a ubiquitous ideological existence, and the fundamental purport and appeal of metaphysics.

The process of design is undoubtedly closely related to the mental schema and ideas of an ethnic group. Hence, art is like an imitation of imitation, a shadow of shadow, seeming to

---

[1] Thilly F. A History of Philosophy [M]. Ge Li (tr). Beijing: Commercial Press, 1995: 66.

be doubly blocked from the reality of idea. Plato rejected literature and art because they were considered an imitation of the natural world, even lower than the natural entity. His thoughts resulted in a binary separation and a contempt for art, which have been criticized by later generations. According to Plato, idea is the fundamental stipulation that exists independently of things. Plato's important enlightenment for creative is that ideas or concepts are the fundamental source of all creative and design expressions. The visual transformation of ideas can be regarded the fundamental way that all designs take place. Of course, idea itself is not enough for designing and producing, as visualization of idea is also necessary in the process.

In this way, idea can become the model, sample or prototype involved in designing, namely, the ideological prototype on which the designed product originally relied. It should also be noted that "Plato's theory of art, that is, art is an imitation of imitation, is inseparable from the 'form' theory he put forward."❶ In the period of Hegel, beauty was still defined as the perceptual manifestation of ideas, so the expressions of art and beauty still had to accept the stipulation of ideas. Accordingly, art lies in expressing ideas with perceptual images for direct observation and vivid sensibility, rather than expressing in forms of thought or pure spirituality. All designs involve the issue of idea, and particularly in conceptual design, the idea has received an extreme emphasis.

Therefore, Hegel's aesthetic and philosophical thoughts are of great significance to the visualization and designing of idea. For Hegel, art is distinguished from religion and philosophy in its intuitive and perceptible qualities. According to him, the original art was a symbolic art. At that stage, humans wanted to express the ideas they recognized, but they could not find a suitable perceptual image, so they symbolized the ideas they wanted to express through the emphasis on form. But Hegel still faced the problems and dilemmas of rational metaphysics. Of course, the symbolic meaning is not limited to Hegel's symbolic art, because in modern and contemporary art expressions and designs, symbols still possess great artistic significance and aesthetic value. By what Hegel called the classical art period, the content and form of art have reached a perfect harmony.

Moreover, the classical art, with its unity of idea and sensibility, has come up to the top of perfect art, while the romantic art appears as a later choice. In the romantic art, the infinite mind finds that finite matter cannot meet the needs of expression, so it retreats from the material world to the spiritual world. In the contemporary design, although the visualization of idea also involves many concept pairs, it is at the same time inseparable from the deconstruction of duality. In fact, as early as ancient Greece, the theoretical idea had already showed in itself the visualized quality, and

---

❶ Wartenberg T E. (ed). The Nature of Art [M]. Li Fengqi, et al (tr). Chongqing: Chongqing University Press, 2011: 15.

the vision, as the most basic sensation, had stipulated and dominated other sensations. Therefore, the visual art of ancient Greece enjoyed a position superior to poetry and music.

It can even be said that art and beauty are always closely related to visual expressions. In ancient Greece, mythology had a profound influence on art and provided the context for the generation of creative and cultural construction. In particular, Homeric epics and the Olympian god system centering around Zeus made preparations for the emergence of Greek art with Greek mythology as the subject matter. In fact, the original meaning of vision is linked with logos. Logos, first intending to expose something to people, that is, to let people see something in a simple way so that they could perceive its being, were later concealed in logic and rational philosophy. However, the creative concepts related to the ethnic mental schema are not limited to any existing concepts and systems. One should note that the earliest reason was derived from logos and related to vision.

It is the sun god Apollo, also the god of light and shape, that sheds light on all beings and make their appearances and forms come into sight. From ancient Greece to modern times, Imitation Theory has always been prevalent in Western art and aesthetics, thus affecting Western realist art style and aesthetic experience. As far as visual art and expression are concerned, imitation mainly refers to the similarity and lifelikeness in shape and appearance. Although in ancient Greece, art could only imitate appearance rather than substance, such imitation cannot be said to have nothing to do with the metaphysical nature. Generally speaking, Plato praised highly of idea and philosophy while looked down upon art, so he advocated the expelling of mad poets from the Republic. Then in Aristotle, all arts were regarded as a kind of representation.

As to art and beauty, although Aristotle also upheld the basic views of imitation, his imitation theory was very different from that of Plato. According to Aristotle, there was only one real world. Art, imitating reality, was as real as the reality, and poetry (art) was even more realistic than history. In fact, the connection between idea and vision has always been an unavoidable issue. But art still involves the relationship between form and material, which is also a problem that artistic creative and design have to face and respond to. Moreover, how to overcome the binary separation between form and material is undoubtedly an important issue in art, design and aesthetic research.

Aristotle believed that reason was divided into theoretical reason, practical reason and poetic (creative) reason. At the same time, he attributed the form of beauty to visual order, symmetry and clarity. Logos stipulate that reason is originally represented as theoretical reason, bound up with insight and vision. As a kind of reflection, reason is related to the reflection of light and stipulates the consistency of seeing and thinking. Seeing is inseparable from light, and light determines the visibility. From the very beginning, visual art has involved the grasping and processing of light.

During Greek and Roman periods, visual art was closely associated to pleasure, utilitarianism, and mundane life. In modern and contemporary times, the visualization of design, through man's expression and interpretation, is concerned with ethnic spirit and cultural characteristics.

Obviously, the visualization of idea is the fundamental stipulation for the generation and realization of creative, and also an indispensable process for the social and cultural construction of design. The new visual culture visualizes things that are not visible in nature, and incorporates them into the visualized context for interpretation. Alexander McQueen integrates into his designing the close connections among fashion, art and concepts, always paying attention to maintaining the balance between beast and civilization, man and woman, technology and nature. In the process of creative designing, the way visualization involving the relationship among different expressions is also inseparable from various ethnic groups' understanding on this relationship. But this emphasis on the importance of visual form to artistic expression doesn't exclude other feelings. Creative is concerned with all kinds of experiences, aiming to visualizing ideas and to construct and integrate experiences through synesthesia.

There is no doubt that the clothing art and fashion design of various ethnic groups are all closely related to traditional visual art. Moreover, fashion creative involves the generative association of various ideas and experiences. As far as fashion creative is concerned, "fashion designers often need to quickly draw and jot down fleeting ideas, to capture short moments, and to conceive enough ideas for the edition of a consistent whole." [1] In visual anthropology, the culture presented in products designed through visual symbols is emphasized. In creative, sketch representation is also the process of visualizing ideas. Visualization is mainly the expression process with basic elements of characters, graphics, and colors. It affects people's feelings with its unique expressions in the spiritual and cultural fields, and makes the aesthetic and cultural construction of people's existence and clothing life.

Visual communication is carried out by means of seeing, and it is also a way of expression and communication through visual language. People of different regions, colors and languages communicate ideas, emotions and culture via creative codes and vision. Obviously, this kind of cross-cultural communication also involves the cultural differences among many ethnic groups. To a certain extent, visual observation and experience can overcome language barriers among people, and eliminate cultural barriers linked with linguistic differences, so as to achieve mutual communication by virtue of visual consensus on patterns and designs. However, how to reveal and understand the visual characteristics of clothing still involves the social and cultural interpretation

---

[1] Jones S J. Fashion Design [M]. Zhang Ling (tr). Beijing: China Textile & Apparel Press, 2009: 82.

on these visual codes.

In fact, visual communication has always been an intuitive way of communication between people, and has a profound influence on the inheritance of human history and culture and the construction of people's spiritual life. Visual expression uses specific media and technique to form the ethnic costume art and patterns, highlighting and constructing the culture of creative related to ethnic characteristics. It should also be noted that "many interdependent connections between thinking and vision cannot be simply divided into a set of parts." ❶ Because all fashion styles have their irreducible characteristics of integrity. Although Italian fashion is famous for its softness and elegance, German fashion its fluffy and gorgeousness, and Spanish fashion its rigidity evolving from elegance, one should realize that the fashion creative of these different ethnic groups is actually inseparable from its social and cultural context, and this kind of contextual connection will melt into the creative designing text.

As a means of communication, visualization certainly has its own expressing ways and skills, and involves different disciplines and perspectives for its understanding and interpretation. People try to see through their own eyes, often combining their understanding of the cultural connotation of images. Therefore, visualizing various regulations and ideas is undoubtedly an important issue of art, design and culture. Since visualization is an intuitive way of cultural dialogue, the two sides of the dialogue should be communicable with the same image symbols. Creative graphics with differences in recognition and understanding can be treated through cultural communication and inclusiveness. Here, visual language can be seen as a set of norms or code systems that convey meaning on the basis of basic elements and principles.

In fact, each ethnic group has its own way of thinking and visual habit, which should be considered in the fashion expression of ethnic elements and culture. In the expression of visual art, the designer always endows classic patterns with traditional meanings, which is the ideological basis and cultural prerequisite for the understanding and communication of creative. "In designs, people can sometimes find visual statements made by designers again and again..." ❷ It is worth noting that creative designing always focuses on how to break through traditional interpretations to obtain a novel fashion effect and interpreting way. Specifically, fashion designing principles concern aspects like layout, contrast, rhythm, balance, unity, etc.. Designers use these principles to convey meaning, but in different ways for different visual designs.

Images with specific meanings are formed by the choice of materials and expression forms

---

❶ Burnett R. Cultures of Vision: Images, Media, and the Imaginary [M]. Zhao Yi, et al (tr). Jinan: Shandong Literature and Art Publishing House, 2008:17.

❷ Dormer P. Design since 1945 [M]. Liang Mei (tr). Chengdu: Sichuan People's Publishing House, 1998:169.

suitable for specific lifestyle and aesthetic needs, and the construction of unique relationship between elements. But visual thinking, not limited to direct perception, has also been widely extended to ethnic aesthetic experiences and cultural construction. Images should be regarded not only as a form of representation, but also a reconstruction of objects and even oneself. The visualization of creative keeps dialogue with ideas, which reveals the generative relationship between ideas and pattern. It may be said that, the visualized representation is only an attempt to reveal the essence of an object. Besides, visualization tries to explore the way of interpreting the social and cultural meanings involved in images, and concerns the connection and dialogue of different races or ethnic groups in matters of creative.

Moreover, this visualization of idea involves the complex generative relationship between presentation and inherence, perceptibility and imperceptibility. During the Renaissance, "the trade and tourism of that time were growing, and people's ideas about fashion got exchanged, but ethnic characteristics were still distinct in clothing."❶ This cross-cultural fashion communication became an important opportunity for ethnic groups to reflect on their own traditions, to consider how to visualize ethnic characteristics in ideas and creative. A cross-cultural communication of clothing and fashion is related not only to the conversion from idea to vision, but also to the exchange and identification of different ethnic elements and cultures. Cultural adaptability has been highlighted in the visualization of fashion creative and cross-cultural fashion communication.

2. Possibility of Visual Transformation of Creative

To a large extent, the theory of idea and its visual characteristics in ancient Greece have defined Western art and aesthetics. The basic style and expression techniques of the Western Renaissance constitute the major tradition of modern visual art and culture. In terms of plastic arts, the Renaissance takes realism as its starting point and basic tradition. In Leonardo da Vinci's view, the art of perspective is a kind of rational expression on the contours of objects converging in human eyes. That is, the lines are under the control of human rationality. The studies on human anatomy and Perspective have been widely used in the creation of visual art. After the Renaissance, visual art with its new meaning has had a profound impact on the visualization of fashion creative.

Modern Perspective and visualization were closely relevant with art and design, which actually resulted from the rationalism and classicism of that time. In advertising and visual communication, classicism often means rationality, order and control. "Perhaps the style of classicism in this advertisement is unusually strong, but the style trend it represents shows typical

---

❶ Nunn J. Fashion in Costume: 1200-2000 [M]. He Tong (tr). Guilin: Guangxi Normal University Press, 2004: 24.

significance in most high-end fashion images."❶ But since the 17th century, Western art has moved from the field of religion to secular world, thus rationality concerns and illuminates the existence of human being. In modern times, René Descartes laid a rational foundation for art and thought, leading to an art and beauty regulated by rationality. In the contemporary period, gradually in-depth studies of human visual perception have greatly expanded the scope and content of Perspective.

In fact, people always interpret and grasp the creative and culture conveyed in designs through the perception and aesthetic experience from ethnic costume and fashion. In the visual transforming of creative, attention should be given to the difference between traditional Chinese artistic expression and Western Perspective, because the understanding and interpretation of different ethnic fashions are involved here. Baumgarten believed that aesthetic appreciation is an ability of perceptual cognition, which can understand and create beauty, and approach its perfection in art. However, Western rationality and understanding in modern times is not enough for a deep understanding on the visualization of different ethnic spirits. Hegel believed that in the art of painting, the light of human rationality weighed much over natural sunlight.

Different from the theoretical rationality of ancient Greece or the practical rationality of the Middle Ages, modern rationality is often related to poetic and creative quality. It should be noted that Hegel interpretation of art and beauty as the perceptual manifestation of idea also bears on the visualization of idea. According to Hegel, all the perceptual manifestations in art are ultimately governed by idea, which, however, does not mean that visual art has nothing to do with perceptual and aesthetic experience, but shows the stipulative influence of rationality in artistic experience. Generally speaking, the beauty of form is generated from the relationship among color, shape, line, sound, and other aspects of things, and it is the fundamental of visual art and aesthetic experience, to be well considered in the visual transformation of creative. In ancient Greece, the law of golden section proposed by the Pythagoras school held that all forms conforming to the ratio of the golden section were beautiful.

As an important rule for formal beauty, the golden section is widely applied to painting, craft, architecture and design in modern times. But modern times explored art and beauty by dealing with the pair of inseparable categories: form and content, which eventually became the conceptual framework for grasping visual art. It is noteworthy that geometry and science have brought a profound impact on visual and artistic expression, and the Perspective based on the principles of science and geometry is widely used in visual art and design. The perspective methods adopted in modern visual art mainly include focus perspective and scattered perspective. Creative is usually

---

❶ Messaris P. Visual Persuasion: The Role of Images in Advertising [M]. Wang Bo (tr). Beijing: Xinhua Publishing House, 2004: 86.

visualized through analogy, which is, different from general forms of analogy, closely linked with mental schema. The visualization of idea made creation possible in the co-relation between material and form.

The visual transformation of creative is based on the visibility of idea. At the very beginning, the meaning endowed in the connection between material and form was just suitable for the creation of object, and later it was transferred to the practice of free art. Borrowing principles and methods of Perspective has expanded the space of expression for visual art. But we must see that "the relationship between visual signifiers and the concepts of divine power is much more complicated than the totem model proposed by Durkheim or Levi-Strauss." [1] In fact, the understanding of vision cannot be separated from the construction of theory and culture. Modern plastic art creates two-dimensional or three-dimensional images out of certain materials through artistic means of composition, perspective, light, etc., which are all indispensable expressing ways for the visual transformation of creative.

The visuality of an idea or concept depends on the cultural imagination and comprehension of an ethnic group, which in turn is inseparable from the inner mental schema of the group. And visuality does not mean that an idea can be seen directly, but that an idea is possible to be transformed into a visual image, and then people can understand idea through the meaning of the image. What visuality emphasizes in its traditional sense is the visual accessibility, and artistic anthropology provides the cultural possibility for different ethnic groups to visualize and understand various ideas. But accessibility is related to creative not only in the level of sight, but also in levels of non-sight factors, such as communication and comprehension across these levels. Visual transformation is a manifestation of physiological and perceptual sensibility, as well as an aesthetic and cultural practice related to ethnicity.

Here, the fundamental question is how an idea can acquire visuality, and visuality often concerns how an idea can be represented in a visual impression and then be understandable to people. However, in today's fashion world, "Some fashion designers, avant-garde in appearance but archaizing at bottom, rarely explore the true meaning of fashion. Instead, they prefer short-lived, self-affected, and meaningless image display." [2] In contrast, ethnical fashion creative and designs involve the way that the historical character of culture could be revealed, and that the ethnic lifestyle could be understood through visual images. In fact, the theoretical reason of

---

[1] Layton R. The Anthropology of Art [M]. Li Dongye, Wang Hong (tr). Guilin: Guangxi Normal University Press, 2009:114.

[2] Cuvillier D. Le Futur de la Mode: Fashion on the Ultimate Cross-Examination [M]. Zhi Qi (tr). Beijing: China Textile & Apparel Press, 2009: 128.

ancient Greece was characteristic of certain visuality, which in a fundamental sense stipulates the visualizing basis of theory.

In the process of accepting expressions of fashion creative, people begin to understand through visual observation the ideas that designs attempt to express, and to reconstruct those visual impressions in certain cultural contexts. The construction of theory and concept cannot put away imagination, which lays some foundation for the expansion of visibility. Imagination is inseparable from intuition, perception and vivid image on one hand, from cognition, theory and thought on the other. The visualizing transformation of creative ideas is related not only to the schema construction through human imagination, but also to the analysis on abstract and conceptual things. And then creative could be transformed into concrete sensibility and visual experience through certain visualizing expressions.

However, there is no so-called pure perceptibility for us to rely on, because without imagination, no abstract concept can ever be understood. In the cognition process, knowledge is formed when intellectuality uses concepts to unify representations. But imagination is different from intellectuality in that, rather than trying to unify representations, it gathers all kinds of sensibility and allows itself to play freely with intellectuality. That is the case with Chinese paintings, as "in the eyes of Chinese painters, any natural landscape picture with its own characteristics corresponds to certain spiritual aspects of human beings."❶ In free games of aesthetics, intellectuality and imagination, though often in conflict, must coexist and coordinate with each other. At the same time, a proper tension must be maintained between the two sides, that is, one cannot be defeated totally by the other. In the process of visualizing ethnic fashion creative, people show their unique ethnic characteristics in psychology and culture.

In nature, abstraction is a process of thought generation in which an idea is separated from the original object, but the relationship between idea and visualization cannot be understood in such conceptual models as that of abstraction and concretization. Therefore, effective understanding and communication on abstract things are often based on communication perception or common experience. The abstracted experiences and sensory impressions need to be reconstructed in the context of artistic expression and product appeal when fashion creative is visualized, and the inner spiritual images must be grasped in the interpretation of these fashions. Unlike abstraction, concretization, in closer relationship with imaginal thinking, human intuition and emotion, necessitates the analysis of the visuality elements in abstract ideas.

But people's visual observation lacks no theoretical support, in other words, it is inseparable

---

❶ Williams C A S. A manual of Chinese metaphor [M]. Li Hong, Xu Yanxia (tr). Changsha: Hunan Science & Technology Press, 2006:178.

from the visual schemas constructed by theories. In the visualization of fashion creative, concretization and abstraction are not separate but closely related and intertwined. Moreover, theories and ideas are extremely significant in people's observation activities, because no observation can be absolutely irrespective of ideas. Ethnic fashion creative often analyzes ethnic elements from various theoretical perspectives and then explores possibilities of visualizing ideas. And these possibilities involve the complex generative relationship between idea and expression, as well as the construction of aesthetic and cultural tensions between them.

In the visualization of creative, all relevant theories and ideas should serve the design purpose. Different designers, or even the same designer, under varying contexts could produce different works or creative ideas. "Rational knowledge, though sometimes useful in forming visual concepts, can play a role only if it can be transformed into visual attributes." [1] Therefore, design transforms invisible creative ideas to visible ones, obscuring the absolute boundary between the invisible and the visible. It should be noted that, due to its abstract and complicated nature, idea is relatively difficult to be grasped through direct vision. Therefore, in the ancient period of Aristotle, form, material and concrete things are all considered substantive.

Then in Descartes, idea is divided into three kinds: natural, external and fictional. And according to Gottfried Wilhelm Leibniz (who opposes empiricism, especially Locke's theory), idea is the potential capability as one's tendency, endowment, habit, or nature. When it comes to George Berkeley, idea is regarded the principle of reality, and things are "collections of ideas." The ideas mentioned above are often abstract, difficult to be perceived by human eyes and ears. Yet idea visualizing also involves the construction of certain visible form. For Heidegger, art, as an ontological existence, forms a relationship of coexistence and mutual generation with the beings of artists and works.

Art and design creative could never ignore historical comment, criticism and cross-cultural communication. And the generative connection between idea and form is actually what the visual expression of creative is trying to achieve. In the visualization of creative, what is called the visual intuition by phenomenology is undoubtedly of great importance and value. "Therefore, to synthesize constitution forms is a kind of thinking activity, and the sense of unity is a spontaneous consciousness, and an insight into the relationship between the elements that can be perceived separately." [2] Among various forms of intuition, the sensible intuition of visual perception is most fundamental. Fdmund Husserl believes that aesthetic object is a kind of intentional object, and

---

[1] Arnheim R. Visual Thinking [M]. Teng Shouyao, Zhu Jiangyuan (tr). Chengdu: Sichuan People's Publishing House, 1998:128.

[2] Santayana G. The Sense of Beauty [M]. Yang Xiangrong (tr). Beijing: People's Publishing House, 2013:72.

the phenomenological intuition is similar to the aesthetic intuition in pure art. The designing and reconstructing of ethnic elements will also be related to the intentional reference defined by ethnic collective unconsciousness.

In the context of art and fashion, post-modernity is a response to the problems and dilemmas faced by modernity. And the complex relationship between modernity and post-modernity is unavoidable for ethnic fashion designing in the era of globalization. Visual sense not only defines creative expressions in a general sense, but also underlies idea conveying and intelligibility constructing. Merleau-Ponty endows intuition with great importance from the perspective of perception. And he regards perception rather than emotional experience as the prior structure of human existence. Moreover, the artistic composition and impression presented by visualization have become an intuitive way to aesthetics, culture and spirit. In contemporary times, people's appeals and expectations for the aestheticization of their living world are often related to fashion creative and its visual expression. With people's vision in the aesthetic process extending, visuality reveals spiritual and cultural concerns on different levels.

The understanding and interpretation of the visuality in creative are bound up with the mental schema of a specific ethnic group, and the dialogue between schemas remains a cross-cultural issue that cannot be ignored in fashion. In fact, aesthetic synesthesia can bring about transferring and interweaving of feelings through association. "Visual design has to do with images, and the function of images is to vividly convey the meaning of signs, symbols, forms and colors, as well as the relationship between them." ❶ It's difficult to rid one's sensation and aesthetic experience of one's own ethnic characteristics, and of the possible communication and identification among different ethnic groups. In addition to resorting to visual sense, fashion makes use of aesthetic synesthesia for the sense of strangeness, which is endowed with ethnic and cultural spirit, as well as ethnic heterogeneity. To explore the possibility of idea visualization, it is still necessary to make artistic and cultural dialogues between ethnic groups.

3. Visual Expression and Schematization of Creative

In art and design, the impressions and experiences presented by visual expressions are usually related to ethnic characteristics, or even to certain mental schema of an ethnic group. The stipulation that human mental schema has for visual expression is represented in the unique meaning and characteristics endowed to art and fashion. Schema, as a transcendental category, is regarded by Kant as a technique hidden deep in the human mind. According to Kant, idea is

---

❶ Munari B. Design as Art [M]. London: Penguin Books Ltd, 2008:33.

something that cannot be fully experienced in daily life. For example, nothing can fully embody the concept of beauty in daily life. And this peculiarity of art that can surpass daily life provides the possibility for the expression of idea.

In the visual expression of ethnic creative, the mental schema stipulates meaning and taste in a fundamental sense. Through experimental research, Jean Piaget gave new meaning to the concept of schema. In Piaget's view, schema is a medium from experience to concept, including a movement structure, an operation structure, as well as a cognitive structure that is dynamic and variable. This schema plays an irreplaceable role in the process of cognition, that is, it can filter, screen, and sort out external stimuli to acquire an organized and overall understanding. Piaget believes that in the process of adapting to the outside world, the schema would get continuously changed, constructed and enriched. However, the fundamental dilemma for his epistemology of binary separation could not be completely overcome. No doubt, the artistic patterns and styles of different ethnic groups are associated with the differences in their mental schemas.

Nevertheless, the hierarchical differences between designs do not necessarily mean the inequality between ethnic groups. Meanwhile, fashion actually involves the rhetoric of signs. For example, "it strives to replace denotation with connotation, using pure rhetoric devices to outline images that may appear inferior in direct reference." ❶ For art design and aesthetic expression, there is also the issue of how to break through cognition for a better effect. But schema is not a simple summation of various parts, but an inseparable and irreversible whole, which is represented in the overall characteristics of fashion brand and style. In terms of visual culture, there are differences of customs that cannot be ignored in ethnic clothing lifestyles.

In fact, schema inherently echoes the spiritual structure of an ethnic group. Ingaden, starting from the work itself, emphasizes the ontological status of the work of art and analyzes the internal structures of different types of works of art. In Ingaden's view, all music works stand on one level, namely, that of sound combination in music; in contrast, painting usually contains two levels – one formed by the schematized view of the reproduced object and the other by the concrete view of reproduced object. According to Roman Ingarden, the concrete view of object, which is what people can actually experience, is in a constant change, while what remains unchanged in identity is the schematized view of object. On the issue of creative schematization, art and design are not only related to the inner spiritual structure, but also to the social, historical and cultural context through the open nature of the structure.

In other words, schema can describe both essential and non-essential features of objects. The

---

❶ Barthes R. Système de la Mode [M]. Ao Jun (tr). Shanghai: Shanghai People's Publishing House, 2000:303.

visualization of schema is made possible just because visual sense itself involves thinking. The rhetorical expression and discourse construction of language manifest that language, speech and thinking are intertwined, and language and schema are mutually transformable as codes. In modern times, simple illustrations of human mental schemas and cultural traditions should above all be overcome in design. And design means that conceptual elements are creatively transformed into visualized images. As a generative context, the visualization of idea provides the conceptual basis and prerequisite for the production of simulacra.

The relationship between perception and understanding, considered a matter of art and aesthetics early in the Middle Ages, was presented as related to perception and reason in modern times. "In neoclassical art and image aesthetics, the concept of 'thought' is inseparable from images or engraved marks, which are the 'ideal' impressions in one's imagination left by experiences, especially visual experiences."[1] The visualized expression of creative is transformed into a concrete and direct image, which is inherently linked to the spiritual structure of humans. However, the rigorous and ideal presupposition on this connection has encountered challenges in the expressions of modern art and fashion. Anyway, symbols come from various human activities, and human society and culture are generated and interconnected with the aid of symbols.

In the visualized expressions of fashion creative, one can often find various codes and symbols, the generation and reconstruction of which in the contemporary context are inseparable from the spirit and culture of specific ethnic group. It may be said that, the schematic representations of creative are based on human spirit and culture, as ethnic culture has generated the characteristics of creative expression and provided the base for creative schematization, which is often achieved through visual means. Ingaden emphasizes the metaphysical qualities of aesthetics such as sublimity, sacredness and peacefulness, which also have something to do with the schematization of fashion creative.

Ferdinand de Saussure believes that a sign includes two inseparable components, the signifier and the signified, whose connection is the central issue in the expression of signs. Therefore, a visualized signifier always points to something signified with certain meaning. For example, in Polhemus' view, "Brands of geographical regions visualize their own symbolic meanings through ethnic clothing (such as Indian sari and Brazilian bikini), and fashion is to weave regularly the narrative of a regional or ethnic brand into the sign structure of its utopian vision."[2] Saussure points out that language signs are characteristic of arbitrariness and their linear sequence. In addition to language, an extremely important example in semiotic systems, things like text signals,

---

[1] Mitchell W J T. Iconology: Image, Text, Ideology [M]. Chen Yongguo (tr). Beijing: Peking University Press, 2012:154.

[2] Berg, et al. The Power of Fashion [M]. Wei Xiaoqiang, et al (tr). Beijing: Science Press, 2014:272.

rituals, customs, etc., are of the similar nature.

However, the connection between the signifier and the signified will lose its certainty with the dispelling of the signified, consequently making many visual expressions become games on the signified in the postmodern era. This kind of game, of course, comes from the diversity of the signifier. It should be noted that the dualism of feeling and idea is usually linked with the supremacy of idea, which believes that in cognitive activities, it is not feeling but idea that dominates. But in the process of visualizing creative, the supremacy of idea cannot walk out of its epistemological and metaphysical limitations. The arbitrariness of the sign actually means that, the relationship between the signified and the signifier is random rather than inherent and natural.

Of course, once the relationship between the signifier and the signified is established, it acquires the characteristics of historical continuity, which is just the basis for the encoding and decoding of creative expressions. Rudolf Arnheim believes that the symbolic meaning should be directly conveyed to the visual sense through composition. Take the Bullfighting Festival in Spain for example. "Aren't the golden ornaments of costume and the red blood of bull symbolizing the colors of Spanish flag?"[1] According to Arnheim, visual sense is of thinking quality as it is a thinking style in itself. And ethnic elements and traditional cultures always permeate through daily lives and festival activities. Arnheim absorbs the idea of Gestalt psychology, that is, visual image is not a mechanical grasp of perceptual materials, but a creative interpretation of reality. Different from linguistic signs, symbols are never completely arbitrary.

To understand the visualization of ethnic concepts, it is important to grasp the established relationship between the signifier and the signified, which, in a sense, is the relationship between feeling and idea. Visual narration, as an important way of visualizing fashion creative, involves historical, social and cultural issues. Roland Barthes believes that narrative is suitable for any occasions, such as literary works, paintings, movies, comics, social stories, and conversations. Of course, ethnic costumes, as well as relative legends and stories, are narrations of clothing lives and cultures. For example, the folk narratives about Xilankapu (a brocade of Tujia people) can be visualized and schematized on clothing designs.

Usually, narration is achieved through spoken or written languages, fixed or movable pictures, gestures, or combinations of all these means. Semiotics consists in a hierarchical analysis on the signifying system, and the system can be divided into a deep structure, a surface structure and an expression structure. For example, the choice and interpretation of fabrics involves different levels and structures. "Dior tends to choose luxurious and fine fabrics like jacquard satin, taffeta, Turkish

---

[1] Benedicte Lapeyre [M]. Liu Yuli (tr). Beijing: China Renmin University Press, 2015:86.

silk, wool crepe and velvet, as these materials are popular among the public for their good visual effects and ..." ❶ This kind of signifying is expressed through visualization, involving different levels and structures in creative design. Based on the semantic research in linguistics, semiotics is enriched with contents and analysis methods related to society and culture.

The traditional Chinese pattern, Dragon and Phoenix Bringing Prosperity, use auspicious and divine animals such as dragon and phoenix as the signifier in the decorative pattern, the signified being love, fortune, happy marriage and harmonious relationship. Ethnical costumes and fashion are not only an artistic style, but also a cultural code and symbol. Therefore, the popularity of fashion can be considered a spread of art and culture, often occurring between ethnic cultures. Although ethnic fashion involves various artistic and cultural connections, visualizing those creative ideas is an important way to make designs accessible to the public. Cross-cultural communication of ethnic fashion will undoubtedly involve issues of cultural identity as well as social, historical and cultural contexts, with the visualization of creative as their generative basis.

Now, narratology has developed from exploring the deep structure at the story level to analyzing the narrative structure at the discourse level. And the visualized expression of ethnic creative is the very process of generating symbol and narrative discourse, involving various spiritual and cultural aspects. In fact, "In the masked performance, mask and costume change the image of the mask wearer, but only temporarily," ❷ because once the masked performance is over, the wearer will return to his daily appearance and life. In the cross-cultural communication of fashion, it is a must to understand and interpret creative schema. To generate fashion sense, creative could be combined with ethnic narratives through expressions of visual illusion.

However, traditional narratology is often limited to myths, folk stories, especially narrative works like novels that use written language as the carrier, needing to be expanded by including various visual codes and graphic narratives. In the process of visualizing creative, mind maps of visual art help to communicate clearly and effectively through graphical means, but the designs of these maps are not meaningless for communication, or merely in pursuit of beauty. The graphicalization of ethnic fashion creative has much to do with the life and narration of an ethnic group, and even if entering the field of visual narratives composed of non-verbal materials, this kind of creative would still take for reference the studies on narratives using language as the carrier. In order to convey the intention of creative effectively, original concepts and ideas are analyzed and integrated in visualization and aesthetization, and expressed visually in unfamiliarized ways.

---

❶ Marsh J. History of Fashion: New Look to Now [M]. Shao Lirong, Xu Qianqian (tr). Jinan: Shandong Pictorial Publishing House, 2014:14.
❷ Mack J. (ed). Masks: The Art of Expression [M]. Yang Yang (tr). Guangzhou: Nanfang Daily Press, 2011:20.

Iconography studies the meaning of art works in its historical and cultural context. This kind of research and interpretation is based on the interpretation of the image itself and its meaning. Here, iconography aims to discover and explain the inner meaning and symbolic meaning of artistic images, as well as the formation and changes of images, and the thoughts and concepts they express or imply. In this image age, "we need a visible past, a visible continuum, and a visible origin myth, which eliminates our doubts about purpose." ❶ But the problem of vision and schematization and its representationalism However, art and design urgently need to respond to and overcome difficulties. It should also be noted that unlike iconography's description and interpretation of the content of artistic works, iconography focuses on discovering and revealing the more essential things behind the pure form, image, motif, and plot of the work.

Section 2　Visual Culture of Ethnic Fashion Creative

In the research on ethnic fashion creative and design, we must not only propose innovative ideas and feasible programs, but also explore the relationship between conceptual cultural elements and visual expressiveness. And it is very necessary to elucidate this relevance in the context of ethnic life history and visual culture. In fact, there is no lack of novelty in many design ideas, but they have not been realized fully in terms of visual expressiveness. In the setting of daily life and popular culture, how to deal with the unique artistic and cultural styles of each ethnic group is undoubtedly of great significance to the aesthetic expression of ethnic fashion creative. Moreover, visual culture makes a creative interpretation and generative construction of creative ideas of ethnic fashion by incorporating them into the discourse of contemporary fashion art and aesthetics. In global artistic and cultural context, the construction of visual culture is related to the ethnic characteristics of clothing life and fashion culture, as well as contemporary aesthetic and cultural reconstruction of these ethnic fashion texts.

1. Ethnic Existence, Creative and Culture

The existence and life style of an ethnic group are never separable from the specific natural environment and cultural context. On the issue of existence, Heidegger emphasized the unavoidability of the world for one's being. Heidegger tried to reveal the nature and the meaning of existence itself through the analysis on the living state of there-being. For a specific ethnic group, its ethnic being is, in nature, its being in the world, and this world is rather a relevant living world

---

❶ Baudrillard J. Simulacra and Simulation [M]. Ann Arbor: The University of Michigan Press, 1995:7.

than an objective outside one. In fact, Heidegger always bore in mind the generative connection between there-being and the world in his exploration on issues of existence. Actually, there-being means existing in the world, namely, in an indivisible whole.

Of course, various factors such as geographical environment, cultural tradition and social mentality affect from different levels lifestyles, hence characteristics of visual culture displayed in fashion creative. "In the pure sense, the so-called clothing in the primitive period of human beings was nothing more than a shabby winter garment, probably made of heavily worn animal skins and barely playing the role of clothing."❶ But with the changes in human existence and life, various functions of clothing have been gradually realized and the appeal for creativity and culture strengthened, which greatly promotes the subsequent beautification of clothing. If we distinguish simply the identity of human as animal from that as cultural being, we can never fully understand the complexity of human nature. In fact, to make this absolute distinction is not possible at all.

It can be said that animality and cultural quality are always intertwined in human bodies and lifestyles, but civilization tries to limit this animality to the lowest degree. Anthropology tends to examine the physical, social and cultural diversity of human races, with the goal of clarifying the relevance between human body and culture. By the Paleolithic Age, when people can make clothes freely according to their needs due to the increase of productivity, clothing had broken away from its original budding state. Then in the Neolithic Age, especially with the invention of primary textile technology, clothing materials turned into artificially woven fabrics, clothing styles underwent corresponding changes, and clothing functions were better realized and greatly improved.

In the Neolithic Age, in addition to one-piece clothing, there appeared caps, boots, headdresses and accessories, which have been discovered from some pottery relics. Then in the period of fishing, hunting, animal husbandry and agriculture, people began to develop the sense of beauty on dress. They not only sought the suitability of clothing styles, but also beautified various accessories attached to clothes. After the advent of textiles, one-piece gown had become a typical clothing style in primitive Chinese society, and been adopted for a long period of time among many ethnic groups in a very broad area, replacing the part-clothing of the Paleolithic Age. In fact, cloak-style clothing such as one-piece gown has become a conventional dress style. In different regions and historical periods, the generative relevance between clothing and human existence and creativity obviously shows irreplaceable artistic and cultural characteristics.

Because costumes are extremely difficult to preserve, primitive pottery paintings, figure

---

❶ Grau F M. Histoire du Costume [M]. Zhi Qi (tr). Beijing: China Textile & Apparel Press, 2009:13.

sculptures, as well as figure jade carvings, have become precious materials for studying clothing styles of that time. Clothing is not only an indispensable component of human life as food, housing and transportation are, but also an aesthetic, social and cultural symbol of human identity. Because of that, "although more and more people accept the idea of topless sunbathing, it seems that bikini will not step out of the stage." ❶ Actually, the aesthetic appreciation of clothing is related to the visual habit and cultural psychology of an ethnic group. The production of clothing, the change of style and the generation of creative are all influenced by human living condition, aesthetic concept and culture. In the lifestyle of primitive humans, the functionality of clothing is undoubtedly most crucial. For example, people must wear thicker clothes in order to maintain body temperature and prevent frostbite in the cold.

However, primitive costumes of different ethnic groups continue to influence the fashion creative and costume culture of later ages. Here, body protection and heat preservation can explain the origin of clothing from the perspectives of physiology and survival. But the way of dressing varies in different regions, which affects people's understanding on fashion creative and culture. For example, even ethnic groups living in tropical regions are barely seen naked. With the development of society and the advent of civilized age, people gradually regard clothing as a decorative culture. All ancient and traditional arts and costumes will be reconstructed in the modern context. For example, modern costumes of primitivism appear natural and simple in style, the creative of which is inspired by the primitive totem cultures in places like Africa, Eskimo and Pacific Islands.

In the clothing life of human beings, some objects are worn on the body as amulets to turn ill luck into good, and some are as symbols of specific social status. Then, expressions of creative are closely related to materials (fabrics), for the expression methods and experiences are different for different materials. For example, "in ancient times, flax was the most commonly used fabric fibers, though rush, palm and papyrus were available as well." ❷ As a pure natural fiber, flax is being widely adopted in contemporary fashion design for being absorbent, breathable, and skin-friendly. It should be noted that any single theory on the origin of clothing is just from one perspective of seeing things, impossible to explain all the reasons for the appearance of clothing. And different theories are constructing their specific interpretations on the origin of clothing.

Undoubtedly, clothing creative and design have to do with the specific lifestyle and environment of an ethnic group. For instance, the half-wild people living in tropical rainforest areas often wear minimal-sized clothes, just enough to cover their genitals, but still able to protect them

---

❶ Tucker A, Kingswell T. Fashion [M]. Tong Weiyang, Dai Lianbin (tr). Beijing: SDX Joint Publishing Company, 2014:67.
❷ Harris J. 5000 Years of Textiles [M]. Li Guoqing, et al (tr). Shantou: Shantou University Press, 2011: 16.

from external damage to a considerable degree. The appearance of clothing is in close relation with that of shame sense, but it is difficult to make a simple judgement about which thing came first. On the issue of covering body, especially where to cover first, ethnic groups are different in opinion.

Generally speaking, the one-piece form of the Han people's clothing came out of their agricultural production mode. But for the ethnic minorities in the north, who lived in grasslands, plains, or deserts, the clothing form of upper coat and lower trousers (such as Hu dress) could meet their survival needs of hunting and grazing, being more suitable to their horseback lives and battles. Therefore, the issue of proper dressing is affected by local habits and customs. Then for ancient Egyptians, the symbolic meaning and value of clothing, being the main cause of their dressing, was more important than its function of covering the body. In fact, by wearing clothes human beings tried to do away with their sense of shame about nudity, but the sense, on the contrary, got emphasized in this behavior.

At the same time, clothes have to do with the mutual attraction between men and women. For primitive humans, clothing was also a code symbolizing the social status of the wearer. In fact, people generally want to show their beauty in clothing to others, and the art of clothing has constructed ethnic clothing life and culture. For example, the embroidery and accessories that some uncivilized people add to their winter clothes of animal skins are actually a unique expression for the beauty of body. Human ancestors also colored themselves and wearing accessories like earrings, jewelry, waist decorations, ankle rings, etc. showing a psychological and aesthetic desire to decorate their bodies, which was as strong as human survival instinct. Although the living environment of mankind today is different from that of previous ages, the relationship between survival and body keeps playing a role in fashion design.

Clothing is inevitably affected and restricted by human spirits and cultures of different historical periods, with clothing styles of various ages branded with historical characters. From a historical perspective, the culture of ethnic costumes is changing constantly, having distinct characteristics of a time, place, and custom, and its artistic expression and design are linked with ethnic peculiarities. "There are indications that the concept of 'tailoring' originated in ancient Crete, because when people in other early civilizations simply wrapped themselves in cloth, the Minoans had been dressed quite smartly." ❶ In certain historical and social context, ethnic fashion creative and design are important ways of constructing ethnic spirit and culture.

In ancient times, people made crude clothes out of any materials coming in handy to protect or modify their bodies. The initial clothes of human beings were often made of animal skins,

---

❶ Cosgrave B. The Complete History of Costume and Fashion [M]. Long Jingyao, Zhang Ying (tr). Shanghai: Oriental Publishing Center, 2006:34.

and the earliest fabrics used for wrapping their bodies were from flax fibers and grass. People in different environments and civilizations vary in understanding of dress and constructing of fashion culture. In the early days of human society, clothing appeared and became an integral part of human life, signifying human culture and spirit. In the primitive society, humans collected wild textile fibers and materials for clothing making. Then the development of crop and animal husbandry has gradually increased the quantity and kind of cultivated textile materials, and the complexity of clothing making tools. The changing trend of clothing is to pay more attention to the beauty of clothing design, aiming to satisfy people's spiritual and cultural demands.

Therefore, creative and design are of great importance to clothing and fashion expressions, and primitive existence and lifestyle of human beings have always been reflected and reconstructed in contemporary design. In fact, various factors could affect the expression of fashion art and aesthetic experience, such as textile texture, color, pattern, grey fabric tissue, shape retentivity, drapability, elasticity, wrinkle resistance, clothing style, etc.. Meanwhile, the raw material, structure and production method of textile are all related to the clothing style. Generally speaking, rough and hard fabrics are only suitable for garments of simple structure, while complex and contoured garments need softer thin fabrics. The Indian-style dress emerging in the United States in the 1960s actually borrowed and reconstructed the characteristics of Indian dress.

As one of the oldest clothing accessories, belt was often used to hang necessary items such as weapons. We might even say that the animal skins, leaves, and braided fabrics on the belt are early forms of skirt. Due to geographic environments with different climates, mountains, rivers, landforms, etc., residents of a place usually have their unique styles and habits. In the long history of human existence, various ethnic groups have formed their own spiritual characteristics and cultural contexts, endowing their clothing lifestyles with colorful ethnic flavors. In some eastern countries, people often show features of their own dresses distinct from those of others through implicit means. Almost since the very origin of clothing, people have embedded their life customs, aesthetic tastes, color preferences, and various cultural mentalities and beliefs into the artistic expression and design of clothing.

In particular, when the basic function of clothing gets satisfied, aesthetic, social and cultural appeals will also be answered in creative design. As the pursuit of art and beauty is natural to human being, the use of clothing in human life is not only to cover and protect the human body, but also to beautify and symbolize the social being of human. Of course, "As to beauty and utility, no matter which one is more important, beauty will penetrate in all aspects of design."[1] Human

---

[1] Clay R. Beautiful Thing: An Introduction to Design [M]. Yin Tao (tr). Jinan: Shandong Pictorial Publishing House, 2010:7.

ancestors struggled to cross the threshold of the civilized era after bidding farewell to apes, and they created a clothing lifestyle carrying civilization.

Moreover, human beings can identify the messages embedded in clothing codes, which, in close relationship with human lifestyles, could be interpreted creatively in the context constituted through ethnic psychology and cultural accumulation. If different aesthetic interests and cultural connotations can be interpreted from the attitudes that various ethnic groups hold to same clothing or accessories, then it is quite possible for the wearer to stimulate unexpected emotional reactions from others. In fact, every ethnic group or country has the fashion creative connected with its own culture, presenting a unique artistic and aesthetic style in expression. However, ethnic or local fashion cannot be limited within the life circle of an ethnic group, it inevitable involves the cross-cultural communication between ethnic groups, as well as their mutual interpretation on clothing and culture.

Each ethnic group concerns in a unique manner issues of aesthetics and culture in the clothing lifestyle, as they are related to the inherent spiritual characteristics of each ethnic existence, and indicative of the idiosyncrasy of each ethnic civilization. "...For example, fashion of France is generally luxury and high-end, of Italy proud and elegant, of Britain fantastic and strange, of Japan functional and useful, of China classical and delicate, of Africa primitive and simple, and of Australia pragmatic and sensible." ❶ Actually, survival requires not only natural and physical space, but also social and cultural one. Of course, fashion culture could not be constructed through blind inheritance, that is, analysis, reflection and cultural criticism on local culture are always necessary in the process. In brief, the distinction made between fashion styles is but relative and historical.

The differences in creative and design between ethnic groups could be regarded as the distinctions in art and cultural anthropology between them. As creative and expressions of art and fashion originate from human creativity, skills and talents, it may well be said that human culture is the very product of creativity and innovation. However, if one ethnic group just insists on its own culture and rejects other ones, it will be caught in closed and rigid local culture, with its art and costume culture greatly restricted in inheritance and development. Later anthropological construction aiming to understand creative finds it necessary to relocate the creative and design characteristics of an ethnic group historically into the original lifestyle of that people. Also, holding fast to ethnic culture involves the relationship among different ethnic cultures and the mutual identification made in these cultures.

---

❶ Perna R. Fashion Forecasting [M]. Li Hongwei, et al (tr). Beijing: China Textile & Apparel Press, 2000: 144.

2. Cultural Context for Creative Visualization

Fashion creative and design are obviously inseparable from visualized expression. Although vision is not the only relevant sensory perception, it is often considered indispensable and stipulative for clothing art. Therefore, to have some idea about art, we must first study the structure and characteristics of human perception. Rudolf Arnheim believes that in human cognitive and aesthetic activities, visual thinking can be the most effective way of perception, which at the same time has the rational function of thinking. The visualization of ethnic clothing creative is an activity to construct social meaning, happening in a specific cultural context. It should be noted that for the reconstruction of ethnic elements in creative, the visualized cultural context is undoubtedly an indispensable foundation.

The designing of ethnical clothing and fashion not only takes cultural context as its important historical basis, but also concerns the characteristics of different ethnic cultures and their inter-relationship. It is worth noting that "the pure perception of sense organs, which is not touched by our past experience, our education and training, our points of view or other kinds of knowledge, does not exist at all." [1] In light of their connection with thinking activity, art and aesthetics need to be studied from a Gestalt approach, and their relationship with visual perception should be analyzed to start with. Vision is not an isolated part in artistic and aesthetic activities, and how to acquire a specific meaning through vision in those activities has much to do with cultural intervention. Of course, visual thinking is not limited to the scope of direct perception. Perception in a broad sense also covers the connection between mental images and direct sensibility.

Here, clothing art, ethnic fashion and cultural creative are all inseparable from the cultural implications embedded in visual expressions. Image, though not only the sole content of visual culture, is an important concern of it. Of course, visualization cannot be attributed to an existing model simply, because people interpret pictures in open and diverse manners, influenced by historical and contextual elements. More importantly, we should not regard image merely as a representation, namely, a visualized artifact that imitates an object, but as something closely related to the object, or even as an equivalent visual substitute of it.

Openness means we can not only construct a text by absorbing language, but also transform one text into the context of another one. There is undoubtedly a generative relationship between ethnic fashion text and cultural context. The structure of art is formed in the cultural context of ethnic existence, expressing in an artistic way the structuring of human activities, thus revealing the unique meaning of ethnic culture in its related context. It should be noted that "the formal

---

[1] Berleant A. Art and Engagement [M]. Li Yuanyuan (tr). Beijing: Commercial Press, 2013: 125.

elements of text do not exist independently, for they need a context to be meaningful."❶ The so-called cultural creative on clothing elements transforms abstract ethnic elements and cultural heritage into visualized expressions, making them interpreted in a certain social, historical and cultural context.

In other words, creative tries to integrate originality, change and strangeness into ethnical elements and culture with spiritual characteristics. The generation of artistic text is not simple association and aggregation of abstract elements, but meaningful and symbolic representation of cultural elements. Moreover, the generation game of costume and artistic creative demonstrates a unique cultural nature. For different social and historical periods, people's inclination for novelty and the ethnic collective unconsciousness have always generated the relevant context of fashion art and culture, so fashion has become an indispensable cultural consumption in modern society. Here, fashion art and culture can reflect certain political and economic forms, which will in turn be internalized into textual factors.

To a certain extent, new visual creative embodies the trend of cultural generation and construction, as it is often novel, cutting-edge and active. Fashion art and culture are always closely related to mass media, which is an important field for fashion generation and dissemination. Meanwhile, the visualization of creative is bound up with times and culture. For example, "before the 1960s, hat used to be a part of the traditional dressing."❷ In the daily life of general public, clothes can fully satisfy people's consumption desires for fashion. However, the generation and realization of this fashion consumption are inseparable from the specific habit and cultural context of an ethnic group. At the same time, fashion inevitably plays a role in deconstructing and reconstructing traditional culture.

In the daily life, various ethnic groups regard clothing not only as their practical necessities, but also as the means to construct the social and cultural meanings of their living, although this construction is sometimes ignored by people. For example, the new generation of hip-hop fashion culture focuses on displaying individuality and expressing true self through various creative and techniques. Moreover, the fashion subculture is often sporadic, changing and participatory, which seems to demand no professional or special technical training for common people to engage in its spreading. And like all other forms of subculture, fashion is inherently characteristic of competitiveness.

Considering that creative and design express meaning through communication and dialogue,

---

❶ Alexander V D. Sociology of the Arts [M]. Zhang Hao, Shen Yang (tr). Nanjing: Jiangsu Fine Arts Publishing House, 2009:329.

❷ Ffoulkes F. How to Read Fashion [M]. New York: Rizzoli International Publications, Inc. 2013:176 .

cultural context is an unavoidable issue in fashion studies. In contemporary times, popular fashion culture generally advocates freedom and self-expression, and creative often start from personal feelings to construct the so-called free lifestyle. According to Galliano, the inspiration of fashion creative comes from diverse cultures of different periods and places. But in the mass culture stipulated by technology, uniformity is exactly what ethnic creative and design should respond to and dispel. Creative visualization involves the visual transformation of concepts and ideas. This transformation is related to the lifestyle and culture of certain ethnic group, and concerns ways of echoing with the specific culture.

But it should also be noted that dressing is a daily event for all ethnic groups, so creative and design need not over-consider cultural issues, at least not be too straightforward in illustrating relevant cultural elements. Although the age of consumption is that of picture reading which focuses on visual spectacles, the importance of text and context should not be ignored. In fact, both image and text are important forms of expression, and "for the things we talk about with their extended meaning, peoples without texts express them with their original meaning." ❶ How to interpret creative from the existence and culture of an ethnic group without texts is also a question to be considered in ethnic fashion design. The centralized subject constructed by traditional visual centralism will inevitably be dissolved and deconstructed in the sight weaving of today.

When people read images, produce creative and express ideas, words exert profound social and cultural influences that cannot be ignored. While Jacques Lacan mainly put the construction of the subject back to his cultural and language environment through the psychoanalysis of his desire, Michel Foucault revealed the power operation mechanism by which the subject is constructed in his cultural and language environment. In fact, modern visual experiences are mostly technology-based, and the world is encoded into images through the visual machine. In the generation of creative, the vital thing is to transform ideas into visual simulacra bearing on the culture of a specific ethnic group. This image simulation constructed by creative visualization also needs to be responded in a cultural sense. Visualization provides a fundamental context for the production of simulacra, which, however, also rely on experiences related to generativism.

Different from general phenomenology, generativism regards the generation of experience as a matter of phenomenology, and provides the possibility for this generation. Here, the visualized idea must be transformed into a kind of visual experience, which is not only the activation of idea, but also the meaning product of the idea visualization. And the realistic and impressionistic styles of creative visualization are distinguished from each other on one hand, interwoven

---

❶ Lévi-Strauss C. Regarder Ècouter Lire [M]. Gu Jiachen (tr). Beijing: China Renmin University Press, 2006:174.

aesthetically and culturally with each other on the other hand. The meaning product mentioned above is the fundamental source of creative simulacra, and it puts creative simulacra back into the relevant cultural contexts for the sake of construction. At the same time, relevant cultural contexts themselves can be reconstructed into ethical fashion texts too.

Therefore, cultural context is extremely important in the visualization of creative, and it is even an indispensable foundation for all ethnic fashion creative and designs. In fact, the visualization of idea has always been contextual. Taking various factors as relevant for understanding, it provides artistic and intellectual experience for creative. "Although art is characteristic of representation, it illustrates the real similarity between visual and verbal expressions through the meaning of its examples in the establishment of a visual communication system, which underlines the importance of cultural traditions."[1] People also need to obtain visual experiences about the world through images with the aid of specific machine or technology. There is undoubtedly a complex generative relationship between people's behavior, image and machine. For the visualization of ethnic creative, visual understanding and interpretation is also related to various non-visual contextual factors.

Moreover, what the designer wants to express is transmitted through visual experience to those who can receive this experience. In that sense, visual experience plays a role in communication and cultural dissemination. Many fields are involved in the designing of visual communication, including various creative designs. Because of its vividness and perceptibility, visual culture generally could attract people's attention and hold psychological appeals for them. Of course, different ethnic groups have different psychological and cultural understandings of visual experience. As the context for the visualization of ethnic creative, ethnic culture is extremely complicated in its composition and its forms of openness and generation. At the same time, the conflict and reconciliation between the visualized and the real worlds are also issues to be responded to in fashion creative and designs.

Western culture cannot be simply attributed to individuality, nor Eastern culture collectivity. The difference and complementarity between these two cultures must be taken into full account. Moreover, different political, economic and social contexts have created and changed the concepts and characteristics of art and culture. It is because of the intervention of culture as a context that the visualization of ethnic creative would not fall into emptiness, but help overcome the separation between visual appearance and inner spirit. In this era of globalization, it is urgent to promote the complementation and integration of Eastern and Western arts and cultures. Thanks to the

---

[1] Layton R. The Anthropology of Art [M]. Li Dongye, Wang Hong (tr). Guilin: Guangxi Normal University Press, 2009:129.

mutual generation of Eastern and Western arts and cultures, differences and diversity can co-exist harmoniously in a real sense.

It should also be noted that, the depthless appeal of postmodernist popular culture calls for and praises the art and discourse style which is characteristic of direct and plain visualization and devoid of grand narrative. But only in a certain cultural context with its unique characteristics can ethnic creative and designs avoid homogeneity. Elements involved in creative and designs are undoubtedly diverse, mutually related and generated in various cultural contexts. Moreover, the relevance between creative visualization and cultural context is historical, inseparable from the existence and lifestyle of an ethnic group. "The father of anthropology"Edward Burnett Taylor holds that in the broad sense of ethnography, culture or civilization is a complex whole acquired by people as members of society. Therefore, culture is a spiritual product that people have accumulated and acquired over a long period of time.

Coming from its continuity and inheritance, the historical character of culture helps to reject wonton interference and artificial forgery, and it is inseparable from the lifestyle and spiritual aspirations of an ethnic group. Of course, "Today's life style no longer stops at the boundaries of ethnic cultures."❶ Instead, it often transcends the boundaries and presents its own manners in other cultures. The visualization of ethnic creative should be based on the artistic exchanges and cultural dialogues between ethnic groups, as it is of no substantive significance to make a simple distinction between them. Every ethnic group has its unique cultural symbols, with its ethnic spiritual pattern perfused in those cultural codes.

Of course, the unique cultural symbols of an ethnic group can be presented through ethnic codes and artistic expressions. In terms of clothing culture, every member of the social group is specific and unique in wearing, and individual person put on their dressing on the basis of their specific need and their judgment on the situation. In today's world, we should recognize the humanistic value and meaning of ethnic traditional artistic styles, as well as the diversity of cultures, because they form the indispensable context for the creative composing and design of ethnic fashion. However, it is also undesirable for fashion art and cultural construction if we over emphasize the superiority of certain ethnic group while ignore the peculiarity and cultural characteristics of others. All concepts and creative should be expressed visually in a certain way, but it is extremely important in design whether and to what extent the visual expression fits in with the concept.

We should pay attention to protecting ethnic costumes and cultural traditions in a variety

---

❶ Welsch W. Undoing Aesthetics [M]. Lu Yang, Zhang Yanbing (tr). Shanghai: Shanghai Translation Publishing House, 2002:197.

of ways, in case these traditions should decline or even disappear in the trend of globalization. If different ethnic groups share cultures with each other and fully respect each other's beliefs and cultural differences, they could effectively eliminate ethnic barriers and achieve mutual understanding and tolerance on ethnic existence and culture. Of course, clothing culture can spread across ethnic groups, distinguishing and integrating the lifestyles of different people. It is also worth noting that texts and contexts from different cultures could be transformed into or generated by each other. As the context of a specific ethnic fashion, a culture can become the fashion text of another ethnic group through textualization. Undoubtedly, any creative and its visual expression must be fundamentally based on certain social, historical and cultural context.

3. Visual Expression of Ethnic Creative Culture

Each ethnic group has its own culture of creative, which, as the prerequisite for design, also needs to be generated and expressed through visualization in clothing. It can be said that the culture of creative concerns the understanding and elucidation on creative, and the revelation on the meaning and value of creative. In creative and designs, on one hand, each ethnic group has its irreplaceable characteristics of creative culture; on the other hand, the dialogues of different arts and cultures promote people's understanding of ethnic costume arts and creative designs. Therefore, the visualization of ethnic creative is inseparable from specific cultural context, while the culture of ethnic creative is embodied through visualization in return.

Undoubtedly ethnic creative culture cannot be separated from visual expression, and this expression is the embodiment of creative culture in fashion. In fact, all arts and designs involve the issue of visually expressing culture in proper ways. Among all human senses, vision is often the one with certain stipulation and dominance. Here, "visual language is also like spoken language, passed from culture to culture, from generation to generation."[1] In ethnic costumes and fashion designs, various art schools and styles are constructed through visualization, forming a unique dimension to reveal the culture of creative. In academic norms, art is generally categorized into visual art, and many designs are closely related to vision. It may be said that, all design arts are based on aesthetics and culture.

Different from classical and modern arts, contemporary art emphasizes the unique feelings and individual expression of artist, and various art schools express fashion creative from their specific perspectives. In contemporary times, it is existence rather than reason that prescribes art and thought. At the same time, visual art is closely related to human physical existence, and physicality

---

[1] Bloomer C M. Principles of Visual Perception [M]. Zhang Gongqian (tr). Beijing: Peking University Press, 1987:55.

has even become an indispensable ontological basis for designing. Therefore, it can be said that visual art and beauty are generated in the realm of existence. In other words, nowadays visual art expressions are inseparable from people's living conditions. In the era of visual culture, image representation has become an important way of artistic composition and fashion communication. Different from existence in modern times, postmodern body is generated in discourse construction.

Of course, art and design concern not only visual and aesthetic issues, but also psychological and cultural ones. Moreover, everything about visual art, including its meaning, expression, connection with culture, inner mental schema and stipulation, etc., is historically changed and generated in a certain context. Away from the homogeneity of design, visual expressions of different ethnic creative cultures are absolutely necessary for the generation and construction of cultural heterogeneity. In fact, visual product can not only become a text, but also exist as a response to creative culture. Expression of diversity such as mixing, collage, and global localization is an indispensable way to construct heterogeneous culture. As an important type of industry, cultural creative industry is rapidly emerging and developing.

The cultural industry of ethnic creative is an extension of creative industry to ethnic art and culture, as it is generated and constructed by the combination of creative industry and ethnic cultural characteristics. Of course, creative industries were formed after the industrialization of developed countries in Europe and the United States, when traditional industries began to transform into service industries and high value-added manufacturing ones. In other words, while old industries and cities in developed countries came to decline, the need for economic transformation and cultural development emerged. In the 1960s, large-scale social movements occurred in European and American art and culture, and various subcultures, pop cultures, and social thoughts sprang up, which had great impacts on the traditional structure of industrial society.

At the same time, various arts and cultures have largely affected visual expressions of creative culture. In contemporary clothing and fashion creative, designers try to oppose traditional mainstream culture, promote the liberation of individuality and the generation of new sensibility by emphasizing differences and recognizing alternative cultures that were considered weird previously. Accordingly, art, design and social culture have walked into an increasingly diversified pattern, forming an atmosphere conducive to the production of unique visual creativity. In the visual expressions of creative culture, the issues on physical body in fashion are actually those on society and culture. Since the appearance of its concept at the end of the twentieth century, people have regarded creative industry as an important component of the cultural industry. In fact, creative and cultural industry are different not only from traditional art and design, but also from general industries in concept, attribute and traditional classification.

In the process of visualizing concepts and creative, especially in the designing of fashion patterns, techniques like conceptualizing, arranging, combining, and mix-and-match have been widely used for reference. As far as cultural creative is concerned, the designs and aesthetic expressions of ethnic fashion are always related to various cultures, with technical means and methods served as their basis. On the issue of how to cultivate people's creative abilities, "I suggest the best way of training is to study works in the field of social sciences."❶ because this way can not only help designers construct proper theoretical perspectives, but also enhance their understanding of the lives and cultures of specific ethnic groups.

It is different disciplines and ideas that constitute the multiple perspectives of creative visualization. Meanwhile, one fundamental problem to be solved by cultural creative is, how technology can better reveal the fundamental meaning of culture rather than conceal it with technological expressions. In the era of new media and big data, the visual expression of ethnic creative culture has become a topic in urgent need of attention. If an idea is rapidly disseminated through information technology, without embodying a profound cultural context, then it couldn't become a good form of creative cultural communication, nor reveal the essence of a brand culture. In fact, the aesthetic evaluation on the visual expressions of ethnic creative culture is linked with ethnic psychology and culture.

The expression and dissemination of ethnic creative culture are related to the relationship between commercialization, consumer culture and creative industries, as well as to the understanding and interpretation of the cross-cultural communications of different ethnicities. Moreover, different clothing concepts and cultures between the East and the West inevitably lead to unique understandings on the expression of fashion creative, such as the implicitness of the East and the explicitness of the West. It should also be noted that the inducement from the fashion market may undermine the autonomy of creative, so how to deal with the complex relationship between market, business and creative will have a far-reaching impact on the development of the cultural industry. If creative is completely subject to commerce, market, and consumption, the spiritual characteristics contained in the creative may be weakened greatly, eventually resulting in the disappearance of the daily life foundation and specific cultural context on which the creative industry depends.

With people's art accomplishment and aesthetic taste improving, those fashion expressions lacking spiritual and cultural characteristics will hardly win their favor. Of course, we should keep reflecting popular art, aesthetic experience and fashion culture in a critical way. Cultural

---

❶ Young J W. A Technique for Producing Ideas [M]. Zhu Shiwei (tr). Beijing: China Renmin University Press, 2014:36.

creative industry and cultural industry cannot be confused as equivalent concepts, though visual information and transmission are indispensable to both of them. It can be said that "the diversity in the fashion field is the very product of huge amounts of visual information, which launches visual bombardments to us every day."❶ What we get through vision are various image reconstructions of reality, which then become an intuitive representation of creative culture. It is the inherent appeal of creative design to promote the generation and contemporary construction of ethnic cultural creative on the basis of new artistic concept, aesthetic perspective and cultural context.

Undoubtedly, the innovation of ethnic concepts and thoughts is fundamental to creative culture and its visual expression, for cultural creative is produced by people of wisdom and unique thinking, who interpret traditional elements with contemporary theories and thoughts to make those ideas both feasible and culture-loaded. Any kind of fashion creative and designing, unable to be separated from specific cultural context of an ethnic group, is the visual expression of ethnic mental schema against that context. Different ethnic groups vary in their understanding and interpretation of creative culture and of the generative relationship between creative culture and mental schema. Creative has never been a simplified adoption or copy of traditional culture.

Creative often reconstruct traditional cultural elements in the current context through people's inspiration, imagination, divergent thinking, as well as various expressions. In addition to traditional artistic and cultural elements, the fashion of an ethnic group must also construct and express a specific sense of the present time. Therefore, creative may start with fabrics, styles, colors or details, the expressions of which, however, are closely related to technology and culture. Throughout the history of Chinese clothing, traditional clothing art and culture have shown great diversity due to China's vast territory and numerous ethnic groups. Then, as typical styles of Oriental clothing, ethnic costumes in countries like China, India or Turkey are inevitably influenced by post-colonial orientalist construction in the contemporary era. However, the historical and cultural characters of an ethnic group can actually be seen as the traditional pedigree abided by its ancestors.

The clothing creative and designs of some ethnic group may seem similar to those of others in terms of clothing material and style, but subtle differences worthy of attention can still be found through careful observation. For example, Hanfu, or Han Chinese costume, enjoying a long history, can be divided into formal and informal dress. Although it retains its main forms through ages, it boasts various styles and presents different characteristics in different dynasties. In terms of its diversified styles, there are such types as upper jacket and lower skirt, one-piece robe, jacket

---

❶ Svendsen L. Fashion: A Philosophy [M]. Li Man (tr). Beijing: Peking University Press, 2010:147.

and dress, and so on. The visual understanding and interpretation on the creative culture of Hanfu cannot be separated from its specific form, ritual connotation and costume culture. In creative producing and fashion designing, Hanfu has undergone changes due to the influence of other ethnic groups.

Considering the diverse styles and forms of ethnic costumes, we should pay full attention to the differences in the lifestyle and culture of different ethnic groups. For example, adapting to the wide forests and grasslands with cold and windy weather, the ethnic minorities in north China mostly rely on hunting and pastoralism for their livelihoods; while the ethnic minorities in south China are mostly engaged in farming, because mountains and basins are alternately distributed there, with the weather humid and hot. These geographical and environmental differences between the south and the north are issues not to be ignored in the design of traditional clothing. In other words, certain natural environment, production mode and lifestyle have generated in a sense specific ethnic character, psychological pattern and aesthetic culture, hence come different clothing styles, characteristics and visual expressions of design.

For another example, the ethnic minorities who live on highland meadows and engaged in animal husbandry, such as Mongolian, Tibetan, Kazakh, Kirgiz, Tajik, etc., usually use the fur of livestock in daily clothes designing, edging the collars, cuffs, front part, and lower hem of their clothes with colored cloth or fine fur. For instance, the coats of the Kazakhs are usually wadded with camel hair, feeling very light and warm. And their typical clothes are broad robes with large sleeves, looking thick and solemn. Different from northern minorities, the southern ones live in the areas suitable for flax and cotton planting, so self-woven linen and home-made cloth are the main materials for their dresses. Despite their simple tools, they can produce exquisite fabrics and wonderful patterns. Suited to the hot and humid weather, their dresses are often short, narrow, light, and thin, without covering their chest and legs fully, showing diverse and lively clothing styles. In a word, the visual expressions of creative culture produce specific fashion styles related to specific regions.

To understand and interpret daily clothing life is obviously indispensable for the visual expression of ethnic creative cultures. In fact, different ethnic characteristics are the cultural anthropological basis of ethnic visual expression. For ethnic groups from different regions, it is the distinctions between diverse dressing styles that constitute the art and culture of ethnic minority costumes. In the visual expressions of ethnic creative cultures, various forms and styles construct various aesthetic habits. In modern and contemporary times, as the so-called Other in the mainstream western culture, visual images full of oriental implications are becoming an exotic flavor in the fashion industry. And this exotic pattern and style in turn affects the Eastern creative culture and fashion design.

Generally speaking, the clothes of Chinese ethnic minorities are difficult to make because they need abundant material, complicated decoration and delicate in craftsmanship, which also make them inconvenient to wear and wash. Therefore, many ethnic minorities turn to wear Hanfu, or Han Chinese costume, to the degree that in some areas, ethnic costumes can hardly be seen. In response to this severe situation, we should promptly rescue and classify ethnic minority clothing resources, preventing distinctive ethnic clothing cultures from disappearing. In fact, "visual culture, usually seen as distracting people from serious matters such as text and history, is now a scene for cultural and historical changes."[1] At the same time, the relevance between visual culture and cultural study is receiving increasing attention. At the present stage, ethnic characteristics are not only an issue faced by ethnic minority costume cultures, but also a design topic for the reconstruction of these cultures.

Based on the cultural characteristics of ethnic costumes, creative and design should strive for the taste and elegance of clothes, making them beautiful, simple and practical enough to meet people's needs in production, life and aesthetics. Integrating the relationship between culture and people into the design is very important to the visualization of ethnic creative culture. One problem is that, in diversified expressions of visual creative and design, some designers pay too much attention to the superficial magnificence of artistic effects, while ignore the understanding and interpretation on inner mental schema. In the process of producing fashion creative, any visualization should become a unique revelation of the mental schema, which involves the in-depth participation of theoretical perspectives and thought construction.

In fact, clothing cultures of various ethnic groups or countries often show distinct spiritual characteristics, such as Afghanistan women's chadri which covers the whole body, Japanese kimono, Indian women's sari, Indonesian sarong for both men and women, Scottish men's kilt, Hawaiian loose unbelted Muumuu, and Indian cape-style poncho. Fashion dialogue and cultural exchanges across ethnic groups are undoubtedly indispensable for the visualization of ethnic creative, and the interpretation on ethnic fashion must be integrated into the visualization of ethnic costume creative. Although it is somehow hard for visualization, with a fuzzy demarcation, to express clothing spirit and culture, the series from the invisible to the visible produced by visualization is still essential for revealing and elucidating spiritual and cultural characteristics.

In the process of visualizing, new and invented images are produced and constructed firstly, which would then be infiltrated into the invisible things, so that thoughts and contexts of visual

---

[1] Mirzoeff N. An Introduction to Visual Culture [M]. Ni Wei (tr). Nanjing: Jiangsu People's Publishing House, 2006:39.

culture could be understood and interpreted anew. Merleau-Ponty emphasizes the physical connection and basis of vision and other means of perception. Here the problem is that, besides the different worlds in the eyes of different individuals or ethnic groups, approaching the world itself is an endless process of phenomenological reduction. In the context of postmodernism, the views on the imitating or reflecting nature of images in the dualistic perspective are losing their popularity or even their basic legitimacy. In fact, the Cartesian visual centralism would be inevitably subverted and deconstructed.

Actually, the duality between rationality and sensibility have lost its fundamental meaning and purpose in modern ontology. In terms of the ethnic visualization of creative, there are undoubtedly differences in the mental schemas and special forms of different ethnic groups. On the issue of Orientalism, "Western critics who criticize Orientalism often use antagonistic terms to describe it. Therefore, this enduring Kipling viewpoint considers East and West as polarities hostile forever to each other." [1] If you just borrow the thoughts of linguistic philosophy and understand images as a kind of linguistic symbol, you still cannot ignore the differences between ethnic groups in custom and culture. Even in the post-modern era, expressions and communications on spirit, creative and visualization could keep falling into the predicaments of duality.

Therefore, ignoring the differences in visions and images will inevitably obscure the uniqueness of visual representations, especially the anthropological meaning of this uniqueness. In the context of post-modern art and culture, simulacrum makes a virtual and realistic illusion for the public, and the authenticity of the visual representation on the world is often questioned. To a certain extent, what vision realizes is the deconstruction of concepts such as rationality and order, which results in visual alienation, fictitiousness, and dazing carnival. In fact, the collusion between postmodern thoughts and consumer culture has led to the deconstruction of the realness of visual representation, leading people into an unprecedented visual crisis for human beings. Therefore, the study on ethnic creative culture and its visualization requires us to analyze and overcome the problems in visual representation.

Section 3   Generation of Ethnicity and Visual Expression of Fashion

In the expression of fashion creative, ethnicity is neither tangible being, nor fixed ready-made article, but something constructed in constant change and generation. To understand and elucidate creative visually is undoubtedly the cultural basis for the expression of fashion design, as

---

[1] Clarke J J. Oriental Enlightenment: The Encounter Between Asian and Western Thought [M]. Yu Minmei, Zeng Xiangbo (tr). Shanghai: Shanghai People's Publishing House, 2011:299.

well as the prerequisite for the dissemination and acceptance of fashion culture. In fact, there is no ethnicity readily accepted by everyone, which need manifest itself in continuous construction and reconstruction. Fashion design and visual expression must not only analyze and explore general design issues, but also interpret the generative characteristics of an ethnic group. Fashion creative concerns the existence of an ethnic group, as well as cultural communication and understanding across ethnicities. No doubt, to elucidate the spiritual meaning, cultural value and historical generation of ethnic elements is essential for ethnic costume and creative design.

1. Generation of Ethnicity in Creative

Whether in its free form of general themes, or in the form of fashion and clothing design, art is always an important means to display human culture in some specific field. In the context of Western civilization and culture, visual art has always occupied a dominant position, exerting a stipulative influence on modern fashion creative and design. Therefore, the visual expression of clothing and fashion creative has become an issue not to be neglected in creative culture and industry. In this visual expression and transmission, specific people or ethnic group should be considered as the anthropological being. The ethnicity of creative is not a fixed entity, but something generated in constant construction and reconstruction. Ethnicity is represented and interpreted as the uniqueness of ethnic group in its existence. Meanwhile, ethnicity is in a constant generation, so is the revelation on this ethnic character.

In the generation of ethnic fashion creative, to display ethnicity is undoubtedly an important stipulation, which, however, should not be regarded as immutably deterministic. Fashion creative is often inseparable from the existence of certain ethnic group in its cultural context. It should be noted that "the aesthetic concern for human appearance includes the concern for hairdressing, clothing, or other adornments such as tattoos, scratches, body paintings, accessories, etc." [1] And this aesthetic concern, together with the understanding and interpretation of it, is inseparable from the spiritual and cultural characters of each ethnic group. Therefore, ethnicity and its generative relationship with spirit schema have even become an important source of fashion cultural creative. The expression of ethnic fashion creative involves multiple factors and complex relationships, as well as ubiquitous multicultural context.

No doubt, the way that cultural creative of fashion is linked with ethnic elements should be given serious attention and in-depth exploration. The generation and artistic expression of fashion creative are concerned with the visualization of concepts and ideas, which is the main means to

---

[1] Van Damme W. Anthropology of Aesthetics: Perspective and Methods [M]. Li Xiujian, Xiang Li (tr). Beijing: China Federation of Literary and Art Circles Publishing house, 2015:37.

express fashion art. Specifically, the visual reconstruction of ethnic elements is involved. The existence of an ethnic group with its ethnicity is not only the essential basis for the construction of ethnic culture, but also the inspiring source of ethnic fashion creative. But this does not mean that, there exists a single ethnic character, which regulates in a simple way the generation and expression of fashion creative.

Rather, ethnicity permeates the foundation of all ethnic fashion creative, as well as the composition of all fashion-related elements. At the same time, the ethnicity of any group is actually intangible. Ethnicity is important in fashion because "in this chaotic era full of heterogeneous standards and mechanical noises, what attracts us strongly is the culture of this or that ethnic group." [1] We may also say that ethnicity is the anthropological basis of ethnic fashion creative, and the spiritual and cultural traits that fashion expression tries to reveal. Moreover, costumes and cultures of different ethnic groups are not only distinguished from each other, but also related to each other in their common life and cross-cultural communication. For example, in China's Sui and Tang dynasties, costumes and cultures of different ethnicities learned from and merged into each other in a significant way.

As the fundamental stipulation in ethnic art and culture, ethnicity echoes art and culture through its own generation and construction. More importantly, to penetrate ethnic elements into fashion art, we should consider such problems as how to fashionize those elements, or, how to achieve a fashion sense through specific artistic expressions. For example, the fashion designing of Kenzo Takada takes the forms of kimonos and oriental ethnic costumes as its anthropological basis, supplemented with clothing styles from other parts of the world. In ethnic fashion creative and cultural construction, we should pay full attention to revealing and interpreting the characteristics of ethnic elements. Only through the emphasis on ethnic character, fashion creative could establish an ethnic foundation and cultural heritage, which in turn would be displayed through fashionizing methods.

The boundary between clothing and culture of an ethnic group has never been clear and fixed, for the two sides are in constant historical changes while taking each other as reference. Within a certain geographical area, people living together often have similar lifestyles, customs and cultures, distinguishing themselves from other ethnic groups in thinking mode, lifestyle, behavior habit, and custom. Even in modern and contemporary times when ethnic groups are closely linked with each other, their respective cultural composition could be expressed and responded to in fashion art. In the identity establishing process of human beings, the ethnic and cultural differences, often

---

[1] Benedict R. Patterns of Culture [M]. He Xizhang & Huang Huan (tr). Beijing: Huaxia Publishing House, 1987: 15.

reflected in the whole ethnic group living together, is actually the indispensable ethnicity of each group.

With the historical generation of society and culture, specific habits and traditions have been constructed within each ethnic group, influencing most members of the group, but these habits and traditions are not different from those of other groups in an absolute sense. Therefore, "for the royal families of China's Sui and Tang Dynasties, the cross-cultural communication in ethnic integration and clothing interpenetration was not only a political strategy to govern the country, but in a sense an innate way of life penetration and culture inheritance."[1] Generally, each ethnic group established its lifestyles and dressing behaviors on the basis of its own ethnic character, distinguishing itself from other groups in the field of clothing culture. It is probably the need to survive that drove people to live together in the primitive society.

In other words, it is difficult for isolated individuals to survive at that time, and people within a certain area naturally gathered together to live a common life. In aspects of spiritual pursuit and cultural acquisition, ethnic group members tend to approve their own ethnic traditions and follow the existing dressing paradigm. Therefore, ethnic consciousness and culture constitute the spiritual foundation for the internal connection and integration within the ethnic group. Here, the historical character is not about the time but the foundation and essence of the history. Art and clothing can be regarded related to the existence of an ethnic group in terms of historical character. For example, the men of Chinese Jingpo ethnic group wear white short coats and white turbans with pompons, while the women generally wear black velvet short coats and red knitted floral skirts. Undoubtedly, art and clothing design should be based on specific social, historical and cultural context if ethnicity need to be generated and established.

In the existence and interaction of different ethnic groups, their mutual influence is an issue to be faced and responded to in art and cultural dissemination. In this process, the art and culture of one ethnic group should not suppress and replace those of other groups. For example, "When the Tuoba people in China's Northern Wei Dynasty definitely adopted the surnames, court etiquette and costumes of the Han people, it was considered a high degree of sinicization."[2] It is the mutual respect and equal exchanges between ethnic groups that form the rational basis for design and cultural transmission. Then primitive culture, an original form of culture, provides the source and primary stipulation for the occurrence of art. In other words, art itself is generated and constructed by primitive culture. For instance, in the primitive society, masks were mostly used in religious and

---

[1] Zhang Zhichun. Chinese Costume Culture [M]. Beijing: China Textile & Apparel Press, 2009:228.

[2] Thorp R L, R E. Vinograd. Chinese Art and Culture [M]. Zhang Xin (tr). Beijing: Beijing United Publishing Company, 2014:131.

witchcraft activities, but later they gradually became a prop for opera and dance. Also, early myths explained nature in an imaginative and allegorical way.

The basic topics of mythology consist in the interpretation on the stories with symbolized meanings in a specific culture and the research on the relationship between these similar stories in different cultures, and all these provide a discourse basis for the construction of ethnicity in creative. As a cultural style, costume reveals and highlights people's appeal for non-utilitarian aesthetics, and it is in a relationship of mutual generation and construction with ethnic culture, rather than of part and whole simply. The logical relationship between whole and part, such as including and being included, would inevitably obscures the fundamental relationship of mutual generation between costume and culture. Of course, the expression and aesthetic experience of ethnic art are not necessarily non-utilitarian and free, as they are sometimes closely linked with practicality and life. Folk craft is one such example.

In the process of clothing design, we should not only pay attention to the functional requirements, but also be concerned with the construction of aesthetics and ethnic culture. The generative relationship between creative and ethnicity brings about the mutual generation between synchronicity and diachronicity in design. Moreover, when the historical existence of ethnicity is shown in creative, ethnic art and culture go into the process of reconstruction. For example, as a form of ethnic culture, Tujia culture is a unique product of Tujia people's living conditions, group psychology, and ethnic identity. No doubt, the meaning of ethnic culture is inseparable from ethnic history and cultural heritage. We may ever say that, this culture, though often hidden and concealed in daily life, exists just in the historical development of the ethnic group.

In a certain sense, it is the differences in customs and habits between ethnic groups that constitute the unique existence and spiritual character of ethnic culture. Through their customs and habits, which are often manifested in forms like songs, dances, and costumes, ethnic groups protect and inherit their ethnic cultures and arts. Some ethnic costumes are relatively stable, experiencing little change. For example, "Romanian ethnic costume has hardly changed in centuries of development, with its basic forms and styles inherited to the present."[1] But other ethnic costumes change their art expressions and traditions eventually in the common life with other ethnic groups. Ethnic art and culture not only embody ethnicity and collective unconsciousness, but also reflect cosmopolitan arts and cultures in the ethnic basis. Therefore, we should return to the generation of ethnic art from its text and context, that is, reveal and interpret the generation of art from the perspective of ethnic character.

---

[1] Wu Yanyan (ed). Introduction to European National Costumes [M]. Beijing: China Textile & Apparel Press. 2016:28.

The design of ethnic costume and fashion need consider the lifestyle and acceptance habit of specific ethnic group, as well as the ethnicity formed unconsciously in the inheritance of ethnic culture. The formation of ethnicity for any ethnic group is inseparable from the collective memory and unconsciousness of that group. The intertextual connections between various ethnic elements display the unique style and spiritual character of art and culture. The generation of ethnic art and fashion, which in essence is the mutual generation of construction and deconstruction, reveal and manifest the historical generation of ethnic character. Of course, cultural context doesn't remain fixed and stable, but changes with the existence of the ethnic group and the historical development of culture. In the generation of fashion text and its cultural context, ethnicity has a unique stipulation and cultural influence on the formation of design and aesthetic style.

The game of creative on art and clothing highlights its unique ethnic culture and generative nature. Fashion design can neither be completely separated from the historical character of an ethnic group, nor be reduced to a simple illustration of ethnic character. Here, the historical generation and revelation of ethnicity not only make ethnic art and culture an important cultural style, but also highlight the distinction in art and culture between different ethnic groups. Fashionable clothes in Europe, America, and other regions across the world are actually distinguished from each other with their specific ethnic characters, and these characters have been manifested in unique ways through fanshionization, but the boundaries among them are becoming blurred and indefinite due to intertwining and communication.

As a creative activity with embodiment, clothing design inevitably concerns its relationship with ethnic and epochal characters. It should be said that the ethnic and cultural characters of art text are not just a collection of abstract elements, but a meaningful symbol of various elements with unique inter-relationships, as well as an aesthetic and cultural representation of the specific concerns of fashion creative. For example, "it is well known that Italian fashion is so delicate in matching of color and using of fabrics that it even surpasses French fashion in these aspects, and Italians produce wool fabrics thicker and softer than others do." [1] However, this symbolization of ethnicity should constantly go back to the existence and daily life of the ethnic group. Meanwhile, design activities must also consider the issue of ethnic identity recognition, that is, the contemporary acceptance and realization of ethnic cultural identities.

In the production of ethnic fashion creative, designers should respond to consumers' custom and culture as possible as they could, so that expressions of fashion could reveal and elucidate ethnic characters, and creative ideas based on ethnic characters could be transformed into

---

[1] Jones S J. Fashion Design [M]. Zhang Ling (tr). Beijing: China Textile & Apparel Press, 2009:46.

contemporary fashion arts with historical visual characters. Undoubtedly, ethnic fashion creative with its cultural identity is a cultural prerequisite for the recognition of ethnic character, while openness and mutual tolerance between different ethnic groups constitute the basis for cross-cultural communication. In view of the homogeneity that globalization may bring, the creative and cultural identity of ethnic fashion are particularly important.

Ethnic art and cultural identity are of great significance in opposing Western cultural hegemony. Numerous elements, being in a relationship too complex to be ignored, get involved in ethnic fashion creative, and each element is related to the entire ethnic culture in a specific way. For example, "in the research of fashion, the study on race usually concerns some obvious physical features, such as skin color, hair quality, facial features, etc." [1] Undoubtedly, the anthropological features of race must be considered in creative for the generation of ethnic character. It may be said that, ethnic element and culture demonstrate the potential character of creative, and influence the artistic quality of creative and the generation of specific cultural meaning. As a free creation of an artist, art is related to his/her aesthetic experience and spiritual world.

However, art does not just stay in the spiritual world of the artist, because art always involves the external representation of internal schema. In particular, when it walks out of the ivory tower of aestheticism, art gets involved in the field of social life more extensively and deeply. At the same time, when art is related to various cultures in a multi-dimensional manner, the meaning of its inner mental schema will be presented in numerous aspects bound up with vision. This connection between art and society, history and culture may exist in all artistic expressions and creative designs, but more prominently it will be manifested in fashion art. In the context of anthropology and sociology, the study on the relevance between ethnic fashion creative and ethnic lifestyle is of great necessity for the revelation and elucidation of ethnicity in creative.

2. Visual Generation and Expression of Ethnic Elements

The generation and existence of any ethnic element involves the formation of ethnic spiritual and cultural characters, and various social and cultural meanings could be constructed due to the openness and visual manifestation of these characters. Human beings create visual images to convey information and ideas, so vision has always been the basic means of human communication between people. No doubt, visual art has great significance for the inheritance and contemporary representation of traditional culture, as well as for the construction of human spiritual life. The relationship between fashion, society and culture is helpful for the in-depth research of creative and

---

[1] Kaiser S B. Fashion and Cultural Studies [M]. Guo Pingjian, et al (tr). Beijing: China Light Industry Press, 2016:62.

design. At the same time, the exploration, revelation and contemporary reconstruction of ethnic elements are extremely important in the art and design of ethnic costumes.

Fashion creative not only involves the manifestation of the text itself, but also the social and cultural symbolic meanings of codes. In writing or coded texts, the uniqueness of visual representation is often concealed in abstraction, but the visual expressions of ethnic elements must start from the text itself. "For example, semiotics regards every picture with images as a text, an encoded symbol containing particular intention and custom, and the uniqueness of the image seems to be weakened intentionally, making itself an integrated part of a network of interpretable objects." ❶ Of course, picture itself is a type of text, different from written text but intertextually related to the latter. Meanwhile, visual art expressions, with unique codes and connotations, have much to do with specific social and cultural identity.

The visual generation of ethnic elements considers not only issues of artistic expression and aesthetic experience, but also the relationship among various understandings and identifications. Actually, the visualized expression of ethnic elements and fashion creative tries to solve the problems like how to visualize non-visual things and how to reconstruct tradition. For example, the abstract patterns in central and western Bulgarian clothes do not conflict with modern aesthetic concepts. Ethnic element is usually interpreted as the basic unit that manifests ethnic spirit and cultural characteristics, which, however, cannot be constrained in the dilemma of traditional simple theory on element. Visual culture takes modern culture and post-modern culture as its research object and lays special emphasis on vision and aesthetic experience, but that does not mean the exclusion of senses other than vision.

In traditional visual art and expressions, designers usually display and interpret classic images or patterns, involving not only general issues on the creative and expressions of ethnic elements, but also unique composing techniques and reconstruction methods. In the creative generation of ethnic elements, specific methods based on visual expression are used to present and convey ethnic spirit and culture. Of course, different visual expressions contain different cultural implications. Visual language, mainly composed of visual basic elements following design principles, is a system of signs that conveys meaning under certain norms. And the meanings of these signs are linked with their social, historical, and cultural references.

No doubt, visual elements are indispensable for the reconstruction of ethnic element and the revelation of ethnic spirit and culture. The principles of design generally concern layout, contrast, rhythm, balance and unity, which are methods to convey meaning by organizing and using basic

---

❶ Mitchell W J T. Iconology: Image, Text, Ideology [M]. Chen Yongguo (tr). Beijing: Peking University Press, 2012:197.

elements. For example, "The human-shaped masks and totem poles on the northwest coast of the Americas have become the symbols of certain cultural heritage, popular across the world with the upsurge of tourists." [1] Of course, various art and design methods and principles should consider specific ethnic culture and context when they are applied to ethnic fashion, because only in certain cultural context can we express and interpret the spiritual characteristics contained in visual texts.

To meet specific needs and cultural demands, designers choose suitable materials, expression forms and techniques, reveal and reshape the relationship between elements in a certain context, and finally produce the pattern or style that could convey specific cultural meaning. Moreover, all created patterns and styles would surely provide reference for later designs. In modern clothing design, the composition of ethnic visual elements is diverse, variable, and generative. Designers often integrate points, lines, surfaces and colors according to utilitarian functions, social codes, and cultural appeals for the product. In addition, they should keep exploring various possibilities of visual expressions, including visual attraction, stimulation, manifestation and emotion manifestation, so as to reveal unique artistic characteristics and cultural appeals in a more effective way.

In Rudolf Arnheim's view, the appeal that people perceive from art shows precisely the relevance between the stimulus of the object and its physiological effect on people. And for the generative composition of various ethnic elements, visualization often contains the interweaving process between construction and reconstruction. According to Arnheim, the physical pattern of any work of art would evoke a force pattern similar to its own force structure. Or maybe we should say, design is to express the desire of the audience with creative works, which are produced in accordance with the forms, aesthetic associations, and affective characteristics of elements like points, lines, surfaces, color, etc.. Based on the traditional standard and aesthetic culture of classical art, it is stipulated and expressed by a series of categories and concepts, such as clear theme, well-matched color, and harmonious proportion.

Generally speaking, classical art is an artistic style characterized with grace and elegance, sometimes also sublime and magnificence. In different ethnic clothing styles, certain artistic expression and aesthetics may convey different meanings and tastes. Modernist art, dissimilar to classical art, emphasizes the self-discipline of art and aesthetics. "The production method on ethnic costume can be borrowed in terms of two levels: one is the enlightenment from the outer contour of clothing; the other is the reference on the internal structure of clothing." [2] Meanwhile,

---

[1] Mack J. (ed). Masks: The Art of Expression [M]. Yang Yang (tr). Guangzhou: Nanfang Daily Press, 2011:144.
[2] Ma Rong (ed). The Application of Ethnic Costume Language to Fashion [M]. Chongqing: Chongqing University Press, 2009:52.

references and reconstructions on these two levels are closely related, together providing important methods for ethnic fashion design. It is an unavoidable and irreversible aesthetic trend for artistic expression to go into society and daily life, which has to do with the openness of the artistic text itself, as well as the relevant social, historical and cultural contexts.

Undoubtedly, the expression methods and aesthetic appeals of classical and modern arts are related to modern epistemology, which, however, no longer has the fundamental stipulation on contemporary art. We may say, aesthetic culture is influenced by the generative relations among art, aesthetics and cultures, or, it is the cultural interpretation on artistic creation, appreciation, criticism and aesthetic experience. Obviously, the interpretation on art and design is inseparable from the unique aesthetic culture and lifestyle of certain ethnic group. In terms of the changes in modern and contemporary art expression and aesthetic experience, anti-art and anti-aesthetics, being essentially the generation process of a new art and aesthetic experience, have become a unique way to respond to traditional art and aesthetics.

In a sense, anti-art and anti-aesthetics are an alternative kind of art and aesthetics. They not only break through the standards of traditional art and aesthetics, but also cultivate the generative association of art and aesthetics with text and existence. The aesthetic experience generated by contemporary art is not only an experience concerned with the nature of existence, but also a textual experience about the discourse representation of desire. Moreover, the aesthetic experience of contemporary art affects the unique generation of meaning on visual culture, as well as the visual expression and cultural interpretation of ethnic elements in the contemporary context. Generally speaking, traditional art depends on people's contemplation and intuition. In essence, it does not rely on the participation and intervention of the viewer, or base the aesthetic appreciation on the dialogue and interaction between the artist and the public.

In contemporary art expression and fashion design, various ethnic elements have been introduced into the process from construction, deconstruction to reconstruction. Although the stipulation on art and aesthetics keeps being the fundamental issue that Western metaphysics studies and explores, it is still extremely difficult to answer the academic and theoretical question about what is the nature of art and aesthetics. Especially in the contemporary era, with Western metaphysical system and tradition severely criticized, concepts on the nature and stipulation of art and aesthetics have been toughly challenged and thoroughly deconstructed. As a form of metaphysics existing in art, art metaphysics has also been subject to constant questioning and strong criticism.

As far as creative and design are concerned, in different ethnic groups and times, skirts show different lengths and artistic styles, which forms the pluralistic and changeable characteristics of fashion visual expression. Moreover, the wheel of fashion turns in a certain rhythm and cycle, but constantly changing and breaking through previous restrictions, thus constructing an unexpected aesthetic effect of defamiliarization. It should be realized that visual culture, using visual perception as its expression mode, is not only the direct cultural representation and interpretation of visual impressions, but also the historical deposit of visual events occurring in a culture. But this close relevance between visual art and cultural concept is not limited within the life and cultural tradition of any specific ethnic group, but concerned with the characteristics of cross-cultural communication between all ethnic arts and cultures.

Of course, contemporary art puts more emphasis on the creative concepts occurring currently, rather than traditional rational concepts that are static and closed. This shows exactly the generative nature of visualization of ethnic elements. "As modern consumers, people construct their ethnic identity through the spatial and physical relationships expressed by fashion." ❶ The creative expression of ethnic clothing art cannot just stay at the representational level of visual art, instead, it should enter the deep structure of spirit and culture for better revelation. The problem here is that, contemporary art cannot avoid its focus on representation, and on the basis of which a visual code and a cultural representation system are generated, while this kind of cultural representation has to be faced with the current occurrence of art.

As a direct way of presentation, the visualization of art can be both a manifestation and a concealment of art. Therefore, the visual expression of ethnic elements and the production of clothing reveal and interpret those obscured meanings in a manner of fashion. Usually, ethnic art includes native artistic expressions, as well as art forms and traditions that absorb and incorporate foreign factors. For example, the Chinese art is a unity of artistic diversity, created by various ethnic groups with their respective characteristics. It is noteworthy that this mutual generation between ethnic vision and culture is constructed not only in the existence and life of an ethnic group, but also in the social and cultural context of the art text. Besides, contemporary creative and design of ethnic costumes provide new possibilities for the artistic expression of ethnic elements.

Visual culture based on image and art is actually a specific deposit of artistic concepts, often manifested and realized through visual representations. But the process needs to constantly break through the binary separation that is difficult for representation to get rid of. In the expression of ethnic art, the interweaving and interrelation between visual representation and cultural tradition is fundamental for the creative design of ethnic costume and fashion. If we, by taking ethnic elements

---

❶ Craik J. The Face of Fashion: Cultural Studies in Fashion [M]. Shu Yunzhong (tr). Beijing: Central Compilation & Translation Press, 2000:41.

in art and clothing as clues, makes an analysis on the aesthetic meaning and spirit associated with external expressions, we will better reveal and interpret the ethnicity and constitutive property of fashion creative. With the cross-cultural communication of art and fashion emerging and developing, the distinction and boundary between local culture and foreign culture have become increasingly blurred.

Ethnic minority art of the areas where ethnic minorities live, refers to the various art forms created and preserved by ethnic minorities, including traditional and modern art forms as well as their contemporary reconstructions. While we study Chinese ethnic art with the Han ethnicity as its main anthropological identity, obviously the existence of other ethnic arts and their mutual influences should not be ignored. In fact, any ethnic group, with its unique spiritual and cultural characteristics, is in close communication and intertextuality with others. At the same time, art is an important form in which ideology or mental schema can be expressed, and it often runs through the evolution and history of various ethnic groups. The understanding of ethnic art and culture and the elaboration on its generation are inseparable from the visual expression of ethnic elements, and elements of various ethnicity are inter-related visually and culturally.

Obviously, ethnic elements, art and culture are in an interweaving and generative relationship with each other. And communication, dialogue and mutual reference are indispensable for the creative producing and visualized expressing of ethnic elements. In other words, every kind of element has effect on the whole ethnic identity and existence. Through the revelation and elucidation of ethnic elements, we can grasp their significance and appeal for the study of art and culture. It should be noted that, fashion never falls limited to a particular ethnic identity, and each ethnic group has its own visual expression and aesthetic style, presenting its own fashion-related spiritual character through specific visualized images.

For ethnic groups, the inter-ethnicity of costumes can be interpreted both as a certain difference and as a visual and cultural fusion. In early Mexico civilization, deities in myths and legends were often depicted according to human shapes. Moreover, "deities of different places need to be distinguished from each other by nuances in clothing, making clothing the main part of most deity portraits."[1] Therefore, myths and legends provide visual text and context for the study of clothing art and culture. In China, creative-related inter-ethnicity in traditional art and culture occurs among the Han ethnicity and various ethnic minorities, showing the mutual influence and generation of the arts and costumes of different groups. Ethnic minority costumes and culture contain plentiful unique creative ideas and expression methods, which are richly embedded with

---

[1] Trigger B G. Understanding Early Civilizations: A Comparative Study [M]. Xu Jian (tr). Beijing: Peking University Press, 2014:307.

ethnic spiritual and cultural characteristics.

In the process of creation and design, unique traditional arts and clothing styles of ethnic groups across the world construct and maintain irreplaceable aesthetic and cultural diversity. This diversity, being an anthropological characteristic of contemporary clothing and design art, is a heritage of art and culture that should be protected. In the visual expression of ethnic elements, attention should also be paid to the continuous generation of ethnic art and the reconstruction of traditional culture, as ethnic tradition cannot be regarded as immutable and stable. In cross-cultural communication, how the unique image of ethnic fashion could get artistic expression and cultural construction is an issue to be responded to promptly in elucidating the local character of art and culture under the context of globalization. The tension between nativism and cosmopolitanism is precisely the aesthetic and cultural prerequisite for the contemporary visual expression of ethnic elements.

Actually, the impact of ideology like post-colonialism and ethnicism on fashion image construction, and the means to spread culture through visual expression, are important issues related to the visual generation and artistic expression of ethnic elements. In essence, the visual generation of ethnic elements is the process of producing and constructing ethnic fashion. Although all inherited dress customs were not necessarily fashionable, subsequent fashion reconstruction could never be possible without these clothing customs and traditions.

3. Visual Art and Fashion Expression of Ethnic Creative

For design art and visual expression, the wide variety, beautiful color, long history and local character of ethnic costume are indispensable characteristics to be displayed in the fashion expression of ethnic creative, in some artistic manner, of course. In fact, at the very beginning of creation activities in human history, there appeared the earliest designs or prototypes of design, although not strictly in the sense of modern design. Early art and design traditions of different ethnic groups are often carried on through the historical protection and inheritance of vision. Only when the designer has a unique idea and put it into practice, can creative design be generated and historical context of fashion be established.

Only through design, could style be formed, culture be disseminated, and mental schema contained in creative be explored and revealed. In costume designing, basic elements and forms of visual art can be used to generate and construct ethnic creative. At the same time, abstract geometric figures composed of points, lines, and planes will stimulate various associations in people's subconscious minds. For creative producing and fashion designing, an indispensable foundation consists in that, any point, line, and plane should present certain shape, size, color and texture. But the visualization of various ethnic elements may involve different artistic concepts and understandings on visibility. Therefore, in the visual construction of ethnic elements, the expression of fashion creative can achieve a variety of visual effects.

At the same time, special attention should be given to the current generation of the aesthetic style of ethnic fashion art, and to the construction and dissemination of fashion culture. It should also be noted that "the meanings and associations of concepts may become easier to understand with the help of their images, but once concepts are systematized, they would become abstract ideas, rather than certain image language."❶ Here, concept can be regarded the abstract idea rooted in metaphor. The connection of ethnic creative and fashion design with vision permeates all levels of conception, implementation, transmission and acceptance. To a large degree, creative stipulates and influences the formation of designing style, however, this process can only be fulfilled through a series of visual expressions.

Fashion creative is related not only to various ideas and insights, but also to the expression of art and realization of design. In the fashion expression of creative, the existence of body and its generative connection with art stipulates and restricts fashion design activities to a certain extent. Although some arts are not visually expressed, they can be visually transformed and have a corresponding connection with visual art and culture. The connection between fashion expression and human aesthetic synesthesia, pass down the beauty of artistic shaping and the construction of experience from one style of sense to another. Therefore, how to generate a sense of fashion related to a specific group of people through visualization, is related to the dialogue between different groups or classes on their spirits and cultures.

In fact, ethnic fashion creative is generated in the dissemination of fashion styles that are based on the fusion of feelings. In the visual communication and trends of fashion, it is this synesthesia that brings about the fusion of various human senses. Then, in the clothing lifestyles of different ethnic groups, this aesthetic synesthesia is grasped in a differentiated manner. As fashion art is a kind of culture often related to vision, fashion's concern for synesthesia is inseparable from visual art and relative life and cultural traditions. For example, Chinese Tang suit originally refers to the clothes for the Han people in the Tang Dynasty, but today, the new Tang suit is a kind of contemporary Chinese clothes that retains the cultural meaning and taste of ancient Hanfu.

Fashion art and fashion culture are more generative than art in general, due to the aesthetic qualities in the popularity of fashion, and the association of this popularity with visuality and

---

❶ Allan S. The Way of Water and Sprouts of Virtue [M]. Zhang Haiyan (tr). Beijing: Commercial Press, 2010:36.

culture. While art in general and its aesthetics change over time, the aesthetic experience on fashion art is much more fluid. At the same time, this generative nature of fashion is reinforced by dissemination, for a fashion surely declines with its widespread popularity and becomes the psychological expectation and generator of the next season's fashion. In the fashion expression of ethnic creative, elements are reconstructed based on visual art, and an aesthetic synesthesia related to this visuality is formed. Here, the text of ethnic dress and fashion creative is undoubtedly linked to the existence and cultural context of an ethnic group.

There are different understandings and interpretations on the connection between text and context in the process of artistic and cultural construction. While both emphasizing the practical analysis on real cases of visual culture, "Pierre Bourdieu's theory of cultural production primarily aims to explain text by using context, yet Erwin Panofsky believes that the meaning of the text itself can be used to illuminate the context of its production." ❶ In fact, this traditional distinction between text and context is relative itself, because they are interwoven and intertextual at various levels of visual culture, and text, by virtue of its openness, is generated together with context. For example, in ancient times, the Drung people living Chinese Yunnan province just covered their bodies with the Drung blanket woven from jute fiber, not having clothes in the strict sense, which was closely linked with the living condition and the customary context of that time.

Therefore, the Drung blanket has become a special symbol with its unique style. When a Drung blanket made of five-color jute clothes hangs askew from one's shoulder to knee, it shows a bold artistic style and a primitive beauty. In addition to Drung blanket, other Chinese ethnic costumes such as the sheepskin shawl of the Naxi people and the "chaerwa" (shawl) of the Yi people, all integrate practicality and decorative function together, while maintaining their characteristics in visual expression and aesthetic taste. After creative designing and clothes production, ethnic costume can enter the fields of marketing and communication, which is also closely related to visual art and culture. The popularity and cultural dissemination of ethnic costumes or fashions is based on the recognition of its specific visual style. And the social and cultural identification of clothing styles contributes to the continuous generation and popularity of ethnic fashion.

It is in the context of art and cultural dissemination that ethnic creative and design can become popular and widely imitated. In fact, the visual expression of fashion is always interrelated with the ethnic style, immersing into itself the ethnic spirit and cultural characteristics. In the creative and design of ethnic costumes, clothes and accessories are closely related and constitute a complete

---

❶ Howells R. Visual Culture [M]. Ge Hongbing, et al (tr). Guilin: Guangxi Normal University Press, 2007:77.

yet open form of beauty. Although it involves many elements and compositional issues, the overall beauty of clothing cannot be broken down into parts once it is formed. The unique accessories and costume matching of ethnic minorities are of important meanings and functions, often making a special or even exaggerated impression in terms of visual modeling and expression.

In ethnic costume creative and design, color has played an irreplaceable role of contrast and emphasis for the overall matching. For example, a Black Yi man from Chinese Sichuan province often wears black clothes, black pants, and black shawls. On his left ear is a large wax jade bead strung with red silk thread, on his wrists are silver bracelets with dragon designs, and on his head stands a bun wrapped in black cloth. The high tapered bun stretches out from the cloth, making his image extraordinarily heroic. Besides, the bun tilting to the right and the large bead on the left ear achieve an asymmetrical yet balanced effect. As for his earring, reddish yellow color plays a good role of embellishment and emphasis. In clothing creative and design, items like shawls and back cushions have become an important part of ethnic costumes because of their constant accompaniment to body, and can be classified into accessories in terms of practicality and aesthetics.

No doubt, costumes of different ethnic groups have different aesthetic and cultural characteristics, because ethnic visual habit has a necessary influence on the formation and acceptance of fashion, and established habits and styles even become indispensable constituents of ethnic clothing. It should be noted that fashion styles and their changes reflect the characteristics of fashion in different periods. In Japan, for example, "the luxurious style of court costumes in the Heian period didn't get passed down, and later noble costumes in the Kamakura period were far less extravagant."❶ As a means of expression, design, art and culture are in constant process of communication. And we can never ignore the association and the distinction between fashion expression styles in different periods and various ethnic groups. In ethnic fashion and aesthetics, customs and culture have great anthropological significance and influence.

For example, the clothing of Naxi women who live in Chinese Yunnan province is usually very plain, with little decoration and simple design, among which the most distinctive accessory is the sheepskin shawl used also as a back cushion. This clothing style is undoubtedly associated with the Naxi customs and culture. Various designs and styles of ethnic minority costumes often produce strong decorative and visual effects. Obviously, the visual expression of ethnic creative and design involves the generation of codes and symbols in social and cultural contexts. In the generation and construction of fashion, clothes and accessories are inseparable and intertwined.

---

❶ Fogg M (ed). Fashion: The Whole History [M]. Chen Lei (tr). Beijing: China CITIC Press, 2016:39.

Ethnic accessories add lots of charm to ethnic clothes, having become an important component in the creative and design of ethnic costume. The integration between clothes and accessories is probably the fundamental characteristics of ethnic costume.

The style of ethnic art is the overall visual expression of the ethnic mental schema and cultural characteristics in the long-term historical existence of an ethnic group. For instance, "different from the uniform and graded clothing in the early Ming Dynasty, the clothing after the mid-Ming Dynasty was more innovative and colorful." [1] This shows that the changes of ethnic clothing and fashion in certain historical period need to be explained in the context of society and culture of that time. Due to the differences in geographical locations and cultural contexts of different ethnic groups, their costumes are often endowed with their own aesthetic experiences and style characteristics. Even in those places that are not far apart, there would exist different dressing styles and features.

With the advent of globalization, China and other Eastern countries have merged into its wave, actively or passively, and ethnic fashion has become the artistic and cultural response of an ethnic group to this wave of globalization. Also, the contemporary fashionization of ethnic creative involves the response and criticism to colonialism and post-colonialism. From the hippie style emerging in the 1960s to the ethnic fashion trends reigniting in recent years, ethnic elements and accessories are increasingly strengthening individualized styles. In the process of designing, it is most crucial to transform ideas and concepts into simulacra of creative. According to Plato, imitation is regarded as inferior to its hidden concept or form, while visualization is just that kind of imitation. Visualization provides a fundamental artistic and cultural context for the generation and construction of simulacra.

To avoid the visual representation associated with Western art, fashion simulacra must be produced in light of generative theory and relative experiences. It should be noted that "the imitation of a mode is meaningful only after the formation rule of the mode is explained and the idea itself is described." [2] Of course, this generation of meaning is the fundamental source for the simulacra of creative. Different from general phenomenology, generative theory regards the generation of experience as the thing in itself, and provides the fundamental possibility for the generation that would turn itself into experience. Of course, visualized concept still needs to be transformed into visual experience, and this kind of visual experience is not only the activation and transformation of the idea, but also the visualization of idea and the product of meaning generation.

---

[1] Yang Xiaohong. History of Chinese Fashion Culture (Volume of the Song, the Yuan and the Ming Dynasties) [M]. Jinan: Shandong Pictorial Publishing House, 2011:212-213.
[2] Todorov T. Théories du Symbole [M]. Wang Guoqing (tr). Beijing: Commercial Press, 2004:158.

In fact, the visualization of idea and creative has always been contextualized, and visualized ideas could provide thought experience for creative and design. As a transition from the visualized idea to the simulacra of creative, the product of meaning generation is not only the emergence of creative, but also the construction of simulacra. Or in other words, it is the product in the mutual generation of creative and simulacra. In the visualization of creative, simulacrum concerns and refers to existence itself through the generation of experience text. What's important is that, the textualization of experience and the empiricization of text are mutually generated, and this empirical text itself is a product of art and culture. The reason why the visualization of idea is so important in creative is that visualization has laid a generative foundation for simulacra and representation. Through visualized processing and construction, all ideas are transformed into creative design.

Those costume designs that imitate the prototypes of animals and plants, although having artistic charm and aesthetic meaning, should not be confused with the mimesis that describes the original work. In fact, design is inseparable from the visualization of ideas and the generation of text. This kind of visualization, as the premise, needs to simulate the visual product through design. At the same time, all design contexts can be interpreted as certain code. Actually, "with a few efforts, the coordinates of time and place will be cancelled, surpassed, and converted into signs."❶ But according to phenomenological reduction, signs can be historically related to time and space by returning to existence. Creative and design can also be regarded as a kind of occurrence of simulacra, that is, transforming ideas into simulacra or visual expressions necessary for creative through visualization.

Obviously, ethnic art and fashion are inseparable from ethnic sentiments and customs, and creative styles of different ethnic groups vary from each other. To a large extent, the spiritual characteristics of an ethnic group stipulate its fashion style. However, if clothing intends to become a fashion, it is necessary to emphasize in artistic expressions the signs of popularity, which often have certain symbolic character and contextual connection while conveying fashion and aesthetic experience. In the simulacra of creative, ideas will exist in transformative styles, giving specific visual guidance to design and art. And to complete the entire design and creation activity, it is also required to transform the simulacra of creative into some things of visual communication.

Visual communication is to express and convey the ideas embedded in the design to the audience through artistic techniques. In the visual communication of the design, there is not only the historical deposit and artistic reconstruction of ideas, but also the cultural meaning and purport

---

❶ Hebdige D. Subculture: The Meaning of Style [M]. Hu Jiangfeng & Lu Daofu (tr). Beijing: Peking University Press, 2009: 82.

of simulacra. It may be said that, fashion art often generates unique individuality through various expressions of avant-garde or classic creative, while associations of classic and avant-garde styles will be intertwined and reconstructed in fashion. In fact, the creative and design of ethnic costume, being the product of intervening in art and life by fashion styles, construct the sense of ethnic fashion through visual art and expressions.

The artistic expression and visual communication of fashion design can be understood as the intertextual reconstruction of ideas and simulacra. For ethnic creativity, fashion expression always occurs in visual text, and is responded to and reconstructed contemporarily through artistic expression techniques. "Moreover, text is always in the process of being generated, forever existing and disappearing at the same time." ❶ In the context of generative theory, experience reach existence itself through text, which is like an everlasting game. In creative producing and fashion designing, visualization is not only an important way for idea to exist, but also the basis for art and creative simulacra to occur. Here, the visual communication and artistic expression of simulacra and design, as well as the various appeals manifested in their association, are all in an intertextuality with the visualization of idea.

---

❶ Zhang Xiangen. Introduction to Art Phenomenology [M]. Wuhan: Hubei People's Publishing House, 2015:116.

第三章

全球化语境里的民族时尚与文化认同

在全球化时代，一切历史悠久的民族服饰与文化都亟待建构出自己的时尚文化，并在时尚创意里重构民族的审美文化与当代话语风格。在服饰与时尚创意之中，民族性不仅是艺术与文化认同的精神性基础，同时也是关联与通达世界性的文化前提。作为时尚创意之源，民族性艺术与文化及其认同，显然也是实现世界性通达所不可或缺的。但应注意到，任何对西方元素与文化的简单拿来或拒斥，都是根本不可取的、不应该的与不可能的，否则就会陷入殖民化或狭隘的民族主义而不能自拔。在这里，有助于发掘与激活民族元素的文化意义，以促成民族当代时尚与文化的生成与建构。在全球化的艺术、审美与文化语境里，基于时尚视觉表现的民族审美文化的当代建构，主要包括民族元素的视觉表现、民族审美趣味与接受习惯、民族间的精神与文化及其比较，以及文化认同的对话与理论建构等。在此基础上，研究如何保持与重构鲜明的民族特色与艺术风格，以避免迷失在全球一体化与同质化的潮流之中。

只有在民族性与世界性的关联与融通之中，才能创造出一种颇具民族性特质的世界时尚与服饰文化。与此同时，还要通过民族元素的时尚创意与艺术表现，为全球化时代里民族审美文化认同的建构提供可能性。任何民族元素及其发现、揭示与重构，其实都可能成为时尚元素与创意的文化之源。这种基于民族元素与文化特质的创意与设计，既离不开社会、历史与文化的语境及其构成，同时又是民族时尚及其文化认同得以建构的路径。当然，这里所涉及的时尚的民族性及其揭示与阐发，从来都不是封闭的、僵化的、彼此排斥的，而是经由民族间性通达与融入一种世界性的文化认同。

第一节　时尚创意的民族性与世界性

在时尚创意与设计之中，难免会涉及民族元素及其文化的问题，一种时尚创意与文化往往是基于民族艺术，并以这种民族文化作为其根本性语境与底蕴。但还要考虑到文化的民族性与世界性的关系，因为任何民族都不可能完全离开其他民族而独自存在，同时也难以避免与其他民族的生活往来与文化交流。就文化本身而言，从来都关涉着民族性与世界性及其关系问题。作为一种独特的文化样式，服饰与时尚也同样摆脱不了民族性与世界性关系。在这里，民族时尚创意与设计是民族性的，因此应得到民族文化的承认与认同。与此同时，一切能够被称为时尚的东西往往也具有世界性特质，并在世界性的语境里获得广泛理解与文化认同。正因如此，文化的民族性与世界性及其生成性关联，无疑是时尚创意所要面对与探究的思想与文化问题。

一、从民族性到世界性

在这里，民族可以理解为在一定的历史阶段形成的具有共同的语言与生活地域等，以及具有一致的文化特质与民族心理的稳定共同体。当然，这种共同性一般是针对本民族的成员而言的。虽然说，任何民族都有其独特的精神特质与文化传统，然而，"民族是不能通过单独一种文化就可领会的"。❶ 在服饰与时装的创意与设计之中，民族性具有不可替代的艺术特质与文化意义，同时又与世界性密切地关联与相互生成。基于民族元素的创意与设计，无不涉及民族性与世界性的关系。

而且，独特的民族艺术与审美文化，何以通达世界性也是创意不可忽视的问题。在不同的场合与文化语境里，民族指涉与表达的含义与旨趣也是有所差异的。在广义上来说，民族泛指各种带有族群性与地域性的共同体，民族性无疑是民族的根本性特质与规定。作为民族规定的民族性及其构成，又是一个处于生成与开放状态的复合结构。就世界范围与历史性而言，各民族是人类生存与文化多元化的构成与表征。原始民族、古代民族、近代民族、现代民族、土著民族等，甚至氏族、部落都可以包括在民族构成内。当然，民族往往还用以指一个国家或一个地区的各民族，如中华民族、阿拉伯民族等。

与此同时，民族又用来指各个具体的民族共同体及其成员。如英吉利人、德意志人、法兰西人、汉族人、蒙古族人、满族人、回族人、藏族人等。那些生活于特定环境与文化语境里，并共享精神与文化特质的群体属于特定民族。也可以说，民族是人在人类历史上形成与构成的，同时具有某种一致的情感与意识的群体或共同体。在某种意义上，文化的类别及其划分是与民族的存在密切相关的。而且，文化与族群、人类学的关系与勾连，显然也是文化人类学研究不可忽视的问题。

应当说，民族之间的关联与共同的民族生活，是揭示民族性与世界性关系的存在论基础。还要看到，民族既是历史性生成与发生的，还与人类精神与文化的建构分不开。在原始社会时期，由于受到生物演化及其自然性法则的限制与制约，人类祖先只能以血缘关系组合的形式共同生活。族群内部各成员之间，以及民族内外成员间也会相互影响，成员们都以本能意识自然地维系着相互间的各种关系。到了人类文化卅始形成的时期，原始社会的人们除了劳动与生存外，还生成与建构了最初的生活习惯与风俗文化。

虽然说，民族艺术与文化相关于地域性特质，但却不能将民族性仅仅归结为地域性。一般来说，这里所说的"民族"（Nation）一词除了与地域相关外，"它也有一个原始意义：有关拥有共同血统或被当作拥有共同血统的人民（People）的'品种'（Breed）或'原种'（Stock）"。❷ 因自然生活环境与族群先天条件的不同，同时加上特定地域独特性的限制，使各族群的成员之间在生活方式、行为模式与风俗上产生区分。当然，不同民族在艺术与文

---

❶ 斯蒂夫·芬顿.族性[M].劳焕强，译.北京：中央民族大学出版社，2009：25.
❷ 斯蒂夫·芬顿.族性[M].劳焕强，译.北京：中央民族大学出版社，2009：20.

化上的差异也是在历史中逐渐形成的。毫无疑问，这种民族性特质使一个民族成为自身的内在精神与文化规定。

与此同时，各民族所具备的、难以相互替代的民族性特质，构成了不同民族的区别和差异的历史性存在。事实上，处于各个民族特质之内共同生活的群体构成了民族本身，民族个体及其情感里的共同群体性特质相关于民族意识。在传统的民族生活方式里，民族性特质与文化认同的意识、心理与观念，往往还可以经由着装与衣生活方式表现出来。在长期的民族生活史中，各民族都生成与建构了带有民族性特质的民族文化。与之相关，民族文化也必定表征与彰显在各个地域与族群的生活方式里。在某种意义上，民族文化是民族艺术与精神建构所留下的痕迹，以及在历史性的社会里生成与实现的各种建制与仪式。

对特定的民族来说，民族性一直沉淀在精神生活、礼仪典章与地方文化之中。在相互的传播与影响下，不同民族得以借鉴艺术与服饰样式。此外，"装饰图案的相似并不一定意味着是传播而致。古代彩陶和纺织品中的某些基本图案在毫无关联的文化中都很普遍，如古代中国和秘鲁之间就出现过这种情况"。❶ 任何民族服饰与时尚其实都以其特有的方式表现了与民族性特质相关的艺术与文化意味，并对民族性与世界性的关系加以揭示与回应。还可以说，对民族元素的发现与历史性阐释，离不开对民族生活、文化观念与风俗习惯的研究。

显然，自特定民族共同体在人类历史上形成与建构起来，以其精神和文化特质区别于其他族群并回应世界性问题以来，人类文化总是表现为各不相同乃至千差万别的文化样式。但应意识到，任何文化的发生与文化的历史性传承，其实都是以民族与民族社会为根基的。特别是，文化使民族与民族社会得以形成自己的精神特质，从而为民族生活方式提供了内在的意义与价值体系。而且，民族的与传统的服饰还在各种艺术里得到了表征，如辛亥革命后，以梅兰芳为代表的京剧演员，创制了表现古代女性的新式戏曲服装，即古装衣。除此之外，文学、雕塑与绘画等也不乏对人物着装的表现。

在民族性及其与精神、文化的关联之中，各民族的生活方式得以形成自身的特质并相互区分开来。在民族的文化建构之中，必定会涉及信仰与观念的密切关联，这种关联的生成之物有仪式、信物与旨趣等，这些都促成与导致精神及其在文化里的灌注。当然，各民族在共同的在世生存与存在之中，相似之处必然会越来越多，而民族间的差异性则可能越来越小。实际上，时尚创意也相关于对各种民族特质的关联的回应，如克里斯汀·拉克鲁瓦的时尚创意虽然饱受法兰西文化的熏陶与浸染，但他非常乐于在欧洲其他地区发掘文化风俗，从而汲取来自各个历史时期与不同艺术风格的灵感。

在传统社会里，不同民族的差异既体现在其精神图式上，又表征在外化了的器物与服饰上。与此同时，这种差异往往还会导致民族间的同化与融合的加剧，形成一致性甚至最

---

❶ 迈克尔·苏立文.东西方艺术的交会[M].赵潇,译.上海：上海人民出版社,2014：289.

终导致民族差异的消失。因此，这将涉及由独特的民族性到普适的世界性的问题，而在这一转化过程中难免关联到民族间性的特质。一个民族往往以对本民族的文化理解去表现时尚艺术，并把民族性元素与文化纳入与重构到世界时尚之中。虽然说民族性特质之于任何民族都是不可或缺的，但这种独特的民族性又是与其他民族的民族性相比较而存在的。

应当看到，服饰与时尚创意又力图使民族性特质成为世界时尚创意与表现不可分离的必要构成。在不同民族的衣生活史上，相互借鉴也涉及一个由陌生到适应的过程，这其实就是文化适应性研究应当考虑的问题。就服饰的创意与设计来说，"征服者的衣生活习惯改变了土著民族的衣生活习惯，或者双方的服装文化相互影响、混合；征服者有时也会屈服于当地的环境、风土和气候，不得不改变自己的衣服，产生新的服装文化"。❶还要注意到，某个民族因受其他民族影响而可能丧失本民族的特质，接受与认同其他民族的精神特质与衣生活方式。在这里，文化的同化是民族创意与设计不可忽视的问题。

一般来说，可以将文化同化分为强迫同化与自然同化两种类型。具体而言，强迫同化在此指凭借压制、特权甚至暴力来实现的同化，可能发生来自被同化民族的反对与抵抗。与此不同，自然同化指各民族经由互相影响与文化交织而发生的同化，如在衣生活方式、服饰文化与习俗、审美趣味等方面产生的趋同。在自然同化之中，甚至可能改变某民族的传统习俗与象征符码，进而接受其他民族的服饰传统与衣生活方式。在同化与反同化的过程中，民族间的衣生活与服饰文化建构了审美与文化张力。而且，民族或本土时尚并不能仅仅局限在某一特定民族文化里，往往还涉及由一个民族向另一个民族的跨文化传播。

在此，世界性及其所谓的普适性特质，指那些悬置了各民族特质后的共同剩余物。当然，由民族性而涉及往往带有一致性特质的世界性，还关联到各民族间文化的理解与认同的问题。应当说，民族文化的多样性基于各民族文化的不可替代性之上。文化多样性不仅体现在人类文化遗产通过多种形式来表达、弘扬和传承，也表征在以各种方式进行的观念、创意与设计等生成之中。但任何形式的多样性都不可能离开独特性，这种多样性其实就是对唯一性的否定与消解。因此，在创意中既要认同本民族的文化，同时又要尊重其他民族的文化，力求相互借鉴、求同存异与彼此包容。

毫无疑问，创意与设计要充分尊重世界文化多样性，促成人类文明的历史性传承与当代重构。显然，主张与尊重各民族艺术与文化的多样性，是以对本民族的艺术与文化的认同为基础的，但还要回应不同民族或国家在文化上的差异。譬如说，"在19世纪，西方人认为穿衣标志着文明，不穿衣服的人被认为是野蛮的。然而，到了20世纪和21世纪，半裸则标志着西方的优越性"。❷虽然说一切着装行为仍然是与文化传统相关的，但它同时又影响着世界性时尚的建构。例如，好莱坞的电影把美国的流行文化传播到了全世界。而且，经由各民族的艺术与文化间的沟通与对话，无疑是通达具有包容性的世界性特质的前提。

---

❶ 田中千代.世界民俗衣装：探寻人类着装方法的智慧[M].李当岐，译.北京：中国纺织出版社，2001：33.
❷ Robert J.C. Young. Postcolonialism: A Very Short Introduction [M].Oxford: Oxford University Press, 2003:83.

民族元素、时尚创意与文化认同 Ethnic Elements, Fashion Creative and Cultural Identity

实际上，承认与认同世界各种不同的艺术与文化样式，就应当坚持各民族艺术与文化共生的原则。在艺术与文化的交流之中，尊重差异、理解个性与相互借鉴显然是必不可少的，只有这样才能共同促进世界服饰与时尚文化的多元化。世界文化指世界各地区所呈现出的彼此不同又密切相关的文化，这些众多的世界文化样式往往具有某种共同的一致性。相对于许多地方性艺术与文化来说，世界性的艺术与文化不乏超出地方性的精神特质，但这种世界性又是以各种不同的民族性为基础的。除了文学与艺术等文化样式之外，文化其实还包括日常生活、交往方式、价值体系，以及关于这些方面的传统、信仰与精神旨趣。

在不同的时代与地方，服饰艺术与文化无疑具有各种不同的表现形式，以及与人们内在精神相关的社会与文化特质。其实，艺术与文化的这种多样性及其具体表现，无疑是构成民族与人类的精神特质所必不可少的语境。尽管说，各民族大都具有其独特的服装样式与着装传统，"但大部分国家，人们在日常穿着世界各地流行的服装，到节日或盛典时则穿上自己的民俗衣装，过着双重的衣生活"。❶ 还可以说，这种所谓的双重衣生活方式，有助于在民族性与世界性之间保持一种平衡与张力。虽然不少设计师都注重对民族元素的借鉴与重构，但设计的服饰与产品要得到世界时尚界的认同，还需要创造性地运用国际性的设计话语与创意思维。

从交流与沟通的意义上讲，文化多样性及其所关涉的世界性问题，亟待从历史性传承与当代建构上予以承认与强调，并将之作为族群间相互适应的文化人类学特质。还要意识到，世界各民族无论大小与人口多少，以及处于何种社会与文化建制里，无疑都应在认同自身民族与文化特质的前提下，对其他民族的艺术与文化持有宽容态度。也就是说，各民族应该相互尊重各自的艺术与文化，并于可以共同接受的世界性的基础上，达成与建构相互间的理解和文化认同。其实，文化权利本身就是人权不可或缺的构成，也是人的文化诉求及其实现的权利保障。如今的许多世界性时尚风格，业已融入了各种民族元素及其文化特质。

在这里，每个人其实都具有选择衣装、服饰的权利与自由，只有充分保护与传承各民族的艺术与文化，才有可能保障每个人均能自由使用本民族传统文献。任何民族元素及其揭示与时尚化，都涉及如何将各种文化整合与重构到服饰中去的问题。比如说，韩国服饰最初主要受中国唐代服饰的影响。在唐代，新罗与唐朝交往非常密切，韩国服饰特点几乎与唐朝无异。在当代社会与人们的生活方式里，文化的全球化意味着全世界的各种文化，都不能再孤立与彼此无关地存在，它们无不面临着其他文化的影响和挑战。应当看到，世界性显然离不开民族性而生成自身，与此同时，世界性所谓的普适性也是有条件的、历史性的。

在全球化时代，不同民族的文化之间的交流也会越来越频繁。在相互的交织之中，各

---

❶ 田中千代.世界民俗衣装：探寻人类着装方法的智慧[M].李当岐，译.北京：中国纺织出版社，2001：36.

种服饰与时尚改变着各自的表现方式与风格。但这绝不意味着各种文化间的差异会消除以致形成一种全球完全一致的艺术与文化。相反,不仅艺术与文化的多样性会长期存在,而且还将继续基于多元化来生成特质。"当然,日常生活受影响于广泛的价值观、国际象征性形式、文明、国家意识形态和文化以及地区性的定位。"❶ 在时尚的民族性所在之处,其实也不乏世界性的建构与存在,而在世界性里往往灌注着民族性特质。在独特的民族性与普适的世界性之间,亟待建构出一种相互交融与彼此生成的关系,而不是传统的个别与一般、被包容与包容的抽象化的逻辑关联。

二、关涉世界性的民族创意与认同

在这里,民族认同的这种血缘及其溯源倾向,源于早期民族的血缘性的存在样式,即氏族、部落及其他早期的民族,应当说都是建立在这种血缘性基础上的。民族文化及其认同的传统与积淀,一直延续与扩展到现代甚至当代时期。基于这种原始的血缘性,民族认同往往比其他认同具有更稳定的本能聚合性。在共同生活之中,不同民族间的艺术与文化交往是不可避免的,也就是说,世界性也是任何民族文化认同不可回避的问题。但如果仅仅停留在民族元素曾经的历史性语境里,是不可能建构出具有当代感的世界性时尚文化的。

实际上,民族认同发生的前提在于民族之间的交往,通过交往形成他族不同于我族的对比,从而确立自己的群体归属与族群间的边界区分。一个民族的身份与文化认同,显然是离不开其他民族的存在的。虽然说各民族的生存、生活及其文化语境都有所不同,但所有民族都共在于这个世界之中却是无可置疑的存在论基础,因此,时尚创意的民族文化认同,显然也是相关于民族间性的,不可能脱离这个世界而存在。其实,世界性的文化首先是民族性的文化,如果没有民族性文化的生成与存在,也就没有什么世界性的一般文化的存在。与此同时,文化的世界性不过是民族性文化融入世界文化的生成物。

虽然说民族创意与文化认同往往相关于某一族群的内在精神,但却离不开对特定族群与其他民族乃至世界的关系的回应。在这里,"此在"(Dasein)是指在世界之中的存在,这同样适合于这里所说的民族性此在。其实,"世界的这种属于'在之中'的先行的展开状态是由现身参与规定的"。❷ 在这种现身的参与之中,既有个体性的在场,又离不开群体性的存在。也就是说,世界性的时尚与文化也是各民族的时尚与文化的生成物,这种生成离不开各民族之间的时尚对话与文化交流。甚至可以说,各民族的生存与生活是以这种世界性为基础的。

还要注意到,经由此在通达存在本身,离不开此在生存及其所关切的世界。因为,此在在本性上就是在世界之中存在。当然,世界性不是忽视了差异与个性的一致性。具有世界性特质的人类学此在,总是各种不同民族共在的生成之物。在海德格尔那里,此在的存

---

❶ 詹姆斯·罗尔.媒介、传播、文化——一个全球性的途径[M].董洪川,译.北京:商务印书馆,2012:309.
❷ 海德格尔.存在与时间[M].陈嘉映,王庆节,译.北京:三联书店,1999:160.

在表明某种面向未来的可能性。这也表明了，一个民族性此在及其文化应是开放性的，并面向将来而生成着自身的艺术与文化。这里所说的面向未来，涉及的正是诸多与多样的可能性，这无疑也是流行与预测所关注的趋势问题。民族文化与世界文化之间可以相互贯通、彼此渗透：一方面表现为民族文化的世界化，另一方面表现为世界文化的民族化。

作为民族成员的根本规定，民族性此在也是对主体人的一种悬置，它以其特有的开放性不同于一般的实体。但民族与世界在文化上的相互渗透，其实并不是无条件的情况下轻易实现的。在安德烈·金的韩国时装设计中，既借鉴了中国元素与文化特质，同时又吸收了欧美时尚元素，显得经典、前卫、不张扬，色彩柔和出挑。同时，文化的民族性与世界性的相互关联与交织，也是一种具有交互性的艺术与文化认同的过程。当然，世界性文化不能被当作各民族元素的简单加和，但它却是民族创意与时尚文化所不可或缺的关涉物。也就是说，世界性的文化往往是各民族文化中那些被世界各民族广泛认同与普遍接受的文化。

但是，并不是所有民族性的文化都能自动地被称为世界文化，同时也并非文化越具有民族性就越具有某种世界性。在基于世界性的共在与生成性关联里，各民族不仅是彼此间袪主体的人类学此在，而且还应与万物处于共在与和谐的状态中。尤其是当一种民族文化只是存在于某个封闭与隔绝的地域内，或者只存活在本民族的现实与实际生活中，并没有对其他民族与世界文化产生文化影响，则其民族文化就难以自然而然地成为一种世界性文化。如果一种民族文化尚未渗透到其他民族文化中时，它只能是一种民族的与地域的独特文化样式，还不能直接被视作一种现实的世界性文化。

因此可以说，民族文化并不天然地就是世界性文化，民族文化及其向世界文化的转变与生成，其实也是一个基于世界性的民族文化的重构过程。与此同时，民族创意与文化认同转化为世界创意与文化认同，以及在民族创意与文化的基础上建构世界性关联，无疑是以人类从地域性向世界性的历史生成为前提的。虽然说封闭在一定程度上有助于民族文化的保存，但这种与世隔绝却是根本不可能持续下去的，还会因为封闭而失去历史性传承与对话的可能性。对时尚创意与文化认同来说，还要考虑到特定民族与世界服饰文化的生成性关联。

在这个全球化时代，世界上任何一个民族或族群，都不可能完全摆脱其他民族而离群索居。而且，各个不同民族之间在服饰领域的开放、交流与对话，构成了民族之所以成为世界的不可缺少的必要条件与前提。譬如说，"美国文化和欧洲文化之间在地理意义上的相互渗透从未停止过，无论是音乐还是自然科学领域、文学还是人文科学领域"。❶近现代以来，西方主体论遇到了诸多难以克服的认知问题与困境。为了克服与解构主体论与理性形而上学，海德格尔用此作为传统主体的基础，并以之作为个别性主体的根本性规定。对于各个民族来说，作为群体性主体的规定就是民族性的此在。

---

❶ 阿尔弗雷德·格罗塞.身份认同的困境[M].王鲲,译.北京：社会科学文献出版社,2010：61.

在当代时尚化创意与重构中，民族元素无不是对世界性时尚与文化的一种独特回应，而不能将民族时尚仅仅把握为内在性与封闭性的轮回。其实，时尚创意的民族性认同，当然也是以民族性此在为基础的。山本耀司基于和服与东西审美观的融合，甚至大面积地使用黑色来营造哥特气氛，引发了西方与世界对当今女性身份定位的思考。在共同在世之中，各个民族的生活、艺术与文化，也显现出自身的开放性与共通性。民族性此在不仅是群体性主体的根本性规定，而且其自身也是祛主体的、开放性的与历史性的。

还要看到，民族时尚创意与文化认同，难免发生在世界性的艺术与文化语境里。这里的祛主体化旨在表明，一个民族不应仅从自身的主体或主观出发，也要将其他民族的存在纳入自己的眼光与视野。这种开放性还使各个不同民族间发生交织与融通，从而奠定了一个基于世界的、根本性的多元文化基础。就服饰与时尚创意而言，力求得到的不仅是各个民族自身内部的认同，还要尽可能获得其他民族的理解与文化认可。为此，就需要在不同的民族性此在之间，展开艺术、思想与文化方面的对话与沟通。实际上，特定民族元素的创意与时尚文化的当代重构，必须将其他民族与世界性时尚趋势纳入自身文本里加以对话。

值得提到的是，民族元素与文化之于当代时尚审美的意义，在今天得到了越来越多的设计师与专家学者的关注与看重。各个民族之间的艺术与文化沟通之所以成为可能，是因为民族性与世界性是相互关联与彼此生成的。在这里，此在及其在世界之中存在，以及此在所残存的主体论痕迹，无疑为日常生活的异化克服，进而向存在本身回归提供了可能。反过来，不同民族元素及其时尚重构，显然也不断生成着世界性的时尚。但海德格尔其实并没有停留在对此在及其日常生活的一般把握上，而是将存在作为此在本性通达的根本所指来对待。

随着一些国家的独立，出现了不少新的民族艺术与文化样式。如第二次世界大战以后的非洲即是如此。与此相反，也会发生民族间的结合甚至相互同化的事件。毫无疑问，独立、结合与同化难免影响着世界民族文化及其构成，以及民族服饰与时尚创意产业的生成与当代建构。但在世界范围内，对同一民族元素的创意与设计的理解，还会因民族与地域而发生历史性的变化。在当今的文化多元主义语境里，时尚创意的民族性难以脱离世界性而存在。尤其是在民族服饰与时尚文化的研究上，诸多学科的介入与借鉴是近年来值得加以关注的学术趋势。

当然，世界性本身也给民族性特质带来了问题与挑战，促使人们关注民族艺术与文化的传承与当代重构，以应对与回应世界性艺术与文化复杂与多样的诉求。应注意到，"现在，不仅时装系统本身已经国际化，讨论时装的话语也被国际化了"。❶但在这种所谓国际化的话语生成里，仍然隐藏着各个民族不可忽视的独特声音。各民族时尚创意的艺术与文化认同，以及民族之间的思想对话的可能性，离不开民族性与全球化语境里的世界性的关联。

---

❶ 珍妮弗·克雷克.时装的面貌——时装的文化研究[M].舒允中，译.北京：中央编译出版社，2000：60.

但无论如何，世界性都是民族性认同亟待关注与探究的问题。

在疏离与熟悉之间，时尚从民族性与世界性的生成性关联里获得了张力。一般来说，同一人种的人们往往还可以分成为不同的民族，因为人种是具有共同遗传体质特征的人类群体。民族通常有着自己特定的人种（种族）这种人类学关联，也由此较为稳定地属于一个人种（种族）集团，但文化上的历史与传承也会影响到民族的人类学存在。当然，民族虽然与人种这种自然性特质密切相关，但它又并不局限在这种自然性的基础上，还会涉及精神图式与文化的复杂关联。还可以说，民族指在文化、语言、历史或宗教上，可以与其他民族有所区分的族群或一群人。

但是，对那些带有混合性的过渡类型的民族来说，难免含有复杂的与难以简单区分的民族成分，像部分中亚民族、埃塞俄比亚人、现代美洲民族等。世界性对民族性的超越之处在于，艺术与文化可能在相互借鉴的基础上建构出某种一致性。与之相关，那些具有同一特质的、超越民族性的世界性艺术与艺术潮流，往往会成为今后世界艺术与文化建构的一种趋势。但在任何时候与所有地方，这种具有一致性的所谓世界性趋势都不可能是绝对的。正因为如此，人们的日常着装与衣生活方式，都是各种民族服饰文化互文后的生成之物。

只有在借鉴与吸收外来文化的基础上，对传统的民族艺术与文化加以当代重构，才能使艺术与服饰在世界性语境里突显民族性。毫无疑问，对其他民族或地方的技艺的考查与借鉴是重要的。在阿尔曼·费南迪斯看来，"通过这些参观学习，我们可以研究那个民族的编织技术或造型传统，然后我们就可以通过这些开发出一个服装系列"。❶ 当然，特定民族性的保护与传承不能无视其他民族而进行，而是要在与其他民族艺术与文化对话的基础上，建构全球化时代的服饰创意与时尚文化的认同感。

与此同时，不少民族性特质都会在世界性的生成里发生变化。还要意识到，艺术与服饰的世界性既不等同于美国化，同时也应与欧洲化趋势有所区分。其实，艺术的世界性并不以某一国家或地区的艺术样式为标本，而且这种世界性还随着各民族艺术与文化的发生及其关联来历史性地生成自身。与此同时，艺术与服饰的世界性也不是一成不变的，而是基于不同民族创意的对话而生成自身。只要各民族间的交往与文化对话存在，艺术的交流就可能表征出世界性的特质。应当说，艺术的民族性只有在与其他民族的交往中，才能成为自身并具有某种世界性的文化特质。

任何民族时尚的当代创意与重构，无不将这种世界性回应到设计样式与风格里。虽然说，一个民族的艺术、服饰与文化，并不受制于其他民族或一般的世界性，"然而，随着铁路的四通八达，巴黎时装以及成衣的扩散，迅速地使地方服装沦落到民间服装的程度，成为过往历史中残留的物证痕迹"。❷ 对待西方艺术、服饰与文化，既不可简单地加以拒绝与

---

❶ 杰·卡尔德林.形式·适合·时尚[M].周明瑞，译.济南：山东画报出版社，2011：148.
❷ 弗朗索瓦-玛丽·格罗.回眸时尚：西方服装简史[M].冶棋，译.北京：中国纺织出版社，2009：139.

排斥，也不能一味地模仿甚至趋之若鹜。显然，世界性时尚往往不乏独特与典型的地域与文化，一切地方性艺术与文化都是世界性时尚建构所不可忽视的。

在这里，任何民族的服饰与时尚创意、设计，都应不断吸收其他民族的创意与风格，以促成本民族艺术在不同民族文化的交织中生成自身。还可以说，那些具有世界性特质的艺术与文化样式，往往具有全人类的共性与普世的人文关怀，不乏世界性的眼光与全球化的文化视野灌注其中。在当今的时尚创意过程中，各民族在世界性语境里的艺术与文化，以及所遭遇到的生存状况与文化处境，无疑都是应加以回应与深入探究的，而这种回应还涉及对时尚的独特领悟与符号化传达。实际上，任何民族的时尚都难免被世界潮流所关注与借鉴，而世界性也不可避免地成为民族时尚创意的关涉物。

在全球化时代，既不应简单消解民族性与地方性的存在，也不能以世界性来直接规约与统一民族多样性，而是旨在于民族性与世界性，以及独特性与一般性之间，建构出某种关于审美与文化的张力。在西方文化语境里，所谓的主流意识往往参照一个较低的他者来建构自己。尤其是，"自从后结构主义出现，强调西方文化将所谓边缘的团体编码为他者的方式，这种观念就越来越流行"。❶ 在当代世界性的语境里，重建民族时尚与文化成了重要的艺术与文化问题。或者说，民族创意与认同是在民族性与世界性的对话里实现的，这种对话与沟通还被纳入不同民族的衣生活方式之中。

三、民族性特质与世界时尚的祛同质化

作为一种生活方式，人类的衣生活难免会带上民族与地方的特质，同时又无不相关于其他民族与世界性的问题。实际上，时尚创意与设计离不开民族性这一根本传统。因此，发掘、保存民族与传统服饰的内在文化精神，就成了当代时尚创意的艺术与文化诉求。例如，古朴的秦汉服装、富丽的隋唐五代服装、高雅的宋装、堂皇的明装，以及华贵的清装，这些服装显然都是这种民族性特质的独特表现，其中，最典型的样式与风格莫过于唐代的服装了。应当注意到，在世界性时尚与流行趋势之中，民族性特质在祛同质化过程中具有不可替代的意义与价值。

但随着历史与文化的变迁，许多的民族与传统服装都面临着被淘汰的命运。在这里，民族性特质与民族精神和文化密切相关。在黑格尔看来，作为人类社会最崇高、最永恒的世界精神，常常体现在一些主要民族的民族精神之中。在艺术与时尚里，还涉及不同民族精神特质的关联与相互借鉴。譬如，"东汉末期，忍冬纹随着佛教艺术在我国流传兴起，南北朝时最为流行"。❷ 其实，这种民族性指一个民族的本性与精神特征，以及在艺术与文化里表现出来的、与其他民族不同的特质。随着人类生活条件与方式的变化，民族性特质及其在服饰领域里的体现与表达，也不断发生着与之相关的历史性变化。

---

❶ 丹尼·卡瓦拉罗.文化理论关键词[M].张卫东，张生，赵顺宏，译.南京：江苏人民出版社，2013：117.
❷ 冯盈之，余赠振.古代中国服饰时尚100例[M].杭州：浙江大学出版社，2016：29.

还要看到，民族性特质的生成与建构，与自然环境、社会生活、历史文化分不开。例如，中国北部、西北部与西南部草原牧区的民族，喜欢骑马、住毡房、喝奶茶或酥油茶等，这些习惯无疑是由牧区气候寒冷、牧民长期逐水草而居的特点与历史传统决定的。在民族的生活方式之中，当遇到同一问题或类似情况的时候，各民族往往会采取不同的思维方式，这也影响了民族着装特质的形成。但全球化可能导致的同质化，却是应引起警惕并加以文化批判的问题。与此同时，各种不同的创意方式又会形成衣生活的差异。在全球化时代，民族性特质也是民族在思想与行动上所具有的独特品质。

当然，世界上并没有什么绝对意义上的独特性与差异性，一切特质都是相比较而存在于各民族共同的在世生活中的，但共同的在世生活又可能导致特质与差异的消失。"从这个意义上说，全球化，特别是流行艺术的全球化，被视作在艺术价值的最低层次推动了艺术的同质化。"❶一切民族发自内在精神的文化自信与自觉，有助于克服本民族向其他民族模仿的冲动。应注意到，从独特性、差异性去看一般性、一致性，对世界时尚与文化的生成有所裨益，但还要克服与批判在独特性与一致性之间非此即彼的文化执态。

与此同时，民族性特质都是复杂与多样的，有时可能还是互相冲突的，这涉及各民族艺术与文化之间的沟通问题。在多元化的民族生活方式之中，任何民族都不宜过分强调本民族对于其他民族的优越感。因为，在全球化时代，各民族及其精神与文化特质都为同质化的消解提供了独特的可能性。例如，维吾尔族的服饰不仅花样较多，还非常优美，富有独特的民族特色。在日常生活中，维吾尔族妇女喜用对比色彩，这样就使得红的更亮、绿的更翠。尤其是，维吾尔族是个爱花的民族，人们戴的是绣花帽，穿的是绣花衣、绣花鞋，扎的是绣花巾，背的是绣花袋，衣着服饰无不与鲜花密切相关。而且，维吾尔服饰形式清晰、纹饰多样、色彩鲜明、图案古朴、工艺精湛，充分体现了一个地区与文化的历史沉淀。世界性时尚总是相关于各种民族元素与文化重构，而非简单或直接地搬抄某一民族的传统样式、图式与审美风格。民族元素与文化特质及其重构，仍然要提防陷入全球一致性中。许多民族服饰往往具有显著的民族文化特色与审美接受范式，并可以从中窥见民族服饰的传承性与地域性的习俗。在民族时尚的创意中，不少设计师借鉴了时尚元素与现代设计手法，巧妙地结合并创造性地重构了东西方服饰的特质。

在19世纪，查尔斯·弗莱德里克·沃斯在法国巴黎从事服装设计与经营，因首创服装表演而被誉为"时装之父"。服装与时尚评论家们开展了关于时装含义的讨论，时装概念得以逐步形成并推动了时尚创意与设计的建构。就时尚来说，世界女装发源地是巴黎、米兰以及后起之秀伦敦，男装发源地则是东京和纽约。虽然这些城市都是国际性的时尚大都市，但它们也是以各自的特质融入世界时尚的。在现代服装与时尚界，巴黎、米兰、纽约、伦敦、东京被视为时装之都，许多顶级世界性的时装秀在这些时尚之都定期举行。而且西方

---

❶ 维多利亚·D.亚历山大.艺术社会学[M].章浩，沈杨，译.南京：江苏美术出版社，2009：215.

艺术与时尚的这种深刻影响，可以说一直持续到了当代的世界时尚界。

尽管说，现代性及其对一致性的强调与诉求，在很大程度上导致了同质化的问题，但对特定民族的艺术与文化的过分强调，并由此来贬损其他民族的做法与行为，可能导致另一种同质化的时尚与文化。因此要注意到，"文化史还面临一个社会史不会面临的问题：人们倾向于用人类学家的某些方法来处理文化，对整体做无差异处理"。❶ 从古希腊开始，西方艺术与文化就强调形体美、外在美，而以模特为核心的现代服装表演与发布，强调的其实也是这种形体美和外在美。从法国乃至整个现代西方服饰文化来看，世界各时尚之都一直秉承着西方人对时尚美的独特理解与阐释。

在世界性服装与时尚领域，真正有价值的东西其实不仅是那些新潮的样式与风格，还包括隐藏在这些时尚后面的民族艺术与文化特质。这里的民族文化及其根本特质之所在，其实就是关于文化的民族独特视角，以及建构与阐发的民族话语与风格。在世界性时尚体系里，各个民族的地位与文化影响虽然参差不齐，但生成性与开放性为既尊重民族差异，同时又不仅局限在某些特定民族的特质上，提供了审美与文化的张力与多种可能性。实际上，民族时尚无疑又是不同于日常生活习惯的一种独特表达形式。

当然，特定民族的特质并不是单一的、与其他民族无关的，而是在与其他民族性特质相比较的过程中成为自身的。毫无疑问，东方风格在东方乃至西方影响深远，但是，"在19世纪中期，东方主义耗尽自身的新奇性，欧洲在设计与产品上开始超过东方"。❷ 可以说，法国服装最为显著的特质就是具有民族性，不仅表现了法兰西民族的历史、传统与精神，以及保持着法国宫廷的贵族气息，同时又融入了现代生活的简洁大方，所以法国服装体现出传统与现实的紧密结合。

不仅如此，法国在各方面都保持和重构了过去的传统，包括法国的建筑、城镇风貌甚至语言文学等，莫不如此。虽然说，法国曾经拥有古典主义与现实主义风格的艺术，但是法国人骨子里却具有强烈的浪漫主义色彩。譬如说，即便是巴尔扎克这个现实主义的文学家，其生活经历并没有充满现实的理性，而是表现了浪漫的冲动与激越的人文情怀。在浪漫主义艺术与文化的语境里，法国时尚不够缜密但却极具感染力。这里所谓的"同质化"，指同一大类中不同品牌的商品，在性能、外观，甚至营销手段上相互模仿，以至彼此趋同与难以区分的现象。在产品同质化的基础上，所形成的市场竞争行为称为同质化竞争。

在设计与消费领域，同质化导致了产品的民族性与地方性的式微甚至消失，因此可以通过对多民族与不同地域的文化的关注来消解同质化。对内在经验与个性的关注与强调，无疑也有助于同质化问题的克服。特别是当今快时尚的服饰始终追随迅捷的潮流，个性化的设计与生产都难以得到充分的考究。再加上时尚服饰新品到店的速度奇快，橱窗陈列的变换频率更是一周两次。在对时尚流行趋势的追逐下，快时尚款式差距缩小的趋势是根本

---

❶ 杰克·古迪.神话、仪式与口述[M].李源,译.北京：中国人民大学出版社,2014：69.

❷ Adam Geczy. Fashion and Orientalism [M].London: Bloomsbury Academic, 2013:116.

难以逆转的，因此，只能在细节上创新以表达特定品牌的想法。

而且，出现在不同快时尚品牌中款式相似的服装越来越多，那些引领潮流的快时尚似乎成为某种"标配性"的流行产品。但应当意识到，同质化显然不仅不利于消费者识别某款时装的独特品质，还会导致艺术与文化陷入技术与现代性所诉求的单调与一致之中。在时尚美的揭示中，"个性化走过的漫长路程已经把早期现代美外部的没有争议的古老模式完全改变成内心的个性化的模式"。❶ 个性化风格总是与特定群体或族群相关，从来都不是所有人群共同的喜好与一致的衣生活选择，但这种个性化在现当代设计里也难免受到极大的挑战。而那些无特色、无差异与边界模糊的设计，无疑是差异化消失及其在时尚上的表征。

在对同质化加以克服的过程中，差异化的设计与营销应当从观念与文化入手，尤其是要关注不同地域与民族文化内在精神特质的挖掘与揭示。否则，时尚品牌商品会出现相似、雷同并难以分辨的情况，以及难免陷入同质化的问题与困境中，从而使各种品牌失去自身原始的独特性与优势。因此，要突破同质化就需要在核心观念与技术研发上创新。如果忽视对民族原创性艺术与文化特质的保护与传承，终究会在当代时尚创意与设计里失去话语权。由现代主义与大众文化造成的时尚同质化趋势，正在使时尚艺术与文化走向单调和枯涸。民族特质在时尚与文化里的式微甚至丧失，还会导致设计随着世界性时尚潮流与风格亦步亦趋。

从基于现代性的时尚同质化中解脱出来，走向多元化的创意与表现成了时尚的必由之路。但独具民族特质的个性化设计，应成为一种自觉与主动的文化认同与选择。对于特殊与普遍的关系，"我自己的论点，包含了既对特殊性、差异又对普遍性和同质性保持直接关注的尝试"。❷ 从同质化中解脱出来的根本路径在于，在多元性的传统与民族文化的生成过程中，重新寻找与建构新的艺术与文化精神的诸多可能性。设计还要为当代时尚赋予民族的个性、差异和文化多元性，多元的民族时尚才能因此成为与同质化趋势相抗衡的力量。各民族的艺术与文化及其精神与文化特质，为克服世界范围内时尚的同质化提供了可能。

其实，时尚创意的多元化路径并不是对一致性的简单否弃，而是在差异性与单一性及其相互生成之间，建构与保持一种基于艺术与文化的张力，以克服与消解两者之间的相互否定与非此即彼。同质化是自启蒙主义以来文化的交流，以及技术与理性所带来的普遍性特质。尽管说民族时尚在一定程度上有助于同质化的克服，但愈演愈烈的相互模仿与同质化仍然难以彻底遏制。在时尚艺术及其表现之中，技术并不仅仅局限于工具性这种定位上，甚至可能成为时尚表现与审美的规定性。正因为如此，服饰创意与设计的独特个性成了某种稀有之物，而民族衣装就是民族内在精神与文化的一种独特符码。毫无疑问，创意与设计在这里面临着如何摆脱同质化的问题，为此应当从民族艺术与文化里寻求思想与灵感来源。

❶ 乔治·维加莱洛.人体美丽史[M].关虹,译.长沙：湖南文艺出版社，2007：237.
❷ 罗兰·罗伯森.全球化——社会理论和全球文化[M].梁光严,译.上海：上海人民出版社，2000：144.

也就是说，只有不乏特质的个性化设计才能满足消费者的各种需要，以及不同族群的人们在着装上的差异性与多元化诉求。各民族的服饰与当代时装设计，表现出其独特的心理、审美与文化个性。在汉语及其思想与文化的语境里，艺术与设计并没有陷入西方传统的形而上学困境。譬如说，"中文不但没有单纯地通过添加冠词，进行这种从'美的'到'美'的简易滑动，将美转向一个具有普世性的概念"。❶这种被赋予精神与文化特质的服装与时尚，不仅展现了各民族鲜活而又不可替代的民族个性，同时也有别于其他民族的精神与文化特质。正是在这个意义上，独特的民族时尚与文化不仅是不可或缺的，它本身其实也是克服设计同质化的一种重要文本与话语样式。

第二节　全球化与民族间时尚文化的对话

在服饰与时尚设计中，民族的艺术特质与文化认同的问题，既是一个国家内部各民族自身亟待探究的，同时也是世界上众多国家及其民族所应加以回应的。而且民族文化的认同与时尚文化的历史性传播，不仅要考虑后殖民时代的社会、历史与文化语境，同时还要面对全球化及其可能导致的问题与困境。当然，全球化其实并非只是趋同化与同质化，也涉及多元化及其对文化差异的认同与尊重。在与世界其他民族的交往中，各民族都经由民族间性而与世界性发生关联。不同民族在衣生活与时尚文化上的对话，已呈现出某种开放性、历史性与生成性的特质。这些特质既可促成民族认同与时尚的跨文化传播，还有助于重构基于民族性的世界性时尚文化样式。

一、时尚的民族性、世界性与全球化

在全球化的过程中，传统与民族的服饰及其文化仍然面临极大的挑战，因为民族的独特性往往容易消弭在某种一致性之中。在各民族的时尚创意中，应充分注重传统元素及其特质的挖掘与揭示。在这里，民族性是一个民族创意的精神图式与文化特质所在，同时也是时尚表现力图彰显的艺术与文化内涵。而且民族性与世界性的相互生成，也是全球化时代设计与文化不得不回应的问题。实际上，时尚创意不仅关涉特定的民族存在，而且涉及民族间的文化沟通与理解。毫无疑问，任何民族都不可能孤立地存在于这个世界上。

在各民族共同的在世生存与生活方式里，时尚创意与设计无疑是相互关联与彼此开放的。因此，时尚艺术既要致力于创意的民族性问题的研究与揭示，还要把民族性置身于世界性的文化语境之中。"在世俗的艺术获得独立之前的历史中，艺术的相互对立的解放和保守这两种作用，并没有穷尽审美经验的全部领域。"❷实际上，艺术文本的开放性将自身导向了日常生活世界及其审美化。还可以说，世界性本身就与多元的民族性及其关联不可分

---

❶ 朱利安.美，这奇特的理念[M].高枫枫，译.北京：北京大学出版社，2016：11.
❷ 汉斯·罗伯特·耀斯.审美经验与文学解释学[M].顾建光，顾静宁，张乐天，译.上海：上海译文出版社，1997：234.

离,它往往也是通过各民族的交织与互文来实现自身的。但要注意世界性与民族性及其生成性关联,不再是简单的包含与被包含、一般与个别的逻辑关系。

尤其要加以特别注重的是,在各种元素之中,究竟哪些是各民族共同的或相似的元素。即使是相似的元素,在不同社会与文化语境里,其含义与理解也可能是有差异的。与此同时,哪些元素又是不一致的、有差异的,以及各民族对那些相同元素有何独特的理解。另外,还涉及对那些不同的元素与文化特质的关注。将不同民族元素加以关联,旨在促成各民族在时尚创意上的相互借鉴,以及在民族文化语境里的沟通与对话等。对民族认同来说,内部的基本共识及其与其他民族的区分都是不可少的。

各民族的时尚创意既基于民族自身,同时又与其他民族发生生成性关联,达到一种世界范围内的相互理解与沟通。其实,"民族性,从共有的历史遗产这个意义上而言,最终可以整合在不同的国家的民族集团中,甚至在不同国家的公民当中,产生一种文化认同感或意识"。❶也可以说,民族性以其与特定地方、地方性,进而与世界性发生着相互关联与呼应。但那些处于中心与支配地位的文化体系与习惯,往往难免对边缘的文化样式产生压抑,这就需要以多元的文化心态来缓解与调适差异。

当然,这种世界性的服饰与时尚文化,也为民族意识与身份认同的确立提供了可能,而并非简单地否定与排斥一切民族性特质。各民族之间的关联性尤其是互文,在根本意义上表征为某种民族间性特质,这种民族间性既是各民族相关性的彰显,同时又为通达世界性本身提供了根本性可能。正是这种民族间性,使民族之间的文化交流与理解变成可能,同时又使各民族独自与共同的存在得以实现。各个国家都有其独特的民族服装与时尚文化,而这些不同的民族服装又发生相互的借鉴与影响。

在本性上,民族间性就是民族性与世界性的一种对话,以及在这种对话中发生的民族间的文化互文。作为对现代性问题的一种回应,全球化在此既是对现代主义的一种推进,同时也为现代主义提供了反思的可能性。在通常意义上,全球化意味着全球联系的不断增强与日趋密切。在全球化时代,各个族群或国家之间在政治与经济上的互相依存,其实也是艺术、时尚与文化不可脱离的语境性关联。随着服饰与时尚的跨文化传播,尤其是,技术与现代性对一致性的诉求在世界范围内的扩展,人们难免涉及从外在着装来区分不同民族的问题。也就是说,全球化也可以解释为世界的压缩和视全球为一个整体。

无可置疑,民族性与世界性,以及地方性与全球性,其实并不是简单的对立与冲突,而是处于相互关联与彼此生成之中。"当然,亚洲的企业家都觉得他们是被迫学习西方科学,了解盎格鲁-撒克逊商务实践的基础,熟练使用英文或法文,穿西装打领带的。"❷因此,民族的共在与相互交往,显然不是消解各民族时尚与文化的差异,以寻求某种简单与空洞的文化一致性。与此同时,还要承认与认同各民族独特的文化个性,促进文化的交织

---

❶《第欧根尼》中文精选版编辑委员会.文化认同性的变形[M].北京:商务印书馆,2008:14.
❷乔尔·科特金.全球族[M].王旭,译.北京:社会科学文献出版社,2010:17.

和对话的有效生成与建构。实际上，完全与彻底的全球化既没必要也不可能实现。

在这里，跨文化的艺术与时尚传播，在不断消解不同民族间的界限，建构出一种既融合了各个民族的特质，同时又不局限于某一民族的流行趋势。互文性为文化认同中的坚持与包容，以及民族之间的相互信任与理解的达成，奠定了不可或缺的社会、历史与文化语境。尽管说，不同民族的区分正在缩小与式微，但还远没有达到消失与可以忽视的程度。对当代服饰艺术与时尚文化而言，既不能以一种民族性否定民族多样性与世界性，同时也不能用全球化去限定与宰制地方性文化。即使在全球化时代，世界性的时尚对各民族元素与文化的关注，无疑正在成为一种新的文化自觉与当代传统认同。

而且，各民族的元素与文化，既是独特的与敞开的，更是彼此关联与相互影响的。显然，文化的交流与沟通促成了不同的民族在时尚创意与服饰文化上的彼此借鉴，并对人们日常生活的审美产生了深刻的影响。可以说，"今天的文化人类学家通常并不采用全球视角，甚至经常反对社会文化现象研究中的普遍性视角和比较方法"。❶ 正因如此，民族文化及其独特性的认同并非可有可无，但这种认同也离不开跨文化的交流与思想对话，这就需要不同族群或国家的广泛参与和深刻介入。

人们应从生成论视角，理解全球化给民族性艺术与文化带来的影响。在全球化过程中，国际分工与世界经济的形成和不断建构，促成了各种知识体系的生成，以及意识形态和宗教世界范围的广泛影响。信息化、互联网与新媒体等当代技术，加速冲破了不同族群或国家之间的传统边界。全球化还缩小了各国和各地的空间距离，使整个世界越来越融为被技术规定与建构的地球村。虽然说，各民族的艺术与文化难免受到深刻的影响，但人们的衣生活方式与审美经验及其建构，并不简单地受制于社会经济的规限与限制。但全球化在为少数发展中国家提供历史机遇的同时，也难免对传统艺术与文化造成冲击甚至解构。

在这里，经济与文化的一体化带有整合与趋同的意思，但实际上根本不可能出现一个单质世界，所以全球化并不能只理解为全球一体化。民族性与世界性的复杂关联，无论是冲突，还是和解，都是全球化不可回避的问题。而且，对全球化的理解与阐发总是在某种文化语境里实现的。虽然说，经济与科技全球化往往表征为一体化趋势，但对各种艺术、文化、宗教与生活方式来说，相互之间的关联与影响其实并不意味着全球化。在全球化的文化语境里，时尚创意不仅是民族性的与地方性的，因此亟待得到民族文化的认同与接受。

而且，各民族的艺术与文化还应尽可能得到其他民族的理解与认同。在这个全球化时代，民族性服饰与时尚会受到世界性趋势的影响而走向时尚化，而当代的世界性时尚风格也离不开对各民族的元素与文化特质的重构。当然，时尚化与重构的发生及其理解与阐释，通常也是经由民族间性来建构与实现的，而民族文化就生成与共在于世界性文化之中。但这里的世界性艺术、服饰与文化，并不是某种单一的、纯而又纯的样式，它本身就含有民

---

❶ 范丹姆.审美人类学：视野与方法[M].李修建，向丽，译.北京：中国文联出版社，2015：131.

族文化及其多样性特质。还要意识到,民族性经由民族间性而通达世界性,这一过程其实是有条件的与语境性的,显然并不是绝对的、必然的与一定如此的。

应当说,民族性向世界性的这种可通达性,取决于民族性自身的开放性、历史性与生成性,这无疑也是民族间性与世界性得以可能成为自身的前提。在现代社会,各种思想的表达彼此相异并呈现出多元化,"尽管其内容的确非常不同,但对整体性的痴迷却是处处一如既往"。❶ 而且,世界性本身并不是民族性的终结或消失,而是对多元的民族文化的包容与接纳。当然,多民族的艺术与文化在世界性文化中的融合,仍然关涉各民族自身的精神与文化特质。特别是,20世纪80年代以来,时装风格呈现出多样化的审美与文化态势。

如果一个民族的民族性是封闭的、非历史性的,那么,时尚创意就不可能在各民族之间得以沟通。虽然说,开放也可能给某种传统带来挑战与风险,但一味地对外封闭却更容易导致文化生命的丧失。封闭的民族时尚创意也不可能是世界性的,它仍然只是限定在该民族的本土生活方式之中。观念及其视觉化表现不仅是艺术性的,同时也是一种关切于精神与文化的创意发生。时尚文化不仅关联于艺术及其审美表现,它还关切于各个民族自身的精神与文化,以及与时尚相关的诸多社会与历史语境。民族艺术与文化的历史性是基于时间性的,但当这种历史性被视为具有历史意义时,却是传统成为传统不可或缺的生成论基础。

当然,不同民族、族群对时尚创意的文化认同,不可能摆脱自身的集体无意识与前理解。一个民族的时尚创意与设计制作的生成,要成为一种世界性与全球性的艺术与文化样式,它首先就要足够明确地彰显与该民族特质相关的文化。民族性既是民族创意认可得以可能的根本基础,也是民族时尚文化成为世界性文化的前提。民族间性使不同民族之间的理解得以可能,并为世界性的时尚文化认同作出奠基。在这里,民族间性使多元的时尚艺术与文化的对话得以可能,同时也为世界性当代时尚与文化建构提供了生成论奠基。

即使当民族时尚创意不仅只是存在,而且通达了世界可理解性的时候,也并不意味着这种创意就是高度一致与一体化的东西,而是一种以民族性为基础的世界性创意文化。在全球化时代,世界性文化应成为内含民族性特质的多元文化。实际上,全球化的时尚创意与设计,大都以各民族及其文化特质为隐性语境,而不应以牺牲独特的民族性或地方性为代价,但也不能只是民族性元素与文化的简单移植与再现。一切民族都应在时尚创意与设计里,建构出本民族的话语风格与审美文化特质。毫无疑问,东方时尚主要源于东方自身的艺术与文化传统,这种文化意识与自觉使得东方时尚在当代的重构成为可能。

这是因为简单的非此即彼的文化执态,都不可避免地陷入殖民化或狭隘的民族主义而难以自拔。应当看到,"我们正步入一个创意时代,创意无所不在,并渗透到经济与社会各方各面,并不仅表现在高科技产业创新的异军突起"。❷ 时尚的艺术与文化甚至进入了文化

---

❶ 沃尔夫冈·韦尔施.重构美学[M].陆扬,张岩冰,译.上海:上海译文出版社,2002:148.
❷ 理查德·佛罗里达.创意阶层的崛起[M].司徒爱勒,译.北京:中信出版社,2010:64.

产业的内在构成里，极其重要的就是去激活民族元素及其文化意义。在时尚创意过程中，还涉及如何建构与重构民族精神与文化意义的问题，因为只有这样才能使世界性的时尚与文化建基在民族性基础之上。与此同时，时尚风格的轮回性也是不可忽视的问题。

在20世纪60年代，曾经流行的迷你风格时尚，到了90年代再次成为一种时尚。应当说，时尚的这种轮回也有关于民族风格及其文化的重构。在全球化的艺术与文化语境里，基于时尚视觉表现的民族审美文化的当代建构，主要包括民族间的价值观比较、民族元素的视觉表现、民族的审美趣味与接受习惯、文化认同的理论基础与对话机制，以及研究如何生成与建构民族特质等。全球化是民族时尚与文化认同不可回避的问题，任何对西方采取简单的拿来或排斥的态度都是不可取的。在当代衣生活方式里，世界性时尚正是在民族性特质里来发掘话语与风格的。

二、全球化创意：同质化，还是多元化

只有具有某种特质的艺术与文化，才不至于迷失在全球一体化与同质化的潮流之中。全球化是第二次世界大战以来，特别是20世纪90年代以来，世界经济与文化不可逆转的根本趋势。应当看到，"当我们谈文化持续地国际化时，我们会谈到这种情况，而文化的国际化甚至在最不可能的领域里也已经变得十分明显——在日常生活里：饮食习惯、服装式样、居住场所，还有在艺术里"。❶ 与此同时，全球化还对文化与时尚创意产业带来了根本性的影响。在全球化时代，服饰与时尚面临的同质化与多元化的交困是绕不过去的设计问题。

其实，现代性及其对一致性的根本性诉求，导致了同质化的问题与困境的出现，这就为在全球化时代，以多元化来回应同质化而提出文化诉求。全球化在很大程度上是资本与文化的全球化，同时也是生产社会化和经济关系国际化的趋势。在本性上，全球化与艺术、时尚、创意文化产业分不开。在全球化时代，各国经济相互依存、彼此渗透的程度大为增强，而阻碍生产要素自由流通的壁垒不断削弱，经济运行的国际规则逐步形成并不断发生重建。毫无疑问，全球化是一个历史性生成与重建的过程，其萌芽可追溯到十六世纪至十八世纪的西方。

值得注意的是，工业革命以后，资本主义商品经济与现代工业、交通运输业迅速发展，世界各国间的贸易往来大大超过历代水平。"当然，从某种角度来说，我们的确目睹了世界的多极化，也目睹了被一些人称为文化全球化的东西：单一性的世界文化的形成。"❷ 而且，随着互联网与各种新媒体的出现，民族时尚易于从其他民族与世界性创意中去借鉴，而各民族建构与重构出来的民族服饰与时尚文化，实际上又无不渗透着世界性的艺术与文化影响。全球化的突出表现在于，国际分工从过去以垂直分工为主，发展到以水平分工为主的新阶段，世界贸易增长迅猛和多边贸易体制得以建构。

---

❶ 伊曼纽尔·沃勒斯坦.变化中的世界体系[M].王逢振,译.北京：中央编译出版社,2016：211.
❷ 乔纳森·弗里德曼.文化认同与全球性过程[M].郭健如,译.北京：商务印书馆,2003：149.

民族元素、时尚创意与文化认同

Ethnic Elements, Fashion Creative and Cultural Identity

与经济全球化一样，文化全球化也是一种世界性动向与趋势，但文化交流仍然与不同民族间的文化认同相关，以至于达致各民族在艺术与文化上的相互理解。还要意识到，这种全球化甚至成为一种不可逆转的文化趋势。在全球化的语境里，同质化指商品在性能、外观甚至营销手段上的相互模仿，最后导致逐渐趋同与差异的式微甚至消失。这种同质化也对民族时尚与创意的多样性造成威胁，甚至致使民族独特的精神图式与传统文化濒临消失。其实，全球化及其对现代性的强调与不断推进，并以同质化给民族时尚带来了挑战与抑制，但全球化也可能为各民族多元化创意带来机遇。

当然，如果只是将全球化理解为绝对一致性的宿命，则难以揭示与阐明后现代主义语境所提供的批判视角。不可否认，全球化创意也将凭借文化多样性的执态，为不同民族与国家的时尚创意与设计，提供了获得肯定与认可的诸多可能性。在马克尔·富马罗利看来，"将活生生的独特性僵化为枯燥乏味的'同一性'严密地保护起来无非是'同一性'行将灭亡的最后一刻"。❶ 在此应特别强调的是，通过民族时尚创意的独特表现，促成全球化时代民族艺术与文化认同的建构。在时尚的创意与设计过程中，民族元素及其文化多样性特质有助于不同民族之间的相互沟通、理解与认同。

对创意与设计而言，同质化指某些大致相同的款式、形制与风格等，这是缺乏原创与一味地相互模仿甚至抄袭所导致的。在产品同质化的基础上，所形成的市场竞争行为称为同质化竞争。就时尚来说，同质化不利于消费者在不同设计间加以有效识别，因为，无特色、无差异与极其相似导致差异性与多元化的式微。全球化时代的创意与时尚设计，无疑是对一致性与差异性及其关系的回应与建构。即使是那些尚有强劲的竞争力的知名品牌，仍需对产品加以差异化创意与设计。但对于一般的服饰品牌，同质化显然避免不了残酷的价格战。

对那些有品牌意识的设计而言，如要突破同质化就必须在创意上别出心裁，以及提前对于终端消费市场做出预判，率先作出变革以求从同质化里脱颖而出。比如中国设计师张肇达的时尚创意始终没有离开中国与东方的民族性，这也就建构了他华美、高雅与大气恢宏的设计风格。由于不少设计师缺乏判断与创新的独特能力，所以只好仿效甚至抄袭别人的创意与设计思路，这样就可能导致同质化的出现与差异性的终结。甚至连一个明显失败的创意表现与设计，都难免有很多设计师在极力模仿与抄袭。相似甚至极其雷同的设计作品的大量出现与屡禁不止，导致人们在创意与设计上陷入单一化的境地。

但应当意识到，随着社会、经济及创意文化的发展，设计的趋同性并没有得到克服甚至还更加突出。人们往往从资料中吸收别人现成的表现手法，而不注意分析创意思想与原创精神之所在。同时还要看到，"需要推翻工业化时代的后遗症，因为它导致市场中千篇一律地描述大部分的商品的特点"。❷ 而且，任何简单的模仿甚至直接拿来，都难免使设计仅

---

❶《第欧根尼》中文精选版编辑委员会.文化认同性的变形[M].北京：商务印书馆，2008：35.
❷ 托马斯·洛克伍德.设计思维[M].李翠荣，李永春，等译.北京：电子工业出版社，2012：100.

仅停留在视觉表象上，根本不可能深入民族的精神特质中去。针对同质化的问题，差异化思维与设计在时尚中具有重要的意义。

在这里，对创意与设计及其民族性的关注，是实现差异化设计的重要样式与文化基础。对于设计而言，差异化是克服同质化极为有效的策略，其实，对差异的强调本身就是对一致性与同质化的消解。在时尚差异与设计之中，针对性地满足个人情感与体验的需要无疑是非常必要的。亟待研究的课题仍然是，怎样才能激活这些民族元素及其精神与文化特质，进而促成与实现民族时尚创意与文化的当代创新。缺乏民族性与个性的时尚创意与设计，难免陷入雷同而得不到审美与文化上的认同。应当提到的是，中国设计师马可的"例外"品牌表明了与一般时尚的区分，她又以"无用"表达了对精神的诉求与向传统文化的回归，两者相互生成并共同实现着对中国风的当代审美与文化重构。

全球化并非简单的一体化、同质化，而是差异化创意与多元文化的并存。实际上，趋同的与同质化的时装创意与设计，导致了艺术与文化特质的式微甚至消失。自20世纪80年代以来，世界文化多元化已成为一种不可逆转的历史趋势。"倘若任由这种以贬损其他社会为代价的现象过度膨胀，那么，这不但会危及对东方世界的客观理解，而且，也要危及对西方世界的正确理解。"❶ 因此，创意亟待激发人们的民族意识和对民族文化的认同感。每一种独特的民族艺术与衣生活方式，其实都具有其他文化所没有的精神与文化特质。

在西方理性哲学与形而上学之中，二元分立的克服也是服饰艺术与时尚文化建构的基础。因此，文化的多元共存与相互生成，为各种文化的交流、取长补短提供了条件。与此同时，各种文化在彼此借鉴与相互生成里建构着共生性，从而形成了彼此各异与魅力无穷的人类文化景观。在时尚与文化的多元化过程中，处在同一时代、同一文化体系里的多元文化各自具有独特的民族特色，但各种文化彼此之间又发生着相互交流、互文与融合。在西方生活史上，时尚是以各种不同的样式而存在的，这些样式通常表征为各种不同的时尚艺术流派。

但还注意到，在相互间的融合与彼此生成过程中，每一种文化都按照自己的价值观念和标准进行自主的选择，吸纳来自不同民族特质或异质文化的特质。实际上，文化在任何时候都是一个动态的、开放的与变化的系统，它的历史性生成永远离不开与其他文化的交流、沟通，以及彼此间的跨文化的艺术、审美与文化传播。流行趋势与时尚的生成，既是对既有同质化问题的克服，同时又难免陷入重新同质化之中。因此，差异与多元对同质化的反离是永无止境的。但在文化融合的过程中，没有冲突就没有意义的融合与交织，而且融合本身就包含着冲突或矛盾。

虽然说在西方思想史上，同一性往往在统一性之中显现与表征。但是，这种统一是在存在论上的相互关切，而不是在存在者层面上的彼此相似。在不同民族的时尚创意之间，

---

❶ 杰克·古迪.西方中的东方[M].沈毅，译.杭州：浙江大学出版社，2012：250.

并非一种天然与简单的对立关系，而是一种相互渗透、对话与融合，以及对冲突与争执的一种和解。"但这种统一性绝不是那种单调的空洞，那种在其自身中没有任何关系、只是一味地持守于一种千篇一律的东西的空洞。"❶ 正是各民族不同的价值观和思维方式，塑造与生成了各民族的风俗习惯、文化心理与行为模式等。在当代，各种民族元素发生着彼此借鉴与混搭，生成了基于互文的多元化的国际时尚风格。

从某种意义上来讲，多元化就是价值观与思维方式的多元化。多元化的文化保持其生命力的途径有待于正视冲突，吸收借鉴其他文化的有益成分与元素，使自身文化得以传承与在当代更新。在2009春夏伦敦时装周上，全球化概念通过各种东西方融合的设计得到了体现与回应。对艺术与时尚流派而言，各种视角往往通过特定的风格加以表征，而视角及其风格的表征其实都是语境性的。即使在对差异与多元的主张与强调之中，创意也不是为了差异而差异、为了多元而多元，否则民族元素及其表现就会停留在视觉表象上。实际上，对文化多元化的理解其实也是多层次的，并表征在各种不同的维度与层面之中。

在全球化时代的艺术、审美与文化语境里，各民族文化是一种基于各自独特性的共在，而任何特定民族的传统文化与其他民族文化也是互文的。还可以说，不同民族的艺术与文化之间都是互为他者的，但它们又在互文里克服自我与他者的二元分立。其实，"拒斥宏大叙事、总体世界观、绝对基础，以及随之而来对于破碎性、差异性和不可通约性的强调，都将后现代主义与现代主义的启蒙区分开来"。❷ 在不同的与多元的创意活动之中，主体间性往往表征为共在于世的生活方式，以及由此而生成的民族性与世界性及其和解与张力。在全球化的创意与设计过程中，对同质化与多元化及其关联的回应是不可忽视的问题。

三、创意的对话与全球性的文化认同

一个民族的存在与成为自身，绝不能失去本民族特有的精神与文化特质，同时也不能以其他民族特质来替代本民族的独特性。通过对民族元素的创意与设计，旨在揭示、表现与阐发民族的艺术与文化特质。任何民族都不可能完全与世隔绝地生存，而是在不同民族的共同生存与生活里，依凭相互间的艺术交流与文化对话，来寻求民族自身的创意、表现与设计，以表达关于民族内在精神图式的设计样式。在全球化时代，各民族在创意与设计上的思想与文化对话，对于相互间的沟通与理解都是必不可少的。与此同时，全球性的文化认同也离不开对差异与多元的包容与尊重。

如果一个民族只是简单地移植和借用其他民族的东西，那就是脱离本民族精神与文化特质的舍本逐末，无疑还会丢失本民族的创意、设计与文化传统。随着全球化的日趋深入与拓展，各民族文化的对话、碰撞、交流与融合已成不可阻挡之势。对种族偏见与歧视的克服，是时尚界应加以重视的文化任务。英国时装委员会曾致函各大时装品牌，要求设计

---

❶ 马丁·海德格尔.同一与差异[M].孙周兴,陈小文,余明锋,译.北京:商务印书馆,2011:29.
❷ J.J.克拉克.东方启蒙:东西方思想的遭遇[M].于闽梅,曾祥波,译.上海:上海人民出版社,2011:305.

师考虑多采用少数族裔模特儿,从而在时装周上体现与包容种族多样性。还应看到,文化交往的全球化给民族创意带来了冲击与影响,因此亟待对民族性特质可能消弭的情况加以思考与回应。在这里,互为异质的各民族文化的碰撞体现在生活的各个层面,它既体现了人类文明的多元化视角与格局,同时又隐藏着不同文化之间的冲突与对立。

正因如此,应经由跨文化交流与思想对话,克服与消解各民族艺术与文化间的冲突,进而建构当代时尚多元化的民族性基础。当然,世界性文化不是基于唯我独尊的西方文化专制,而是关于人类生存与价值体系的多元文化共同体。在全球化的社会与文化语境中,任何作为主体的族群不应再被极端个体化,而是民族个性及其与世界性的相互共属。作为一种回归中的传统及其重构,民族时尚不仅传递着传统精神与文化的特质,还生成与建构着民族文化的当代韵致和气韵,从而成为传统文化在当代的艺术与文化符码。

全球化时代的到来,仍然和各民族艺术与文化间的对话息息相关。在这里,跨文化既指跨越了各民族传统界限的文化,同时也是对这种边界的一种文化跨越。但是,"西方服装系统和殖民地本土服装系统之间的关系不是互相排斥的关系,而是一种互相改变、互相争夺文化吸引力的动态过程"。❶全球化时代的创意与设计,亟待回应不同文化归属的人们之间的交往,并从各种民族元素与文化里得到灵感与启示。在全球化的语境里,民族间的文化变迁、文化冲突与文化融合,以及在当代的继承与重构等各种复杂关系,无疑都是不可忽视的创意、设计与文化的问题。

其实,各民族在精神与文化上的差异与融合,影响着人们的价值观念、思维特质与衣生活方式。在全球化这个不可逆转的进程中,民族文化所呈现出的新趋向与流行时尚,正在成为世界性时尚多样性的构成要素。在时尚界,汤米·希尔费格的"完全美国味"的服装,因其实用与风格朴素,受到美国年轻人的喜欢。但当代服饰创意与设计所关联的,不再只是一种民族习俗与生活方式及其再现式还原,而是与其他民族发生着世界性的跨文化交流与对话。对各民族的精神与文化来说,全球化其实也强化了各民族文化的相互依赖性,因此迫切需要建构民族文化的开放性与世界性关联。

在这里,日常生活审美化中的民族时尚,应当说是当代民族文化的生成之物。不同样式的艺术风格与审美经验及其建构,正在广泛与深入地介入人们的衣生活方式。民族服饰元素之所以能够成为世界性的时尚元素,其实是因为,在艺术与文化的地方性与全球性之间,存在着不可或缺的内应、外化、转换与重构。而且,"由于全球变暖已经成为大众普遍关注的重大议题,因此时尚界也开始将焦点转向环保服饰"。❷在全球化时代,传统的民族服饰与所有的文化遗产,包括着装礼仪、服饰制度、风俗习惯等,都面临着如何保护、传承与当代重构的问题。民族时尚的创意与设计的表现,也是民族艺术与文化在当代生成的一种样式,并难免被注入不同民族乃至世界性的精神与文化特质。

---

❶ 珍妮弗·克雷克.时装的面貌:时装的文化研究[M].舒予中,译.北京:中央编译出版社,2000:51.
❷ 哈里特·沃斯里.100个改变时尚的伟大观念[M].唐小佳,译.北京:中国摄影出版社,2013:204.

因此，只有坚持以开放与包容的心态看待各民族文化，艺术、思想与文化间的对话才能实现，从而生成与建构各民族间的彼此认同与相互理解。尤尔根·哈贝马斯认为，现代性根本不是丧失活力、了无生机，而是一项正在进行中的、尚未完成的事业，还不断地发生着协商与思想对话。其实，反全球化运动构成全球化的一种对冲力量，它强调全球化可能带来民族生活方式与文化传统的丧失。而且，跨文化的理解并不是主体对客体的理解，而是各主体之间的相互理解与彼此沟通，它主张与强调的是以主体间性替代主体性。

更确切地说，各民族之间的创意与文化对话，显然是以民族间性为人类学基础的，而这种对话又在各个维度与层面上展开。在这里，民族间性可表征为不同民族间的对话及其发生。在跨文化的艺术与文化对话中，参与者不只依赖自己的代码、习惯、观念与行为方式，而是也经历和了解对方的代码、习惯、观念与行为方式。在哈登看来，任何地方人类的心智，都习惯于一定的地方图案、造型与结构。因此，与艺术相关联的审美经验也难免带上民族性差异。但无论是民族主义，还是殖民主义，它们都没有恰当地对待民族时尚文化。而那些徘徊在民族主义与殖民主义间的思想，也都具有自身特定的艺术与文化的视角与维度。

但对民族服饰与文化的理解与阐释，不应忽视不断生成与建构的创意方式，以及创意与设计方式所关联的文化特质。因此，"我们在自己的文化内交流，或者与其他文化中的人交流时，务必要记住，在成熟的过程中，每一种文化都处在常恒不断的变化之中"。❶ 在民族性问题上，不少的设计师仍然侧重民族主义情结，还有些则一直带有殖民主义的艺术风格，但都难免涉及民族性与世界性的关系问题。在许多前卫与先锋的时尚里，也不乏对民族主义或殖民主义的反思。在创意与设计中，相互学习与借鉴早就发生在各民族之间。

譬如，在清代，衣冠形制保持了满族的风格与审美特征，并将汉人的宽衣大袖改为紧身窄袖。这里旨在表征的是，各民族与文化的独特性虽然是不可忽视的，但民族的东西又不可能是绝对纯粹与单一的。作为殖民主义的一种新样式，后殖民主义更多的是一种文化意义上的殖民。在后殖民主义的语境里，曾经的殖民地可能放弃对本民族的文化坚守，认同殖民主义者所带来的生活方式与殖民文化。而且，人们的民族意识也难免在全球化过程中式微，更缺乏对本民族艺术与文化及其特质的深入思考。

与全球化相关的问题还有，时尚的同质化趋势也越来越明显，独特的传统图式与风格正在消失。正因为如此，不少中国与东方设计师的地域与民族意识在觉醒，并没有简单地追随西方的趋势与对流行的表现，而在时装设计中引入与融会了东方元素与文化。其实，"认同的建构是一个精致的至为严肃的镜子游戏。它是多重的识别实践的复杂的时间性互动，这种识别发生于主体或人群的外部和内部"。❷ 中国设计师梁子在他的时装设计中，将东方元素与国际时尚完美结合，并将天人合一的和谐之美作为根本诉求。其实在西方当代

---

❶ 迈克尔·普罗瑟.文化对话：跨文化传播导论[M].何道宽，译.北京：北京大学出版社，2013：32.
❷ 乔纳森·弗里德曼.文化认同与全球性过程[M].郭健如，译.北京：商务印书馆，2003：213.

时尚设计中，东方的元素与文化也正在受到西方世界从未有过的重视。

比如，男士的西服、衬衫和裤子，女士的连衣裙、套装、衬衫和裙子，这类服饰甚至成为通用于世界各地的国际服装，而在许多公共场所也难以再见到民族性着装。虽然说，全球化与现代性、殖民主义是不可分离的运动，但全球化在带来问题、挑战与困境的同时，也为多民族的共生与时尚提供了文化契机与机遇。因此，简单地放弃民族的时尚传统与衣生活方式，其实也是对文化历史性及其存在的忽视与遗忘。注重对各民族服饰元素的整理与挖掘，对民族艺术与文化的保存与重构来说既是必不可少的，更是民族传统文化及其世界性认同所必需的。但如果只是秉持固执一端的狭隘民族心理，无疑是一种失之偏颇的心理与文化执态。

可以说，后殖民主义时代的多民族性与文化多样性问题，既是全球化所要面对与回应的问题，当然也是各民族文化认同得以发生的前提。

应当充分强调的是，各民族在生存与文化权利上应该是平等的，同时还要包容各民族的艺术、信仰与文化差异。全球化不应是艺术与文化的趋同化与同质化，而是多元化及其对文化差异的认同与尊重。"全球化的一个重要结果是，个体民族意识苏醒和独特性的追寻，这看起来好像与之明显相悖。与自由和人权需求的增长相伴，要求保护和尊重文化遗产和传统的呼声越来越高。"❶对弱势民族的艺术与文化的妖魔化，成为后殖民主义时代典型的话语风格，而这往往又是以西方强势民族优越的文化心理为前提的。其实，民族内在的文化认同与各民族彼此间的文化认同，以及世界范围内的文化相互适应都是不可或缺的。

在不同的社会、历史与文化语境里，东方的元素在西方乃至世界所彰显出的意义与旨趣也有所差异。因此，对"东方风"时尚艺术与文化的理解与阐释，显然也涉及不同民族与文化间的对话。但在这并不是说，民族的艺术与文化不应接受来自异质文化的批评，而是强调了对差异化与多元化的文化认同。在独特性与地域性之间的审美与文化张力，是东方时尚的当代建构与东方主义批判所不可或缺的。在这个全球化时代，一致性与差异性之间的文化张力及其建构，既是民族美学当代建构与不断重构的思想诉求，同时也是民族内在精神与特质建构的文化语境。

实际上，民族文化认同既是一个国家内部各民族自身的事情，同时也是世界上众多国家及其民族共同面对的文化问题。在主体与自我的关系问题上，"茱莉亚·克里斯蒂娃认为，主体对其自我的发现是一个悖论，因为主体只有在放弃自我的某些东西中来相关于我们发现自己的另一个"。❷其实，许多服饰与时尚本身就融合了不同民族、国家的文化。而且，民族文化的认同与跨文化传播，不仅要考虑后现代的文化语境，还要应对全球化的根本问题与困境。传承与保护好各个民族的服饰文化，这对于文化多样性来说也是非常重要的。

---

❶ 彼得·史密斯，等.跨文化社会心理学[M].严文华，权大勇，译.北京：人民邮电出版社，2009：339.
❷ Kevin O'Donnell. Postmodernism[M]. Gibraltar: Lion Publishing Limited, 2003:80.

民族元素、时尚创意与文化认同

Ethnic Elements, Fashion Creative and Cultural Identity

任何民族的服饰元素与文化不仅属于本民族，还应成为世界性服饰元素与文化多样性的独特组成部分。在全球化之中，传统与民族的服饰及其文化的保存仍然面临极大的挑战，因为民族的独特性可能消弭在对一致性的诉求中。在现代化过程中，泰国、菲律宾等国家还将自己的民族服装的造型与风格，作为一种罕见的生活方式与传统文化保存下来。艺术、服饰与文化的多元性特质，其实是所有民族都必须面对与回应的问题。与此同时，任何非此即彼的严格界限与区分，以及缺乏不同文化特质的整合与同质化，都是民族元素与文化认同应加以警惕与批判的。

在当代，不同民族的衣生活与时尚文化之间的对话，已呈现出开放性、历史性与生成性特质。各民族之间的承认与世界性的文化认同，涉及差异性与相似性的审美与文化张力的重构。普罗瑟认为，"尽管如此，研究和有效践行跨文化传播中的一个固有的命题是，我们要学习和应用相似性和差异性两极之间的平衡"。❶ 其实，民族的生活与时尚并不是隔绝的和排他的，而是人类共同的生活世界不可分离的构成。为此，应对不断促成与建构民族的自我认同与民族间的文化传播，进而在全球化语境里重构基于民族性的世界性时尚文化。

与此同时，对西方所谓的东方主义与后殖民主义文化的批判，以及对民族自信与文化自觉的强调与当代建构，无疑正是中国与东方世界性时尚建构所不可或缺的。作为身份识别与归属确立的一种符号与意义的赋予过程，文化认同在不同的层次与维度上都有着独特的性质、方式和效果预期。民族间的相互沟通、对话与理解，以及文化的相互适应都是一个历史性过程。应当看到，民族认同是全球认同的文化基础与人类学前提，而民族认同所建构的审美经验、价值诉求与社会意义，无疑是艺术与服饰的跨文化传播与全球认同的必要语境。在一定意义上，全球文化认同既不能脱离各民族自身的认同，也不可能无视民族间的相互认同与承认。也就是说，全球文化认同无疑是基于民族间性与跨文化传播的。

---

❶ 迈克尔·H.普罗瑟.文化对话：跨文化传播导论[M].何道宽，译.北京：北京大学出版社，2013：13.

CHAPTER 3

Ethnic Fashion and Cultural Identity in the Context of Globalization

In the era of globalization, all long-standing ethnic costumes and cultures need to construct their own fashion cultures, and reconstruct their aesthetic cultures and contemporary discourse styles in the fashion creative. In costumes and fashion creative, ethnicity is not only the spiritual foundation of art and cultural identity, but also the cultural prerequisite for access to the globality. As the source of fashion creative, identity on ethnic art and culture is indispensable for acquiring the globality. However, it is noteworthy that any simplified adoption or rejection of Western elements and culture is fundamentally undesirable, improper and impossible, as it will plunge us deeply into colonialism or narrow ethnicism. Here, to explore and activate the cultural meanings of ethnic elements is helpful to the generation and construction of contemporary ethnic fashion and culture. In the artistic, aesthetic and cultural context of globalization, the contemporary construction of ethnic aesthetic culture, which is based on the visual expression of fashion, mainly includes such aspects like the visual expression of ethnic elements, ethnic aesthetic tastes and acceptance habits, comparisons in ethnic spirits and cultures, dialogues and theoretical constructions on cultural identity. On that basis, researches are made on ways to maintain and reconstruct distinctive ethnic characteristics and artistic styles, and to avoid losing them in globalization and homogeneity.

Only in the connection between ethnicity and globality could we create a kind of world fashion and clothing culture with ethnic characteristics. At the same time, through the fashion creative and artistic expression of ethnic elements, we provide the possibility for the construction of ethnic aesthetic cultural identity in the era of globalization. Any revelation and reconstruction of ethnic elements may become the cultural source of fashion elements and creative. This kind of creative and design based on ethnic elements and cultural characteristics, being inseparable from the context of society, history and culture, is a means by which ethnic fashion and cultural identity can be constructed. Of course, the revealing and interpreting of fashion ethnicity is never closed, rigid and exclusive, rather, it gets accessed and integrated to a cosmopolitan cultural identity through inter-ethnicity.

Section 1   Ethnicity and Globality of Fashion Creative

Fashion creative and design inevitably involves issues of ethnic elements and culture, for a certain fashion creative and culture is often based on ethnic art and takes this ethnic culture as its fundamental context and connotation. Meanwhile, the relationship between the ethnicity and globality of culture must be considered, because it is impossible for any ethnic group to exist independently of other groups, or to avoid exchanges of life and culture with others. Culture, in itself, has always been related to the relationship between ethnicity and globality, so clothing and fashion, as a unique cultural style, can never get rid of this relationship. Ethnic fashion creative and design concerns ethnicity, hence should be recognized and recognized by ethnic culture; but at the same time, things classified into fashion often have cosmopolitan characteristics, gaining broad understanding and cultural identity in a worldwide context. Therefore, the generative relationship between ethnicity and globality of culture is undoubtedly an ideological and cultural question that fashion creative must face and explore.

1. From Ethnicity to Globality

An ethnic group can be understood as a stable community that is formed through a certain historical period, and common in language, living area, cultural characteristics and ethnic psychology. And generally, this commonality applies to most members of the ethnic group. Although every ethnic group has its unique spiritual characters and cultural traditions, it "cannot be understood through a single culture."[1] While ethnicity has irreplaceable artistic characteristics and cultural significance in fashion creative and design, it is closely related to and mutually generated with globality. The creative and designs based on ethnic elements invariably involve the relationship between ethnicity and globality.

Moreover, how the unique ethnic art and aesthetic culture can find their way to globality should also be considered in creative. The meaning and purport of ethnic expressions vary with cultural contexts. In a broad sense, ethnic group refers to any community with common ethnic and regional characteristics, and ethnicity is undoubtedly the primality that defines an ethnic group. The composition of this ethnicity is a compound structure in an open state of generation. In terms of geographic and historical scope, ethnic group is the composition and representation of the diversity of human existence and culture. Ethnic group in its broad range can be composed of primitive ones, ancient ones, modern ones, contemporary ones, aboriginal ones, etc., or even clans and tribes. Of course, ethnic groups can often make up a multi-ethnic ethnic group or country, such as the Chinese ethnic group and the Arab ethnic group.

Therefore, the term ethnic group can refer to both a multi-ethnic community and its specific members, such as the English, the German, the French, the Han for the former kind, and the

---

[1] Fenton S. Ethnicity [M]. Lao Huanqiang, et al (tr). Beijing: China Minzu University Press, 2009:25.

Mongolian, the Manchu, the Hui, the Tibetan for the latter kind. Those people living in a specific environment and cultural context and sharing spiritual and cultural characteristics belong to a specific ethnic group. It may be said that, an ethnic group is a community formed by people in human history with a similar kind of feeling and mentality. In a sense, division on the types of culture is closely related to the existence of ethnic groups. Obviously, the relationship between culture, ethnic group and anthropology is an issue not to be ignored in the study of cultural anthropology.

In fact, the connection between ethnic groups in a common ethnic life is the ontological basis for showing the relationship between ethnicity and globality. As ethnic group is historically generated, it is inseparable from the construction of human spirit and culture. In the primitive society, due to the restrictions of biological evolution and the laws of nature, human ancestors could only live together by relying on blood relations. There were mutual influences among the members within the ethnic group, as well as between the members within and without, and people maintain relationships with each other naturally by instinct. By the time when human culture began to take shape, people in the primitive society had formed earliest living habits, customs and cultures, out of their work and survival.

Although ethnic art and culture are related to regional characteristics, ethnicity cannot be attributed only to the latter. Generally speaking, besides its connection with region, the term ethnic group also has "an original meaning: related to the 'breeds' or 'stock' of people who have, or regarded as having, a common descent." ❶ Due to the restrictions of natural living environment, innate ethnic condition, and regional uniqueness, members of different ethnic groups have different lifestyles, behavior patterns and customs, which also brings about their distinctions in art and culture formed gradually through history. Undoubtedly, this ethnicity is the spiritual and cultural stipulation that defines an ethnic group.

At the same time, irreplaceable ethnic characters of various ethnic groups constitute different historical existences of them. In fact, the people living together with the same ethnicity constitute the ethnic group itself, and the collective character in the emotions of ethnic individuals is related to the ethnic consciousness. In traditional ethnic lifestyle, the consciousness and concept of ethnicity and cultural identity can often be expressed through clothing and dressing lifestyles. In the long history of ethnic life, all ethnicities have produced and constructed their cultures with specific ethnic characteristics. Accordingly, ethnic culture must be represented and manifested in various regions and lifestyles of ethnic groups. In a sense, ethnic culture is the trace left by ethnic

---

❶ Fenton S. Ethnicity [M]. Lao Huanqiang, et al (tr). Beijing: China Minzu University Press, 2009:20.

art and spiritual construction, including various institutions and rituals that have been generated in historical societies.

For a specific ethnic group, ethnicity has always been deposited in spiritual life, etiquette and local culture. Under mutual influences in communication, different ethnic groups can learn from each other on arts and clothing styles. However, "the similarity of decorative patterns does not necessarily come from mutual communication. Some basic patterns in ancient painted pottery and textiles are similar between unrelated cultures, such as between ancient China and Peru."❶ In a specific way, ethnic clothing and fashion expresses the artistic and cultural meanings related to ethnic character, and reveals or responds to the relationship between ethnicity and globality. In other words, the discovery and historical interpretation of ethnic elements are inseparable from the study of ethnic life, cultural concepts and customs.

Since specific ethnic communities were formed in human history, distinguished from each other and responding to globality with their spiritual and cultural characteristics, human culture has manifested vastly different cultural patterns. Actually, the generation and the historical inheritance of any culture build its base on the ethnic group and society. And culture enables an ethnic group and society to form its own spiritual characteristics, thereby providing inherent meaning and value system for the ethnic lifestyle. Moreover, traditional ethnic clothing has been manifested in various arts. For example, after the Revolution of 1911 in China, Peking opera actors represented by Mei Lanfang, a master actor, created a new style of opera costume to characterize ancient women. Also, art like literature, sculpture, and painting gives expressions on the dressing of artistic characters.

In the connection between ethnicity and spirit and culture, various ethnic groups form their own characteristics in lifestyle and distinguish themselves from each other. The ethnic cultural construction must be closely related with beliefs and ideas. And this connection brings about some rituals, tokens and purports, which help the infusion of certain spirits into culture. Of course, in the common existence of ethnic groups, there will be more and more similarities, while less and less differences between them. In fact, fashion creative also responds to the connections of various ethnic characteristics. For example, although Christian Lacroix's fashion creative is influenced greatly by French culture, he is very willing to exploit cultural customs in other parts of Europe and to learn from inspirations of different historical periods and artistic styles.

In traditional society, the differences of ethnic groups are reflected not only in their mental schema, but also in externalized artifacts and costumes. However, assimilation among ethnic groups is intensifying, and uniformity may even lead to the disappearance of ethnic differences.

---

❶ Sullivan M. The Meeting of Eastern and Western Art [M]. Zhao Xiao (tr). Shanghai: Shanghai People's Publishing House, 2014:289.

Therefore, it is a question how to make unique ethnicity transition properly to universal globality, and this process inevitably involves the issue of inter-ethnicity. An ethnic group usually expresses fashion art from the perspective of its own culture, meanwhile reconstructs and incorporates ethnic cultural elements into the world fashion. Ethnic character, though indispensable to any ethnic group, exists only in comparison between ethnic groups.

Clothing and fashion creative tries to make ethnicity an essential component of world fashion creative and expression. In the clothing life history of different ethnic groups, mutual learning involves a process from strangeness to familiarity, which is an important issue for study of cultural adaptability. As far as clothing creative and design are concerned, "the dressing habits of the conquerors usually change those of the indigenous peoples, or the clothing cultures of the two sides influence each other and get mixed together. Sometimes the conquerors, succumbing to the local environment and climate, have to change their own clothes and produce a new clothing culture." ❶ It is noteworthy that due to the influence of other ethnic groups, certain group may lose its own ethnic character, and accept the spiritual characters and clothing lifestyles of others. In that case, the assimilation of culture should not be ignored in ethnic creative and design.

Generally speaking, cultural assimilation can be divided into two types: forced assimilation and natural assimilation. Specifically, forced assimilation is often achieved by repression, privilege or even violence, but may be faced by opposition and resistance from the assimilated side. In contrast, natural assimilation usually occurs with the mutual influence and cultural interweaving between ethnic groups, such as the convergence in clothing lifestyle, clothing culture, and aesthetic tastes. Natural assimilation may even change the traditional customs and symbol codes of an ethnic group, and make it accept the clothing traditions and lifestyles of other groups. In the process of assimilation and anti-assimilation, the clothing lives and cultures among ethnic groups construct aesthetic and cultural tensions. Local ethnic fashion cannot be limited within a specific ethnic culture, rather, it often involves cultural communication across ethnic groups.

Here, globality with its universality refers to the common sediment after the suspension of various ethnic characteristics. Of course, from ethnicity to homogeneous globality, the process is related to cultural identity and understanding among ethnic groups. Actually, the diversity in ethnic culture is based on the irreplaceability of each kind of it. Cultural diversity is not only reflected in manifold expressions and promotions of human cultural heritage, but also in the generation of various ideas, creative and designs. However, diversity can never be separated from uniqueness, but be realized by negating and dispelling uniqueness. Therefore, creative should not only identify

---

❶ Tanaka, Chiyo. World Folk Costume: Exploring the Wisdom of Human Dressing Ways [M]. Li Dangqi (tr). Beijing: China Textile & Apparel Press, 2001:33.

with local ethnic culture, but also respect the cultures of other ethnic groups, so that different peoples can learn from each other, seek common ground, and be more inclusive to differences.

No doubt, creative and design should fully respect the cultural diversity of the world, and promote the historical inheritance and contemporary reconstruction of human civilization. While the respect for the artistic and cultural diversity is based on the artistic and cultural identity of local ethnic group, it needs to respond to the cultural differences between ethnic groups or countries. For example, "In the 19th century, Westerners thought that dressing properly was a symbol of civilization, and people with no clothes on were considered barbaric. However, in the 20th and 21st centuries, half-nakedness has become a mark of Western superiority."[1] On one hand, all dressing behaviors are still related to cultural traditions; on the other hand, they affect the construction of world fashion, just like Hollywood movies spread American popular culture to the world. Of course, communication between ethnic groups on art and culture is a prerequisite for accessing the inclusive globality.

To identify with various artistic and cultural styles of the world, we should adhere to the principle of symbiosis of arts and cultures of different ethnic groups. In the communication of arts and cultures, it is fairly necessary to respect differences, understand individuality and learn from each other, so that we can jointly promote the diversification of world clothing and fashion culture. World culture refers to different yet closely-related cultural patterns presented in various regions of the world, which often exhibit a certain commonality. Compared with local arts and cultures, cosmopolitan arts and cultures usually have spiritual characteristics going beyond locality, despite their roots in various ethnic characters. In addition to such cultural forms as literature and art, culture also includes daily life, communication method, value system, as well as relative tradition, belief, and spiritual purport.

In different times and places, clothing art and culture have different forms of expression, as well as social and cultural characteristics related to people's inner spirit. In fact, the specific manifestations of this artistic and cultural diversity are the indispensable context for forming the spiritual characteristics of ethnic groups and mankind. All ethnic groups have their own unique clothing styles and dressing traditions, "but in most countries, people lead a double life of clothing, by wearing clothes popular across the world in their daily life and folk costumes at their festivals or ceremonies."[2] In a way, this double clothing life helps maintain a balance and tension between ethnicity and globality. Although many designers pay much attention to the adoption and

---

[1] Young R J C. Postcolonialism: A Very Short Introduction [M]. Oxford: Oxford University Press, 2003:83.

[2] Tanaka, Chiyo. World Folk Costume: Exploring the Wisdom of Human Dressing Ways [M]. Li Dangqi (tr). Beijing: China Textile & Apparel Press, 2001:36.

reconstruction of ethnic elements, they need to rely on international design discourse and creative thinking so that their designs and products could be recognized by the world's fashion industry.

In terms of communication, issues of globality, which are related to cultural diversity, need to be recognized and emphasized in historical inheritance and contemporary construction, and to be regarded as cultural anthropological characteristics out of mutual adaptation among ethnic groups. Undoubtedly, every ethnic group in the world, regardless of size, population, or social and cultural institution, should have a tolerant attitude towards the arts and cultures of other groups, on the premise of identifying with its own ethnic and cultural characters. In other words, all ethnic groups should respect each other's arts and cultures, and construct mutual understanding and cultural identity on the basis of an acceptable globality. In itself, cultural right is an indispensable component of human rights, as well as the guarantee of realizing human's cultural appeals. Today, many styles of world fashion have integrated with various ethnic elements and cultural characteristics.

Everyone has the right and freedom to choose apparel and accessories. And only by fully protecting and inheriting ethnic arts and culture, can we make sure that traditional ethnic documents can be freely accessible to everyone. The revealing and fashionizing of ethnic elements involve the question of how to integrate various cultures into clothing. For example, the clothing of South Korea got its initial influence mainly from that of the Tang Dynasty in China, when ancient Silla was in close contact with China, so that the characteristics of Korean costumes were almost the same as those of the Tang costumes. In contemporary society, cultural globalization means that all cultures in the world, facing mutual influences and challenges of each other, must exist in connection with each other. Obviously, globality must be achieved in its relation with ethnicity, and the universality of globality is built on historical conditions.

In the era of globalization, cultural exchanges between ethnic groups will become more and more frequent. In the interweaving trend, clothing fashions are changing in expression and style, which, however, in no way means that the differences between cultures will be eliminated and a globally uniformed art and culture will be formed. On the contrary, arts and cultures will maintain their diversity for long, and develop their characteristics on the basis of diversity. "Of course, daily life is affected by a wide range of values, international symbolic forms, civilization, ethnic ideology, as well as cultural and regional positioning." [1] Where the ethnicity of fashion lies, there is no lack of the construction of globality, as the latter is often perfused with the former. It is urgent to construct a relationship of mutual integration and generation between the unique ethnicity and

---

[1] Lull J. Media, Communication, Culture: A Global Approach [M]. Dong Hongchuan (tr). Beijing: Commercial Press, 2012:309.

the universal globality, which is not as traditional as the logical relationship between generality and individuality, including and being included.

2. Ethnic Creative and Identity Related to Globality

The tendency of kinship tracing in ethnic identity originates from the existence pattern of early ethnic groups, namely, clans, tribes and other forms of early ethnic groups were built on the basis of kinship. Undoubtedly, the tradition and inheritance of ethnic cultural identity have continued and extended into modern and contemporary periods. Based on this primordial kinship, ethnic identity tends to have a stabler instinctive cohesion than other kinds of identity. In the common life, the artistic and cultural exchanges between ethnic groups are necessary, which also means globality is unavoidable in the cultural identity of any ethnic group. However, it is impossible to construct a fashion culture characteristic of contemporary world if we keep staying within the bygone context of ethnic elements.

In fact, the prerequisite for ethnic identification lies in the communication between ethnic groups. Through the communication, the contrast between ethnic groups can be formed, hence one's group affiliation be acquired and the boundary between ethnic groups be established. The cultural identity of an ethnic group is obviously inseparable from the existence of other groups. Despite their differences in existing, living and cultural contexts, all ethnic groups co-exist in this world, which is an unquestionable foundation of ontology. Therefore, the cultural identity of fashion creative is related to inter-ethnicity, unable to occur in isolation from this world. Actually, cosmopolitan culture is first and foremost an ethnic culture, because the two things exist on condition of each other. Or we can say, cosmopolitan culture is nothing but the product of integrating ethnic culture into world culture.

Although ethnic creative and cultural identity are often related to the inner spirit of an ethnic group, they cannot avoid responding to the relationship between one group and other groups or the world. Dasein (there-being), meaning the existence in the world, is also a suitable term for the existence of the ethnic group. In fact, "the antecedent there-being state of the world is stipulated by its presence and participation." ❶ And this kind of participation manifests the presence of both individuality and collectivity. In other words, cosmopolitan fashion and culture are also the products of various ethnic fashions and cultures, unable to be separated from fashion dialogues and cultural exchanges between ethnic groups. As it were, the existence and lives of ethnic groups are based on this globality.

---

❶ Heidegger M. Sein und Zeit [M]. Chen Jiaying, Wang Qingjie (tr). Beijing: SDX Joint Publishing Company, 1999:160.

To reach the state of Dasein is inseparable from the existence itself and the world to which it is related, because in essence Dasein is the existence in the world. Of course, globality does not ignore the homogeneity of differences and individualities, and the anthropological Dasein with cosmopolitan characteristics is always the result of the coexistence of various ethnic groups. According to Heidegger, Dasein indicates a future-oriented possibility, which shows that an ethnic group should be open in its Dasein and culture, and face the future to generate its own art and culture. Here, being future-oriented indicates diverse possibilities, which undoubtedly involves the issues of trend concerned by popularity and forecasting. Ethnic culture and world culture can be interpenetrated, which is manifested as the globalization of ethnic culture on one hand, and the ethnicization of world culture on the other hand.

As the fundamental stipulation on ethnic group members, ethnic Dasein is also a suspension of the subject person, being different from general entities in its unique openness. However, the cultural interpenetration between ethnic groups and the world could not be easily achieved without any condition. For example, the Korean fashion designs of Andre Kim draw on Chinese elements with cultural characteristics, as well as European and American fashion elements, presenting soft yet attractive colors, and classic, restrained, yet avant-garde styles. At the same time, the interweaving of cultural ethnicity and globality is a process of mutual identify with arts and cultures. Cosmopolitan culture cannot be regarded as a simple summation of various ethnic elements, but it is closely related to ethnic creative and fashion culture. In other words, cosmopolitan culture, existing among ethnic cultures, is the one that is widely recognized and generally accepted by various ethnic groups of the world.

However, we should neither think that all ethnic cultures will go into the world culture automatically, nor that the more ethnic a culture is, the more cosmopolitan it will be. In the cosmopolitan coexistence and generative association, ethnic groups form the anthropological Dasein, dispelling the subject role of each other on one hand, co-existing in harmony with all things on the other hand. If an ethnic culture exists only in a closed and isolated area, or in the reality and actual life of that ethnic group, exerting no cultural influence on other groups or on the world, it would have great difficulty in becoming a cosmopolitan culture. When an ethnic culture has not penetrated into other cultures, it is just a unique style of ethnic and regional culture, and cannot be directly regarded as a real cosmopolitan culture.

Therefore, an ethnic culture is not naturally a cosmopolitan culture, and the transformation of the former into the latter is actually a reconstruction of ethnic culture based on globality. At the same time, the transformation into cosmopolitan creative and cultural identity from ethnic ones, and the construction of a worldwide connection on the basis of ethnic ones, occur on the prerequisite that human beings are historically generated from nativism to cosmopolitanism. Although isolation helps the preservation of ethnic culture to a certain extent, it cannot keep the world away forever, and it might eliminate the possibility of historical inheritance and dialogue. For fashion creative and cultural identity, it is still necessary to consider the generative relationship between specific ethnic group and the world in terms of clothing culture.

In this era of globalization, it is impossible for any ethnic group to be completely away from other groups and live in isolation. Moreover, open exchanges and dialogues between ethnic groups in the field of clothing constitute the necessary prerequisite for the transformation from ethnicity to globality. For example, "the interpenetration between American culture and the European culture in the geographical sense has never stopped, whether it is in the fields of music, natural sciences, literature or humanities."[1] Since modern times, Western subjectivism has encountered formidable cognitive problems and dilemmas. In order to overcome and deconstruct subjectivism and rational metaphysics, Heidegger uses Dasein as the basis of traditional subject, and as the fundamental stipulation of individual subject. Then for each ethnic group, the ethnic Dasein is the stipulation of a group subject.

In contemporary fashion reconstruction and creative, ethnic elements are unique responses to cosmopolitan fashion and culture, so ethnic fashion cannot be grasped as an internal and closed recurrence. In fact, the ethnic identity of fashion creative is also based on the ethnic Dasein. For example, based on the fusion of Eastern and Western aesthetics in kimono, Yamamoto Yohji used black color on a large scale to create a Gothic atmosphere, causing the Western or the whole world to reflect on the identity of today's women. In the coexistence, various ethnic groups show their openness and commonality in life, art and culture. Ethnic Dasein is the fundamental stipulation of the group subject, but meanwhile, it dispels the fixed subject in an open and historical manner.

Inevitably, ethnic fashion creative and cultural identity occur in the context of cosmopolitan art and culture. Here, subject-dispelling aims to show that an ethnic group should not only start from the perspective of its own subject, but also incorporate the existence of other groups into its vision. This kind of openness enables different ethnic groups to interweave and connect with each other, thus laying a foundation for a diversified culture based on globality. It is not only internal ethnic identity but also cultural understanding and recognition from other ethnic groups that clothing and fashion creative strive to obtain. Therefore, it is necessary to develop dialogue and communication between different ethnic Dasein in terms of art, thought, and culture. To produce the creative on its own elements and to reconstruct fashion culture in contemporary times, a

---

[1] Grosser A. Les Identités Difficiles [M]. Wang Kun (tr). Beijing: Social Sciences Academic Press, 2010:61.

specific ethnic group must make dialogues with other groups in the world by incorporating their fashion trends into its own clothing texts.

Nowadays, more and more designers and experts are paying attention to the significance of ethnic elements and culture to contemporary fashion aesthetics. The art and cultural communication among ethnic groups is made possible because ethnicity and globality are related to and generated by each other. Here, Dasein existing in the world, as well as the remaining traces of subjectivism in Dasein, provides the possibility to overcome the alienation of daily life, and to return to the existence itself. In turn, the fashion reconstruction on different ethnic elements keeps generating cosmopolitan fashions. But Heidegger does understand Dasein in daily life in a general sense, but treats existence as the fundamental signified of Dasein in essence.

With the independence of some countries, many new styles of ethnic art and culture have emerged, such as in Africa after the Second World War. Meanwhile, there will be integration or even assimilation among ethnic groups. And undoubtedly, phenomena of independence, integration and assimilation will affect the composition of ethnic cultures in the world, as well as the generation and contemporary construction of ethnic clothing and fashion creative. Worldwide, the understanding on the creative and design of the same ethnic element would undergo historical changes due to differences in ethnicity and region. In today's context of cultural pluralism, it is difficult for the ethnicity of fashion creative to exist without being cosmopolitan. Then in the study of ethnic costumes and fashion culture, it is noteworthy that many other disciplines have been introduced and used for reference in recent years.

Of course, globality brings problems and challenges to ethnic characteristics, prompting people to focus on the inheritance and contemporary reconstruction of ethnic art and culture, so as to respond to the complex and diverse demands of cosmopolitan art and culture. It should be noted that "nowadays, not only the fashion system itself but also the discourse on fashion has been internationalized."[1] However, in the discourse generation of this internationalization, there are still unique voices of various ethnic groups not to be ignored. The artistic and cultural identity of fashion creative of various ethnic groups, as well as the possible ideological dialogue between ethnic groups, are inseparable from the connection between ethnicity and globality in the context of globalization. In any case, globality is an issue to be noted and explored in ethnic identity.

Between alienation and familiarity, fashion obtains tension from the generative relationship between ethnicity and globality. Generally speaking, people of the same race can be divided into different ethnic groups, because race is a human group with common genetic characteristics. An

---

[1] Craik J. The Face of Fashion: Cultural Studies in Fashion [M]. Shu Yunzhong (tr). Beijing: Central Compilation & Translation Press, 2000:60.

ethnic group usually has its own anthropological connection with a specific race, and therefore belongs to a race group in a relatively stable way, yet cultural history and inheritance will also affect the anthropological existence of an ethnic group. Although an ethnic group is closely related to the natural characteristics of a race, it is not limited to this natural basis, but involves the complex connection with mental schema and culture. In all, an ethnic group refers to a group of people that can be distinguished from other groups in terms of culture, language, history, or religion.

However, there are some ethnic groups with mixed characteristics, like those located in Central Asian, Ethiopia, or American continent, who contain ethnic components that are too complex to be distinguished clearly. The transcendence of globality over ethnicity is that arts and cultures may construct a certain homogeneity by means of mutual reference. Accordingly, those cosmopolitan art trends that transcend ethnicity with their similar characteristics may become a trend of constructing world art and culture in the future. But whenever and wherever it is, this cosmopolitan trend with certain homogeneity cannot go in an absolute sense, so people's daily dress and clothing styles are the products of intertextuality between ethnic clothing cultures.

Only by referring to and absorbing foreign cultures, and making the contemporary reconstruction on traditional ethnic art and culture, can we highlight the ethnicity of art and clothing in the global context. Undoubtedly, it is very important to investigate and adopt the skills of other ethnic groups or regions. In Arman Fernandez's view, "Through visiting and learning, we can study the weaving technology or modeling tradition of that ethnic group, and then develop a costume series on that basis." [1] Of course, in the protection and inheritance of its own ethnicity, one ethnic group cannot ignore the characteristics of other groups, rather, it should establish a sense of identity on clothing creative and fashion culture in the era of globalization through dialogues with other ethnic groups in art and culture.

At the same time, ethnic characteristics will change in the generation of globality. We must also realize that the globality of art and clothing is neither equivalent to Americanization nor to Europeanization. In fact, the globality of art does not take the artistic style of a certain country or region as a specimen, but generate itself historically through connection with the occurrence of ethnic arts and cultures. Meanwhile, the globality of art and clothing is not static, but based on the dialogue between ethnic groups in creative. As long as this kind of cultural dialogue between ethnic groups exist, artistic communication may display the characteristics of globality. In other words, only in the communication among ethnic groups can the ethnicity of art become itself and

---

[1] Calderin J. Form, Fit, Fashion [M]. Zhou Mingrui (tr). Jinan: Shandong Pictorial Publishing House, 2011:148.

possess certain cultural characteristics of globality.

Contemporary creative and reconstruction of ethnic fashion will always respond to this globality in the design style. It is generally thought that the art, clothing and culture of one ethnic group are not subject to other ethnic groups or globality, "however, with the spread of railways, Paris fashion and ready-to-wear clothing, local clothing has quickly fell down to the level of folk clothing, becoming a trace of physical evidence left by the past." ❶ As for the western art, clothing and culture, we should neither reject them simply nor follow them blindly. Obviously, cosmopolitan fashion often contains unique and typical characteristics of regions and cultures, and all local arts and cultures cannot be ignored in the construction of globalized fashion.

Any ethnic group should constantly absorb creative styles of other groups into its own clothing creative and design, so as to promote the generation of its ethnic art in the interweaving of various ethnic cultures. Usually, those artistic and cultural styles with cosmopolitan characteristics have common and universal humanistic care, and are infused with global cultural vision. Today, when producing fashion creative, we should respond to and explore in depth the existing conditions of various ethnic arts and cultures in the global context, as well as the unique understanding and symbolic communication of fashion. In fact, any ethnic fashion will finally be seen and used for reference by the world trends, and globality will inevitably become the focus of ethnic fashion creative.

In the era of globalization, we should neither simply dispel ethnic and local characters, nor directly replace ethnic diversity with globality. Instead, we aim to construct a tension between aesthetics and culture by handling the relationship between ethnicity and globality, uniqueness and generality. In the context of western culture, the mainstream ideology often constructs itself by referring to a lower other. In particular, "Since the emergence of post-structuralism, which emphasizes the way that western culture encodes the so-called marginal group as the other, the idea has become more and more popular." ❷ In contemporary global context, the reconstruction of ethnic fashion and culture has become an important artistic and cultural issue. We may say, the identification with ethnic creative is achieved in the dialogues between ethnicity and globality, and this kind of communication has been incorporated into the clothing lifestyles of various ethnic groups.

3. Ethnic Characteristics and De-homogenization of World Fashion

As a way of life, the clothing life of one ethnic group is inevitably endowed with local

---

❶ Grau F M. Histoire du Costume [M]. Zhi Qi (tr). Beijing: China Textile & Apparel Press, 2009:139.
❷ Cavallaro D. Critical and Cultural Theory: Thematic Variations [M]. Zhang Weidong. et al (tr). Nanjing: Jiangsu People's Publishing House, 2013:117.

characteristics, and related to other ethnic groups and globality at the same time. In fact, fashion creative and design are inseparable from the fundamental tradition of ethnicity. Therefore, discovering and preserving the inner cultural spirit of traditional ethnic costumes have become the artistic and cultural appeal of contemporary fashion creative. For example, the costumes with unique expressions of ethnic characteristics include: the plain costumes of the Qin and Han dynasties, the sumptuous ones of the Sui, Tang and Five Dynasties, the elegant ones of the Song, the magnificent ones of the Ming, and the gorgeous ones of the Qing. Among them, the clothing of the Tang Dynasty is particularly unique in style. It should be noted that in the trend of globalized fashion, ethnic characteristics have an irreplaceable significance and value for de-homogenization.

However, with culture changing in history, many ethnic groups and traditional costumes are confronted with the danger of being eliminated. Here, ethnicity is closely related to ethnic spirit and culture. In Hegel's view, the most noble and eternal cosmopolitan spirit of human society is often embodied in the ethnic spirits of some major ethnic groups. Art and fashion also involve the relationship and mutual reference between spiritual characters of different ethnic groups. For example, "In the late Eastern Han Dynasty, the honeysuckle pattern emerged in China along with Buddhist art, and became most popular during the Southern and Northern Dynasties."[1] In fact, ethnicity refers to the nature and spiritual character of an ethnic group, as well as artistic and cultural characteristics different from those of other groups. Responding to the changes in human living conditions and ways, the manifestation of ethnicity in the field of clothing undergoes constant and historical changes.

It should be noted that ethnicity is generated and constructed in the close connection with natural environment, social life, history and culture. For example, people in the pastoral grasslands of northern, northwestern, and southwestern China get used to riding horses, living in yurts, drinking milk tea or butter tea, etc., which can be attributed to the cold climate in the pastoral areas, and the historical tradition of herdsmen living where there is water and grass. In their lifestyles, when encountering same or similar situations, different ethnic groups may apply different ways of thinking, which also affects the formation of ethnic dressing characteristics. However, the homogeneity that globalization may bring about is an issue worthy of vigilance and cultural criticism. Meanwhile, a variety of creative will lead to differences in clothing life. In the era of globalization, ethnicity is the unique quality that an ethnic group shows in its thoughts and behaviors.

Of course, there is no absolute uniqueness and otherness in the world, for all peculiarities

---

[1] Feng Yingzhi, Yu Zengzhen. 100 Cases of Fashion of Ancient Chinese Clothing [M]. Hangzhou: Zhejiang University Press, 2016:29.

exist through comparison in the common life of ethnic groups, while this common life, in turn, may leads to the disappearance of peculiarity and difference. "In this sense, it is thought that globalization, especially the globalization of pop art, has promoted the homogeneity of art at the lowest level of artistic value."❶ The cultural confidence and consciousness out of the inner spirit of any ethnic group, is helpful for it to overcome the urge of imitating other groups. As we know, examining generality and uniformity from the perspective of uniqueness and otherness is beneficial to the generation of cosmopolitan fashion and culture, so we should overcome and criticize the either-or cultural attitude to the relationship between uniqueness and uniformity.

At the same time, the ethnic characters of different groups are complex and diverse, sometimes even in conflict with each other, which necessitates the communication between ethnic groups in art and culture. In diversified ethnic lifestyles, no ethnic group should overemphasize its own superiority over others, because in the era of globalization, all ethnic groups could provide unique possibilities for the elimination of homogeneity with their own spiritual and cultural characters. For example, Uyghur costumes are beautiful and full of unique ethnic characteristics with their myriad patterns. In daily life, Uyghur women like clothes of contrasting colors, making each color denser and brighter to human eyes. And Uyghur people are keen on flowers, so they wear all kinds of apparel and accessories embroidered with flower patterns, including hats, clothing, shoes, waist bands, and back bags. Moreover, Uyghur clothing is characteristic of clear forms, diverse patterns, bright colors, primitive styles, and exquisite craftsmanship, fully reflecting the historical flavor of a region and culture. Cosmopolitan fashion always involves the reconstruction of various ethnic elements and cultures, rather than a simple and direct copying of the traditional pattern and aesthetic style of some ethnic group. Still, the reconstruction of ethnic element and cultural character should be guarded against global uniformity. Many ethnic costumes have distinctive cultural characteristics and aesthetic acceptance paradigms, from which the tradition of ethnic costumes and regional customs can be manifested. In the creative of ethnic fashion, many designers have used modern fashion elements and design techniques for reference, ingeniously combining and creatively reconstructing the characteristics of both Eastern and Western clothing.

In the 19th century, Charles F. Worth was engaged in costume design and management in Paris, France, and was hailed as the "Father of Fashion" for initiating fashion show. Since then, clothing and fashion critics have carried out discussions on the meaning of fashion, and the concept of fashion has gradually formed and helped constructing fashion creative and design. As

---

❶ Alexander V D. Sociology of the Arts [M]. Zhang Hao & Shen Yang (tr). Nanjing: Jiangsu Fine Arts Publishing House, 2009:215.

far as fashion is concerned, the birthplaces of women's wear of the world are Paris, Milan, and the rising star London, while those of men's are Tokyo and New York. All these cities are international fashion metropolises, but they show their own characteristics while integrating themselves into the world fashion. In modern clothing and fashion industry, these cities, being regarded as fashion capitals, hold top-level world fashion shows regularly. We can say, the profound influence of Western art and fashion has continued into contemporary world fashion industry.

Although modernity, with its emphasis on and demand for uniformity, has caused the problem of homogeneity in a large degree, overemphasizing the art and culture of a particular ethnic group and belittling those of other groups may lead to another kind of homogenous fashion and culture. Therefore, we should be aware that "cultural history is still faced with a problem that doesn't face social history: we are inclined to deal with culture by using anthropological methods, treating the whole in an undifferentiating manner." [1] Since ancient Greece, Western art and culture have emphasized physical beauty and external beauty, which actually are still highlighted in modern clothing shows with models as the core. From the perspective of modern clothing culture in France or even the entire western world, all fashion capitals of the world have been adhering to the westerners' unique interpretation on the beauty of fashion.

In the field of cosmopolitan clothing and fashion, real value lies not in those trendy styles but in the ethnic artistic and cultural characteristics hidden behind fashions. And the fundamental characteristics of ethnic culture are in fact the unique ethnic perspective on culture, as well as the ethnic discourse and style constructed and interpreted from that perspective. In cosmopolitan fashion system, although ethnic statuses and cultural influences of various groups are uneven, the generativity and openness of the system provide aesthetic and cultural tensions and possibilities, which respect ethnic differences on one hand, and go beyond specific ethnic characteristics on the other hand. Undoubtedly, ethnic fashion is a unique form of expression different from habits in daily life.

Of course, the character of an ethnic group is not onefold and irrelevant to other groups, instead it comes into being in the process of comparing itself with the ones of other groups. For example, Eastern style has a profound influence in both the East and the West, however "in the mid-nineteenth century, the novelty of Orientalism went exhausted, and Europe began to surpass the East in design and product." [2] It is admitted that French clothing is most characteristic of its ethnicity, which not only shows the history, tradition and spirit of France, maintains the aristocratic atmosphere of the French court, but also incorporates the elegant simplicity of modern life, hence a

---

[1] Goody J. Myth, Ritual and the Oral [M]. Li Yuan (tr). Beijing: China Renmin University Press, 2014:69.
[2] Geczy A. Fashion and Orientalism [M]. London: Bloomsbury Academic, 2013:116.

close combination of tradition and reality.

Not only that, France has maintained and reconstructed its past traditions in all aspects, including French architecture, townscape, language and literature. Although France once had classicism and realism in the style of art, French people have strong romanticism at heart. For instance, though Balzac was a realist writer, his life experience shows romantic impulses and passionate humanistic feelings rather than realistic rationality, but. In the context of romantic art and culture, French fashion is not rigorous but highly infectious. Then again, "homogeneity" refers to the phenomenon that products of different brands in the same category imitate each other in performance, appearance, or even marketing, so that they become similar to and indistinguishable from each other. And the market competition based on product homogenization is called homogeneous competition.

In the field of design and consumption, homogenization has led to the decline or even disappearance of the ethnic and local characters of products, therefore it could be eliminated by us paying more attention to the cultures of multiple ethnic groups and regions. Meanwhile, focus and emphasis on inner experiences and individuality would also help overcome homogenization, particularly when today's clothing of fast fashion constantly follows the swift trend and the consideration on individualized design and production is far from enough. In addition, new fashion products arrive at the store so quickly that window displays change even twice a week. Under the pursuit of fashion trends, it is fundamentally difficult to prevent fast fashion styles from converging. As a result, only innovation in details can express the ideas of a particular brand.

Besides, more and more clothes of similar styles have appeared in different fast fashion brands, and it seems those fast fashions leading trends are becoming "standardized" popular products. However, it should be noted that homogenization not only hinders consumers from identifying the unique quality of certain fashion, but also drives art and culture into the monotony and uniformity caused by technology and modernity. In the revelation of fashion beauty, "the long journey of individuation has completely changed the outer uncontroversial model of early modern beauty into an inner individuated model." [1] Individuated style, always related to a specific group or people, has never been the common preference and identical choice of clothing for all people, inevitably would face great challenge in modern and contemporary designing. And those designs without characteristics, distinctions, and clear boundaries are undoubtedly the manifestation of homogenization in fashion.

To overcome homogenization, design and marketing should be differentiated in concept and

---

[1] Vigarello G. Histoire de la beauté [M]. Guan Hong (tr). Changsha: Hunan Literature and Art Publishing House, 2007:237.

culture, focusing on the exploration and revealing of the inner spiritual characteristics of various regions and ethnic cultures. Otherwise, products of fashion brands would appear similar and indistinguishable, fall inevitably into problems and predicaments of homogeneity, and deprive their brands of original uniqueness and advantages. Therefore, the elimination of homogeneity requires innovation in core concept and technology research and development. If we ignore the protection and inheritance of ethnic original art and cultural characteristics, we will eventually lose the right of speech in contemporary fashion creative and design. The trend of homogenization of fashion caused by modernism and mass culture are making fashion art and culture monotonous and dried up. Also, the declining or even loss of ethnicity in fashion and culture will cause designs to follow blindly the cosmopolitan fashion trends and styles.

It is the only way for fashion to go out of the modernity-based homogenization and into diversified creative and expressions. And individuated designs with unique ethnic characteristics should become a kind of conscious and active cultural identification and choice. Regarding the relationship between specificity and universality, "my opinion contains an attempt to maintain direct attention to both particularity and universality, difference and homogeneity."❶ The fundamental path out of homogenization is, to seek and construct once again various possibilities for artistic and cultural spirits in the generation of diversified traditions and ethnic cultures. Design must also endow contemporary fashion with ethnic individuality, distinction and cultural diversity, so that plural ethnic fashions can become a force to counteract the trend of homogenization. In all, the spiritual and cultural characteristics of ethnic arts and cultures provide the possibility to overcome the homogenization of fashion worldwide.

In fact, the diversification of fashion creative is not a simple rejection of uniformity, but the construction and maintenance of a tension of art and culture in the mutual generation between differences and unity, in order to dissolve their negation of each other. Homogeneity is the universal character brought by the cultural exchange, technology and rationality since the Enlightenment Movement. Although ethnic fashion helps to overcome homogenization to a certain extent, mutual imitation and homogeneity are growing too intensified to be completely contained. In the expression of fashion art, technology, not confined to its instrumentality, may even become the stipulation of fashion expression and aesthetics. Therefore, the individuality of clothing creative and design becomes a rare thing, and ethnic clothing is a unique code of the inner spirit and culture of an ethnic group. There is no doubt that creative and design are faced with the problem of getting rid of homogeneity, and to this end we should seek ideas and inspirations from

---

❶ Robertson R. Globalization: Social Theory and Global Culture[M]. Liang Guangyan (tr). Shanghai: Shanghai People's Publishing House, 2000:144.

ethnic art and culture.

In other words, only individuated designs with unique characters can meet the various needs of consumers, as well as the appeals for dressing diversity of different ethnic groups. Contemporary fashion designs and costumes of various ethnic groups show their psychological, aesthetic and cultural individualities. In Chinese context of language, thoughts and culture, art and design have not fallen into the metaphysical dilemma of the Western tradition. For example, "Chinese language does not make the simple sliding from 'beautiful' to 'beauty' just by adding an auxiliary word, thus turning beauty into a universal concept."❶ This kind of clothing and fashion endowed with spiritual and cultural characters, not only shows the vivid and irreplaceable ethnic individuality of each group, but also distinguish one ethnic group from another in terms of spiritual and cultural character. It is in this sense that unique ethnic fashion and culture are indispensable, being an important text style able to overcome the homogenization of design.

Section 2   Globalization and Inter-ethnic Dialogue on Fashion Culture

In clothing and fashion design, the issues of ethnic artistic character and cultural identity need to be explored and answered not only within an ethnic group or a country, but also across the wider world. Moreover, the identification of ethnic culture and the historical communication of fashion culture must consider the social, historical and cultural context of the post-colonial era, as well as potential problems and dilemmas arising from globalization. Of course, globalization means more than assimilation and homogenization, also it involves recognition and respect for cultural differences and diversity. In its communicating with the world, each ethnic group gets access to globality through inter-ethnicity. The dialogues between ethnic groups in clothing life and fashion culture have shown characteristics of openness, historicity and generativity, which can promote ethnic identity and cross-cultural fashion communication of fashion, and help reconstruct the global fashion culture on the basis of ethnicity as well.

1. Ethnicity, Globality and Globalization of Fashion

In the process of globalization, traditional ethnic costumes and culture are still facing great challenges, because ethnic uniqueness is often eliminated in a certain homogeneity. In their fashion creative, various ethnic groups should pay full attention to the manifestation and interpretation on the characteristics of traditional elements. Here, ethnicity is the spiritual schema and cultural

---

❶ Jullien F. Cette Étrange Idée Du Beau [M]. Gao Fengfeng (tr). Beijing: Peking University Press, 2016:11.

character that ethnic creative depends on, as well as the artistic and cultural connotation that fashion expressions strive to highlight. Moreover, the mutual generation between ethnicity and globality is an issue that designing and cultures have to respond to in the era of globalization. In fact, fashion creative concerns not only the existence of a specific ethnic group, but also cultural communication and understanding between ethnic groups. Undoubtedly, no ethnic group can exist in this world in complete isolation.

In the common existence and lifestyle of ethnic groups, fashion creative and designs of them are interrelated and open to each other. Therefore, fashion art must research and disclose issues on ethnicity of creative, and locate this ethnicity in the global cultural context. "In the history before secular art gaining independence, the two opposite functions of art, namely, liberation and conservation, did not exhaust areas of aesthetic experience."❶ In fact, the openness of artistic text leads itself to the aestheticization of daily life. And then, it can be said that globality itself is in close relationship with diverse ethnic characters, and it is often realized through the interweaving and intertextuality between ethnic groups. However, it should be noted that the generative relationship between globality and ethnicity is not a simplified logical one between including and being included, generality and particularity.

In particular, we should pay attention that among those various ethnic elements, which ones are common or similar to all ethnic groups, because despite the similarity of some elements, their meanings and interpretations may vary in different social and cultural contexts. Meanwhile, it is also noteworthy that which elements are different and unique, endowed with special cultural characters. The aim of associating elements among different ethnic groups is to promote the mutual learning between ethnic groups in fashion creative, as well as their communication in the context of ethnic culture. For ethnic identity, both consensus within an ethnic group and distinction between ethnic groups are indispensable.

On the basis of ethnicity, fashion creatives of various ethnic groups build generative connections with each other, thus achieving their mutual understanding and communication on a worldwide scale. In fact, "ethnicity, in terms of shared historical heritage, can eventually generate a sense of cultural identity or awareness among ethnic groups, or even among citizens, of different countries."❷ In other words, ethnicity is interrelated with and echoed globality with its local character. However, those cultural systems and habits in the central and dominant position may

---

❶ Yauss H R. Aesthetic Experience and Literary Hermeneutics[M]. Gu Jianguang. et al (tr). Shanghai: Shanghai Translation Publishing House, 1997: 234.

❷ Editorial Board of Diogenes Chinese Edition (ed). Transformation of Cultural Identity [M]. Beijing: Commercial Press, 2008:14.

repress marginal cultural styles, which requires easement and adjustment with diversity in cultural mentality.

Of course, cosmopolitan fashion culture makes possible the establishment of ethnic consciousness and identity, rather than simply denying and repelling ethnic characteristics. The connection, especially the intertextuality, between ethnic groups, is characterized fundamentally as a kind of inter-ethnicity, which not only manifests the relevance between ethnic groups, but also provides a possible access from ethnicity to globality. It is this inter-ethnicity that promotes cultural exchanges and understanding between ethnic groups, and maintains their individuality in their common existence. Each country has its unique fashion culture and ethnic costume, and these different ethnic costumes learn from and influence each other.

In essence, inter-ethnicity is a dialogue between ethnicity and globality, or we can say, a cultural intertextuality between ethnic groups occurring in this dialogue. As a response to the issue of modernity, globalization is not only a promotion, but also a reflection, of modernism. In the usual sense, globalization means global connections ever-increasing and ever-closer. In the era of globalization, the political and economic interdependence among ethnic groups or countries constitutes a contextual relationship inseparable for art, fashion and culture. With the cross-cultural communication of clothing and fashion, especially the worldwide strengthening of the uniformity appeal made by technology and modernity, people inevitable will consider how to distinguish ethnic groups from each other through external clothing. In other words, globalization can be interpreted as the compression of the world and the integration of the globe.

No doubt, ethnicity and globality, as well as nativism and cosmopolitanism, are not in a simple opposition and conflict, but in a mutual generation and correlation. "Usually, entrepreneurs in Asia have a feeling that they are obliged to study Western science, to understand the foundations of Anglo-Saxon business practice, to speak English or French fluently, and to wear a suit and tie." ❶ But obviously, ethnic co-existence and communication do not aim to seek simple and vain cultural uniformity by dissolving the fashion and cultural differences between ethnic groups. It is equally important to recognize and identify with the unique cultural characters of ethnic groups and promote effective cultural interweaving and dialogues among them. In fact, complete globalization is neither necessary nor possible.

Cross-cultural art and fashion communication is dispelling the boundaries between ethnic groups and constructing a fashion trend that integrates various ethnic characteristics. Intertextuality lays an indispensable social, historical and cultural context for inclusive cultural identity and

---

❶ Kotkin, Joel. Tribes [M]. Wang Xu, et al (tr). Beijing: Social Sciences Academic Press, 2010:17.

mutual trust and understanding among ethnic groups. The distinctions between ethnic groups are still present and far from the degree of being negligible, though they keep shrinking and fading. Contemporary costume art and fashion culture can neither deny ethnic diversity and globality with ethnicity, nor limit and repress local culture with globalization. Even in the era of globalization, cosmopolitan fashion still pays much attention to ethnic elements and cultures, which is becoming a new cultural consciousness and a contemporary identity with the tradition.

Elements and cultures of different ethnic groups are not only unique and open in nature, but also interrelated and interactional to each other. Obviously, cultural exchanges and communication facilitate different ethnic groups to learn from each other in fashion creative and clothing culture, exerting a profound impact on their aestheticization of daily life. It should be pointed out that "today's cultural anthropologists seldom take a global perspective, and often even oppose applying universal perspective and comparative approach to the study of socio-cultural phenomena."[1] Therefore, the identity with the uniqueness of ethnic culture is not inessential, and this identity is inseparable from cross-cultural communication and ideological dialogues, requiring the extensive participation and profound involvement of different ethnic groups or countries.

We should understand the influence of globalization on ethnic art and culture from the perspective of generative theory. In the process of globalization, international division of labor and the world economy are in a continuous construction, which contributes to the formation of various knowledge systems, as well as the world-wide influence of ideology and religion. Contemporary technologies such as informationization, internet and new media, have accelerated the breaking down of traditional boundaries between ethnic groups or countries. Globalization has also narrowed the spatial distance between countries and regions, increasingly integrating the whole world into a global village defined and constructed by technology. Although different ethnic arts and cultures get profound influence in that process, people's clothing lifestyle and aesthetic experiences are not constructed simply in subjection to social and economic constraints. However, globalization inevitably impacts, or even deconstructs, traditional art and culture, despite the historical opportunities it may provide for some developing countries.

Here, the integration of economy and culture seems to mean uniformity and convergence, but in fact, it is impossible to have a homogeneous world, so globalization cannot only be interpreted as global integration. The complex relationship between ethnicity and globality, whether conflicting or reconciliatory, is an unavoidable issue of globalization. Moreover, the understanding and interpretation of globalization are always realized in a certain cultural context. Although economic

---

[1] Van Damme, W. Anthropology of Aesthetics: Perspective and Methods [M]. Li Xiujian, Xiang Li (tr). Beijing: China Federation of Literary and Art Circles Publishing house, 2015:131.

and technological globalization is often characterized as a trend of integration, the co-relation and interaction among various arts, cultures, religions and lifestyles do not mean globalization. In the cultural context of globalization, fashion creative, being more than ethnic and local, is in urgent need of being recognized and accepted by ethnic culture.

Moreover, the art and culture of one ethnic group should try as hard as possible to win the recognition of other groups. In this era of globalization, ethnic clothing would become fashionable from the influence of globalizing trend, and contemporary world fashion develops its style from the reconstruction of ethnic elements and cultural characteristics. Of course, the reconstruction and interpretation of fashion are usually realized through inter-ethnicity, and ethnic culture is generated in the common existence of world cultures. However, this cosmopolitan art, clothing and culture is not simplex and pure in style, but contains ethnic cultural diversity in itself. Then one should realize that, it is only in certain context that ethnicity gets its access to globality through inter-ethnicity, and this process is definitely not necessary and inevitable.

It may be said that, the accessibility from ethnicity to globality depends on the open, historical and generative nature of ethnicity itself, which is also the prerequisite for inter-ethnicity and globality to come into being. In the modern world, where ideas are expressed in diverse ways, "the obsession with the wholeness keeps the same everywhere, despite the great difference in their content." [1] Moreover, globality does not mean the end or disappearance of ethnicity, but the tolerance and acceptance of diverse ethnic cultures. Of course, the mixing of multi-ethnic arts and cultures in the cosmopolitan culture still concerns the spiritual and cultural characteristics of each ethnic group. In particular, since the 1980s, fashion styles have shown diversified trends of aesthetics and culture.

If ethnicity is closed and non-historical in nature, it would be difficult for ethnic groups to communicate on fashion creative. Although opening up may bring challenges and risks to certain traditions, blind mind-closing to the outside world is more likely to destroy cultural life. Closed ethnic fashion creative can never be cosmopolitan, but limited to the local lifestyle of an ethnic group. The visualized expression of concept, being artistic, is the generation of creative concerning spirit and culture. It may be said that, fashion culture involves aesthetic expression of art, ethnic spirit and culture, as well as relative social and historical context. The historical character of ethnic art and culture has its temporal basis, but when this character is regarded as of historical significance, it becomes the indispensable basis for the generation of tradition.

Of course, an ethnic group cannot achieve its cultural identify on fashion creative by

---

[1] Welsch W. Undoing Aesthetics [M]. Lu Yang, Zhang Yanbing (tr). Shanghai: Shanghai Translation Publishing House, 2002:148.

casting off its collective unconsciousness and pre-understanding. And an ethnic group must clearly manifest its culture characteristics in its fashion creative and design production, so that its artistic and cultural style could become cosmopolitan and global. Ethnicity is not only the basis for the recognition of ethnic creative, but also the premise for ethnic fashion culture to go to the world. And inter-ethnicity makes cross-ethnic understanding possible and lays a foundation for cosmopolitan fashion identification. In other words, inter-ethnicity promotes the dialogue between diverse fashion arts and cultures, and provides the generative basis for the contemporary construction of global fashion and culture.

Even when ethnic fashion creative has gained access to global comprehensibility in its existence, it does not mean that such creative is highly identical and integrated to others, but that it is cosmopolitan with a basis of ethnicity. In the era of globalization, global culture should be diversified with ethnic characteristics. In fact, fashion creative and design are usually globalized against the implicit context of ethnic and cultural characteristics, neither sacrificing its unique ethnicity, nor transplanting its ethnic elements simply. All ethnic groups should construct their own ethnic discourse styles and aesthetic characters in fashion creative and design. Undoubtedly, oriental fashion mainly originates from its own artistic and cultural tradition, and this cultural consciousness enables oriental fashion to be reconstructed in the contemporary era.

The simplified either-or cultural attitude makes one inevitably fall into colonialism or narrow ethnicism and get trapped there. It should be noted that "we have entered an era that creative permeates all aspects of economy and society, not just manifested in emergence of high-tech industry innovation." [1] As fashion art and culture has entered the inherent composition of the cultural industry, it is extremely important to activate the cultural significance of ethnic elements. Fashion creative should be concerned with how to construct and reconstruct ethnic spirit and cultural significance, because only in this way can cosmopolitan fashion and culture be established on the basis of ethnicity. At the same time, the recurrence of fashion style should not be ignored.

The mini-fashion style, once popular in the 1960s, returned again in the 1990s. It should be said that this cycle of fashion is also related to the reconstruction of ethnic cultural style. In the artistic and cultural context of globalization, the contemporary construction of ethnic aesthetic culture on the basis of fashion visualization, mainly concerns such aspects like: value comparison between ethnic groups, visualization of ethnic element, ethnic aesthetic taste and reception habit, theory foundation and dialogue mechanism of cultural identity, and construction of ethnic character. Globalization is an unavoidable issue of ethnic fashion and cultural identity, and it is

---

[1] Florida R. The Rise of Creative Class [M]. Situ Aiqin (tr). Beijing: China CITIC Press, 2010:64.

inadvisable to adopt a simplified attitude of taking or rejecting the West. In contemporary clothing lifestyle, the world fashion explores its discourse and style precisely from ethnic characteristics.

2. Globalized Creative: Homogenization, or Diversification

Only by maintaining certain characteristics can art and culture avoid being lost in the trend of global integration and homogenization, considering globalization has been an irreversible trend in the world economy and culture since the Second World War, especially since the 1990s. "When we speak of the continuing internationalization of culture, we find that this trend has become so evident even in the most unlikely areas – in daily life: such as eating habits, clothing styles, and living places; and also, in art."❶ At the same time, globalization has exerted a fundamental impact on cultural and fashion creative industries. In the era of globalization, clothing and fashion has to face the designing dilemma between homogenization and diversification.

In fact, modernity with its fundamental appeal for uniformity has brought about the problem of homogenization, which needs to be responded to with diversification in the era of globalization. To a large extent, globalization means the globalization of capital and culture, as well as the socialization of production and the internationalization of economic relations. And by nature, globalization is inseparable from art, fashion, and creative cultural industries. In the era of globalization, countries are strengthening their economic dependence and influence on each other, while barriers hindering the free flow of production factors are being weakened, and international rules for economic operation are gradually formed and constantly reset. No doubt, globalization is a historical process of generation and reconstruction, and its origin can be traced back to the West in the period from the 16th to the 18th century.

Since the industrial Revolution, commodity economy, modern industry and transportation industry have developed rapidly, and trade contacts between countries across the world have been more frequent than ever. "In a sense, we do witness the multi-polarization of the world, and also the so-called cultural globalization: the formation of a homogeneous world culture."❷ Moreover, with the emergence of the Internet and new media, it is relatively easy for the world creative to learn from certain ethnic fashion, or vice versa. What's most conspicuous in globalization lies in that, with international division of labor changing its direction from vertical to horizontal, world trade has grown rapidly and multilateral trade system has been established.

Like economic globalization, cultural globalization is also a worldwide trend, but cultural

---

❶ Wallerstein I. Geopolitics and Geoculture: Essays on the Changing World-System [M]. Wang Fengzhen (tr). Beijing: Central Compilation & Translation Press, 2016:211.

❷ Friedman J. Cultural Identity and Global Process[M]. Guo Jianru (tr). Beijing: Commercial Press, 2003:149.

communication is still related to the cultural identity among ethnic groups, which means mutual understanding in art and culture. And this globalization has become a cultural trend irreversible. In the context of globalization, homogenization refers to the phenomenon that goods imitate each other in performance, appearance or even marketing method, leading to a gradual decline or disappearance of their differences. This kind of homogenization poses a threat to the diversity of ethnic fashion and creative, and even places unique ethnic mentality and traditional culture on the verge of extinction. While globalization, emphasizing and promoting modernity, offers challenges to ethnic fashion with homogenization, it may also bring opportunities to the diversification of ethnic creative.

If globalization is just understood as an inevitable path to absolute uniformity, we can hardly reveal and clarify the critical perspective provided by the context of postmodernism. Undeniably, globalized creative, with a positive attitude for cultural diversity, will provide possibilities for ethnic fashion creatives and designs to gain identity and recognition. In Marc Fumaroli's view, " if we fossilize living uniqueness into dull 'identity' and give it a rigid protection, this 'identity' would soon meet its doom." [1] What should be emphasized is that it is through the unique expressions of ethnic fashion creative that ethnic art and cultural identity could be constructed in the era of globalization. In creative producing and fashion designing, ethnic elements characterized with cultural diversity contribute to the communication, understanding and identification between ethnic groups.

For fashion creative and design, homogenization refers to the phenomenon that clothes become very similar in design, shape and style, which is caused by blind imitation or even plagiarism for lack of originality. The market competition based on product homogenization is called homogeneity competition. As far as fashion is concerned, homogenization does not help consumer to make valid distinction between different designs, because extreme similarity for want of characteristics and differences leads to the decline of otherness and diversity. Fashion creative and design in the era of globalization is undoubtedly a response to the relationship between uniformity and difference. Even those well-known brands with strong competitiveness still need differentiable creative and designing of products. And for general clothing brands, homogenization obviously leads to cruel price wars.

For those designs with brand awareness, if they want to break through homogeneity, they must be unique in their creative, make proper predictions about the terminal consumption market, and take the lead in making innovation to stand out. For example, the Chinese designer Zhang

---

[1] Editorial Board of Diogenes Chinese Edition (ed). Transformation of Cultural Identity [M]. Beijing: Commercial Press, 2008:35.

Zhaoda has never abandoned the ethnicity of China and the East in his fashion creative, hence forming his gorgeous, elegant and magnificent designing style. As they lack the special ability to make judgement and innovation, many designers have to imitate or even plagiarize others' designing ideas and thoughts, leading to the emergence of homogeneity and the end of difference. Even an apparently failed creative expression or design may bring about the imitation or plagiarism of many designers. Large numbers of similar or even identical designs keep appearing despite repeated prohibitions, pushing creative and design into a predicament of homogeneity.

It should be noted that the convergence of design has not been overcome with the development of society, economy and creative culture; instead, it has been more and more prominent. People tend to absorb ready-made ideas from others' expressions, without paying attention to where creative idea or original spirit lies. Meanwhile we must see that "the legacy of the industrialization era needs to be removed, for it has resulted in the cookie-cutter characteristics of most commodities in the market." ❶ Moreover, any simplified imitation or even direct adoption will inevitably make designing only stay in its visual appearance, rather than penetrate deeply into the ethic spirit. To deal with the problem of homogenization, differentiated thinking and design are of great significance in fashion.

Here, the attention to the ethnicity of creative and design is an important stylistic and cultural basis for the realization of differentiated design. For design, differentiation is an extremely effective strategy to overcome homogeneity. In fact, the emphasis on difference is itself the counteraction against uniformity and homogeneity. In differentiated fashions and designs, it is very necessary to meet the needs of personal emotions and experiences in a targeted manner. The topic in urgent need of study is how should we activate the ethnic elements with their spiritual and cultural characteristics so as to promote the contemporary innovation of ethnic fashion creative and culture. Fashion creative and design lacking ethnicity and individuality will inevitably fall into homogeneity and miss aesthetic and cultural recognition. One fashion brand worthy of mentioning is "Exception" created by the Chinese designer Ma Ke, who expresses her appeal to spirit pursuit and traditional culture with the notion of "uselessness", realizes the contemporary aesthetic and cultural reconstruction on Chinese style, and makes the brand stand out from general fashions.

Globalization does not bring forth simplified integration and homogenization, but differentiated creatives and coexistence of multiculturalism. In fact, the convergence and homogeneity of fashion creative and design have led to the decline or even disappearance of artistic and cultural characteristics. Since the 1980s, the world cultural diversity has become a

---

❶ Lockwood T. Design Thinking [M]. Li Cuirong, et al (tr). Beijing: Publishing House of Electronics Industry, 2012:100.

historical trend irreversible. "If this phenomenon at the expense of derogating other societies is allowed to expand overly, it will jeopardize not only the objective understanding of the Eastern world, but also that of the Western world." ❶ Therefore, creative is in urgent need of stimulating people's ethnic awareness and cultural identity. Each unique ethnic art and clothing lifestyle actually has spiritual and cultural characteristics that are not owned by other cultures.

To overcome the binary separation in western rationalistic philosophy and metaphysics is also the basis for the construction of costume art and fashion culture. Therefore, multi-cultural coexistence and mutual cultural generation provide conditions for cultural exchanges and mutual learning. At the same time, various cultures construct their symbiosis through mutual learning and generation, thus forming human cultural landscapes that are charming in unique ways. In the diversification of fashion and culture, multiple cultures in the same era and cultural system keep their own ethnic characteristics, but communication, intertextuality and integration are found among each other. In the history of western life, fashion has been existing in various styles, which are usually characterized by various schools of fashion art.

One noteworthy point is that in the process of mutual fusion and generation, each culture makes independent choices according to its own values and standards, and absorbs characteristics from other ethnic groups or cultures. In fact, culture is always a dynamic, open and changing system, and its historical formation is never separable from the communication with other cultures in art, aesthetics and other aspects. The generation of fashion trends is on one hand the overcoming of existing homogenization, one the other hand an inevitable falling into re-homogenization. Therefore, the counteraction of difference and pluralism against homogeneity is never-ending. But in the process of cultural fusion, there is no meaningful fusion and interweaving without conflicts, and fusion contains conflicts or contradictions in itself.

Although in the history of western thought, identity is often manifested and represented in unity, this unity is an ontological mutual concern rather than a mutual similarity at the existent level. The fashion creatives of different ethnic groups are not in a natural and simplified opposition, but in a mutual penetration, dialogue and integration, as well as a reconciliation of conflicts and disputes. "But this unity is by no means the kind of monotonous emptiness, which bears no relations with others but blindly clings to stereotypes in itself." ❷ It is the different values and thinking modes of different ethnic groups that have shaped their unique customs, cultural psychology and behavior patterns. In contemporary times, various ethnic elements are influencing and mixing with each other, resulting in diversified international fashion styles based

---

❶ Goody J. Myth, Ritual and the Oral [M]. Li Yuan (tr). Beijing: China Renmin University Press, 2014:250.
❷ Heidegger M. Identität und Differenz [M]. Sun Zhouxing. et al (tr). Beijing: Commercial Press, 2011:29.

on intertextuality.

In a sense, diversification refers to that of values and thinking modes. The way for a diversified culture to maintain its vitality is to face up to conflicts, absorb beneficial elements from other cultures, and make its own culture inherited and updated in the contemporary era. At 2009 Spring/Summer London Fashion Week, the concept of globalization was reflected and responded to through a variety of east-west-fusion designs. Schools of art and fashion often represent various perspectives thought specific styles, which occurs actually in some context. Even in the advocacy for difference and diversification, creative is not made different for the sake of difference, or diversified for the sake of diversification, otherwise the expressions of ethnic elements would stay only on the visual appearance. In fact, the understanding on cultural diversity is multi-level, represented in various dimensions and levels.

In the artistic, aesthetic and cultural context of globalization, various ethnic cultures are in a coexistence based on their uniqueness, and the traditional culture of any ethnic group is intertextual with other ethnic cultures. It can also be said that various ethnic groups take the arts and cultures of each other as others, meanwhile they overcome the binary separation between self and others in their intertextuality. In fact, "the rejection of grand narrative, overarching worldview and absolute foundation, as well as the attendant emphasis on fragmentation, difference, and incommensurability, distinguish postmodernism from modernist enlightenment." ❶ In diverse creative activities, intersubjectivity is often characterized by the lifestyle of coexistence in the world, as well as by the reconciliation and tension between ethnicity and globality. In the producing of globalized creative and designs, the response to the relationship between homogeneity and diversity should never be ignored.

3. Creative Dialogue and Global Cultural Identity

To exist as itself, an ethnic group should never lose its unique spiritual and cultural characteristics, nor replace its uniqueness with characteristics of other ethnic groups. The creative and design involving ethnic elements aim to reveal, express and elucidate the artistic and cultural characteristics of an ethnic group. Any ethnic group cannot exist in complete isolation from the world, instead it is in the common existence and life of different ethnic groups. And from its artistic and cultural dialogues with others, the ethnic group seeks the creative, expression and design of its own ethnic characteristics, so as to present the designing style concerning its inner mental schema. In the era of globalization, the ideological and cultural dialogues among various ethnic groups

---

❶ Clarke J J. Oriental Enlightenment: The Encounter Between Asian and Western Thought [M]. Yu Minmei & Zeng Xiangbo (tr). Shanghai: Shanghai People's Publishing House, 2011: 305.

in creative and design are essential for their mutual communication and understanding. At the same time, global cultural identity is inseparable from the tolerance and respect for difference and diversity.

If an ethnic group just transplants and borrows elements from others in a simplified way, it will abandon its own ethnic spirit and cultural character, and losing its ethnic creative, design and cultural tradition, which equals attending to trifles to the neglect of essentials. With the expansion of globalization, the communication, collision, and fusion of various ethnic cultures have become an irresistible trend. Overcoming racial prejudice and discrimination is a cultural task that the fashion industry should take seriously. The British Fashion Council once sent letters to major fashion brands, asking designers to consider using more models of ethnic minority, to reflect and accommodate racial diversity at the Fashion Week. It should also be noted that as the globalization of cultural exchange has brought impact on ethnic creative, it is urgent to respond to the possible elimination of ethnic characteristics. Here, the collision of different ethnic cultures is reflected in all aspects of life, not only reflecting diverse perspectives and patterns of human civilization, but also implying the conflict and opposition between cultures.

Therefore, it is necessary to dissolve the conflicts between various ethnic groups in art and culture through cross-cultural communication and ideological dialogue, and construct the ethnic basis for contemporary fashion diversity. Of course, cosmopolitan culture is not the tyranny of Western culture based on Western centralism, but the multicultural community concerning human existence and value system. In the social and cultural context of globalization, any ethnic group as a subject should no longer be extremely individualized, rather, its ethnicity is in a relationship of mutual belonging with globality. As a reconstruction of returning tradition, ethnic fashion not only conveys traditional spirit and cultural character, but also generates the contemporary charm of ethnic culture, thus becoming a contemporary artistic and cultural code of traditional culture.

The arrival of globalization era is connected with artistic and cultural dialogues between ethnic groups. Here, cross-culture refers both to the culture that spans the traditional boundary between ethnic groups, and to a cultural transcendence over this boundary. However, "the western clothing system and the colonial native clothing system are not in a mutually exclusive relationship, but in a dynamic process of mutual changing and competing for cultural attraction."[1] Creative and design in the era of globalization need to respond to communication between peoples of different cultural belonging, and get inspiration from various ethnic elements and cultures. In the context of globalization, various complex relationships such as cultural change, cultural conflict

---

[1] Craik J. The Face of Fashion: Cultural Studies in Fashion [M]. Shu Yunzhong (tr). Beijing: Central Compilation & Translation Press, 2000:51.

and cultural fusion between ethnic groups, as well as cultural inheritance and reconstruction in contemporary times, are undoubtedly issues not to be ignored in creative, design and culture.

In fact, the differences and integration between ethnic groups in spirit and culture influence people's values, thinking mode and clothing lifestyle. In the irreversible process of globalization, new trends and fashions presented by ethnic cultures are becoming constitutions of world fashion diversity. In the fashion world, Tommy Hilfiger's "Absolutely American" clothing is loved by American youths for its practicality and simplicity. However, contemporary clothing creative and design involve not just a recurrence and restoration of some ethnic custom or lifestyle, but a worldwide cross-cultural communication and dialogue between ethnic groups. In terms of ethnic spirits and cultures, globalization has strengthened the interdependence between ethnic cultures, so there comes an urgent need to construct the openness and cosmopolitan relevance of ethnic cultures.

Here, the ethnic fashion in aestheticized daily life could be considered the product of contemporary ethnic culture. The construction of different artistic styles and aesthetic experiences are widely and deeply influencing people's clothing lifestyle. That ethnic costume elements can become global fashion elements is actually because there occurs indispensable internal response, externalization, transformation and reconstruction between the nativism and the cosmopolitanism of art and culture. Moreover, "as global warming has become a major issue of public concern, the fashion industry begins to turn its focus to environmentally friendly clothing." [1] The era of globalization is faced with the problem of how to protect, inherit and reconstruct traditional ethnic clothing and all other cultural heritages, including dress etiquette, clothing system, customs, habits, and etc. The expression of ethnic fashion creative and design is also a style of ethnic art and culture generated in the contemporary era, and inevitably injected with ethnic or even cosmopolitan spiritual and cultural characteristics.

Therefore, only by treating various ethnic cultures of groups with an open and inclusive mind, can we make dialogues between arts, thoughts and cultures, thus constructing mutual recognition and understanding among ethnic groups. For Jürgen Habermas, modernity has not lost its vitality and life at all; rather, it is a work in progress to be finished, in which negotiations and ideological dialogues keep taking place. In fact, the anti-globalization movement constitutes a counteracting force against globalization, emphasizing that globalization may bring about the loss of ethnic lifestyle and cultural tradition. Moreover, cross-cultural understanding is not the subject's understanding on the object, but the mutual understanding and communication between the

---

[1] Worsley H. 100 Ideas that Changed Fashion [M]. Tang Xiaojia (tr). Beijing: China Photographic Publishing House, 2013:204.

subjects, which advocates and emphasizes the replacement of subjectivity with intersubjectivity.

To be more precise, the dialogue between ethnic groups in creative and culture, occurring at various dimensions and levels, takes inter-ethnicity as its anthropological basis. Here, inter-ethnicity can be characterized as the dialogue between different ethnic groups. In the cross-cultural artistic and cultural dialogue, one ethnic group need not only rely on the codes, habits, concepts and behaviors of itself, but also experience and understand those of other groups involved. In Harden's view, the human mind of any place is accustomed to certain local patterns, designs and structures. Therefore, the aesthetic experience accompanying art will inevitably bear ethnic differences. But neither ethnicism nor colonialism has properly treated ethnic fashion culture. And those thoughts hovering between ethnicism and colonialism take on specific artistic and cultural perspectives or dimensions.

However, the interpretation on ethnic costume and culture should not ignore the ways of creative which are in continuous generation and construction, as well as the cultural characteristics related to creative and design methods. Therefore, "when we communicate with people either within our culture or from other cultures, we must remember that as it matures, every culture is in constant change." ❶ On the issue of ethnicity, though some designers still pay particular emphasis on the ethnicism complex, and some others present the artistic style of colonialism, inevitably they have to deal with the relationship between ethnicity and globality. In many avant-garde fashions, there is no shortage of reflections on ethnicism or colonialism. In creative and design, mutual learning and reference have long existed among various ethnic groups.

For example, in the Qing Dynasty of China, the dress maintained the Manchu style and aesthetic characteristics, and the loose clothes of the Han people with wide sleeves were changed to tight-fitting clothes with narrow sleeves. Here the point is that, although the uniqueness of each ethnic group and culture cannot be ignored, ethnic things cannot be kept absolutely pure and single. As a new form of colonialism, postcolonialism is more of a cultural colonization. In the post-colonial context, former colonies may give up the culture of their own ethnic group and identify with the lifestyle and the colonial culture brought by the colonialists. Moreover, people will inevitably find their ethnic awareness fading away in the process of globalization, and there is a lack of in-depth thinking on the artistic and cultural characteristics of their own ethnic group.

Another problem related to globalization is that the trend of fashion homogenization is increasing, while unique traditional patterns and styles are disappearing. Therefore, many Chinese and oriental designers are awakening to their regional and ethnic awareness. Instead of simply

---

❶ Prosser M H. The Cultural Dialogue: An Introduction to Intercultural Communication [M]. He Daokuan (tr). Beijing: Peking University Press, 2013:32.

following western trends and fashion expressions, they have introduced and integrated oriental elements and culture into fashion design. In fact, "the construction of identity is a most exquisite and serious mirror game. It is a complex temporal interaction of multiple identification practices, and this kind of identification occurs outside and inside a subject or group." [1] For example, the Chinese designer Liangzi has perfectly combined oriental elements and international fashion in his fashion designs, with the beauty of the harmony between man and nature being his fundamental appeal. In western contemporary fashion design, oriental elements and culture are actually receiving more attention than ever from the western world.

Some clothes, such as men's suits, shirts and trousers, women's dresses, outfits, shirts and skirts, have become international clothing used universally, and ethnic costume rarely appears in many public places. Although globalization, being inseparable from modernity and colonialism, brings about many problems and dilemmas, it also provides cultural opportunities for multi-ethnic symbiosis and fashion. Therefore, simply giving up ethnic fashion tradition and clothing lifestyle is actually a neglect of the historical significance of culture. Paying attention to the sorting and exploration of ethnic costume elements is essential not only for preserving and reconstructing ethnic art and culture, but also for the worldwide identity of ethnic traditional culture. Undoubtedly, the narrow ethnic mentality that adheres to one culture stubbornly is a biased and extreme psychological and cultural attitude.

It may be said that, ethnic and cultural diversity in the post-colonial era is not only the problem that globalization has to face and respond to, but also the premise for the identification with various ethnic cultures.

It should be fully emphasized that all ethnic groups should be equal in terms of subsistence and cultural rights, and their differences in art, belief and culture should also be permitted. Globalization should not be about the convergence and homogenization of art and culture, but about diversification of culture, as well as recognition and respect for cultural differences. "An important consequence of globalization is the awakening of ethnic consciousness and the pursuit for uniqueness, which seems to be rather paradoxical. Accompanied by the increasing need for freedom and human rights, there are growing calls for the protection and respect of cultural heritage and traditions." [2] The demonization to the art and culture of disadvantaged ethnic groups has become a typical discourse style in the post-colonial era, which is often premised on the superiority cultural psychology of advantaged ethnic groups in the West. In fact, it is of great

---

[1] Friedman J. Cultural Identity and Global Process[M]. Guo Jianru (tr). Beijing: Commercial Press, 2003:213.
[2] Smith P, et al. Understanding Social Psychology across Cultures [M]. Yan Wenhua & Quan Dayong (tr). Beijing: Posts and Telecom Press, 2009:339.

necessity that cultural identity exists both inside an ethnic group and between ethnic groups, and cultures around the world are adapted to each other.

In different social, historical and cultural contexts, Chinese and other eastern elements have different meanings and purports for the West or even the world. Therefore, the interpretation of "oriental style" fashion art and culture involves the dialogue between different ethnic groups and cultures, which, however, does not mean that ethnic art and culture should not receive criticism from heterogeneous cultures, but emphasizes cultural identification with difference and diversity. The aesthetic and cultural tension between uniqueness and regionality is indispensable to the contemporary construction of oriental fashion and the criticism of orientalism. In this era of globalization, constructing cultural tension between uniformity and difference is not only the ideological appeal made by contemporary continuous reconstruction of ethnic aesthetics, but also the cultural context for the construction of inner ethnic spirit and characteristics.

In fact, ethnic cultural identity is both a matter appearing within a country of various ethnic groups, and a cultural issue faced mutually by most countries and ethnic groups across the world. On the relationship between a subject and their self, " Julia Christeva holds that the process that a subject discovers their self is a paradox, since the subject can only find the other of themselves by giving up something in themselves."[1] In fact, many costumes and fashions have integrated to themselves the cultures of different ethnic groups and countries. Moreover, ethnic cultural identify and cross-cultural communication must not only consider the postmodern cultural context, but also deal with the fundamental problems and difficulties of globalization. Properly inheriting and protecting ethnic costume cultures is very important for cultural diversity.

Any ethnic costume element and culture should not only belong to its own ethnic group, but also become a unique composition of world costume elements and cultural diversity. Globalization poses great challenges to the preservation of traditional ethnic costumes and cultures, because ethnic uniqueness may be lost in the pursuit for uniformity. In the process of modernization, countries like Thailand and the Philippines have preserved the designs and styles of their ethnic costumes as a rare way of life and traditional culture. Artistic, clothing and cultural diversity is actually a problem that all ethnic groups must face and respond to. At the same time, any strict distinguishing between one and the other, as well as the integration and homogenization in want of various cultural characteristics, should be avoided and criticized by cultural identification with ethnic elements.

In contemporary times, the dialogue between ethnic groups in clothing life and fashion culture

---

[1] O'Donnell K. Postmodernism [M]. Gibraltar: Lion Publishing Limited, 2003:80.

are becoming open, historical and generative in nature. Recognition among ethnic groups and worldwide cultural identity involve the reconstruction of aesthetics and cultural tension between differences and similarities. Prosser believes that "anyway, an inherent proposition in the study and effective practice of cross-cultural communication is that we have to learn and apply the balance between the poles of similarity and difference." [1] In fact, ethnic life and fashion are not isolated and exclusive, but an inseparable composition of the common living world of mankind. Hence, we should keep constructing ethnic self-identity and promoting cross-ethnic cultural communication, and then reconstruct the global fashion culture based on ethnicity in the context of globalization.

Undoubtedly, the criticism of the so-called orientalism and post-colonial culture in the West, as well as the emphasis on ethnic self-confidence and cultural self-consciousness, are indispensable to the construction of globalized fashion in China and the East. As a process of endowing symbol and meaning to identity recognition and establishment, cultural identity has unique qualities, methods and effect expectations at different levels and dimensions. The communication and understanding among ethnic groups, as well as the mutual adaptation of cultures take place in a historical process. It should be noted that, ethnic identity is the cultural basis and anthropological premise for global identity, while the aesthetic experience, value appeal and social meaning constructed by ethnic identity provide the essential context for the cross-cultural communication and global identity of art and clothing. In a sense, global cultural identity can neither break away from the identity within each ethnic group, nor ignore the mutual identity and recognition across ethnic groups. In other words, global cultural identity is based on inter-ethnicity and cross-cultural communication.

---

[1] Prosser, M. H. The Cultural Dialogue: An Introduction to Intercultural Communication [M]. He Daokuan (tr). Beijing: Peking University Press, 2013:13.

结　语

　　对民族元素与时尚的当代重构来说，全球化所涉及的民族性与世界性的审美与文化张力是不可或缺的。在此要注意到，全球认同并非淡化甚至忽视民族与国家认同，恰好相反，它是以对各民族认同的包容与尊重为前提的。在经济全球化与文化多元化的时代，有着悠久历史的中华文明理应关注自己的时尚文化，同时也亟待在当代时尚创意与设计表现中，建构起基于传统的民族审美文化与话语风格。因此，基于民族自身的艺术风格与文化传统进行民族间的跨文化对话是民族时尚创意的前提。实际上，只有保持鲜明的民族特色与文化特质，才不至于迷失在全球一体化与同质化的潮流之中。

　　与此同时，所有对民族性与世界性非此即彼的文化执态都是不可取的。其实只有经由跨文化传播与文化认同，各民族间的时尚创意与设计的对话，才得以生成与建构并富有文化多样性特质。在克拉克看来，"毕竟，东西方对话在敞开心灵面对更宽、更普遍的同情之际，曾经也同时发现并复活了本土的传统"。❶ 对于民族时尚创意而言，有助于激活这些民族元素及其文化特质。与此同时，还要生成与重构民族的创意与当代时尚文化。在全球化语境里，基于时尚视觉表现的民族审美文化的当代建构，主要包括民族间价值观比较、民族元素的视觉表现、民族的审美趣味与接受习惯、文化认同的理论基础与对话机制等。

　　对当代时尚艺术与文化而言，既不应以一种民族性否定民族多样性与世界性，同样也不能用全球化去限定与宰制地方性文化。在时尚创意过程中，视觉的审美表现与人的各种感觉相交融，并在民族文化上生成与建构出自身的意义，而意义的建构又离不开地方性与全球性的关联。2017年，复古风潮在纽约、伦敦、巴黎与米兰的时装周上得到了充分的展示。应注意到，那些只有肤浅与刻板的视觉表象，而缺乏民族精神图式与文化特质的设计，以及只是借助世界性的抽象符码来简单拼凑的时尚手法，是毫无品位与情调可言的。正是民族的精神与文化认同，构建了民族时尚创意的文化基础与语境。

　　其实，任何元素及其发现、揭示与重构，无疑都可能成为时尚创意的文化之源。但应当注意到，新的时尚创意往往会对旧的文化认同构成挑战，以寻求与建构新的时尚表现及

---

❶ J.J.克拉克.东方启蒙：东西方思想的遭遇[M].于闽梅，曾祥波，译.上海：上海人民出版社，2011：311.

其文化认同的方式与路径。尤其是时尚创意既在元素之内，同时又在元素之外，因此，民族时尚建构与元素的开放性相关。时尚消费不仅是一种生活方式，更是对时尚生活的理解与认同。在时尚的消费过程中，不仅会涉及功能、技术与实用性问题，还关联到符码、能指及其象征意味。在民族时尚与文化里，实用与非实用的互文也是设计应着力回应的问题。

对不同的民族来说，可时尚化的元素当然也是有所区分的，而且，这些不同的民族元素及其在当代的重构，正是世界性时尚生成不可忽视的文化语境。但时尚的视觉表现不应停留在一般的表象上，否则它最多也就是一种浅表的视觉印象。在时尚创意过程中，视觉表现还应成为一种关切族群的审美文化，也只有这样的视觉表现才有民族文化的底蕴，并促成时尚创意与设计得到世界性的文化认同。毫无疑问，这里所涉及的时尚的民族性及其文化特质，其实也是在各民族跨文化传播与对话里生成的。

加强民族的时尚创意及其与文化认同关联的研究，揭示与建构既有民族自身特质的，又关切于世界当代时尚的民族文化认同，显然是民族时尚研究重要的学术、思想与文化任务。实际上，任何艺术与设计都离不开历史与传统文化，即使那些反传统的当代设计也是如此。在全球化的创意与设计语境里，世界性时尚文化应当成为基于民族性的多元时尚文化。对所有民族元素与艺术、文化的关注，以及在此基础上生成的民族间文化对话，将有助于反对任何样式的文化殖民与霸权主义。

总而言之，全球化民族时尚创意的生成与当代建构，无疑是以民族独特性与多样性为前提，它显然不能以牺牲独特的民族精神与文化为代价。而且，民族时尚创意与设计的建构与实现，就是文化的民族性与世界性相互生成的过程。时尚的民族性与世界性及其生成性关联不可或缺，并在当代服饰与时尚文化里重构这种关联的意义。所有富有浓郁民族意味与特色的时装，象征着悠久的时尚历史与服饰文化。民族时尚创意还亟待在这个全球化的时代里，坚持与彰显着民族面向世界的艺术与文化自信。在全球化的趋势与过程中，文化的趋同性与多元化之间的相互交织与彼此互文，正是时尚的跨文化传播与文化认同相关联的生成性语境。

Conclusion

Indispensable for the contemporary reconstruction of ethnic elements and fashion are the aesthetic and cultural tensions between ethnicity and globality involved in globalization. It should be noted that global identity does not downplay or even ignore ethnic or national identity, but takes as its premise the tolerance and respect for the ethnic identity of different peoples. In the era of economic globalization and cultural diversification, the time-honored Chinese civilization should pay attention to its own fashion culture, and construct on the basis of tradition its ethnic aesthetic culture and discourse style in contemporary fashion creative and design expression. Therefore, ethnic fashion creative is premised on the intercultural dialogue between ethnic groups which occurs on the basis of ethnic artistic style and cultural tradition. In fact, only by maintaining distinct ethnic and cultural characteristics can we avoid getting lost in the trend of globalization and homogenization.

At the same time, it is undesirable to hold an extreme cultural attitude and make an either-or choice between ethnicity and globality. In fact, only through cross-cultural communication and cultural identity, the dialogue between ethnic groups in fashion creative and design can occur and be characterized by cultural diversity. In Clark's view, "after all, the East and the West have discovered and revived their respective traditions while they make dialogues and open to a wider and more general sympathy."[1] For ethnic fashion creative, these dialogues help to activate ethnic elements and their cultural characteristics. At the same time, it is necessary to generate and reconstruct ethnic creative and contemporary fashion culture. In the context of globalization, the contemporary construction of ethnic aesthetic culture based on fashion visualization mainly includes: the comparison of ethnic values, the visualization of ethnic elements, ethnic aesthetic tastes and acceptance habits, the theoretical basis and dialogue mechanism of cultural identity, etc.

---

[1] Clarke J J. Oriental Enlightenment: The Encounter Between Asian and Western Thought [M]. Yu Minmei, Zeng Xiangbo (tr). Shanghai: Shanghai People's Publishing House, 2011:311.

Contemporary fashion art and culture should neither deny ethnic diversity and globality with one type of ethnicity, nor suppress regional culture with globalization. In the generation of fashion creation, the aesthetic expression of vision blends with various human senses to generate its own meaning in ethnic culture, and this construction of meaning is inseparable from the connection between nativism and cosmopolitanism. In 2017, retro trend was fully highlighted at the fashion weeks in New York, London, Paris and Milan. It should be noted that, no taste or emotional appeal would come from those designs that only give superficial and rigid visual appearance, lacking ethnic spiritual schema and cultural characteristics, or from those designing methods that piece simply together globalized abstract symbols. It is ethnic spirit and cultural identity that construct the cultural foundation and context for ethnic fashion creative.

Actually, the discovery, revelation and reconstruction of any element could become the cultural source of fashion creative. However, new fashion creative often poses challenges to former cultural identity, so as to seek and construct new ways of fashion expression and cultural identity. We may say, fashion creative lies both inside and outside elements, so the construction of ethnic fashion has something to do with the openness of elements. Fashion consumption is not only a way of life, but also an understanding and recognition of fashion life. The process of fashion consumption involves not only function, technology and practicality, but also sign, signifier and symbolic meaning. In ethnic fashion and culture, the intertextuality between practicality and impracticality is also a problem that designing should especially respond to.

For different ethnic groups, elements that could be fashionable are also different, and the contemporary reconstruction of these different ethnic elements provides the unignorable cultural context for the generation of global fashion. But the visual expression of fashion should not rest on the level of general appearance, otherwise it will be a superficial visual impression at best. In fashion creative and design, visual expressions should form an aesthetic culture that is concerned with ethnic groups, and only such visual expressions can manifest the heritage of ethnic culture and promote the global cultural identity on fashion creative and design. Here, the ethnicity and the cultural characteristics of fashion are actually generated in the cross-cultural communication and dialogue between ethnic groups.

Strengthening the research on the relationship between ethnic fashion creative and cultural identity, and constructing the ethnic cultural identity that is concerned both with ethnic characteristics and with world contemporary fashion, are obviously important academic, ideological and cultural tasks of ethnic fashion research. In fact, all arts and designs, even those anti-traditional contemporary ones, cannot go away from history and traditional culture. In the context of globalized creative and design, cosmopolitan fashion culture should become a multiculture of fashion based on ethnicity. Undoubtedly, attention to all ethnic elements, arts and cultures, and inter-ethnic cultural dialogues on that basis, will help to oppose any form of cultural colonization and hegemony.

All in all, the generation and contemporary construction of globalized ethnic fashion creative is premised on ethnic uniqueness and diversity, at no expense of individual ethnic spirit and culture. Moreover, constructing and realizing ethnic fashion creative and design is a process that cultural ethnicity and globality get mutually generated. The generative relationship between fashion ethnicity and globality is of great importance, and the meaning of this relationship can be reconstructed in contemporary clothing and fashion culture. All fashions with strong ethnic flavor and characteristics symbolize long history of fashion and clothing culture. In this era of globalization, ethnic fashion creative should demonstrate an artistic and cultural confidence with which an ethnic group would face the world. In the trend and process of globalization, the interweaving between cultural convergence and diversification is exactly the generative context in which cross-cultural communication of fashion gets related to cultural identity.

参考文献

[1] 阿多诺.美学理论[M].成都：四川人民出版社，1998.

[2] 鲁道夫·阿恩海姆.视觉思维——审美直觉心理学[M].成都：四川人民出版社，1998.

[3] 鲁道夫·阿恩海姆.艺术与视知觉[M].成都：四川人民出版社，1998.

[4] 夸梅·安东尼·阿皮亚.认同伦理学[M].南京：译林出版社，2013.

[5] 艾兰.水之道与德之端——中国早期哲学思想的本喻[M].北京：商务印书馆，2010.

[6] 本尼迪克特·安德森.比较的幽灵：民族主义、东南亚与世界[M].南京：译林出版社，2012.

[7] 本尼迪克特·安德森.想象的共同体——民族主义的起源与散布[M].上海：上海人民出版社，2016.

[8] 休·昂纳.中国风：遗失在西方800年的中国元素[M].北京：北京大学出版社，2017.

[9] 罗兰·巴特.流行体系——符号学与服饰符码[M].上海：上海人民出版社，2000.

[10] 艾伦·巴纳德.人类学历史与理论[M].北京：华夏出版社，2006.

[11] 马尔科姆·巴纳德.理解视觉文化的方法[M].北京：商务印书馆，2005.

[12] 马尔科姆·巴纳德.艺术、设计与视觉文化[M].南京：江苏美术出版社，2006.

[13] 邦尼·英格利希.时尚[M].杭州：浙江摄影出版社，2012.

[14] 彼得·伯克.什么是文化史[M].北京：北京大学出版社，2009.

[15] 朗·伯内特.视觉文化——图像、媒介与想象力[M].济南：山东文艺出版社，2008.

[16] 伯格，等.时尚的力量[M].北京：科学出版社，2014.

[17] 乔纳森·鲍德温，卢西恩·罗伯茨.视觉传播：从理论到实践[M].沈阳：辽宁科学技术出版社，2010.

[18] 克莱夫·贝尔.艺术[M].南京：江苏教育出版社，2005.

[19] 沃伦·贝格尔.像设计师一样思考[M].北京：中信出版社，2011.

[20] 阿诺德·贝林特.艺术与介入[M].北京：商务印书馆，2013.

[21] 露丝·本尼迪克.文化模式[M].北京：华夏出版社，1987.

[22] 北京大陆桥文化传媒.时尚帝国[M].北京：北京出版社出版集团，2005.
[23] 比梅尔.海德格尔[M].北京：商务印书馆，1996.
[24] 包铭新，曹喆.国外后现代服饰[M].南京：江苏美术出版社，2001.
[25] 卞向阳.服装艺术判断[M].上海：东华大学出版社，2006.
[26] 卡洛琳·M.布鲁墨.视觉原理[M].北京：北京大学出版社，1987.
[27] 帕尔塔·查特吉.民族主义思想与殖民地世界：一种衍生的话语？[M].南京：译林出版社，2007.
[28] 布鲁斯·G.崔格尔.理解早期文明：比较研究[M].北京：北京大学出版社，2014.
[29] 丹纳.艺术哲学[M].合肥：安徽文艺出版社，1998.
[30] 斯蒂芬·戴维斯.艺术哲学[M].上海：上海人民美术出版社，2008.
[31] 若昂·德让.时尚的精髓[M].北京：三联书店，2012.
[32] 蒂埃里·德·迪弗.艺术之名——为了一种现代性的考古学[M].长沙：湖南美术出版社，2001：66.
[33] 埃伦·迪萨纳亚克.审美的人[M].北京：商务印书馆，2004.
[34] 马克·第亚尼.非物质社会——后工业世界的设计、文化与技术[M].成都：四川人民出版社，1998.
[35] 《第欧根尼》中文精选版编辑委员会.文化认同性的变形[M].北京：商务印书馆，2008.
[36] 雅克·德里达.一种疯狂守护着思想——德里达访谈录[M].上海：上海人民出版社，1997.
[37] 米·杜夫海纳.美学与哲学[M].北京：中国社会科学出版社，1985.
[38] 杜朴，文以诚.中国艺术与文化[M].北京：北京联合出版公司，2014.
[39] 彼得·多默.1945年以来的设计[M].成都：四川人民出版社，1998.
[40] 彼得·多默.现代设计的意义[M].南京：译林出版社，2013.
[41] 埃克伯特·法阿斯.美学谱系学[M].北京：商务印书馆，2011.
[42] 范丹姆.审美人类学：视野与方法[M].北京：中国文联出版社，2015.
[43] 斯蒂夫·芬顿.族性[M].北京：中央民族大学出版社，2009.
[44] 冯盈之.汉字与服饰文化[M].上海：东华大学出版社，2008.
[45] 冯盈之，余赠振.古代中国服饰时尚100例[M].杭州：浙江大学出版社，2016.
[46] 理查德·佛罗里达.创意阶层的崛起[M].北京：中信出版社，2010.
[47] J.G.弗雷泽.金枝——巫术与宗教之研究[M].北京：商务印书馆，2013.
[48] 帕特里克·弗兰克.视觉艺术原理[M].上海：上海人民美术出版社，2008.
[49] 乔纳森·弗里德曼.文化认同与全球性过程[M].北京：商务印书馆，2003.
[50] 玛尼·弗格.时尚通史[M].北京：中信出版社，2016.

[51] 保罗·福塞尔.格调：社会等级与生活品味［M］.北京：世界图书出版公司，2011.
[52] 格罗塞.艺术的起源［M］.北京：商务印书馆，1984.
[53] 阿尔弗雷德·格罗塞.身份认同的困境［M］.北京：社会科学文献出版社，2010.
[54] 安·格雷.文化研究：民族志方法与生活文化［M］.重庆：重庆大学出版社，2009.
[55] 弗朗索瓦-玛丽·格罗.回眸时尚：西方服装简史［M］.北京：中国纺织出版社，2009.
[56] 奥蒂莉·戈弗雷.复古时裳［M］.北京：北京时代华文书局，2015.
[57] 欧文·戈夫曼.日常生活中的自我呈现［M］.北京：北京大学出版社，2008.
[58] 杰克·古迪.神话、仪式与口述［M］.北京：中国人民大学出版社，2014.
[59] 杰克·古迪.西方中的东方［M］.杭州：浙江大学出版社，2012.
[60] 多米尼克·古维烈.时尚不死？——关于时尚的终极诘问［M］.北京：中国纺织出版社，2009.
[61] 多米尼克·古维烈.在时尚中融化［M］.桂林：漓江出版社，2013.
[62] 简·艾伦·哈里森.古代艺术与仪式［M］.北京：三联书店，2008.
[63] 詹妮弗·哈里斯.纺织史［M］.汕头：汕头大学出版社，2011.
[64] 阿尔弗雷德·C.哈登.艺术的进化：图案的生命史解析［M］.桂林：广西师范大学出版社，2010.
[65] 奥斯汀·哈灵顿.艺术与社会理论——美学中的社会学论争［M］.南京：南京大学出版社，2010.
[66] 海德格尔.存在与时间［M］.北京：三联书店，1999.
[67] 马丁·海德格尔.同一与差异［M］.北京：商务印书馆，2011.
[68] 本·海默尔.日常生活与文化理论导论［M］.北京：商务印书馆，2008.
[69] 芮乐伟·韩森.丝绸之路新史［M］.北京：北京联合出版公司，2015.
[70] 理查德·豪厄尔斯.视觉文化［M］.桂林：广西师范大学出版社，2007.
[71] 大卫·赫斯蒙德夫.文化产业［M］.北京：中国人民大学出版社，2007.
[72] 迪克·赫伯迪格.亚文化：风格的意义［M］.北京：北京大学出版社，2009.
[73] 阿格妮丝·赫勒.日常生活［M］.哈尔滨：黑龙江大学出版社，2010.
[74] 尼娜·加西亚.我的100件时尚单品［M］.北京：中信出版社，2010.
[75] 杰·卡尔德林.形式·适合·时尚［M］.济南：山东画报出版社，2011.
[76] 杰伊·卡尔德林.时装设计100个创意关键词［M］.北京：中国青年出版社，2012.
[77] 丹尼·卡瓦拉罗.文化理论关键词［M］.南京：江苏人民出版社，2013.
[78] 苏珊·B.凯瑟.时尚与文化研究［M］.北京：中国轻工业出版社，2016.
[79] 史蒂文·康纳.后现代主义文化——当代理论导引［M］.北京：商务印书馆，2002.
[80] 罗伯特·克雷.设计之美［M］.济南：山东画报出版社，2010.
[81] 珍妮弗·克雷克.时装的面貌——时装的文化研究［M］.北京：中央编译出版社，

2000.

[82] 保罗·克劳瑟.20世纪艺术的语言：观念史［M］.长春：吉林人民出版社，2007.

[83] J.J.克拉克.东方启蒙：东西方思想的遭遇［M］.上海：上海人民出版社，2011.

[84] 普兰温·科斯格拉芙.时装生活史［M］.上海：东方出版中心，2006.

[85] 乔尔·科特金.全球族［M］.北京：社会科学文献出版社，2010.

[86] 本内迪克特·拉佩尔.欧洲脸谱［M］.北京：中国人民大学出版社，2015.

[87] 詹姆斯·拉韦尔.服装和时尚简史［M］.杭州：浙江摄影出版社，2016.

[88] 马克·拉索尔.向着大地和天空，凡人和诸神：海德格尔导读［M］.北京：中信出版集团，2015.

[89] 罗伯特·莱顿.艺术人类学［M］.桂林：广西师范大学出版社，2009.

[90] 诺埃尔·帕洛莫·乐文斯基.世界上最具影响力的服装设计师［M］.北京：中国纺织出版社，2014.

[91] 保罗·利科.活的隐喻［M］.上海：译文出版社，2004.

[92] 保罗·利科.作为一个他者的自身［M］.北京：商务印书馆，2013.

[93] K.马尔科姆·理查兹.德里达眼中的艺术［M］.重庆：重庆大学出版社，2016.

[94] 克洛德·列维-斯特劳斯.看·听·读［M］.北京：中国人民大学出版社，2006.

[95] 刘国联.服装心理学［M］.上海：东华大学出版社，2007.

[96] 刘天勇，王培娜.民族·时尚·设计——民族服饰元素与时装设计［M］.北京：化学工业出版社，2010.

[97] 楼慧珍，吴永，郑彤.中国传统服饰文化［M］.上海：东华大学出版社，2004.

[98] 罗兰·罗伯森.全球化——社会理论和全球文化［M］.上海：上海人民出版社，2000.

[99] 罗姆巴赫.作为生活结构的世界——结构存在论的问题与解答［M］.上海：上海书店出版社，2009.

[100] 詹姆斯·罗尔.媒介、传播、文化——一个全球性的途径［M］.北京：商务印书馆，2012.

[101] 托马斯·洛克伍德.设计思维［M］.北京：电子工业出版社，2012.

[102] F.大卫·马丁，李·A.雅各布斯.艺术导论［M］.上海：上海社会科学院出版社，2011.

[103] 维克多·马格林.设计问题——历史·理论·批评［M］.北京：中国建筑工业出版社，2010.

[104] 琼·马什.时尚设计史：从"新风貌"到当代［M］.济南：山东画报出版社，2014.

[105] 约翰·马克.面具：人类的自我伪装与救赎［M］.广州：南方日报出版社，2011.

[106] 乔治·E.马尔库斯，弗雷德·R.迈尔斯.文化交流：重塑艺术和人类学［M］.桂林：广西师范大学出版社，2010.

［107］马蓉.服装创意与构造方法［M］.重庆：重庆大学出版社，2007.

［108］马蓉.民族服饰语言的时尚运用［M］.重庆：重庆大学出版社，2009.

［109］凯瑟琳·麦克德莫特.设计：核心概念［M］.北京：清华大学出版社，2014.

［110］提姆·麦克雷特.设计的语言［M］.沈阳：辽宁科学技术出版社，2015.

［111］H.A.梅内尔.审美价值的本性［M］.北京：商务印书馆，2001.

［112］若斯·吉莱姆·梅吉奥.列维-斯特劳斯的美学观［M］.天津：天津人民出版社，2003.

［113］保罗·梅萨里.视觉说服：形象在广告中的作用［M］.北京：新华出版社，2004.

［114］温尼·海德·米奈.艺术史的历史［M］.上海：上海人民出版社，2007.

［115］W.J.T.米歇尔.图像学：形象，文本，意识形态［M］.北京：北京大学出版社，2012.

［116］尼古拉斯·米尔佐夫.视觉文化导论［M］.南京：江苏人民出版社，2006.

［117］戴维·米勒.论民族性［M］.南京：译林出版社，2010.

［118］安古拉·默克罗比.后现代主义与大众文化［M］.北京：中央编译出版社，2001.

［119］琼·娜.服饰时尚800年：1200-2000［M］.桂林：广西师范大学出版社，2004.

［120］唐纳德·A.诺曼.设计心理学［M］.北京：中信出版社，2010.

［121］马里奥·佩尔尼奥拉.仪式思维［M］.北京：商务印书馆，2006.

［122］丽塔·裴娜.流行预测［M］.北京：中国纺织出版社，2000.

［123］迈克尔·普罗瑟.文化对话：跨文化传播导论［M］.北京：北京大学出版社，2013.

［124］苏·詹金·琼斯.时装设计［M］.北京：中国纺织出版社，2009.

［125］乔治·桑塔耶纳.美感［M］.北京：人民出版社，2013.

［126］拉里·A.萨默瓦，理查德·E.波特.跨文化传播［M］.北京：中国人民大学出版社，2004.

［127］维克托·什克洛夫斯基，等.俄国形式主义文论选［M］.北京：三联书店，1989.

［128］安东尼·史密斯.民族主义——理论、意识形态、历史［M］.上海：上海人民出版社，2011.

［129］彼得·史密斯，等.跨文化社会心理学［M］.北京：人民邮电出版社，2009.

［130］休斯顿·史密斯.人的宗教［M］.海口：海南出版社，2013.

［131］拉斯·史文德森.时尚的哲学［M］.北京：北京大学出版社，2010.

［132］纳丹·施郎格.论技术、技艺与文明［M］.北京：世界图书出版公司，2010.

［133］理查德·舒斯特曼.实用主义美学［M］.北京：商务印书馆，2002.

［134］彭妮·斯帕克.设计与文化导论［M］.南京：译林出版社，2012.

［135］迈克尔·苏立文.东西方艺术的交会［M］.上海：上海人民出版社，2014.

［136］苏永刚.服装时尚元素的提炼与运用［M］.重庆：重庆大学出版社，2007.

［137］瓦迪斯瓦夫·塔塔尔凯维奇.西方六大美学观念史［M］.上海：译文出版社，2006.

[138] 安德鲁·塔克,塔米辛·金斯伟尔.时装[M].北京:三联书店,2014.

[139] 梯利.西方哲学史[M].北京:商务印书馆,1995.

[140] 田中千代.世界民俗衣装:探寻人类着装方法的智慧[M].北京:中国纺织出版社,2001.

[141] 茨维坦·托多罗夫.象征理论[M].北京:商务印书馆,2004.

[142] 汪芳.中国传统服饰图案解读[M].上海:东华大学出版社,2014.

[143] 伊曼纽尔·沃勒斯坦.变化中的世界体系[M].北京:中央编译出版社,2016.

[144] 哈里特·沃斯里.100个改变时尚的伟大观念[M].北京:中国摄影出版社,2013.

[145] 沃尔夫冈·韦尔施.重构美学[M].上海:译文出版社,2002.

[146] 沃特伯格.什么是艺术[M].重庆:重庆大学出版社,2011.

[147] 乔治·维加莱洛.人体美丽史[M].长沙:湖南文艺出版社,2007.

[148] C.A.S.威廉斯.中国艺术象征词典[M].长沙:湖南科学技术出版社,2006.

[149] 温克尔曼.希腊人的艺术[M].桂林:广西师范大学出版社,2001.

[150] 吴妍妍.欧洲民族服饰概论[M].北京:中国纺织出版社,2016.

[151] 肖世孟.先秦色彩研究[M].北京:人民出版社,2013.

[152] 西美尔.时尚的哲学[M].北京:文化艺术出版社,2001.

[153] 奚传绩.设计艺术经典论著选读[M].南京:东南大学出版社,2002.

[154] 理查德·谢弗.社会学与生活[M].北京:世界图书出版公司,2009.

[155] 徐复观.中国艺术精神[M].北京:商务印书馆,2010.

[156] 维多利亚·D.亚历山大.艺术社会学[M].南京:江苏美术出版社,2009.

[157] 詹姆斯·韦伯·扬.创意的生成[M].北京:中国人民大学出版社,2014.

[158] 汉斯·罗伯特·耀斯.审美经验与文学解释学[M].上海:译文出版社,1997.

[159] 戴维·英格利斯.文化与日常生活[M].北京:中央编译出版社,2010.

[160] 邦尼·英格利希.时尚[M].杭州:浙江摄影出版社,2012.

[161] 雅科伏列夫.艺术与世界宗教[M].北京:文化艺术出版社,1989.

[162] 杨孝鸿.中国时尚文化史(宋元明卷)[M].济南:山东画报出版社,2011.

[163] 叶立诚.服饰美学[M].北京:中国纺织出版社,2001.

[164] 弗雷德里克·詹姆逊.布莱希特与方法[M].北京:中国社会科学出版社,1998.

[165] 张志春.中国服饰文化[M].北京:中国纺织出版社,2009.

[166] 张繁文,韩雪松.中国时尚文化史(清民国新中国卷)[M].济南:山东画报出版社,2011.

[167] 张星.服装流行学[M].北京:中国纺织出版社,2006.

[168] 张贤根.艺术现象学导论[M].武汉:湖北人民出版社,2015.

[169] 钟志金.民族文化与时尚服装设计[M].石家庄:河北美术出版社,2009.

[170] 朱利安. 美，这奇特的理念 [M]. 北京：北京大学出版社，2016.

[171] Jean Baudrillard. Simulacra and Simulation [M]. Ann Arbor: The University of Michigan Press, 1995.

[172] Malcolm Barnard. Fashion as Communication [M]. London: Routledge, 1996.

[173] Umberto Eco. Art and Beauty in the Middle Ages [M]. New Haven: Yale University Press, 1986.

[174] Fiona Ffoulkes. How to Read Fashion [M]. New York: Rizzoli International Publications, Inc, 2013.

[175] Adam Geczy. Fashion and Orientalism [M]. London: Bloomsbury Academic, 2013.

[176] Bruno Munari. Design as Art [M]. London: Penguin Books Ltd, 2008.

[177] Kevin O'Donnell. Postmodernism [M]. Gibraltar: Lion Publishing plc, 2003.

[178] Jakub Petri. Performing Cultures [M]. Kraków: Wydawnictwo LIBRON, 2015.

[179] George Ritze. Postmodern Social Theory [M]. New York: The McGraw-Hill Companies, Inc, 1997.

[180] Agnes Rocamora, Anneke Smelik. Thinking Through Fashion [M]. London: I. B. Tauris, 2016.

[181] Robert Sokolowski. Introduction to Phenomenology [M]. Cambridge: Cambridge University Press, 2000.

[182] Robert J.C. Young. Postcolonialism: A Very Short Introduction [M]. Oxford: Oxford University Press, 2003.

Bibliography

(Rearranged according to the names of the authors.)

[1] Adoeno T W. Asthetische Theorie [M]. Wang Keping (tr). Chengdu: Sichuan People's Publishing House, 1998.

[2] Alexander V D. Sociology of the Arts [M]. Zhang Hao, Shen Yang (tr). Nanjing: Jiangsu Fine Arts Publishing House, 2009.

[3] Allan S. The Way of Water and Sprouts of Virtue [M]. Zhang Haiyan (tr). Beijing: Commercial Press, 2010.

[4] Anderson B. The Spectre of Comparisons: Nationalism, Southeast Asia and the World [M]. Gan Huibin (tr). Nanjing: Yilin Press, 2012.

[5] Anderson B. Imagined Communities: Reflections on the Origin and Spread of Nationalism [M]. Wu Ruiren (tr). Shanghai: Shanghai People's Publishing House, 2016.

[6] Appiah K. A. The Ethics of Identity [M]. Zhang Rongnan (tr). Nanjing: Yilin Press, 2013.

[7] Arnheim R. Visual Thinking [M]. Teng Shouyao (tr). Chengdu: Sichuan People's Publishing House, 1998.

[8] Arnheim R. Art and Visual Perception: A Psychology of the Creative Eye [M]. Teng Shouyao, Zhu Jiangyuan (tr). Chengdu: Sichuan People's Publishing House, 1998.

[9] Barthes R. Système de la Mode [M]. Ao Jun (tr). Shanghai: Shanghai People's Publishing House, 2000.

[10] Barnard A. History and Theory in Anthropology [M]. Wang Jianmin, et al. (tr). Beijing: Huaxia Publishing House, 2006.

[11] Barnard M. Fashion as Communication [M]. London: Routledge, 1996.

[12] Barnard M. Approaches to Understanding Visual Culture [M]. Chang Ningsheng (tr). Beijing: Commercial Press, 2005.

[13] Barnard M. Art, Design and Visual Culture [M]. Wang Shengcai, et al. (tr). Nanjing: Jiangsu

Fine Arts Publishing House, 2006.

[14] Baldwin J, L. Roberts. Visual Communication: From Theory to Practice [M]. Chen Jin, Liu Xiaolin (tr). Shenyang: Liaoning Science and Technology Press, 2010.

[15] Bao Mingxin, Cao Zhe. Postmodern Costume Abroad [M]. Nanjing: Jiangsu Fine Arts Publishing House, 2001.

[16] Baudrillard J. Simulacra and Simulation [M]. Ann Arbor: The University of Michigan Press, 1995.

[17] Beijing Continental Bridge Corporation (ed). Fashion Empire[M]. Beijing: Beijing Publishing House, 2005.

[18] Bell C. Art [M]. Xue Hua (tr). Nanjing: Jiangsu Education Publishing House, 2005.

[19] Benedict R. Patterns of Culture [M]. He Xizhang, Huang Huan (tr). Beijing: Huaxia Publishing House, 1987.

[20] Berger W. Design Thinking [M]. Li Xin (tr). Beijing: China CITIC Press, 2011.

[21] Berleant A. Art and Engagement [M]. Li Yuanyuan (tr). Beijing: Commercial Press, 2013.

[22] Berg, et al. The Power of Fashion [M]. Wei Xiaoqiang, et al. (tr). Beijing: Science Press, 2014.

[23] Bian Xiangyang (ed). Judgement on Costume Art [M]. Shanghai: Donghua University Press, 2006.

[24] Biemel W. Heidegger [M]. Liu Xin, Liu Ying (tr). Beijing: Commercial Press, 1996.

[25] Bloomer C M. Principles of Visual Perception [M]. Zhang Gongqian (tr). Beijing: Peking University Press, 1987.

[26] Burke P. What is Cultural History [M]. Cai Yuhui (tr). Beijing: Peking University Press, 2009.

[27] Burnett R. Cultures of Vision: Images, Media, and the Imaginary [M]. Zhao Yi, et al (tr). Jinan: Shandong Literature and Art Publishing House, 2008.

[28] Calderin J. Form, Fit, Fashion [M]. Zhou Mingrui (tr). Jinan: Shandong Pictorial Publishing House, 2011.

[29] Calderin J. 100 Keywords of Creative in Fashion Design [M]. Cao Shuai (tr). Beijing: China Youth Publishing House, 2012.

[30] Cavallaro D. Critical and Cultural Theory: Thematic Variations [M]. Zhang Weidong, et al. (tr). Nanjing: Jiangsu People's Publishing House, 2013.

[31] Chatterjee P. Nationalist Thought and the Colonial World: A Derivative Discourse [M]. Fan Muyou, Yang Xi (tr). Nanjing: Yilin Press, 2007.

[32] Clarke J J. Oriental Enlightenment: The Encounter Between Asian and Western Thought [M].

Yu Minmei, Zeng Xiangbo (tr). Shanghai: Shanghai People's Publishing House, 2011.

[33] Clay R. Beautiful Thing: An Introduction to Design [M]. Yin Tao (tr). Jinan: Shandong Pictorial Publishing House, 2010.

[34] Connor S. Postmodernist Culture: An Introduction to Theories of the Contemporary [M]. Yan Zhongzhi (tr). Beijing: Commercial Press, 2002.

[35] Cosgrave B. The Complete History of Costume and Fashion [M]. Long Jingyao, Zhang Ying (tr). Shanghai: Oriental Publishing Center, 2006.

[36] Craik J. The Face of Fashion: Cultural Studies in Fashion [M]. Shu Yunzhong (tr). Beijing: Central Compilation & Translation Press, 2000.

[37] Crowther P. The Language of Twentieth-Century Art: A Conceptual History [M]. Liu Yiping, et al. (tr). Changchun: Jilin People's Publishing House, 2007.

[38] Cuvillier D. Le Futur de la Mode: Fashion on the Ultimate Cross-Examination [M]. Zhi Qi (tr). Beijing: China Textile & Apparel Press, 2009.

[39] Cuvillier D. Les Femmes Sont-Elles Solubles Dans La Mode? [M]. Zhi Qi (tr). Guilin: Lijiang Publishing Limited, 2013.

[40] Davies S. The Philosophy of Art [M]. Wang Yanfei (tr). Shanghai: Shanghai People's Fine Arts Publishing House, 2008.

[41] DeJean J. The Essence of Fashion [M]. Yang Ji (tr). Beijing: SDX Joint Publishing Company, 2012.

[42] Derrida J. A Madness Guards Thought – A Collection of Interviews with Derrida [M]. He Peiqun (tr). Shanghai: Shanghai People's Publishing House, 1997.

[43] Diani M. The Immaterial Society: Design, Culture, and Technology in the Postmodern World [M]. Teng Shouyao (tr). Chengdu: Sichuan People's Publishing House, 1998.

[44] Dissanayake E. Homo aestheticus: Where art comes from and why [M]. Lu Xiaohui (tr). Beijing: Commercial Press, 2004.

[45] Dufrenne M. Esthetique et Philosophie [M]. Sun Fei (tr). Beijing: China Social Sciences Press, 1985.

[46] Duve T D. Au Nom de L'art: Pour une Archéologie de la Modenité [M]. Qin Haiying (tr). Changsha: Hunan Fine Arts Publishing House, 2001.

[47] Dormer P. Design since 1945 [M]. Liang Mei (tr). Chengdu: Sichuan People's Publishing House, 1998.

[48] Dormer P. The Meaning of Modern Design [M]. Zhang Bei (tr). Nanjing: Yilin Press, 2013.

[49] Eco U. Art and Beauty in the Middle Ages [M]. New Haven: Yale University Press, 1986.

[50] Editorial Board of Diogenes Chinese Edition (ed). Transformation of Cultural Identity [M].

Beijing: Commercial Press, 2008.

[51] English, B. Fashion Design [M]. Huang Hui (tr). Hangzhou: Zhejiang Photography Publishing House, 2012.

[52] Faas, E. The Genealogy of Aesthetics [M]. Yan Jia (tr). Beijing: Commercial Press, 2011.

[53] Fenton, S. Ethnicity [M]. Lao Huanqiang. et al. (tr). Beijing: China Minzu University Press, 2009.

[54] Feng Yingzhi. Chinese Characters and Clothing Culture [M]. Shanghai: Donghua University Press, 2008.

[55] Feng Yingzhi & Yu Zengzhen. 100 Cases of Fashion of Ancient Chinese Clothing [M]. Hangzhou: Zhejiang University Press, 2016.

[56] Ffoulkes, F. How to Read Fashion [M]. New York: Rizzoli International Publications, Inc, 2013.

[57] Florida, R. The Rise of Creative Class [M]. Situ Aiqin (tr). Beijing: China CITIC Press, 2010.

[58] Fogg, M (ed). Fashion: The Whole History [M]. Chen Lei (tr). Beijing: China CITIC Press, 2016.

[59] Frazer, J.G. The Golden Bough: A Study in Magic and Religion [M]. Wang Peiji, et al. (tr). Beijing: Commercial Press, 2013.

[60] Frank, P. The Principle of Visual Art [M]. Chen Lei, Yu Yu (tr). Shanghai: Shanghai People's Fine Arts Publishing House, 2008.

[61] Friedman, J. Cultural Identity and Global Process[M]. Guo Jianru (tr). Beijing: Commercial Press, 2003.

[62] Fussell, P. Class: A Guide through The American Status System [M]. Liang Lizhen, et al. (tr). Beijing: World Publishing Corporation, 2011.

[63] Garcia, N. The One Hundred: A Guide to the Pieces every Stylish Woman must Own [M]. Lü Fangxing (tr). Beijing: China CITIC Press, 2010.

[64] Geczy, A. Fashion and Orientalism [M]. London: Bloomsbury Academic, 2013.

[65] Godfrey, O. Vintage Fashion [M]. Ouyang Suye (tr). Beijing: Beijing Times Chinese Press, 2015.

[66] Goffman, I. The Presentation of Self in Everyday life [M]. Feng Gang (tr). Beijing: Peking University Press, 2008.

[67] Goody, J. The East in the West [M]. Shen Yi (tr). Hangzhou: Zhejiang University Press, 2012.

[68] Goody J. Myth, Ritual and the Oral [M]. Li Yuan (tr). Beijing: China Renmin University

Press, 2014.

[69] Grau F M. Histoire du Costume [M]. Zhi Qi (tr). Beijing: China Textile & Apparel Press, 2009.

[70] Gray A. Research Practice for Cultural Studies: Ethnographic Methods and Lived Culture [M]. Xu Mengyun (tr). Chongqing: Chongqing University Press, 2009.

[71] Grosse E. The Beginnings of Art [M]. Cai Muhui (tr). Beijing: Commercial Press, 1984.

[72] Grosser A. Les Identitès Difficiles [M]. Wang Kun (tr). Beijing: Social Sciences Academic Press, 2010.

[73] Hadden A C. Evolution in Art: As Illustrated by the Life-Histories of Designs [M]. Agazuoshi (tr). Guilin: Guangxi Normal University Press, 2010.

[74] Hansen V. The Silk Road: A New History [M]. Zhang Zhan (tr). Beijing: Beijing United Publishing Company, 2015.

[75] Harrington A. Art and Social Theory: Sociological Arguments in Aesthetics [M]. Zhou Jiwu, Zhou Xueping (tr). Nanjing: Nanjing University Press, 2010.

[76] Harris J. 5000 Years of Textiles [M]. Li Guoqing, et al. (tr). Shantou: Shantou University Press, 2011.

[77] Harrison J E. Ancient Art and Ritual [M]. Liu Zongdi (tr). Beijing: SDX Joint Publishing Company, 2008.

[78] Hebdige D. Subculture: The Meaning of Style [M]. Hu Jiangfeng, Lu Daofu (tr). Beijing: Peking University Press, 2009.

[79] Heidegger M. Sein und Zeit [M]. Chen Jiaying, Wang Qingjie (tr). Beijing: SDX Joint Publishing Company, 1999.

[80] Heidegger M. Identität und Differenz [M]. Sun Zhouxing, et al. (tr). Beijing: Commercial Press, 2011.

[81] Heller A. Everyday Life [M]. Yi Junqing (tr). Harbin: Heilongjiang University Press, 2010.

[82] Hesmondhalgh D. The Cultural Industries [M]. Zhang Feina (tr). Beijing: China Renmin University Press, 2007.

[83] Highmore B. Everyday Life and Cultural Theory: An Introduction [M]. Wang Zhihong (tr). Beijing: Commercial Press, 2008.

[84] Honour H. Chinoiserie: The Vision of Cathay [M]. Liu Aiying, Qin Hong (tr). Beijing: Peking University Press, 2017.

[85] Howells R. Visual Culture [M]. Ge Hongbing, et al. (tr). Guilin: Guangxi Normal University Press, 2007.

[86] Inglis D. Culture and Everyday Life [M]. Zhang Qiuyue, Zhou Leiya (tr). Beijing: Central

Compilation & Translation Press, 2010.

[87] Iskin R E. Modern Women and Parisian Consumer Culture in Impressionist Painting [M]. Meng Chunyan (tr). Nanjing: Jiangsu Fine Arts Publishing House, 2009.

[88] Jameson F. Brecht and Method [M]. Chen Yongguo (tr). Beijing: China Social Sciences Press, 1998.

[89] Jones S J. Fashion Design [M]. Zhang Ling (tr). Beijing: China Textile & Apparel Press, 2009.

[90] Jullien F. Cette Étrange Idée Du Beau [M]. Gao Fengfeng (tr). Beijing: Peking University Press, 2016.

[91] Kaiser S B. Fashion and Cultural Studies [M]. Guo Pingjian, et al. (tr). Beijing: China Light Industry Press, 2016.

[92] Kotkin Joel. Tribes [M]. Wang Xu, et al. (tr). Beijing: Social Sciences Academic Press, 2010.

[93] Lapeyre B. Francois, Peter, Maria, Hendrik Et Les Autres [M]. Liu Yuli (tr). Beijing: China Renmin University Press, 2015.

[94] Lavel J. Costume and Fashion: A Concise History [M]. Lin Weiran (tr). Hangzhou: Zhejiang Photography Publishing House, 2016.

[95] Layton R. The Anthropology of Art [M]. Li Dongye, Wang Hong (tr). Guilin: Guangxi Normal University Press, 2009.

[96] Lévi-Strauss C. Regarder Ècouter Lire [M]. Gu Jiachen (tr). Beijing: China Renmin University Press, 2006.

[97] Liu Guolian (ed). The Psychology of Clothes [M]. Shanghai: Donghua University Press, 2007.

[98] Liu Tianyong, Wang Peina. Ethnicity · Fashion · Design - Ethnic Costume Elements and Fashion Design [M]. Beijing: Chemical Industry Press, 2010.

[99] Lockwood T. Design Thinking [M]. Li Cuirong, et al. (tr). Beijing: Publishing House of Electronics Industry, 2012.

[100] Lou Huizhen, et al. Chinese Traditional Costume Culture [M]. Shanghai: Donghua University Press, 2004.

[101] Lovinski N P. The World's Most Influential Fashion Designers [M]. Zhou Meng, Zheng Shanshan (tr). Beijing: China Textile & Apparel Press, 2014.

[102] Lull J. Media, Communication, Culture: A Global Approach [M]. Dong Hongchuan (tr). Beijing: Commercial Press, 2012.

[103] Mack J (ed). Masks: The Art of Expression [M]. Yang Yang (tr). Guangzhou: Nanfang Daily Press, 2011.

[104] Ma Rong (ed). Costume Creative and Construction Methods [M]. Chongqing: Chongqing University Press, 2007.

[105] Ma Rong (ed). The Application of Ethnic Costume Language to Fashion [M]. Chongqing: Chongqing University Press, 2009.

[106] Marcus G E, F R. Myers. The Traffic in Art and Culture: A Critical Ethnography of Art [M]. Agazuoshi, Liang Yongjia (tr). Guilin: Guangxi Normal University Press, 2010.

[107] Marglin V. (ed). Design Discourse: History, Theory, Criticism [M]. Liu Sha, et al. (tr). Beijing: China Architecture & Building Press, 2010.

[108] Marsh J. History of Fashion: New Look to Now [M]. Shao Lirong, Xu Qianqian (tr). Jinan: Shandong Pictorial Publishing House, 2014.

[109] Martin F D, Jacobs L A. The Humanities through the Arts [M]. Bao Huiyi, Huang Shaoting (tr). Shanghai: Shanghai Academy of Social Sciences Press, 2011.

[110] McCreight T. Design Language [M]. Liu Zhuangli (tr). Shenyang: Liaoning Science and Technology Press, 2015.

[111] McDermott K. Design: The Key Concepts [M]. Wang Lu (tr). Beijing: Tsinghua University Press, 2014.

[112] McRobbie A. Postmodernism and Popular Culture [M]. Tian Xiaofei (tr). Beijing: Central Compilation & Translation Press, 2001.

[113] Merquior J G. L'Esthtique de Lévi-Strauss [M]. Huai Yu (tr). Tianjin: Tianjin People's Publishing House, 2003.

[114] Messaris P. Visual Persuasion: The Role of Images in Advertising [M]. Wang Bo (tr). Beijing: Xinhua Publishing House, 2004.

[115] Meynell H A. The Nature of Aesthetic Value [M]. Liu Min (tr). Beijing: Commercial Press, 2001.

[116] Miller D. On Nationality [M]. Liu Shuhui (tr). Nanjing: Yilin Press, 2010.

[117] Minor V H. Art History's History [M]. Li Jianqun, et al. (tr). Shanghai: Shanghai People's Publishing House, 2007.

[118] Mitchell W J T. Iconology: Image, Text, Ideology [M]. Chen Yongguo (tr). Beijing: Peking University Press, 2012.

[119] Mirzoeff N. An Introduction to Visual Culture [M]. Ni Wei (tr). Nanjing: Jiangsu People's Publishing House, 2006.

[120] Munari B. Design as Art [M]. London: Penguin Books Ltd, 2008.

[121] Norman D A. The Design of Everyday Things [M]. Mei Qiong (tr). Beijing: China CITIC Press, 2010.

[122] Nunn, J. Fashion in Costume: 1200-2000 [M]. He Tong (tr). Guilin: Guangxi Normal University Press, 2004.

[123] O'Donnell K. Postmodernism [M]. Gibraltar: Lion Publishing plc, 2003.

[124] Perna R. Fashion Forecasting [M]. Li Hongwei, et al. (tr). Beijing: China Textile & Apparel Press, 2000.

[125] Perniola M. Ritual Thinking [M]. Lv Jie (tr). Beijing: Commercial Press, 2006.

[126] Petri J. (ed). Performing Cultures [M]. Kraków: Wydawnictwo LIBRON, 2015.

[127] Prosser M. H. The Cultural Dialogue: An Introduction to Intercultural Communication [M]. He Daokuan (tr). Beijing: Peking University Press, 2013.

[128] Richards K M. Derrida Reframed [M]. Chen Si (tr). Chongqing: Chongqing University Press, 2016.

[129] Ricoeur P. La Métaphore Vive [M]. Wang Jiatang (tr). Shanghai: Shanghai Translation Publishing House, 2004.

[130] Ricoeur P. Soi-même Comme Un Autre [M]. She Biping (tr). Beijing: Commercial Press, 2013.

[131] Ritze G. Postmodern Social Theory [M]. New York: The McGraw-Hill Companies, Inc,1997.

[132] Robertson R. Globalization: Social Theory and Global Culture[M]. Liang Guangyan (tr). Shanghai: Shanghai People's Publishing House, 2000.

[133] Rocamora A, A Smelik (eds). Thinking Through Fashion [M]. London: I.B. Tauris, 2016.

[134] Rombach H. Die Welt als lebendige Struktur: Probleme und Losungen der Strukturontologie [M]. Wang Jun (tr). Shanghai: Shanghai Bookstore Publishing House, 2009.

[135] Santayana G. The Sense of Beauty [M]. Yang Xiangrong (tr). Beijing: People's Publishing House, 2013.

[136] Samovar L A. & R. E. Porter. Communication between Cultures [M]. Min Huiquan, et al. (tr). Beijing: China Renmin University Press, 2004.

[137] Schaefer R T. Sociology [M]. Liu Hequn, Fang Zhihui (tr). Beijing: World Publishing Corporation, 2009.

[138] Schlanger N (ed). Techniques, Technology and Civilization [M]. Mengyangshanren (tr). Beijing: World Publishing Corporation, 2010.

[139] Shklovsky V, et al. Selected Literary Theories of Russian Formalism [M]. Fang Shan, et al. (tr). Beijing: SDX Joint Publishing Company, 1989.

[140] Simmel G. The Philosophy of Fashion [M]. Fei Yong, Wu Yan (tr). Beijing: Culture and Art Publishing House, 2001.

[141] Shusterman R. Pragmatist Aesthetics [M]. Peng Feng (tr). Beijing: Commercial Press, 2002.

[142] Smith A. Nationalism: Theory, Ideology, History [M]. Ye Jiang (tr). Shanghai: Shanghai People's Publishing House, 2011.

[143] Smith H. The World's Religions [M]. Liu Anyun (tr). Haikou: Hainan Publishing House, 2013.

[144] Smith P, et al. Understanding Social Psychology across Cultures [M]. Yan Wenhua, Quan Dayong (tr). Beijing: Posts and Telecom Press, 2009.

[145] Sokolowski R. Introduction to Phenomenology [M]. Cambridge: Cambridge University Press, 2000.

[146] Sparke P. An Introduction to Design and Culture: 1900 to the Present [M]. Qian Fenggen, Yu Xiaohong (tr). Nanjing: Yilin Press, 2012.

[147] Sullivan M. The Meeting of Eastern and Western Art [M]. Zhao Xiao (tr). Shanghai: Shanghai People's Publishing House, 2014.

[148] Su Yonggang (ed). The Refinement and Application of Fashion Elements [M]. Chongqing: Chongqing University Press, 2007.

[149] Svendsen L. Fashion: A Philosophy [M]. Li Man (tr). Beijing: Peking University Press, 2010.

[150] Taine H A. Philosophie de L'art [M]. Fu Lei (tr). Hefei: Anhui Literature and Art Publishing House,1998.

[151] Tanaka, Chiyo. World Folk Costume: Exploring the Wisdom of Human Dressing Ways [M]. Li Dangqi (tr). Beijing: China Textile & Apparel Press, 2001.

[152] Tatarkiewicz W. Dzieje Szesciu Pojec (A History of Six Ideas) [M]. Liu Wentan (tr). Shanghai: Shanghai Translation Publishing House,2006.

[153] Thilly F. A History of Philosophy [M]. Ge Li (tr). Beijing: Commercial Press, 1995.

[154] Thorp R L, R E. Vinograd. Chinese Art and Culture [M]. Zhang Xin (tr). Beijing: Beijing United Publishing Company, 2014.

[155] Todorov T. Théories du Symbole [M]. Wang Guoqing (tr). Beijing: Commercial Press, 2004.

[156] Trigger B G. Understanding Early Civilizations: A Comparative Study [M]. Xu Jian (tr). Beijing: Peking University Press, 2014.

[157] Tucker A, T Kingswell. Fashion [M]. Tong Weiyang, Dai Lianbin (tr). Beijing: SDX Joint Publishing Company, 2014.

[158] Van Damme, W. Anthropology of Aesthetics: Perspective and Methods [M]. Li Xiujian,

Xiang Li (tr). Beijing: China Federation of Literary and Art Circles Publishing house, 2015.

[159] Vigarello G. Histoire de la beauté [M]. Guan Hong (tr). Changsha: Hunan Literature and Art Publishing House, 2007.

[160] Wallerstein I. Geopolitics and Geoculture: Essays on the Changing World-System [M]. Wang Fengzhen (tr). Beijing: Central Compilation & Translation Press, 2016.

[161] Wang Fang. Interpretation of Chinese Traditional Costume Patterns [M]. Shanghai: Donghua University Press, 2014.

[162] Wartenberg T E (ed). The Nature of Art [M]. Li Fengqi. et al. (tr). Chongqing: Chongqing University Press, 2011.

[163] Welsch W. Undoing Aesthetics [M]. Lu Yang, Zhang Yanbing (tr). Shanghai: Shanghai Translation Publishing House, 2002.

[164] Worsley H. 100 Ideas that Changed Fashion [M]. Tang Xiaojia (tr). Beijing: China Photographic Publishing House, 2013.

[165] Williams C A S. A manual of Chinese metaphor [M]. Li Hong, Xu Yanxia (tr). Changsha: Hunan Science & Technology Press, 2006.

[166] Winkelmann J. Geschichte der Kunst des Altertums [M]. Shao Dazhen (tr). Guilin: Guangxi Normal University Press, 2001.

[167] Wrathall M. How to Read Heidegger [M]. Jiang Yihui (tr). Beijing: China CITIC Press, 2015.

[168] Wu Yanyan (ed). Introduction to European National Costumes [M]. Beijing: China Textile & Apparel Press, 2016.

[169] Xi Chuanji (ed). Selected Classical Readings on Design Art [M]. Nanjing: Southeast University Press, 2002.

[170] Xiao Shimeng. Colors in the Pre-Qin Period [M]. Beijing: People's Publishing House, 2013.

[171] Xu Fuguan. Chinese Art Spirit [M]. Beijing: Commercial Press, 2010.

[172] Yakovlev E. Art and World Religions [M]. Ren Guangxuan, Li Donghan (tr). Beijing: Culture and Art Publishing House, 1989.

[173] Yang Xiaohong. History of Chinese Fashion Culture (Volume of the Song, the Yuan and the Ming Dynasties) [M]. Jinan: Shandong Pictorial Publishing House, 2011.

[174] Yauss H R. Aesthetic Experience and Literary Hermeneutics[M]. Gu Jianguang, et al. (tr). Shanghai: Shanghai Translation Publishing House, 1997.

[175] Ye Licheng. Fashion Aesthetics [M]. Beijing: China Textile & Apparel Press, 2001.

[176] Young J W. A Technique for Producing Ideas [M]. Zhu Shiwei (tr). Beijing: China Renmin

University Press, 2014.

[177] Young R J C. Postcolonialism: A Very Short Introduction [M]. Oxford: Oxford University Press, 2003.

[178] Zhang Zhichun. Chinese Costume Culture [M]. Beijing: China Textile & Apparel Press, 2009.

[179] Zhang Fanwen, Han Xuesong. History of Chinese Fashion Culture (Volume of the Qing Dynasty, the Republic of China & the People's Republic of China) [M]. Jinan: Shandong Pictorial Publishing House, 2011.

[180] Zhang Xing. Study on Fashion Trends [M]. Beijing: China Textile & Apparel Press, 2006.

[181] Zhang Xiangen. Introduction to Art Phenomenology [M]. Wuhan: Hubei People's Publishing House, 2015.

[182] Zhong Zhijin. Ethnic Culture and Fashion Design [M]. Shijiazhuang: Hebei Fine Arts Publishing House, 2009.